The Gay Detective Novel

The Gay
Detective Novel

Lesbian and Gay
Main Characters and
Themes in Mystery Fiction

JUDITH A. MARKOWITZ

foreword by Katherine V. Forrest

McFarland & Company, Inc., Publishers
Jefferson, North Carolina, and London

Pub
2004

LIBRARY OF CONGRESS CATALOGUING-IN-PUBLICATION DATA

Markowitz, Judith A.
   The gay detective novel : lesbian and gay main characters and
themes in mystery fiction / Judith A. Markowitz ; foreword
by Katherine V. Forrest.
       p.   cm.
   Includes bibliographical references and index.

   ISBN 0-7864-1957-1 (softcover : 50# alkaline paper) ∞

   1. Detective and mystery stories, American—History and
criticism.   2. Gays in literature.   3. Detective and mystery
stories, English—History and criticism.   4. Homosexuality and
literature—English-speaking countries.   5. Commonwealth
fiction (English)—History and criticism.   6. Gays' writings,
American—History and criticism.   7. Gays' writings, English—
History and criticism.   8. Lesbians in literature.   9. Gay men
in literature.   I. Title.
PS374.H63M37   2004
813'.087209352664—dc22   2004019458

British Library cataloguing data are available

Cover photograph ©2004 Photodisc

Manufactured in the United States of America

McFarland & Company, Inc., Publishers
   Box 611, Jefferson, North Carolina 28640
      www.mcfarlandpub.com

To the authors:
By putting your words on paper
you make us visible and reaffirm our lives

Acknowledgments

My deepest thanks go to the authors who took the time to share their insights and views about their books. Their thoughtful answers and other comments are the rarest and most valuable part of this book. I wish I could have included every word they said.

Katherine V. Forrest was the guiding light for the book. Her suggestions and critiques helped give the book its direction and structure, and her confidence in this work made it easier for me to gain access to other authors I wanted to interview.

Susan Franz, my partner of almost twenty-five years, provided critical editing and proofreading of the manuscript. As a result of her efforts the book is stronger and more cohesive. Needless to say, however, I have removed all red pencils from our home.

I want to thank Michael Bronski, Christine Cassidy, Don Cullina of Alyson, Rhonda and Gerry Duncan, Barbara Grier of Naiad, Marie Kuda, Chris Willis, Bonnie Zimmerman and others who allowed me to tap their prodigious knowledge. I also appreciate the encouragement Barbara D'Amato gave me when I was formulating the early series analyses. Thanks also to Cornelius Sippel and Charles Kitchell for allowing me access to their personal library of gay mystery authors and to both Gerber Hart Library and the Chicago Public Library for their tremendous collections of gay/lesbian mysteries.

Contents

Foreword

That this particular overview of gay/lesbian detective fiction has come along just now could not be more opportune. A half century of gay and lesbian visibility—the first categorically recorded period of this subculture's existence on the planet—has produced a history so eventful and tumultuous, so dramatic in its highs and lows and anguish and triumph, that only now can we glean some perspective, some sense of how a community managed to emerge from this crucible, and the shape of that community.

In her creation of this book, Judith Markowitz's great achievement is her sheer grasp of the dimensions of what has been accomplished: *The Gay Detective Novel* emerges as both blueprint and portrait of a community on an upward trajectory in its demand for justice.

For a subculture virtually bereft of in-print images of itself up until the midpoint of the twentieth century, today's plethora of gay and lesbian literature is astonishing, and its expanding presence in American literature is a publishing phenomenon. Within this flourishing body of writing, the subset of gay detective fiction is both unique and of unusual significance. Because of the very nature of this genre, with its focus on the quest for justice in an unjust society, no other body of work in the current store of gay and lesbian literature contains so basic and rich a chronicle of the growth of a community and its painful struggle for the right to exist.

This book rewards everyone interested in any element of the formation, development, growth, range and themes of gay/lesbian detective literature. While scholars and researchers will be gratified by the book's depth and historical scope, this is no pedantic tome. A significant work of thoroughgoing scholarship, *The Gay Detective Novel* is also clearly a labor of love. Thanks to Dr. Markowitz's thoughtful interviews (I speak from experience), the voices of the writers engage us in all their variety

1

and individuality. Any reader will enjoy the sparks of wit and humor; all readers can place full confidence in the analysis, assertions and conclusions in these pages.

With its insights, its scope, and its keen observations into a unique period in the literary history of America as well as an emergent community, this book will surely become as much a part of history as the works Dr. Markowitz showcases in her invaluable study.

Katherine V. Forrest
San Francisco, California

Preface

Whenever I would tell someone I was writing a book about mystery series with gay and lesbian main characters, the most common response I received was an amazed, "Are there really enough of them to write a book?" In fact, my research found one hundred series, as well as countless stand-alone mysteries.

The Gay Detective Novel provides a systematic analysis of this literature from its onset in 1961 through the first quarter of 2003. The object of this effort is to make that body of work visible to mystery readers and scholars who might otherwise be only marginally aware of its existence.

The book contains only those series with main characters who are decidedly lesbian or gay. Series with characters whose sexual orientation is implied, coded, or (as yet) undetermined (e.g., Rita Mae Brown's Sneaky Pie Brown series) are not included. Similarly, this book does not cover series with heterosexual main characters who operate in strongly gay/lesbian contexts, such as Steven Saylor's series about Gordianus the Finder. These publications are suited to another book with different objectives.

Because so many stand-alone gay/lesbian detective novels exist, coverage of single-effort works is limited to those of historical or political significance, such as Lou Rand's 1961 pulp novel, *Gay Detective*, the first novel-length mystery with a gay main character. Gertrude Stein's 1933 mystery *Blood on the Dining Room Floor* is not among them, however, since it lacks three core attributes of mystery novels: it involves no detecting, uses no clues, and has no solution.

Part I, "The Gay and Lesbian Crime-Fiction Scene," lays the groundwork for the subsequent chapters. It includes a brief historical review of mainstream subgenres, such as traditional and hard-boiled mysteries. Of greater significance, however, are its exposition of the elements that make gay/lesbian detective mysteries unique and its insights about the cultural

3

diversity found in this body of literature. Part I concludes with an examination of the kinds of humor found in these mysteries.

Part II, "The Authors and Their Characters," examines the mystery series, grouped according to the professions of the main characters: police; private investigators (PIs); "professional sleuths," who are journalists, attorneys, and other trained investigators whose work involves them in criminal cases; amateur detectives; and "partners"—series with multiple detectives who may or may not be working as a team. Each of these groupings has a cross-series discussion related to that type of fictional investigator. The discussion includes historical information and trends within the gay/lesbian detective literature. It is followed by descriptions of the series that fall into the grouping.

The series analyses in each group are arranged alphabetically by author—either the author's real name or the pseudonym that appears on the series. Each series' heading (author's name, main character's name, beginning and ending dates of the series) is followed by a brief biography of the author, identification of the publisher, and a list of awards garnered by the series. This is followed by a descriptive analysis of the series. If the author was interviewed, much of the analysis is expressed in her or his own words.

Part III, "Themes Across the Series," covers issues that are addressed across series. Its primary focus is on lesbian and gay themes, such as homophobia and sexism, but it is not limited to them. The discussion of each theme includes references to series and individual novels that highlight it.

Every attempt has been made to provide comprehensive coverage of the gay/lesbian detective subgenre. I recognize that, despite these efforts, there may be a series or a stand-alone book of historical significance that has not been included. Such omissions are the start of another body of work that perhaps I or someone else will write about in the near future.

I

The Gay and Lesbian Crime-Fiction Scene

... the detective story ... is you might say the only really modern novel form that has come into existence....

Gertrude Stein[1]

The detective story is one of the most popular novel forms, and gay /lesbian detective stories—those with overt gay and lesbian main characters—are among the most dynamic and diverse novels of the genre. Despite that, so little has been written about gay/lesbian detective fiction that many mystery aficionados are virtually unaware of its existence.

Gay/Lesbian Detective Mysteries

Writers of any good mysteries would probably agree with most of Barbara Sjoholm's (formerly known as Barbara Wilson) response to the question *Why do you write?*

> I write to pay attention, to indulge my curiosity, to give something back. I write to make lesbian life visible. I write to ask questions and make connections. I write because I love words and pictures made of words. I write because literature is my home.[2]

Like any good mysteries, gay/lesbian detective novels are written to entertain, to enlighten, and to challenge the reader to match wits with the fictional sleuth. The questions asked and the connections that are made in gay/lesbian detective stories—including plots, characters, and dialogue —are comparable to those found in mysteries with heterosexual main characters. Many authors of gay/lesbian detective series also consciously write in ways designed to attract a broad readership. For example, in an autobiographical article, Joseph Hansen described his approach to writing the Dave Brandstetter series: "My aim was to write a book about a homosexual that heterosexuals would want to read, and there's no form that keeps readers turning pages like a mystery."[3]

Despite the attempt to reach a crossover audience, gay/lesbian detective fiction remains ghettoized, unlike mysteries featuring African American and heterosexual women main characters. Furthermore, mainstream bookstores still allocate very little shelf space to gay/lesbian mysteries—either as part of a separate gay section or integrated with other mysteries—and have thereby made it difficult for these books to make their way into the hands of non-gay mystery aficionados. The end result is continued invisibility of this body of literature which, in turn, restricts the visibility of lesbian and gay life as a whole.

Making Lesbian and Gay Life Visible

Within the gay and lesbian community, gay/lesbian detective fiction has experienced enormous popularity and has played a tremendous role in making gay and lesbian life visible. Joseph Hansen recalls that, as a young man,

> I was always alert for any sign of homosexual presence in a novel or story or play. The rarity surely was part of the reason why. We were outsiders, misfits, a dirty secret—but here was a sign someone knew we were in the world. It might not be much, but it was better than nothing. Today's popular fiction, even in such formerly staid and stuffy venues as *The New Yorker*, teems with gay characters. And today's gay male readers probably would find passing strange the excitement ink-on-paper homosexuals stirred in readers of my youth.[4]

Hansen's Brandstetter series, which debuted in 1970, was one of the forces behind the change.

Visibility begins with the sexual orientation of the detective, but Mark Richard Zubro, who writes two series with gay main characters, argues that true visibility means that "The entire spectrum of our lives needs to be portrayed—not just little bits and pieces."* That is what really distinguishes gay/lesbian detective fiction from other mysteries. It presents the positive, negative, and highly personal aspects of lesbian and gay life: loving and contentious relationships; friendship; parenting; and emotion-laden issues, such as the closet, coming out, family rejection, and gay/lesbian bashing.

According to Patricia Boehnhardt (aka Ellen Hart), "The gay and

---

All unattributed author citations come from interviews with authors for this book.

lesbian community is not a monolith. If we truly believe it's important to embrace diversity, we should also embrace diversity within our own ranks." Gay/lesbian detective fiction presents a diversity of lesbian and gay lifestyles which enables a wide variety of gay and lesbian readers to see themselves and their worlds woven into the stories. Some main characters are constructed with this in mind. Barbara Johnson's Colleen Fitzgerald, for example, is designed to be "someone readers can see parts of themselves in—whether it's what they like in a person or how they, themselves, looked or acted." In describing her main character, Lindsay Gordon, Val McDermid says, "I was conscious growing up of the complete lack of any sort of lesbian role model, anything out there that would make young women growing up gay feel less like a freak, so I wanted Lindsay to be a kind of Everydyke."

Gay/lesbian detectives are butch, femme, straight-acting, and "just me." Some have close ties to families, lovers, and friends; others are loners. Most are white Americans but there are Hispanic, African American, Native American, and mixed-race sleuths—plus one cat.* There are also gay/lesbian detectives who are Canadian, British, Australian, and New Zealander. Their ages range from sixteen to the mid-sixties (plus one ageless vampire), although the majority are in their thirties or forties. They come from working class, middle class, and privileged backgrounds; and they have financial situations that range from impoverished to wealthy. Some have minimal educations while others have PhDs. They were raised Catholic, Protestant, Jewish, Native American, and Wiccan which they currently embrace, ignore or reject.

They live in big cities, small towns, and in rural areas. Jean Hutchison and Marcy Jacobs, who constitute the *Jean Marcy* identity, placed their PI, Meg Darcy, in a largely heterosexual environment because "a lot of gays and lesbians are not in big cities or are in situations where a lot of their friends and family are straight. They are not immersed in a gay community." Series with plots that have little or no connection to the gay/lesbian community sometimes shift gay and lesbian issues to the main character's personal life and professional interactions. This is the situation for Katherine V. Forrest's police detective, Kate Delafield; Randye Lordon's PI, Sydney Sloane; and Lauren Maddison's attorney/sleuth Connor Hawthorne. As Maddison says:

> While Connor's lesbianism is not the central issue of any of these mystery novels, it *is* an important quality of *her* character. Her conflicts with her

---

Sue Slate is Lee Lynch's feline PI. Sneaky Pie Brown, Rita Mae Brown's cat-detective, is not included in this book. Sneaky Pie's sexual orientation may be implied but it is not made explicit.

mother and dozens of other people in her life have arisen from that one aspect of who she is. Her calm determination to be exactly who she is colors her interactions with others.

Some main characters live and work largely within the confines of one or more segments of the lesbian/gay community. Those segments are as heterogeneous as the gay bars where bartender Daniel Valentine (the creation of author Nathan Aldyne)* works; the new-millennium, youth/party scene in which bar-dancer/personal-trainer Scotty Bradley (Greg Herren) lives; Matty Sinclair's (Tony Fennelly) wealthy gay-male social circle; the SM/leather worlds of Larry Townsend's and Kate Allen's main characters; and the highly political, lesbian-feminist community of Pam Nilsen (Barbara Sjoholm, fka Wilson).

Most gay/lesbian detectives are called upon to investigate crimes motivated by hatred, fear, jealousy, lust for power or money, misplaced love, and social ills that could easily appear in non-gay/lesbian mysteries. Some authors, such as Joan Drury, also exploit the mystery format to educate readers about gay, feminist, socialist, race-related, or other types of issues: "I knew that people who knew none of the statistics about violence against women would be reading my books if I wrote them as mysteries." Barbara Sjoholm (fka Wilson) created Pam Nilsen because "I wanted to see what a mystery could do in terms of tackling social issues." Richard Lipez (writing as Richard Stevenson) tries "to give readers a funny take on a moral stance on gay life in America and American society more generally."

Some gay/lesbian detective series are embedded in gay or lesbian culture. Kate Allen's Alison Kaine series, for example, is so immersed in lesbian-separatist and leatherdyke subcultures that the criminals in those novels manipulate the practices and beliefs of those cultures to accomplish their goals undetected.

Series that have strong ties to the gay or lesbian community often deal with crimes associated with homophobia. For Richard Lipez (aka Stevenson), whose PI Donald Strachey works on gay-related cases within and outside of the gay community,

> The big theme in all of the books—the overarching theme—in one way or another is that the villain is always homophobia. That includes irrational fears of homosexuality, misunderstanding of homosexuality, attempts to stamp out homosexuality.

These novels also address the noncriminal homophobia that lesbians and gay men encounter every day. R.D. Zimmerman recalls:

Author names are in parentheses.

> A straight person recently said to me "Oh, you're the cook in the family. Does that mean you're the girl in the family?" It is so weird that straight people don't get the broad spectrum of talent and issues the LGBT community brings to our lives.

Experiences like Zimmerman's reflect the misguided, homophobic belief that gay men who do chores generally assigned to women, such as cooking, or who have feminine mannerisms or interests that are considered feminine must want to be women. This applies to men who are *bottoms* in intercourse as well. In the following example, lesbian PI Micky Knight (J.M. Redmann) learns that gay men understand the sexist implications of these assumptions.

> Blond Boy tapped me on the shoulder, "Hey, honey, you want me to drive this thing?"... I did realize that his attempted insult was nervous tension, flailing back at that macho thing that 'real men' aren't bottoms. Everyone in the car knew he was going to be fucked by another man.[5]

The internalization of homophobia and the sexism associated with it often take the form of negative characterizations of feminine gay men. It even surfaces in series that provide positive images of effeminate gay men, such as hairdresser/sleuth Stanley Kraychik (Michael Mesrobian writing as Grant Michaels).

> My sudden windfall of money gave me the luxury of choice ... and my first act of so-called choice was to embark on a quest to become a full-fledged man. That's a big decision for someone like me, a congenital sissy.[6]

Lesbians have internalized sexism and homophobia as well, which accounts for the preponderance of lesbian butch detectives in the literature. Kate Allen says:

> I think it's because butch is seen as strong and capable while femmes are always having to battle that "incapable" stereotype. I did it myself with Alison—if I had been as strongly femme identified at the time I wrote the series as I am now Stacy might have been the protagonist.

Forging New Images

The diversity found in gay/lesbian detective fiction provides the entire spectrum of gay and lesbian life that Zubro wanted. In doing so, gay/lesbian mysteries have provided new, more accurate images of lesbians and gay men than those generally found in mainstream literature and popular media. Those new images include gay and lesbian characters who are intelligent, ethical, and self-confident adults. They also include sensitive portrayals of uniquely lesbian and gay archetypes, such as drag queens and kings, ultra-butch lesbians, leathermen/dykes, transvestites, and transsexuals.

Many authors use the mystery format to uplift as well as to divert and instruct. They create handsome, honorable, and brave role models for readers living in a world that discounts and demeans them. "Both as a publisher and a writer," says Joan Drury, "my tendency is to always look for characters who could be role models, rather than characters who are in flux." Authors like Drury describe their characters using terms like *integrity, very courageous, self-accepting, strong,* and *decent.* Vicki P. McConnell considers her reporter/sleuth Nyla Wade to be someone who "pursues solutions to problems and injustices that would probably intimidate me sufficiently to stop me in my tracks." Kaye Davis describes her forensic pathologist Maris Middleton as "She's comfortable being a lesbian.... She's very courageous, especially in the presence of physical danger." Lev Raphael says about his amateur sleuth Nick Hoffman, "I see him as a man with a strong sense of justice and injustice—and a strong sense of the ridiculous connected to that." Even most of the flawed detectives have a strong sense of justice or a desire to set the world right as best they can.

Strong characters who are feminine lesbians and gay men fly in the face of the sexist elements of homophobia. Drag queens/kings and transvestites violate gender norms. Gay hairdresser Stanley Kraychik, mentioned earlier as a self-described *sissy,* is not only an effective sleuth, his "limp wrist" technique earns him marksmanship awards in the Boston PD police academy. "Then some of my toughest colleagues asked me to teach them my 'soft-hand' technique."[7] Barbara Johnson describes her goal in creating femme insurance investigator Colleen Fitzgerald in these terms.

> I'm a self-identified femme, and I wanted to give femme readers someone they could identify with as a character rather than someone they wanted to sleep with. Having her be a femme character also gave me an opportunity to expand on people's comprehension of the butch-femme dynamic and to challenge their assumptions. The general stereotype of femmes is that they need to be taken care of, but here is somebody who ends up being very strong and can take care herself.

Similarly, Outland's gay transvestite, Doan McCandler, is out, proud, and an effective leader. "In a more tolerant world, wherein sexuality would be irrelevant, Doan would have been a general."[8]

Many of these new gay and lesbian images are presented as heroes and *sheroes.* R.D. Zimmerman says that in his Todd Mills series he "was trying to make heroes out of people that I've known and issues that I've seen." Sometimes main character s/heroes assume mythic attributes. Lauren Maddison and Linda Kay Silva describe their main characters as *knights,* Jack Dickson refers to his Jas Anderson as an *alpha male,* and there is a category of gay/lesbian police characters who are so powerful that this book calls them *supercops*. Like the heroes of the Blacksploitation films of the 1970s, these new, super-human images of lesbians and gay men constitute a powerful antidote to the homophobic stereotypes that still thrive in our daily lives.

Authors and Publishers

Like their characters, the authors included in this book differ in age, culture, experience, philosophy, citizenship, and economic and educational background. They also differ in sexual orientation. In addition to lesbian and gay authors, there are those whose sexual orientation is not specified and those who are clearly heterosexual.

The mention of heterosexual authors of gay/lesbian detective series often provokes a debate about whether they are capable of accurately portraying lesbian or gay characters. Non-lesbian Laurie R. King responds

> I wouldn't say it's difficult, certainly less so than writing a male character, which is what I did in *Keep Watch*. It might be more so if there were more of an emphasis on that side of her life, but there isn't…. Writing about a lesbian is a bit like writing about a Roman Catholic in England: identifying a character with that particular minority makes for a clear-cut identity and unarguable sense of apartness.

The debate will no doubt continue, but it would be more useful if it were recast to examine *how well* an author portrays characters who are members of any groups to which the author does not belong.

The publishers who created the detective subgenre have tended to be small, independent lesbian and gay presses. According to Barbara Grier of The Naiad Press, "It has always been the small gay and lesbian presses who have supported the industry and move it forward." Among the most active are Alyson Publications, Banned Books, Cleis, Daughters, Firebrand, Gay Men's Press, Naiad, New Victoria, Seal Press, Second Story Press, Spinsters Ink, and The Women's Press. These publishers and their editors established the readership for gay/lesbian detective literature. They were later joined by larger presses, such as Kensington, Berkley, New Victoria Publishers and St. Martin's, who heightened the visibility of the subgenre.

A History of the Modern Detective Story

In general, the series that are described in the following chapters fall into one or more of the mystery styles presented below. Despite their differences they all adhere to a common, highly structured format that includes a crime that is investigated and solved by one or more detectives. The crime is usually murder, and the investigation uncovers clues and misdirections (sometimes called *red herrings*). Usually, the perpetrator is exposed at the end of the novel, although *inverted* mysteries reveal the identity of the criminal early in the story, as in television's *Columbo* series. Some mysteries are inverted so that the author can focus on how the detective arrived at the truth or how a case is built against the perpetrator. Other inverted mysteries, such as Patricia Highsmith's *Strangers on a Train*, follow the criminals as they plan and execute their crimes.

Although the basic structure of crime—investigation—solution still holds, gay/lesbian authors, like their mainstream counterparts, no longer adhere to strict guidelines such as those in S.S. Van Dine's 1928 article "Twenty Rules for Writing Detective Stories."[9] They obey the demands of their creative muses, experiment, violate genre boundaries, and forge unique blends with suspense, horror, science fiction, fantasy, and romance.

The First Great Detectives (1841–1918)

Edgar Allan Poe is often called the father of the modern mystery because his short story "Murders in the Rue Morgue" (1841) introduced elements that characterize mystery fiction more than 150 years later. Its plot is a puzzle—a whodunit—that can be solved by paying attention to clues and avoiding red herrings designed to mislead the unwary. Since the murders occur in a locked room, the puzzle includes discovering how the murderer got in and out. Poe's detective, August Dupin, is an outsider skilled in observation and logic. He's accompanied by an admiring colleague dedicated to recording Dupin's brilliant activities for posterity.

Dupin's successors in this early period of mystery include

- Inspector Bucket (Charles Dickens) in "Bleak House" (1853), the first mystery short story published in England.
- Monsieur Lecoq of the French Sûreté (Emile Gaboriau) in *Monsieur Lecoq* (1868) which used forensic techniques (e.g., footprint analysis).
- Sgt. Cuff of Scotland Yard (Wilkie Collins) in *Moonstone* (1868), considered to be the first modern British detective novel.
- NYPD Officer Ebenezer Gryce (Anna Katharine Green) in *The Leavenworth Case* (1878), the first American mystery novel and the first mystery novel published by a woman and the first serial detective. Green is called the mother of modern mystery.

- Lady Molly of Scotland Yard (Baroness Emmuska Orzcy) in *Lady Molly of Scotland Yard* (1912).
- Sherlock Holmes (Arthur Conan Doyle) starting with "A Study in Scarlet" (1887).

Like Dupin, these early detectives tend to be infallible geniuses whose powers of observation and scientific deduction separate them from ordinary humans. Some, including Holmes, are also eccentrics.

Today, detectives of this type are rare. They generally resurface as extensions of the original great detectives, such as Laurie R. King's *Beekeeper's Apprentice* series and Nicholas Meyer's *Seven Percent Solution*. A vestige of these early mysteries has been retained, however, in stories that emphasize forensics, such as Kaye Davis' series about a lesbian forensic chemist.

The Golden Age (1919–1939)—The Traditional Mystery

By the end of World War I, genius detectives had been supplanted by a spectrum of fallible amateur and professional sleuths in more complex, plot-oriented mysteries that later became known by a number of names, including *classic, traditional* and *cozy*. Inverted mysteries in which the criminal is the main character aren't included in this book because they perpetrate crimes rather than solve them. Criminal main characters range from gentleman thieves, such as E.W. Hornung's Raffles, to not-so-gentlemanly criminals, such as Patricia Highsmith's Mr. Ripley. Some of those villains were described in Anthony Slide's 1993 *Gay and Lesbian Characters and Themes in Mystery Novels* because they are thinly veiled gay men.

The traditional mystery introduced some of the most enduring detectives. Among the best known are

- PI Hercule Poirot and amateur Jane Marple (Agatha Christie)
- PI Violet Strange and amateur Amelia Butterworth (Anna Katharine Green), the first female PI and the first elderly female amateur
- PI Philo Vance (S.S. Van Dine)
- amateurs Harriet Vane and Lord Peter Wimsey (Dorothy Sayers)
- amateur Father Brown (G.K. Chesterton)
- amateur Dr. John Thorndyke (R. Austin Freeman), the first inverted mysteries
- amateur Albert Campion (Margery Allingham)
- police Inspector Roderick Alleyn (Ngaio Marsh)
- police consultant Dr. Gideon Fell (John Dickson Carr)

They are students of human nature who apply logic (Poirot's "little grey cells") to information gathered from physical evidence and behavior. Some, like Nero Wolfe, are called armchair detectives, because they do virtually nothing but think.

Traditional mysteries adhere to rules of "fair play" designed to enable readers to solve the crimes themselves. Plots are novel-length puzzles filled with red herrings and sometimes the least likely suspect as perpetrator. Crimes occur in confined settings (e.g., locked room, country manor house, small town, professional conference) populated by a well-defined group of characters who know each other. There's little violence and gore, no sex, and resolution of the crime generally restores moral order to the world.

Interest in traditional mysteries declined in the 1950s and 1960s in favor of less puzzle-like novels (e.g., Mary Roberts Rinehart's *Had-I-But-Known* school which blended gothic romance and terror with mystery) but resurged in the 1970s and has remained strong among mainstream and gay/lesbian writers and readers. Gay/lesbian author Michael Craft says:

> Though I'm unblushing about the erotic content of my stories (I doubt that Mrs. Christie would approve) ... I have no taste whatever for violence or, as it translates into pop culture, "action." So my mysteries most closely resemble the cozy genre, but with an erotic twist, because that's what suits my own temperament.

Lesbian-feminist and *gay positive*** authors, such as Joan Drury and Mark Richard Zubro, have adopted the traditional mystery format to create mysteries that attack the status quo rather than support it. This is sometimes called *subverting* the mystery genre. They do so by creating strong and intelligent gay and lesbian main and supporting characters (sometimes accompanied by weak or corrupt heterosexuals). They give those characters problems to unravel and mysteries to solve that expose flaws in the status quo, such as child molestation, gay/lesbian bashing, rape, and other by-products of homophobia, sexism, and racism. Sometimes, resolution of the crime not only fails to restore the established world order, it actually offers the possibility of a new social order in which homophobia, sexism, racism, and other social ills are eliminated. For example, at the end of *Last Rites* Tracey Richardson writes:

> like a ray of sunshine after a horrendous storm ... it soon filled her with a reverence that was majestic in capacity ... not reverence for the church or

There is no single term equivalent to feminist *that expresses the philosophy of authors interested in presenting positive images of gay men and lesbians that contradict the stereotypes. This book adopts the term* gay positive *to serve that purpose because* gay activist *seemed too strong to reflect the work of authors who have no strong political agendas.*

religion, but at all that was good and right and hopeful.... All the ugliness here was over now, of that she was sure.[10]

That spirit was responsible for creating the lesbian-mystery genre in the 1980s. Lesbian-feminist writers, such as Vicki P. McConnell and Barbara Sjoholm (fka Wilson), introduced strong female detectives who solved crimes tied to sexism, homophobia, and other social/political problems. In some novels, such as Sjoholm's *Murder in the Collective,* distrust for patriarchal authority, feminist solidarity, and other factors lead the detective to violate the traditional mystery stricture of handing the perpetrator to the authorities. *Closed in Silence,* the final book in Drury's Tyler Jones trilogy, goes even further by not fully disclosing the murderer's identity.

Hard-Boiled and Noir (1930–1950)

While British authors were creating amateur and professional detectives for traditional mysteries, American writers were writing about macho lone-wolf private eyes and other alienated main characters. Their short fiction, primarily in *The Black Mask* magazine, and pulp novels came to be known as "hard-boiled" and "noir." The best known hard-boiled detectives are PIs, such as Three Gun Terry and Race Williams (Carroll John Daly), the first hard-boiled PIs; Sam Spade and Continental Op (Dashiell Hammett); Philip Marlowe (Raymond Chandler); and Michael Shayne (Brett Halliday). The list of hard-boiled detectives also includes reporters (e.g., George Harmon Coxe's Flashgun Casey), attorneys (e.g., Erle Stanley Gardner's early Perry Mason stories), and officers of the law (e.g., Chester Himes' African American police detectives Coffin Ed Johnson and Grave Digger Jones). Noir fiction, a hard-boiled offshoot, features amateur detectives as well including Jeff Jeffries, the nosy neighbor in Cornell Woolrich's "Rear Window," and Charlotte Armstrong's child sleuths.

Tough and streetwise, hard-boiled and noir gumshoes are individualistic products of the working class. With few exceptions they are heterosexual, white men. They live in a violent world where corruption festers at the top and infects all levels of society. Some are solitary knights driven by a personal code of justice while others strive to merely stay alive. The more noir the story, the more iconoclastic and flawed the PI, and the more dangerous and venal the world is.

Some hard-boiled plots adhere to the puzzle pattern of traditional mysteries; others introduce a diverse cast of characters engaged in seemingly unrelated events designed to surprise the reader and propel the story down unexpected paths. There's no explicit sex, which is not surprising because female secondary characters are often portrayed as dangerous -- even deadly. There's also no return to a moral order; at best, the detective can right a wrong. In the process, they expose social ills, consort with criminals, sustain numerous injuries, and spill a great deal of blood.

Hard-boiled fiction remains popular but has become increasingly heterogeneous in both PI and plot. Starting in the 1970s, diversification of PIs based on gender, race, ethnicity, sexual orientation, and other attributes brought new faces and voices to hard-boiled fiction, such as Paretsky's V.I. Warshawski, Buchanan's Britt Montero, Mosley's Easy Rawlins, and Hansen's Dave Brandstetter. Noir, the darkest incarnation of hard-boiled, reached its height in the 1940s and 1950s but continues in the work of mainstream writers, such as Andrew Vachss, and gay/lesbian authors, such as Pat Welch, Jack Dickson and John Morgan Wilson. The publication of Spillane's *I, the Jury* in 1947 ushered in an era of sexually explicit action novels featuring ultra-macho PIs and vigilantes. The 1970s saw the emergence of less alienated gumshoes (sometimes called "soft boiled") whose lives include lovers, friends, and even health clubs. They include mainstream detectives, such as Parker's Spenser and Muller's Sharon McCone as well as a host of gay/lesbian PIs, including Herren's Chanse MacLeod, Lordon's Sydney Sloane, Redmann's Micky Knight, Scoppettone's Lauren Laurano, and Stevenson's Donald Strachey.

The Police Procedural (1945–1960)

The police have always been involved in detective and crime fiction, but Lawrence Treat's *V as in Victim*, published in 1945, is considered to be the first true police procedural. It was the first to focus on the multidisciplinary team effort required to solve crimes. The most famous police procedural is *Dragnet*, a highly successful 1950s radio and TV series starring Jack Webb.* The best known characters of early police procedurals include Det. Mitch Taylor and colleagues (Lawrence Treat, the father of the modern police procedural); Commander George Gideon of Scotland Yard (John Creasey); and the men of the 87th precinct (Ed McBain). These officers of the law are dedicated, working-class police professionals whose goals are to identify the perpetrator of a crime and build a case that will hold up in court. They accomplish those goals using teamwork and realistic police methods that range from high-tech forensics to knock-

---

The NBC radio program ran from 1949 to 1957. The first television series ran from 1951 to 1959. The second series started in 1967 and ended in 1970.

ing on doors and cultivating snitches. These methods include special authority (e.g., to bring someone in for questioning) and special access to information, such as telephone records. Their team encompasses beat officers, forensic experts, medical examiners, psychologists, and others inside and outside of the department whose knowledge and expertise can contribute to solving crimes.

There's a grim realism about police procedurals that views crime as part of society. Consequently, the fight against crime is a never-ending battle. While solving a crime may produce a sense of a job well done it doesn't restore moral order—no matter how heinous the crime. In fact, finding the truth may hurt good people rather than bad. Many of these attributes overlap with hard-boiled and noir novels making the boundaries between those categories extremely fuzzy and leading some to call series like John Sandford's *Prey* series hard-boiled police procedurals.

The personal life of the main detective or team members assumes a prominent position in many police procedurals. They face problems at home and politics at work. They feel hampered by big case loads (they must work on the cases they are assigned), inadequate staffing, colleagues of questionable skill and reliability, rules that seem to tie their hands, and commanders with corrupt or political agendas. They may come to view their job as thankless and some, including Det. Mitch Taylor (Lawrence Treat), fall to temptations criminals dangle in front of them.

The police procedural has undergone diversification comparable to that described earlier for hard-boiled fiction. Chester Himes' hard-boiled detectives Jones and Johnson have been joined by other African American, Latino, Native American, British and European sleuths, heterosexual and lesbian women, and gay men. Main characters have been expanded to include medical examiners and forensics experts, such as Cornwell's Kay Scarpetta and Davis' gay/lesbian detective and forensic chemist Maris Middleton, whose jobs entail working alone as much as working with a team. Gay/lesbian police procedurals by Forrest, McNab, and Zubro add strong social consciousness and romance.

Publication of Joseph Wambaugh's *The New Centurions* in 1970 opened the way to a grimmer view of police work that was realized in violent story lines that include police corruption. The film "Dirty Harry" in 1971 presented a maverick, vigilante police detective who became the inspiration for a new generation of police detectives. Mainstream mavericks, such as Connelly's Harry Bosch, sometimes emulate hard-boiled gumshoes, such as Philip Marlowe, Kinsey Milhone, Spenser, and Matt Scudder, by escaping to the outside world as PIs. Gay/lesbian mavericks, including Dickson's Jas Anderson, Grobeson's Steve Cainen, and Silva's

Delta Stevens, are often "supercops:" superior police officers who generally have ESP or other extraordinary powers that set them apart from everyone else. They exemplify the new gay and lesbian images described earlier.

Humor

> Humor is a gay survival technique—it's an essential part of our lives. To get through this life we need to be able to laugh at ourselves and laugh through the pain—to laugh at the absurdity of being hated for being different.

Many other authors echo this statement by Barbara Johnson, which may account for the wide use of humor in gay/lesbian mysteries. Parodies, satires, farces, screwball comedies, camp, and romps are all well represented. Consequently, the nature of that humor varies considerably. It can be cruel or gentle, subtle or over-the-top, whimsical or slapstick. It can be pure diversion, social commentary, expressed solely through quips, or it can be a plot element. It can appear as intermittent flashes in a story that is basically serious, it can be a thread running through a book, or it can be the spirit of an entire novel or series.

Characters

One of the most frequent approaches to humor is to create one or more comedic characters. Mark Zubro's Chicago PD Det. Paul Turner is surrounded by off-kilter colleagues, including his partner Buck Fenwick. Lauren Laurano, Sandra Scoppettone's PI, is besieged by antagonistic and bizarre New Yorkers. The travels of Cassandra Reilly, Barbara Sjoholm's nomadic translator, bring her into contact with comic figures, some of whom change gender and identity along the way. Mysteries by George Baxt, Stan Cutler, Sarah Dreher, Dean James, Joe R. Lansdale, Mabel Maney, and other authors are filled with wacky characters who do their best to create chaos and confusion. In contrast, Nikki Baker's bitter humor cuts and slashes her characters as in this description of attorney Naomi Wolf's typical party behavior:

> Given twenty minutes she could meet everyone of interest in a convention hall. Between her glad-handing and her political connections, it was no wonder someone was going to make her a judge someday before senility set in.... Like a bloodhound, Naomi had found whatever dirt there was to find at this party and her eyes fairly glowed with fresh intrigue— that or gin.[11]

A number of authors include a larger-than-life, humorous series-character who is generally female. Patricia Boehnhardt (writing as Ellen Hart) describes Cordelia Thorn as "Jane's sidekick. Watson to her Sherlock." Cordelia is large in every regard. She's almost six feet tall, weighs over 200 pounds, dresses in flamboyant clothing, and has a forceful theatrical voice supporting a dominant personality. These attributes not only provide a counterpoint to Jane's seriousness, they make Cordelia a good comedic character. Jean Reynolds is the mother of one of Fred Hunter's investigative duo. She's attractive, sophisticated, wealthy, delightfully British, and a willing participant in her son's adventures. Sydney Sloane's Aunt Minnie (Randye Lordon) and Stoner McTavish's Aunt Hermione (Sarah Dreher) are not only mother figures but dynamic octogenarians who commune with dead relatives and friends. Nicole Albright, the owner of the fashionable Snips Salon in Grant Michaels' Stanley Kraychik series, is a hefty former runway model with a penchant for good food, liquor, and gossip. Independent minded Professor Juno Dramgoole exudes sexuality in Lev Raphael's Nick Hoffman series:

> Beyond the physical, Juno has carte blanche to say what she wants. In a situation where power is wielded so brutally and people can't say the truth, for Nick it's kind of dazzling to have someone who can speak the truth whenever she wants to.

Jeff Barnes, the only male in this group, is Todd Mills' (R.D. Zimmerman) friend. He's large in every way and has an effervescent joie de vivre which contributes to his success as a drag queen.

Humorous characters in Richard Lipez' (writing as Richard Stevenson) Donald Strachey series are tools for making political and social commentary. "I use the humor in the book to make some of the uglier facets of gay life in America—the crassness, intolerance, and stupidity—easier to take. There's also an element in each of the books of revenge fantasy." Similarly, Michael Craft, Kate Allen, Mary Wings, Lev Raphael and others construct humorous character types as a part of the satire in their books. For example, Michael Craft embodies "activist journalism" (the belief newspapers can create news as well as report it) in a self-important prig who dresses "like a character from a French farce, complete with cape and walking stick."[12] The excessive behavior of humorous characters not only helps Kate Allen and Mary Wings lampoon lesbian and gay culture, it also provides clues to murder and other crimes.

Writers whose work is not intended to be light or humorous are among those who include humorous secondary characters. Katherine V. Forrest's Kate Delafield police-procedural series is an example.

> Kate approaches her grim business in pretty grim fashion, but I do like to
> have it in my books.... It sometimes will come from a situation, but most
> often it's just generated from characterization. For example, there's a
> pretty bizarre office worker in *Amateur City*, a faded wreck of an actress in
> *The Beverly Malibu*—these off-center characters have their own skewed
> take on the world, and they were great fun to write.

Although main characters are less likely to be humorous, gay/lesbian
detective fiction is peppered with outrageous and eccentric detectives,
such as Orland Outland's transvestite-detective Doan McCandler; Doan's
socialite partner, Binky Van de Kamp; Grant Michaels' Stan Kraychik,
hairdresser extraordinaire; Nathan Aldyne's Clarisse Lovelace; and Dean
James' Simon Kirby-Jones.

> Simon is, in many ways, the stereotypical "bitchy queen" who comments
> on everyone and everything he sees. If he were heterosexual instead, the
> tone of the books would change completely.

Samuel Steward's Gertrude Stein is imperious; Fred Hunter's Alex
Reynolds and Peter Livesay are hapless heroes; and the naïveté of Mabel
Maney's Cherry Aimless know no bounds.

Humor can come from the relationship between detecting partners.
Joe R. Lansdale's ill-tempered vigilante/sleuths Hap Collins and Leonard
Pine drag each other into and out of outrageous escapades. Stan Cutler
describes his main characters as "cliché characters, by design. Because it
sets up for humor more easily." The humor that is set up comes when
Goodman, a retired PI who is "reactionary, right-wing, semi-alcoholic,"
and yuppy, gay Bradley are forced to collaborate on Goodman's autobiography. Similarly, much of the humor in David Stukas' series comes from
the unlikely alliances among Michael Stark, an ultra-wealthy gay playboy; wimpy Robert Willsop, a struggling advertisement copywriter; and
no-nonsense, lesbian jock Monette.

Situations

Some situational humor arises from the everyday lives of the characters. For example, when Lansdale's two heroes go out hunting squirrel,
one of their prey turns predator.

> We broke and ran. The squirrel, however, was not a quitter. Glancing
> over my shoulder, I saw that it was in fact gaining on us, and Leonard's
> cussing was having absolutely no effect, other than to perhaps further
> enrage the animal, who might have had Baptist leanings.[13]

While in Hungary, Barbara Sjoholm's Cassandra Reilly is invited to
stay with Eva and her aunt.

> Mrs. Nagy gave me a push on the shoulder and pointed in a threatening manner in the direction of the bathroom. It appeared she was telling me not to use the shower. Eva said brightly, "She says, Our home is your home."[14]

Barrister Frankie Richmond (Elizabeth Woodcraft) tapes the statement of a murder witness while she's driving. "We listened to the tape. The quality wasn't good and Saskia's voice was occasionally obscured by my shouting at other drivers."[15] When chicken farmer Letty Campbell (Alma Fritchley) evicts her rooster from a nest he has made in her classic car,

> He batted me with his wings in protest but finally he stalked off complaining loudly to Henrietta whom he pecked for good measure. The end of a beautiful friendship, I suspect.[16]

Humorous situations come out of gay and lesbian life as well. When Mary Wings' PI, Emma Victor, goes to a restaurant with another woman, their waiter pours wine for Emma to taste and approve. "I guessed I was playing the butch that night."[17] As part of their investigation Lou Rand's detectives, Tiger Olsen and Francis Morley, go to a gay nightclub. When Olsen starts for the men's room,

> Several persons spoke, casually inviting him to sit down for a drink. Some, suggested bolder things.... One or two interested men evidently decided that they should powder their noses just at this time, and followed the big man closely.[18]

In Orland Outland's *Death Wore a Fabulous New Fragrance*, gay activist Kenny Wells is trying to out a closeted movie star.

> Jeff Breeze is G-A-Y gay and I want the world to know it! ... he shouted, for the benefit of TV cameras that were as likely to hear and see him as he was to hear and see Breeze.[19]

Dialogue and Language

Humorous dialogues can range from witty to nonsensical. The following example from Sarah Dreher could easily fit into *Alice in Wonderland*.

> The old woman grunted. "I have plenty of names."
> "Oh. Well ... uh ... what should I call you?"
> "Why you want to call me? I'm here."[20]

Scoppettone's PI Lauren Laurano hands a witness her card while gravely advising him

"You think of anything, anything at all, even if it seems unimportant, call me, okay?"

"If it's unimportant how will I know I should call you?"[21]

Writers also play with language in various ways. The titles of Claire McNab's Det. Carol Ashton books are puns on the stories they contain: a famous golfer is murdered in *Death Club*, *Lessons in Murder* is set in a school, and the events in *Cop Out* have a lasting impact on Ashton's career in the Sydney PD. McNab and other authors assign evocative names to characters, locations, and organizations. Dean James spoofs of cozies have characters named Sir Giles, Lady Blitherington, Constable Plodd, and Col. Clitheroe who live in Snupperton Mumsley. Baker's African American detective works at the Whytebread and Greese investment firm, Wings' Emma Victor does a surveillance job for the Guaranteed All Risk insurance company, and Will Powers is a motivational consultant in Outland's series.

Other authors, such as TV script writer Stan Cutler, differentiate the voices of characters. "I was so used to hearing dialogue in my head from working with actors, it came as second nature." In his series, Warren Dunford laughs at the script writing process itself by presenting sometimes mundane dialogues in the form of scripts. In one book his screen writer/detective rewrites the same scene whenever a new witness gives him additional information. Samuel Steward made Gertrude Stein speak like she writes; Lipez captures the speech patterns of a variety of spoken dialects; and Sjoholm's characters are undone by vowels and consonants.

> For example, the jokes about bassoons (fagottos) and liver (fegato) in *The Case of the Orphaned Bassoonists*. It gives the dialogue a kind of vigor as well as creating misunderstandings. There is humor and sometimes the plot is advanced.

Many authors admit that some of the dialogues in their books represent an author's chance to say something they would like to have said in real life. According to Mary Wings

> The French have an expression called *esprit d'escalier* which means *spirit of the stairway*. It refers to when you wish you'd said something in a situation but you didn't and you'll never have another chance. The wonderful thing about being a writer is that the *spirit of the stairway* is yours. You get to actually say all that stuff.

The following example from Lipez/Stevenson's *Death Trick* is no doubt one of them.

> Detective Sergeant Ned Bowman lost no time in showing me his winning personality. "Yeah, I've heard of you.... You're the pouf."

"What ever happened to 'pervert'.... I always liked that one better.... 'Faggot,' too, I was comfortable with. The word had a defiant edge that I liked. 'Fairy' wasn't bad—it made us seem weak, which was misleading, but also a bit magical, which was wrong, too, but still okay. 'Pouf,' on the other hand, I never went for. It made us sound as if we were about to disappear. Which we aren't."[22]

Parody and Satire

Parody imitates the style and characteristic elements of a literary genre, author, or school of writing.* Gay/lesbian parodies of traditional mysteries include Dean James' novels featuring vampire-detective Dr. Simon Kirby-Jones and Mabel Maney's Nancy Clue series. Maney recasts the simplistic young-adult worlds of Nancy Drew and Cherry Ames into a gay-friendly universe in which homophobia, sexism, and racism are aberrations. "I decided to use the basic framework of the Nancy Drew originals—a crime is committed, outfits are selected, daring stunts follow, and the girls are victorious—as a framework in which to work out what I detected between the lines: Nancy's creepy wifelike devotion to her father, the missing mother, Nancy's suffocatingly small world, of which she is always the center, and her life of privilege."

Parodies of the hard-boiled style outnumber those for other mystery styles. The first gay/lesbian detective novel, Lou Rand's 1961 *Gay Detective*, is a parody that turns hard-boiled fiction on its head: it introduces a PI who has "an unconsciously un-masculine air"[23] and plays with stereotypes of gay men and lesbians as well as with hard-boiled conventions.

Most of the other parodies are by lesbian authors writing about butch-lesbian detectives. As with mainstream hard-boiled fiction most of them are PIs (e.g., Emma Victor (Mary Wings), Nell Fury (Elizabeth Pincus), and the four-legged feline Sue Slate (Lee Lynch)), although Hollis Carpenter (Deborah Powell) and Lillian Byrd (Elizabeth Sims) are tough, savvy crime reporters. Each of these women (and one cat) muscles her way through the mean streets of her town on her way to solving crimes.

Unlike parody, satirical humor is always caustic and is used to ridicule vices, pretensions, and foolishness. Mystery writers have also used the genre as a tool for satirizing the foibles and villainies of specific groups. Former academician Lev Raphael takes aim at American academia in his gay/lesbian detective series.

Parody invites readers to laugh at the conventions of a literary style or to create humor by blowing those conventions out of proportion. A sincere attempt to imitate style is called pastiche.

> You know, academia is the real world, despite talk of "the ivory tower."
> It's frequently cruel, authoritarian, inhumane, but it has this surface
> rhetoric of a shared community of knowledge and responsibility to stu-
> dents. Nowadays, most universities talk about "customer satisfaction."
> They think in terms of business and bottom line, and the disjunction
> between reality and rhetoric makes it a great environment for satire.

In *Death Wore a Smart Little Outfit*, Outland satirizes elements of the
art world, and both Kate Allen and Mary Wings lampoon parts of the
gay and lesbian community. Wings says, "I wanted to do something new
under the sun, and no one was looking at our community and satirizing
it."

Camp

Camp is a uniquely gay form of humor. It is a complex phenomenon
in which the intent of the creator and the perception of the reader may
be entirely different. As Orland Outland points out, "Some people go out
and do a movie like *Showgirls* or *Valley of the Dolls* that turns out to be a
camp classic."

David Bergman begins his five-page definition of camp with

> Combining elements of incongruity, theatricality, and exaggeration, camp
> is a form of humor that helps homosexuals cope with a hostile environ-
> ment.[24]

and then he proceeds to say that *camp* defies definition.

The first gay/lesbian mysteries, Baxt's Pharoah Love novels and
Rand's *Gay Detective*, are grounded in incongruity, theatricality, and exaggeration. Baxt's *Topsy and Evil* has an aura of a 1930s musical gone hor-
ribly awry. It is populated by outrageous characters and overflows with
references to literature and motion pictures. For example, a murder victim whispers "Rosebud" before dying, à la *Citizen Kane*. The humor that
is produced is theatrical and acerbic.

The humor in Rand's *Gay Detective* is much lighter. The book is
filled with inverted stereotypes: an "un-masculine" PI, a ballet school
that's really a gym, an androgynous interior decorator in dungarees and
Wellingtons who turns out to be a lesbian, and a heterosexual ex-football
star with a flair for decorating.

> I think that a rough copper drapery with maybe some metal in it would
> do well in here. Walls and woodwork in shades of light green, possibly
> some blue in it, but no yellow. The furniture in off-white leather, a darker
> green broadloom on the floor, bone-white desk, and one or two lamps
> with copper shades....[25]

Mysteries by Nathan Aldyne, Diane Davidson, Mabel Maney, Orland

Outland, and others exhibit attributes of camp humor, per Bergman's definition, and may be perceived as campy—even when camp was not the author's intent. The perception of campiness may arise from their use of humor as a sugar coating on social commentary. After all, explains Maney (whose books contain strong social critiques), "Who wouldn't want to live in an all-girl dorm, giggle late into the night, and wear a starched uniform and jaunty cap?"

The Crime Scene

The gay/lesbian crime scene blends elements that are uniquely lesbian/gay with those that can be found in mainstream detective novels. The gay/lesbian subgenre evolved from the traditions that gave rise to other segments of the genre. Its stories take familiar forms (e.g., traditional, hard-boiled, and police procedural), and they abide by the conventions that govern all mystery fiction, including having a crime to solve, finding clues, encountering red herrings, and arriving at a solution. At the same time, gay/lesbian mysteries provide a view of gay and lesbian life—the dreams, fears, love, hatred, and self-hatred—that are not available in mainstream literature.

Standing at the center of the crime scene are the gay/lesbian detectives. Their roles are police detective assigned to the case, PI with a client, insurance investigator, defense attorney, crime reporter, interested party, or unwilling participant. As the following chapters reveal, they are fearless or neurotic, decisive or dithering, adroit or bumbling. They are loners or work in a team. In the end, however, they all get the job done.

II

The Authors and Their Characters

———————— POLICE ————————

The earliest fictional police detectives are often called "aristocops." They were highly educated and culturally sophisticated scions of upper-class families (e.g., Emile Gaboriau's Monsieur Lecoq of the French Sûreté and Baroness Emmuska Orzcy's Lady Molly of Scotland Yard). They were also brilliant detectives who strongly resembled other great detectives. These artistocops evolved into puzzle-solving professionals who were more suited to traditional mystery. Those more modern aristocops include Colin Dexter's Inspector Endeavour Morse (a Wagner aficionado), Ngaio Marsh's Inspector Roderick Alleyn (his brother is a baronet), and P.D. James' Detective Inspector Adam Dalgliesh (a poet).

There were few early hard-boiled police detectives, largely because the cynical loner with antiestablishment sentiments—a staple of hard-boiled and noir fiction—is ill-suited to working within the quasi-military hierarchy of police departments. Police main characters reemerged in the police procedurals and have continued to be popular. Recent variations of these include forensic specialists and other law-enforcement professionals.* In the late twentieth century, movie and TV figures, such as "Dirty" Harry Callahan, transformed the hard-boiled and police-procedural images into a maverick who favored an ends-justify-the-means approach. Mainstream incarnations of these new cops include Michael Connelly's Harry Bosch and John Sandford's Lucas Davenport. Like them, the newest generation of gay/lesbian cops is action-oriented rather than thought-oriented and street-smart rather than book-smart.

*For more on police procedurals see Part I, "The Gay and Lesbian Crime-Fiction Scene."

Main Characters

The gay/lesbian police subgenre began inadvertently in 1966 with the publication of George Baxt's *A Queer Kind of Death*. New York Police Department (NYPD) Det. Pharoah Love was the detective assigned to the case of a gay hustler murdered in his bathtub. Although Love was not the main character, he was the one readers remembered. Baxt wrote two sequels with Love as the main focus (if not the actual main character). Love was also the first gay/lesbian African American main character and the first transsexual. Eighteen years later Katherine V. Forrest's *Amateur City* introduced the first lesbian police detective.

> I intended to have an amateur sleuth, a young woman whose first day on the job coincides with the murder of the firm's top west coast executive.... I realized though, to my annoyance, that I'd need to have the police on hand to do their bit ... so I decided to have my homicide detective be a woman. Thus Kate Delafield walked onto the page. I immediately perceived ... that here was an opportunity to portray a lesbian in a high visibility, high pressure, and most unusual profession.*

Like Love and Delafield, most of the main characters in this chapter are police detectives. Interspersed among them are beat officers, sheriffs, lieutenants, captains, and police consultants. They approach their responsibilities as great detectives, ordinary working-class cops, and mavericks. Some of their creators are current or former law-enforcement professionals themselves, who embed their own experiences in their novels. Janet McClellan incorporates pieces of cases she handled in her thirty years of police work and her knowledge of departmental politics. Mitchell Grobeson's *Outside the Badge* documents his experience as a gay officer in the virulently homophobic LAPD. Kaye Davis is a forensic chemist who "wanted to make the evidence found and the forensics that were used realistic and within the realm of probability for the crimes."

Aristocops and Ordinary Mortals

The only gay/lesbian aristocop with her own series is Claire McNab's Det. Inspector Carol Ashton, who is from Australia's privileged class. Her novels contain a sizable percentage of well-heeled victims, perpetrators, and other interested parties who accept her as one of their own and try to use their power and influence to achieve their goals. According to her

---

All unattributed author quotes come from interviews for this book.

creator, however, Ashton's "work with Detective Sergeant Mark Bourke is rather closer to a partnership" than is typical of many aristocops.

The traditional mystery format was adapted by feminist authors in the late 1980s and early 1990s but their police detectives are all working- and middle-class lesbians. These authors use the mystery genre to explore feminist issues. Mary Morell's Lucia Ramos series highlights the lifelong damage of incest, Kieran York's Royce Madison series examines racism and homophobia, and Tracey Richardson's Stevie Houston series looks at institutionalized homophobia and sexism. Richardson's series combines the traditional mystery with elements of police procedurals.

Mark Zubro's Det. Paul Turner, Katherine V. Forrest's Kate Delafield, and Laurie R. King's Kate Martinelli are among the main characters in gay/lesbian police procedurals. As in mainstream police procedurals, their successes are based on teamwork, persistence, and both good investiga- tive instincts and techniques. Those novels discuss the politics, person- alities, and procedures that constitute the daily working experiences of their main characters. The personal lives of their main characters also play a major role in these series.

Some main characters are perceived by their departments and cowork- ers as special. Among them are Penny Mickelbury's Gianna Maglione,* Forrest's Det. Kate Delafield, Richardson's Det. Stevie Houston, and McClellan's Det. Tru North. These characters provide positive lesbian/gay models that are tempered to varying degrees by the flaws that plague ordi- nary human beings. Delafield and Maglione are buried so deeply in their closets that they barricade themselves from potential allies, limit the scope of friendships, and threaten relationships with their lovers. North and Houston are young, inexperienced, and sometimes foolish.

Supercops

Gay/lesbian authors who have adopted mavericks as their main char- acters tend to create extraordinary individuals who offer powerful, positive images of lesbians and gay men. These "supercops" are highly intelligent, unusually good looking, remarkably strong or agile, exceptionally coura- geous, and superior law-enforcement officers. Most supercops are also magical in some way. Tenny Mendoza (Melanie McAllester) and Delta Stevens (Linda Kay Silva) have ESP. Mendoza, Pharoah Love (George Baxt), and Jas Anderson (Jack Dickson) have a hypnotic force of per-

*Mickelbury's series is described in the section on partners (pp. 195–233) because Maglione investigates in parallel with reporter Mimi Patterson.

sonality that overwhelms other people. Steve Cainen's (Mitchell Grobeson) eyes are so penetrating that "Even the hardest criminals had squirmed under Steve's intense gaze."[1] Toni Underwood (Diane Davidson) is not hypnotic but she inspires adoration in subordinates as well as hatred in superiors. Stevens is exceptionally strong, and Anderson is "the archetypal 'alpha male'" whose physical durability is nothing short of miraculous.

Supercops follow their own moral compass, and they battle evil much like knights in shining armor on a holy quest. Linda Kay Silva agrees, "For me, that's what Delta is. She is my white knight." These modern knights are very much akin to the superior individuals featured in spy and intrigue novels. Thus, it is not surprising that several of these series have evolved from police stories to stories of intrigue and moved beyond the purview of this book.

Out of Uniform

Sometimes a character shifts from police officer to civilian. Morell's Ramos and Silva's Stevens take leaves of absence. Beat officers Alison Kaine (Allen) and Steven Cainen (Grobeson) do their probing *ex officio* because they lack the authority to investigate crimes officially. All the supercops resign or are driven out of their departments. Although some are happy to be rid of the constraints of the police bureaucracy, they would still echo Ramos' complaint, "I really miss my badge. People have to talk to you when you're a cop."[2] Most out-of-uniform detectives learn how to conduct investigations like PIs and amateurs, including using former police colleagues as resources. On the other hand, being a PI has its benefits.

> Private investigator.... That's the way to live. Take the ones you want to work on and let the rest go. I wish I could get away with that.[3]

Secondary Characters— Heterosexual Police

The police have been involved in detective fiction since Poe's "Murders in the Rue Morgue" appeared in 1841. Who else has the authority to cart evil doers off to jail once the brilliant detective has exposed them? Depiction of the police in mysteries has rarely been restricted to perpetrator disposal, however. Throughout the history of the genre, police inspectors, such as Lestrade and Japp have vied with, aided, and frustrated detectives of all stripes—even other police officers.

Friends and Allies

As in mainstream fiction, gay/lesbian detectives of all kinds often have allies in the police department. Police allies provide the only means by which civilian detectives can obtain certain types of information. Detectives Delia Whitney and Roger Thomas are reporter Lynn Evans' (Claudia McKay) friends and talk with her off-the-record about cases. Officer Terry Ormes becomes an increasingly valuable police resource to gay/lesbian attorney Henry Rios (Michael Nava) as she moves up the police hierarchy. PI Sydney Sloane (Randye Lordon) relies on NYPD Det. Gilbert Jackson, an old friend of the family, for services such as fingerprint checks. Boston PD Det. Vito Branco not only gives amateur detective Stanley Kraychik (Grant Michaels) information, he solicits Kraychik's assistance on cases and encourages him to enter the police academy.

Gay/lesbian police may have allies within their departments. Forrest's Kate Delafield is blessed with good superior officers, and as the series progresses the quality of her partners improves as well. Rookie detectives Stevie Houston (Tracey Richardson) and Kate Martinelli (Laurie R. King) both have seasoned partners who help them blossom into first-rate detectives. Det. Sgt. Mark Bourke is Carol Ashton's (Claire McNab) right-hand man, friend, and confidant. Paul Turner's (Mark Zubro) partner Buck Fenwick is also a good personal friend.

Power and Corruption

> The cops entered with their inimitable style—all heavy feet and loud voices and squawking radios. Their particular kind of intrusion can push anyone's latent hysteria over the edge. They probably plan it that way.[4]

The response of hysteria rather than anger in this excerpt from Grant Michaels' *Love You to Death* is a by-product of the power vested in the police. When applied to the solution of a crime the power to arrest, detain, restrict access, and compel people to provide information is part of what sets the police apart from other kinds of detectives. When power is abused it becomes the basis of the corrupt and brutish stereotypes of police that pervade hard-boiled and noir fiction.

Violent and venal police appear in all categories of gay/lesbian detective fiction. Joseph Hansen's insurance investigator, Dave Brandstetter, uncovers a nest of corruption and abuse of power when he looks into the death claim of a powerful police chief. Mabel Maney's Nancy Clue and her friends discover that the police chief in Nancy's home town is deeply involved in criminal activity. Marion Foster's attorney Harriett Fordham

Croft exposes the abuses of two of Spruce Falls, Ontario's, finest, and an officer in Pat Welch's PI series threatens to deport a Hispanic woman he plans to rape. Benjamin Justice, John Morgan Wilson's investigative reporter, shoots his drunken and abusive father, a veteran police officer, to prevent him from raping his own daughter. Later, Justice himself is raped by a corrupt police officer.

Virtually every police main character encounters police brutality and corruption. Some, like Toni Underwood (Diane Davidson) and Delta Stevens (Linda Kay Silva) root them out from among their own ranks. Others, including Doug Orlando (Steve Johnson) and L.A. Franco (Baxter Clare) are forced to work along side of brutish, corrupt colleagues. Such revelations would not surprise supercop Jas Anderson (Jack Dickson) whose dark and brooding series describes how power breeds corruption. Some authors, including Silva, view corruption as a disease afflicting specific individuals. Her supercop, Delta Stevens, believes that once corrupt cops have been identified they can be extracted from the force like bad teeth. "Taking down dirty cops is bad business, but it's gotta be done.... It's shit like this that gives us all a bad name."[5]

Homophobia

Gay/lesbian detective literature portrays the male-dominated, macho police culture as a nourishing environment for homophobia. Homophobic police exhibit a full spectrum of behaviors extending from obvious discomfort to violence. The literature captures these behaviors when they are directed at the gay and lesbian community and when they are focused on lesbian and gay police officers.

The most common manifestations of police homophobia are overt discomfort and name calling. The following example from Richard Stevenson's *On the Other Hand, Death* shows such a detective interacting with a group of gay men and a lesbian.

> Detective Lieutenant Ned Bowman ... greeted Dot formally, exchanged scowls with McWhirter, suffered through an introduction to Timmy— homosexuals not wearing pleated skirts always confused Bowman—then came over to where I stood by the wall phone and whispered "Hi, faggot."[6]

Gay/lesbian bashing and murder by the police are far less frequent and appear mostly in novels by hard-boiled and noir authors such as John Morgan Wilson, Jack Dickson, and Michael Nava. These behaviors are especially vicious when directed against gay police officers. Even Mark Zubro, whose stories are filled with police officers who have no trouble working with gays and lesbians, expresses concern. "Prejudice might be against the law, recruitment of gay officers a desired goal, but in the real world lots of young, straight, male cop wannabes could be vicious."[7]

Female officers exhibit the same attitudes as their male colleagues. Silva's lesbian Delta Stevens mentions the "I know you're a dyke and if you touch me, I'll kill you" routine[8] she often encounters with heterosexual women officers. A female officer in Grobeson's *Outside the Badge* participates in the deadly schemes against gay patrolman Steve Cainen.

The police are usually shown giving tacit approval to the violence others perpetrate against gay men and lesbians. The literature is peppered with examples of contaminated, lost, or uncollected evidence; witnesses who are hounded or ignored; misclassified crimes; and denial that crimes were even committed. In Ellen Hart's *Hallowed Murder*, the police call the drowning of a lesbian college student a suicide because they believe lesbians are prone to suicide. The West Hollywood police in Nava's *The Burning Plain* refuse to make a report on an attack against a gay man so they can claim that such crimes don't happen in their district. Grobeson's *Outside the Badge* describes the LAPD's actual practice of labeling gay-on-gay crimes as NHI or "No Human Involved." Det. Ed Taylor, Kate Delafield's (Katherine V. Forrest) partner, believes such homophobic behavior is justified. "Goddammit, nobody deserves to be killed. But some people fucking ask for it. You know it, Kate."[9]

Responses to Police Homophobia

Gay/lesbian detectives of all types shoulder the responsibility for investigating crimes against lesbians and gay men and for bringing the perpetrators to justice. Joe R. Lansdale's amateur detective Leonard Pine summarizes their viewpoint. "Couple queers aced is almost good business as far as the Chief's concerned.... It's police business when they want to make it their business. They don't make it their business, then I got to make it *my* business."[10] This motive of retribution is the genesis of many gay/lesbian detective novels.

Authors of gay/lesbian police series respond to police homophobia by creating gay and lesbian characters whose intelligence, skill, and dedication defy the premises of such biases. Some go further by offering supercops whose superiority is so evident it makes those prejudices seem ludicrous. These characters are united in their need to find and punish those who have committed crimes against lesbians and gays. They share Doug Orlando's (Johnson) view "that any other cop assigned to the case wouldn't feel his obsessive drive to snare this psycho."[11]

Gay/lesbian police characters disagree about coming out at work. Steve Johnson's Doug Orlando, Davidson's Underwood, and McAllester's Mendoza would support Delta Steven's (Linda Kay Silva) view that "I came out a long time ago because the secret was eating me up inside and making me pretend to be someone I'm not."[12] Forrest's Delafield, McClellan's North, and Mickelbury's Maglione would argue that remaining closeted not only protects their careers but is the only way to accomplish important goals, such as funding a Hate Crimes Unit. Authors with deeply closeted characters make it clear, however, that being in the closet doesn't mean that their colleagues don't know they are gay/lesbian. The LAPD grapevine outs Grobeson's Cainen as decisively as if he had announced his sexual orientation in a press release.

Zubro's Turner and Clare's Franco would likely take a middle ground that Zubro calls "gently out." They are careful about how, when, and how quickly they emerge from the closet.

The response of the lesbian/gay community to police homophobia creates an additional problem for gay/lesbian police. People refuse to answer questions and fail to provide important information. Sometimes, as the following excerpt from Fred Hunter's *Government Gay* illustrates, they won't even report a crime.

> "Are you going to call the police?"
> "Are you kidding?" I said, my eyes going wide. "Going to the police would be like getting bashed again."[13]

Consequently, gay/lesbian police feel wedged between a hostile community and homophobic colleagues, and their jobs are made harder because of it.

Sexism

Like homophobia, sexism in police departments is portrayed as a monster with many heads. At the top, sexist policies funnel female officers into secretarial services, prostitution decoys, and the juvenile department. At the peer level, it's manifested by behaviors ranging from demeaning language to sexual harassment and rape. Richardson's *Over the Line* is about one police department with a systematic program to purge itself of female officers—especially lesbians—by any means available.

Capt. Rhonn, superior officer to McClellan's Det. North, would argue that females, including lesbians, are constitutionally inferior to men. In his opinion, the only way a woman can succeed in the police department is through preferential treatment—getting promotions and assignments that should be going to more deserving men. Examples of such preferential treatment are rare. When they occur, they are generally produced by a blend of twisted sexism and political pressure. Laurie R. King's Det. Martinelli knows her department wanted to assign a woman to a case in *A Grave Talent* because the victims are children. In Diane Davidson's *Deadly Rendezvous* political pressure leads to the assignment of lesbians to a taskforce aimed at catching a serial killer targeting lesbians.

Most lesbian characters respond to this sexism by trying to prove that they can perform any job as well as or better than their male colleagues. Each woman applies her own interpretation of those self-imposed requirements. Forrest's Delafield demands the highest performance of herself and her team. Davidson's Underwood "volunteered for every dirty job, and was determined to prove that women had everything it took to succeed in police work.... Eventually, she had succeeded in proving she was smarter and tougher than most other officers...."[14]

Beyond Sexism and Homophobia

The link between sexism and homophobia is clearly represented in the gay/lesbian police literature. It easily explains the "logic" behind Ed Taylor's (Kate Delafield's partner) statement that gay men can't be "real men" because they want to turn themselves into women.[15] The same thinking lurks behind the expectation by some of Kate Martinelli's (Laurie King) male colleagues that, as a lesbian, she would view women the same way they do. According to LAPD Sgt. Mitchell Grobeson, the author of *Beyond the Badge*

> In many ways, law enforcement actually prefers lesbian officers to heterosexual women. There's a book called *Multicultural Law Enforcement* that talks about this and points out that they are more comfortable with them —even a heterosexual woman who is "masculine" or "butch." They just label her a lesbian.

Kaye Davis, who is also a law-enforcement professional, would argue that there is a limit to such acceptance and that the glass ceiling is lower for lesbians. "Being women pushes Maris and Lauren outside of the inner circle. Being lesbians practically banishes them to the parking lot outside."

Authors also present police sexism and homophobia as manifestations of a constellation of biases that includes racism and anti-Semitism.

Linking fiction to fact in *Apparition Alley*, Katherine Forrest points to real-world groups of officers in the LAPD who want to rid the department of all minorities. McClellan, a former law-enforcement professional, believes little has changed over the years. Her Captain Rhonn

> was part of the new breed of management. They were practiced at using all the right words, and they refrained from sexist or ethnic slander and covered their biases and prejudices with stupefying ease. They still had all the same prejudices the old guard held, but they'd been schooled and trained to hide them under phrases like *organizational necessity, for the good of the order*, and something about *economic necessity*. [16]

Secondary Characters— Lesbian and Gay Police

Reginald Hill broke new ground when, in 1978, he added Sgt. Wield, a then-closeted gay officer to a team led by Superintendent Andrew Dalziel and Det. Insp. Peter Pascoe. He was unique in a series with heterosexual main characters. Originally described as an extremely ugly man who struggled with a personal secret, Wield's homosexuality wasn't revealed until 1980 in *A Killing Kindness*. He was soon joined by a heterogeneous collection of other series characters, including openly gay LAPD Det. Milo Sturgis in the Alex Delaware series (Jonathan Kellerman); angry and deeply closeted Homicide Det. Helen Soileau who becomes Dave Robicheaux' (James Lee Burke) partner; and Kay Scarpetta's (Patricia Cornwell) niece, FBI intern Lucy Farinelli. These officers are described as honest, dedicated professionals. In addition to performing their jobs, they have to contend with official and unofficial homophobia in their agencies.

Gay/lesbian detective fiction abounds with lesbian and gay officers whose roles vary from information resource to lover. Det. Roberta Exline is assigned to reporter Lexy Hyatt's (Carlene Miller) first case and remains a friend and source of information. Det. Jackie Jones adds credibility to Nancy Clue's (Mabel Maney) team of teenaged investigators. Det. Martha Harper is PI Cassidy James' (Kate Calloway) best friend. Det. Sarah Lindstrom is PI Meg Darcy's (Jean Marcy) antagonist, client, and the object of Darcy's affections. Homicide Det. Steve Rawlins becomes journalist Todd Mills' (R.D. Zimmerman) lover; and Officer Allison Sullivan captures mobster Brett Higgins' (Therese Szymanski) heart.

Secondary characters in gay/lesbian police fiction are generally colleagues in the main character's department. Very few of them are corrupt.

Notable exceptions are a gay-bashing blackmailer in Joe R. Lansdale's *Bad Chili*; a sexist detective in Rose Beecham's *Introducing Amanda Valentine* who is a party to kidnapping, prostitution, and murder; Samuel Steward's sadistic Parisian gendarme in *Caravaggio Shawl*; and a revenge-crazed lesbian detective in Therese Szymanski's *When the Dancing Stops* who will do anything to kill main character Brett Higgins. Most secondary characters serve as gay and lesbian role models, such as Officer McCreedy in Gianna Maglione's (Penny Mickelbury) Hate Crime Unit.

> Tim McCreedy was as close to a perfect specimen of male pulchritude as Gianna had ever seen…. And he was one hell of a good cop…. Tim McCreedy was also happily, openly, and joyously gay. Tim McCreedy was a flaming queen and proud of it.[17]

KATE ALLEN: *Alison Kaine* (1993–1999)

Kate Allen (1957–; pseudonym, real name undisclosed) lives in Denver with four cats and a house bunny. She grew up in the west and southwest and has been writing since she was six years old. She's published books for children and young adults and is working on a crossover mystery. Like Alison Kaine, Allen battles fibromyalgia syndrome largely through the practice of yoga.

Detective: Officer Alison Kaine, Denver PD

Setting: Primarily Denver, Colorado. Time period is contemporary with publication dates

Books: *Tell Me What You Like* (1993); *Give My Secrets Back* (1995); *Takes One to Know One* (1996); *Just a Little Lie* (1999)

Publisher: New Victoria Publishers

This series satirizes lesbian politics, mores, language, and behavior. Officer Alison Kaine is a police officer who stands at the intersection between antagonistic groups. She's a feminist whose increasing involvement in the leathergirl scene puts her in direct conflict with her separatist friends. Murder and mayhem arise directly from those two lesbian subcultures and cannot be fully understood outside of them. In *Tell Me What You Like* the lesbian-feminist practice of replacing birth names with woman-identified names (e.g., Seven Yellow Moons) has the unintended effect of concealing the identity of a serial killer preying on lesbians.

A primary theme flowing through the series is intolerance, and the prejudice in the lesbian community against S&M was a reason she began writing the series. "I did want to write about leathergirls who had lives that included other aspects than just sex…. Alison was a police officer in a dream. It helped me understand a great deal more about lesbian SM."

Takes One to Know One lampoons the rigidity of lesbian separatism.

"I want them to understand that through feminism we have formed a tool that should be used to dig and create with—not beat each other over the head with. I also wanted to show that your politics don't make you a superior person." *Just a Little Lie* levels comparable charges of narrow-mindedness against the leather community. For example, "Alison, when discussing the phenomena of women switching from butch to femme to fit the occasion, felt completely queasy about the whole topic."

Intolerance appears outside of the lesbian community in the form of gay-bashing skinheads, religious zealots with reprogramming programs, and homophobic police officers.

> On the one side were the straight and narrow boys in uniform who thought ... no goddamn queer should be disgracing the uniform. On the other side were the dykes and fags who, every time she showed up anywhere in uniform, took it upon themselves to confront her about every atrocity ever committed by the boys in blue, from Rodney King to Stonewall. [18]

In fact, police rarely appear unless they are being homophobic. "Somebody else could get killed tonight and the police don't care. They don't care about women, and they especially don't care about dykes."[19] Such convictions drive Kaine to begin her own *ex officio* investigations supported only by friends, family, and lovers who overcome their mutual dislike to help and protect her.

Allen's approach to writing is cathartic. "When I am in a good writing space, I carry a notebook and am writing in it constantly. Ideas, snatches of conversation, things I see and think are interesting or provocative. My head is popping with ideas like a popcorn popper, and the ideas just keep rolling out like a gumball machine. I may be working on two or three stories at once, but eventually one will dominate and when it does, it will have a character attached to it. I know this sounds silly, but a lot of my stuff feels as if it was 'ghost written'—that is, the first draft rolls out with characters and plot twists that I didn't know were coming at all." A similar process occurs with characters. "I often have a hard time explaining the personal motives of my characters—they really do take over and do a lot of things that I didn't plan at all on their own."

GEORGE BAXT: *Pharoah Love* (1966–1968, 1994–1995)

George Baxt (1923–2003) was a native New Yorker. His first published novels were the Pharoah Love mysteries which were rereleased for the eighth time in 1998. He's best known for mysteries featuring crime-solving movie stars. He also wrote numerous short stories (e.g., for *Ellery Queen* mystery magazine), plays, and TV scripts (e.g., The Defenders, Kraft TV Theater).

Detective: Pharoah Love, detective, New York City Police Department

Setting: New York City. Time period is contemporary with publication dates

Books: *A Queer Kind of Death* (1966); *Swing Low, Sweet Harriet* (1967); *Topsy and Evil* (1968); *A Queer Kind of Love* (1994); *A Queer Kind of Umbrella* (1995)

Publishers: Simon & Schuster (1998 release is by Alyson Publications)

The Pharoah Love books were written in two subseries that were separated by more than twenty-five years. *A Queer Kind of Death* was a book of many firsts: the first book to have a gay police detective main character, the first to have a gay African American main character, the first main character who becomes a transsexual, and the first gay Native American supporting character.

NYPD Det. Pharoah Love is a flashy, ultra-cool dude who calls everyone "Cat" and who has an aura of mystery that captivates both women and men. He's also a supercop with strong ties to the criminal underworld. Love was not the main character of *A Queer Kind of Death*. He was simply the police detective assigned to the case. Love's forceful personality caused Baxt and his publisher to reposition him as the focus of the series, even when he's not physically present.

Much of the action in these books takes place among criminals. Although he is an engaging character, Love is a crooked cop in the first subseries. In *A Queer Kind of Death,* Love covers up a murder and then blackmails the murderer into becoming his lover. When his activities are uncovered, he's drummed out of the NYPD. By the end of *Topsy and Evil,* Love's larceny has blossomed into depravity, and he dies as flamboyantly as he lived.

At the insistence of his publisher, Baxt resuscitated Love for two novels and several short stories in the mid 1990s. Love retains his beguiling personality and his penchant for flashy clothes and witty replies, but he's more complex, mature, and ethical. The tone of these books is more subdued and the humor more subtle although action still generally takes place among criminal elements who are, once again, engaged in nefarious activities.

The stories, particularly those in the first subseries, are peppered with literary and movie nostalgia. In *Topsy and Evil* (which was Baxt's favorite book) the murder victim whispers "Rosebud" before dying, à la *Citizen Kane;* and Topsy Alcott's daughters are Jo, Meg, Beth, and Amy (another set of "little women"). The books teem with stock characters (e.g., the prostitute with the heart of gold) and eccentric, greedy, self-absorbed schemers engaged in improbable intrigues and snappy dialogue. Characters who spout racial, homophobic, and ethnic epithets are invariably evil. In the early subseries, most of the gay characters, including Love, are evil or deeply flawed, which reflects the attitudes of the period in which the books were written.

Gay issues, notably homophobia and AIDS, bubble to the surface and burst as strong, brief statements. Among them is Love's bitter reflection on "the sneers and jeers and snide remarks of my fellow officers" that were heaped upon him when he came out of the closet. The appearance of gay issues reflects the sensibilities and sensitivities of the 1990s but no gay issues are pursued, allowing the focus of the books to remain on the humor.

ROSE BEECHAM: *Amanda Valentine* (1992–1996)

Rose Beecham (1958–; pseudonym for Jennifer Fulton) is from New Zealand and divides her time between Wellington, New Zealand, and Melbourne, Australia. Under her real name, she has written a number of lesbian romances, including *Passion Bay* and *True Love*.

Detective: Inspector Amanda Valentine, Wellington, New Zealand, Criminal Investigation Bureau

Setting: Wellington, New Zealand. Time period is contemporary with publication dates

Books: *Introducing Amanda Valentine* (1992); *Second Guess* (1994); *Fair Play* (1996)

Publisher: The Naiad Press

This series places sexism at the root of many of the crimes that Valentine investigates. Sexism also surfaces repeatedly in Amanda's dealings with the public, the media (which seems to be preoccupied with her appearance), and her police department.

> Sexism certainly existed, especially among the top brass, and she was well aware tokenism had played a role in her fast-track career. "I still get asked to give the 'feminine perspective' on a case."[20]

Introducing Amanda Valentine begins five years after Amanda has moved from the United States to Wellington, New Zealand. Her emigration followed the murder of her lover by a crazed criminal who entered Amanda's precinct house, guns blazing. In New Zealand, Valentine joined the Wellington police department and her skill and experience fighting crime in a big city put her on a fast track. By the start of the series Inspector Valentine is already chief of detectives. She's proven her effectiveness in that highly visible position by establishing good rapport with the press and the public. Because the Wellington PD is small, Valentine is expected to personally investigate high-profile cases, such as capturing a serial killer who dismembers victims and deposits them in garbage dumps and solving the murder of a debutante that took place in a lesbian bar.

The story lines are loaded with red herrings and crimes that are not always what they appear to be. Plot twists and surprise endings are made possible by interesting characterizations combined with investigations that expose many facets of victims' lives. Subplots, romance, and social commentary add depth to the stories.

Lesbian/gay themes, such as the closet, homophobia, and internalized homophobia, figure in both main and subplots. The portrayal of lesbians and gay men is polarized. On one side are Amanda's lover, friends, and colleagues who are closeted, middle-class professionals. Characterizations of lesbians and gay men who do not belong to Amanda's inner circle are overwhelmingly negative. Some of them are outright criminals (e.g., a corrupt police detective, a gay con artist, and a pair of lesbian rapists). Many of the gay men are closeted, married to women, and sexist. The lesbian and gay community appears rarely. When it does, it's unfriendly. Valentine is resigned to being isolated. "As if a cop would ever find easy acceptance in the lesbian community. It was almost as likely as the police force welcoming lesbians to the ranks."[21]

Even if the community did cast a friendly eye in her direction, it's highly unlikely Inspector Valentine would welcome it. She's deeply closeted and seemingly with good reason. She battles sexism in her job on a daily basis, and it appears the closet is her only protection against homophobic harassment as well. Being in the closet adds to the sexual tension in the romantic subplot of *Introducing Amanda Valentine* when equally closeted TV journalist Debbie Daley begins her pursuit and seduction of Inspector Valentine.

BAXTER CLARE: *L.A. Franco* (2000–CURRENT)

Baxter Clare (1959–; pseudonym for Vicki Trautman) has lived in many U.S. and Latin American locations, including Nicaragua and Argentina. After completing a degree in Parks and Recreation she worked as a ranger for the National Park Service. She has a master's degree in biology and is recognized as an expert on Kitt foxes, an endangered species. Clare lives in southern California with her partner of over thirteen years and divides her time between writing and working as a wildlife consultant on endangered and threatened species.

Detective: Lt. L.A. (Frank) Franco, LAPD

Setting: Los Angeles. Time period is contemporary with publication dates

Books: *Bleeding Out* (2000); *Street Rules* (2003); *Cry Havoc* (2004)

Publisher: Bella Books

Lt. L.A. Franco belongs to the new breed of maverick cops that are populating crime fiction. "She's a Dirty Harry personality stuffed into a Martina Navratilova body." She's an effective, dedicated officer who lives for her work. "She loves it and she loves the people who work for her. To her, work is play: finding a mystery and solving it. She has a lot of psychological motivation for that, although she doesn't realize it. She'd never be that introspective." Her independence has grown out of necessity rather than defiance. "She's not a department person. She knows they're never going to stand behind her. That still surprises her, though, because she still hopes for the best. Part of her wants to belong to this group but it's a pipe dream."

Franco immerses herself in work to avoid dealing with emotional wounds, such as the deaths of her father and her lover. "I had to start Frank off so detached and so removed from herself that I could give her room to grow.... Here's this woman who has no life. All she has is work and booze. What a wretched little existence that is.... She's on the trajectory that was planned for her: to show how we can move beyond our personal issues and become fully actualizing humans."

That personal evolution is the overriding theme of the series, but other themes emerge as a by-product of the violent, gritty, and unjust world where Frank lives and works. The sexism in street culture restricts the roles females can play to sexual trophies, prostitutes, and mothers; in the department sexism keeps women at lower ranks, making Lt. Franco an anomaly. Racism promotes a laissez-faire attitude towards violence in the poor, Hispanic district where Franco works, and homophobia keeps Frank in the closet. "Obviously, in her job as a high-ranking LAPD officer, she has reason to hide and to not talk about it" even though she knows that the department is aware of her sexual orientation and could use it against her if they so choose.

"Each book is an epiphany.... I usually weave the plot around what's going on with Frank rather than weave Frank around the plot. I start each book with an idea that mutates at some point so the finished product is very often not like the first attempt at all.... The plots are always just agony for me. I never know what to do with them. Usually some sort of inspiration hits and I go with it. I leave it open.... I have a horror of sitting down at the computer at first, in the morning. I usually give myself some sort of time line because it's hard to divorce myself from Vicki Trautman and become L.A. Franco.... Once I'm there I get into a groove where it's doing its own thing and I'm just a typist. Then, when I'm done writing at the end of a day, it's a lot easier to slip into it again the next morning....

"I never planned to write this series. The character was there. I was surprised to find myself writing a police procedural when I know nothing about any of this. Perhaps she's my alternate ego, my dark twin. She let's me get to be a cop and live in a big city and things like that."

DIANE DAVIDSON: *Toni Underwood* (1994–CURRENT)

Diane Davidson (1933–; pseudonym for Diane Bunker) is a single parent who was born and still lives in southern California. The Toni Underwood mysteries are the only novels she's published.

Detective: Lt. Toni Underwood, detective, Riverwood, California, PD

Settings: Various locations in the western United States. Time period is contemporary with publication dates

Books: *Deadly Rendezvous* (1994); *Deadly Gamble* (1997); *Deadly Butterfly* (2001)

Publisher: Rising Tide Press

Each novel in this series has a distinct flavor. *Deadly Rendezvous* incorporates elements of police procedurals and feminist mystery. *Deadly Gamble* is a raucous romp filled with high drama and humor that mirrors the flamboyance of its Las Vegas setting. *Deadly Butterfly* is equal parts horror, romance, and whodunit set in the dark and stormy Northwest.

Toni Underwood is a supercop. She's six feet tall, muscular, and ruggedly handsome with a finely chiseled jaw. She's also a talented leader who understands how to motivate subordinates. She has a reputation for never giving up on a case, but her tendency to ignore established procedures—to "go solo" on investigations—doesn't sit well with her superiors. Although she's out of the closet and has experienced homophobia, she sees entrenched sexism as a greater barrier to her continued advancement in law enforcement.

As the series begins, Underwood realizes she's burning out but complies with the assignment to capture a serial killer. It requires enlightening her homophobic partner, Sgt. Sally Murphy of the Palm Beach PD, as well as working the case. They discover that the victims are lesbians who belong to an organization that combats spousal and child abuse. The killer is an abusive husband who fears exposure.

The investigation also uncovers rampant abuse of power and high-level corruption in two law-enforcement agencies. These revelations and the murder of Underwood's lover drive Underwood out of law enforcement. At the conclusion of *Deadly Rendezvous,* she leaves the Riverwood PD. In *Deadly Gamble* she reluctantly investigates threats to people close to her as a private citizen, but by *Deadly Butterfly* she describes herself as "committed to helping those who may be suffering some silent pain or anguish."[22]

Davidson employs stereotypical characters to establish a clear separation between the forces of evil and the forces of good. Included among the forces of good are Toni's Aunt Vera, an ex-brothel madam with a big heart and an Auntie Mame-like personality, and Vera's best friend Royce, a drag queen turned hairdresser. Evil characters include Alfonse Colombo, a big-time Italian Mafioso from Chicago; Arthur Van Buren, a charismatic preacher who spouts anti-gay slogans but who is a closet case and a chicken hawk; and Aaron Blake, a monster so menacing that it seems that "he had no face, just two pieces of coal were where eyes should be."[23]

The danger of using stereotypes is that they can reinforce existing biases about lesbians and gay men. For example, although Aunt Vera's friend Royce is portrayed as a good man, he is a screaming queen. In *Deadly Rendezvous,* Nicky Carter is not so fortunate. She's a mannish lesbian and sexual predator who seduces innocent young lesbians and subjects them to S&M sex and rape. At the same time, stereotypes make it easier to portray societal ills, such as homophobia, sexism, and spousal abuse, as evils that can be eradicated. This view of the world gives the series an upbeat feeling even though it addresses serious issues.

KAYE DAVIS—*Maris Middleton* (1997–1999)

Kaye Davis (1956–) is a criminalist with twenty-three years of experience working in a Texas Department of Public Safety regional crime laboratory. Her areas of expertise include drug analysis, shoe prints, and tire track evidence. She's testified in court over five hundred times and has participated in innumerable crime scene investigations. Davis lives in the Dallas area with her partner of almost twenty years and three dogs.

Detective: Maris Middleton, self-employed forensic chemist

Setting: Allen, Texas (near Dallas). Time period is contemporary with publication dates

Books: *Devil's Leg Crossing* (1997); *Possessions* (1998); *Until the End* (1998); *Shattered Illusions* (1999)

Publishers: Bella Books, The Naiad Press

This series is equal parts forensics, mystery, and romance starring

Maris Middleton, a self-employed forensic chemist. "I wanted to tell the stories from the point of view of a forensic chemist rather than a private detective, police detective, or even a medical examiner.... Related to that, I wanted to make the evidence found and the forensics that were used realistic and within the realm of probability for the crimes. Oftentimes you will read something that is so off-the-wall that there's not an instrument or chemist in the world that could do the analysis."

The series also follows the evolution of Maris' relationship with FBI Agent Lauren O'Connor. "You have two people who are very busy, who work long hours and are both under a lot of stress. Sometimes, they may not have time to communicate as effectively as they should." Since both women are in law enforcement, their personal and professional lives sometimes intersect. "By having a partner who's a law-enforcement officer there is someone who can get ... things for her.... It's kind of a two-edged sword when they work together, though. In some ways, they work well together, but it also causes conflict."

Themes are not planned. "They pop up in the story because I've told it the way it would happen—like the homophobia in law enforcement. It is there if you tell a realistic story. Law enforcement, in general, is still hard for women and extremely hard for lesbians. They both know that if Lauren comes out at work it could cause her a lot of problems with the FBI. Yet, Lauren would be happier and Maris would be more comfortable if Lauren came out." The situation is complicated by Lauren's homophobic family. "She wants their love and acceptance but is afraid to stand up to them and demand they recognize her relationship with Maris.... Fair or not, Maris sees this as a test of Lauren's love."

Maris is comfortable with her lesbianism and "as an 'out' lesbian, Maris can cut through some of the smoke surrounding the power dynamics of male/female relationships.... Also, I write about topics like child abuse and spousal abuse. Women see things differently from men and lesbians see them differently from straight women. It is easier for Maris to see some of the horrors and inequities."

Davis generally fits Maris into events that interest her. "In *Devil's Leg Crossing* I was interested in an East Texas case about missing teenage girls. There were rumors linking their deaths to Satanism.... With *Possessions*, I wanted to research sexual predators and serial killers.... I wanted to write something a little different afterwards, so I incorporated two stories into *Until the End*, which is my favorite book. A friend told me about her grandmother who became a border patrol agent back in the thirties. I was also interested in the story of a man who lived near Dallas who'd stolen some Nazi treasure during World War II.... *Shattered Illusions* was very loosely influenced by the yogurt shop murders in Austin. I thought how hard it would be to lose a child that way."

JACK DICKSON: *Jas Anderson* (1998–CURRENT)

Jack Dickson (1959–) grew up in a small coastal town in western Scotland. He has written pornography under the pseudonym Jack Gordon but now uses his real name for all his work. He currently writes novels for a living augmented by travel journalism and plans to write for motion pictures. Dickson lives in Glasgow with his partner of twenty years.

Detective: Det. Sgt. James (Jas) Anderson, Glasgow police department

Setting: Glasgow, Scotland. Time period is contemporary with publication dates

Books: *FreeForm* (1998); *Banged Up* (1999); *Some Kind of Love* (2002)

Publisher: Gay Men's Press

This series does nothing to dispel the notion that Scots are dour and Scotland is a dark and brooding place. Violence permeates the stories which have been called *noir, gritty,* and *hard-edged* by various reviewers and by the author himself. The S&M sex scenes are the gentlest interpersonal interactions in the series that includes male-on-male rapes and beatings.

At the start of *FreeForm,* Det. Jas Anderson has been suspended from the Glasgow PD. By the end of the book he's been expelled from the force, and fifty pages into *Banged Up* he is in prison, framed for drug pushing. When he emerges from these experiences, he's been transformed into a dangerous enemy of corrupt officials. "I see the man himself as the archetypal outsider—the maverick—in the noir tradition. He's alienated from everything, partly because he's gay but more because of his specific sexual interests, namely the SM."

Corruption permeates every institution that Jas encounters, including the police, Glasgow's political structure, and the prison hierarchy. Even Jas' police mentor has fallen prey to it, leaving Jas alone and driven by his quest for personal justice. He's aided by criminals and prostitutes—the groups who are most reviled and despised by society. Despite being unreliable and self-serving, they appear far more civilized than their supposed social betters. Dickson explains that "what interests me is confounding preconceptions and exposing hypocrisy. In any class-based system, there is scope for abuse of power.... I do believe the most damaging behavior comes from those who should 'know better': bosses, those employed ostensibly to protect, etc."

The blond, blue-eyed and handsome Anderson is "the archetypal 'alpha male'—or your 'supercop,' the intention being that whatever sets him apart from society also gives him his edge on it, be that edge his gayness or his SM proclivites." He's so dominant that he transforms a rabid gay basher into a willingly submissive sex partner after a single encounter. He also has amazing powers of recovery. Jas requires only the healing properties of urine followed by a shower to mend the damage inflicted by a vicious beating and gang rape. "If it wiz good enough fur the Romans tae bleach their togas wi', it's good enough for me!"[24]

"The themes I tackle come out of Jas himself and what interests me. I try to take him places which will interest the reader too, of course. I live where Jas lives, in the type of accommodation he lives in, and we see the same things every day.... In a wider sense, though, the character of Jas and the story he is involved in, in any given novel, are paramount."

Homosexual S&M is a core theme of the series and one of the defining attributes of its protagonist. It is part of Anderson's strongly dominant relationships with other men and a large part of their hatred of him. At the same time, it is the most dependable window to his personal vulnerability. "Throughout the series, Jas is searching for something I think we all search for: a way of being himself with those around him, a way of living and loving that works for him....

"I probably consider the prime theme I want to communicate as, oddly enough, diversity.... I'm writing for other gay men and women, some of whom presumably enjoy detective fiction and want to see something other than a heterosexual man or woman as protagonist, some of whom are into SM and want to see this theme explored—and some of whom who just want a good read."

KATHERINE V. FORREST: *Kate Delafield* (1984–CURRENT)

Katherine V. Forrest (1939–) is an award-winning and internationally best-selling writer of lesbian mysteries, science fiction, and novels. Her novel *Curious Wine* is one of the best-selling lesbian novels of all time. She was senior editor with The Naiad Press for ten years. Forrest received the Lesbian Rights Award from Southern California Women for Understanding and the Lambda Pioneer Award for her contributions as a writer, editor, and spokesperson. She lives with her partner in San Francisco.

Detective: Kate Delafield, homicide detective, LAPD

Setting: Los Angeles, California. Time period is contemporary with publication dates

Books: *Amateur City* (1984); *Murder at the Nightwood Bar* (1987); *The Beverly Malibu* (1989); Lambda Award—Best Lesbian Mystery (1989); *Murder by Tradition* (1991); Lambda Award—Best Lesbian Mystery (1991); *Liberty Square* (1996); Finalist Lambda Award—Best Lesbian Mystery (1996); *Apparition Alley* (1997); Finalist Lambda Award—Best Lesbian Mystery (1997); *Sleeping Bones* (1999); Finalist Lambda Award—Best Lesbian Mystery (1999)

Publishers: The Berkley Publishing Group, The Naiad Press (rereleases by Alyson Publications)

Kate Delafield is a detective, senior grade, in the LAPD who is often assigned cases that highlight gay positive and feminist issues. "All my stories about her begin with a dramatic situation I want to explore with Kate as my principled explorer."

Delafield was the first lesbian police detective to have her own mystery series, but that was not Forrest's original plan. "It was to be one mystery, not a series. I simply wanted to use my background in business ... to explore the issue of abuse of power.... In my position in management I saw, on a daily basis, what I called 'spiritual deaths' because of the acts perpetrated by those in positions of power. So I decided to have an actual death, but with the tables turned—one of the abused turns on the abuser." In that book, *Amateur City*, Delafield is the police detective on the case but the real sleuth is an amateur detective. "I immediately (smart me) perceived that SHE was the interesting character, and that here was an opportunity to portray a lesbian in a high visibility, high pressure, and most unusual profession."

Abuse of power continues to be a major recurrent theme, but after *Amateur City* the mysteries became theme-rich police procedurals. Among these is Kate's lesbianism. "Kate's sexual identity is central; the series revolves around it, and Kate has made personal and career decisions solely because of it, because of her internal view of herself and her sexuality." Plots and subplots in all the novels intersect with Kate's lesbianism from gay bashing to her tenuous link with the lesbian community via the Nightwood Bar. "Being a lesbian police officer has offered an additional dynamic and has allowed introduction of many issues of interest to a wide range of readership." Some of those issues involve Kate's personal life, such as her relationship with her lover Aimee Grant and, more recently, her rapprochement with her family.

The closet—the dominant recurring theme in the series also derives from Kate's lesbianism. "Kate's a decent, admirable person and a fine, dedicated police officer. Her central chord is integrity, and it's a powerful element in her; it imbues her actions and responses personally as well as professionally. Still, with all that integrity, she remains deeply flawed because of her perception that she must be closeted." Kate clings to the closet and to the belief that her colleagues are unaware she's a lesbian—even though she was outed in a courtroom early in the series. She's blind to other obvious indicators that her secret is out even if *she* isn't, such as the presence of her name at the top of a list of gay and lesbian LAPD officers that is given to her in *Apparition Alley*. "She's edged more and more out of the closet, but in seven novels about her she has yet to see that the closet's hold on her has isolated her on the job, has limited her life choices and her relationship with the woman she loves, and is sowing the seeds of real jeopardy to that relationship." Fortunately for Kate, she has recently begun to move, albeit slowly, towards greater personal integration and self-acceptance.

MITCHELL GROBESON: *Steve Cainen* (2000)

Sgt. Mitchell Grobeson (1958–) has been featured on *60 Minutes* and other TV shows about being the first openly gay officer in the LAPD and the first officer in the country to sue a law enforcement agency to stop antigay harassment and discrimination.

Despite risking his career by challenging the LAPD academy's practice of maliciously injuring women cadets to prevent them from graduating, Grobeson earned the highest overall scores in physical fitness, academics, shooting and self-defense. Afterwards, Grobeson was the only officer in his division to provide protection to a black family targeted by white supremists and the first officer to come forward about the beatings and false arrests of Latinos prior to the "Rampart Scandal." In addition to writing, Grobeson provides free cultural diversity training on sexual orientation to high schools, colleges, municipal organizations and law enforcement agencies.

Detective: Officer Steve Cainen, LAPD

Setting: Los Angeles. Time period is contemporary with publication date

Book: *Outside the Badge* (2000)

Publisher: Vantage Press

Outside the Badge is a supercop thriller about the homophobic, sexist, and racist practices of the LAPD, from the chief of police down to the beat officers. "People who know me or know my story know that the discrimination and harassment against the gay officer in the book are things that actually happened to me at the hands of the LAPD." Grobeson wrote the book because "I had death threats from the LAPD and

LAPD officers. I had even been pulled over at gunpoint by rookie officers who'd been told that I was a wanted felony suspect. A couple of times I was almost killed. I decided I wanted the story out there just in case anything happened to me."

The book tracks Officer Steve Cainen's investigation into the serial killings of gay hustlers and the harassment he endures at the hands of his homophobic colleagues. "I wanted to keep the readers interested but at the same time educate them. As long as I could keep them reading the story line, I could throw in all this information about how the LAPD actually treats gay men and lesbians in the public and how it treats gay and lesbian officers." *Outside the Badge* also describes the hustler culture, including the belief "that they were heterosexuals who were exploiting the gay community for money."[25] The LAPD, on the other hand, views them as gay and labels the murders NHI (no human involved).

Cainen is maneuvered into accepting the undercover assignment of posing as a hustler, but there's no police backup when he's abducted. "What happened in the book was exactly what happened in real life to me. My captain was deposed and admitted that my fellow officers refused to provide me backup, that they 'were not responding to emergency calls that have some element of danger when they were given to Grobeson.' They had a meeting at a donut shop, and from that moment on everyone was given that message. Even the few officers who would have backed me up, didn't. So, when I went on a robbery alarm, which was the second highest call on which officers are killed or seriously injured, I was alone. Then, when I went on a foot pursuit, even the dispatcher was yelling on the radio 'Where's his backup? What the hell's going on?' I was surrounded by gang members, and not a single officer would back me up. LAPD had 8,000 gay officers and nobody would back me up. That's a fear that gay officers have even in 2003.

"The bottom line is that I want it to be easier for the next generation. I want them to feel good about themselves so that they don't fall into drug or alcohol abuse or wind up with suicide or unsafe sex.... I want them to have a freedom of choice that I didn't have when I joined LAPD. That's what books with role models can do."

Cainen is, indeed, a role model. He's so physically, intellectually, and morally superior that even he believes "he might possibly be the reincarnation of a Samurai warrior."[26] The fact that Mitchell Grobeson can be described in the same terms is a reminder that gay and lesbian heroes exist in the real world as well as in the pages of fiction.

STEVE JOHNSON: *Doug Orlando* (1992–1993)

Steve Johnson earned a baccalaureate in English Literature from UCLA and has lived in Los Angeles.

Detective: Homicide Detective Doug Orlando, Brooklyn, NYPD

Setting: Brooklyn, New York. Time period is contemporary with publication dates

Books: *Final Atonement* (1992); *False Confessions* (1993)

Publisher: Penguin Books

This theme-rich series pits strong gay positive and feminist messages against institutionalized homophobia, sexism, and racism. Brooklyn PD Homicide Det. Doug Orlando, supported by his lover, family, friends, and a phalanx of gay and heterosexual activists, first exposes and then tries to combat institutionalized bigotry. The main targets are religion and the police department.

Final Atonement begins after Orlando has violated the police code of silence. He has testified against a fellow detective whose use of excessive force against minorities culminated in the death of an African American teen. Orlando, a 20-year veteran of the department, is shunned by his colleagues, given the worst cases by his lieutenant, and subjected to constant homophobic harassment. "He'd always been closeted on the force, and though there'd been whispers and titters, it hadn't affected his treatment on the job. Probably because nobody really believed it…. But after his testimony, it all fit together. *That snitch was a queer.* It all made sense."[27]

The campaign against Orlando is spearheaded by the crude and violent white supremacist Det. Briggs, who personifies the ugliness of bigotry. Briggs' death and the imminent exposure of his neo-Nazi police enclave at the end of the series offer a sliver of hope for Orlando and the police department as a whole.

No comparable ray of hope shines on intolerance and abuse of power in religion. A spiritual leader is found murdered in each of the two books in the series: an extremist Hasidic rabbi and a guilt-ridden, gay Catholic priest. Orlando's quest to find their murderers uncovers the personal devastation created by homophobia, sexism, and racism promulgated in the name of God.

Counterbalancing those themes are strongly positive images of gay men and lesbians. Orlando and his lover Stewart, a university professor, have had a loving and mutually respectful relationship for twelve years. The relationship between Orlando's best friend, medical examiner Ronnie Bell, and her partner Sally is just as enduring and has been extended to a child. Strong feminists, Ronnie and Sally are active in the lesbian community and are friends of the women who operate a women's clinic that was bombed by the murdered rabbi. One gay man provides a role model and legitimate work environment for troubled gay teens. Although the editor of a leftist gay newspaper, and Anthony, a Queer Nation activist, are abrasive, they are portrayed sympathetically.

The subcultures Orlando encounters in his investigations add meat to the plots and characters. In *Final Atonement*, Hasidic traditions and beliefs provide the clues that lead Orlando to the rabbi's killer. In *False Confessions*, American Catholicism and the homophobic doctrines of the church provide the context for understanding why the priest was murdered. Gay youth counterculture is the backdrop for the serial killings in *False Confessions*, and Ronnie Bell struggles to understand the shift from the lesbian-feminism of her youth to the antifeminism of the young lesbians she meets in that book.

LAURIE R. KING: *Kate Martinelli* (1993–CURRENT)

Award winner Laurie R. King is a best-selling author whose Bee-Keeper's Apprentice and Kate Martinelli novels are approaching two million in sales worldwide. She has degrees in religious studies and wrote her master's thesis on feminist theology. She's received awards for her novels and short stories as well as other honors, including an honorary doctorate. King is a San Francisco Bay Area native who has lived in twenty countries on five continents. She and her husband have homes in California and Oxford, England.

Detective: Homicide Inspector Katarina (Kate) Martinelli, San Francisco PD

Settings: San Francisco and northern California. Time period is contemporary with publication dates

Books: *A Grave Talent* (1993); Edgar—Best First Novel (1993); John Creasey Award (1993); Finalist Anthony—Best First Novel (1994); *To Play the Fool* (1995); *With Child* (1996); Finalist Edgar and Orange Awards (1996); *Night Work* (2000)

Publisher: Bantam Books

Inspector Kate Martinelli is a homicide detective in the San Francisco Police Department. She begins the series as a dour, intense, and deeply closeted young detective working her first big case. "With each book she has become more confident, personally and professionally, until with *Night Work* she is simply a cop doing her job. Actually, that was one of the toughest books to write, and only when I finished did I realize why: It's because Kate IS just doing her job, not immersed in personal catastrophe or angst. Heaven only knows what I'll do with the next one. Kill off someone close to her, I suppose, to keep her on the edge....

"Kate came about because I wanted to write about a world-rank woman artist, which didn't seem to go with the historical Mary Russell milieu I had already developed, so I took that idea and set it into a part of the world I knew well and in a time I didn't have to research.... Later, I wanted to write about a holy fool ... and the rather stilted personality of Kate seemed a perfect foil for Erasmus' embodiment of chaos.... I have to admit that I found Kate's repressed humorlessness trying, and had in fact not intended to write another after *A Grave Talent*. But then Brother Erasmus demanded to be written, and his presence seemed to shake her loose a bit. I like her better now, but wouldn't say she's exactly the life of my particular party. Although some of my lesbian friends would beg to differ....

"As a defining part of who Kate is, her being a lesbian is nearly as important as the fact that she is a woman. And yet, the books are not about a lesbian, but about a woman cop who, among other things, happens to be a lesbian." Nor does Kate's lesbianism represent an unusual writing challenge. "I wouldn't say it's difficult, certainly less so than writing a male character, which is what I did in *Keep Watch*. It might be more so if there were more of an emphasis on that side of her life, but there isn't.... Perhaps if I were a lesbian myself, Kate's sexual identity might play a more central role in the books, but I don't think so.... In most of my books, including the Martinellis, sex is a private thing. Which is a round-about way of saying that restrictions and liberations, sexually at any rate, tend to be innate to the individual book, not from an external pressure." Yet, the impact of Kate's lesbianism extends beyond the character. "She enables me to look at male power structures within an essentially military structure such as the police department, not only because she's a woman, but because she's not apt to fall in love with one of the male cops, and can therefore preserve her clear-eyed view of the department."

Communities play an important role as well. The artist accused of murdering children in *A Grave Talent* lives in a closed, traditional community that must contend with an onslaught of outsiders. In *To Play the Fool*, San Francisco's homeless community faces the loss of Brother Erasmus, their spiritual leader, who is implicated in a murder. In *Night Work*, the lesbian-feminist community is involved in vigilante attacks but not in the murders. In *With Child*, Martinelli's department stands solidly behind "one of their own" when the media imply the lesbian cop is a sexual predator.

"One of the great strengths of a mystery series is its ongoing dependence on relationships, using them not only to flesh out the characters, but also to add depth and resonance to the plot elements ... *Night Work*, for example, rests solidly on the friendship between Kate and Roz..." and Kate's relationship with her lover Lee Cooper is continually evolving. "Maybe the next one will find Lee finally getting her say."

MELANIE MCALLESTER: *Tenny Mendoza* (1994–1996)

Melanie McAllester (1962–) spent ten years as a police officer for the Palo Alto Police Department in the San Francisco Bay area. She specialized in crisis resolution intervention and hazardous materials response. She has a bachelor's degree in political science and a master's degree in public administration. McAllester has since moved with her partner to the Seattle area.

Detective: Sr. Homicide Det. Elizabeth (Tenny) Mendoza, Los Palos, California, PD

Setting: Northern California and Brazil. The time period is contemporary with publication dates

Books: *The Lessons* (1994); *The Search* (1996)

Publishers: The Naiad Press, Spinsters Ink

Elizabeth "Tenny" Mendoza is one of the few mixed race main characters in the gay/lesbian literature. The youngest child of an African American mother and a "European looking" Mexican father, Mendoza is a stunningly beautiful and talented professional with a reputation for fighting for justice. Although she is only in her thirties, she has established herself as a dynamic leader who inspires people to work together. Her nickname, Tenny, was given to her because she would tenaciously pursue a case until she got results. Mendoza also appears to have ESP and can sense when something bad will happen. Thus, it is not surprising that other characters in these stories use terms like "magical" and "mystical" to describe her.

In *The Lessons*, Mendoza has been assigned to head a task force formed to capture a serial rapist who targets lesbians. Her team consists of openly lesbian Ashley Johnson and sexual-assault officer Steve Carson who is equally open about his beliefs that homosexuality is immoral and that lesbians are the "dregs of womanhood." The task force apprehends the rapist despite interpersonal conflict, police brass attempts to disband it, and a community up-in-arms. In the process Mendoza, Johnson, and Carson learn to respect each other as professionals and individuals.

Early in *The Lessons*, Tenny begins a transformation that is carried into *The Search*. At first, she begins to question the value of her work as a police officer. By the end of *The Lessons*, Mendoza has become obsessed with capturing the rapist and with discovering why he attacks lesbians. "I know I'm not supposed to let things become a personal battle, but that's an unrealistic expectation of cops. The pain we see, the death, the destruction, it's all personal. Sometimes when you have an opportunity to change a little piece of all that, you have to seize it."[28]

The transformation is completed at the beginning of *The Search* when Mendoza's ex-lover asks Tenny to help find her kidnapped daughter. Unable to comply with a direct order to stop working on that case, Tenny resigns from the police force. The book concludes with a dramatic gun battle on a Brazilian beach involving Mendoza, an assassin, the kidnappers, and Mendoza's two former task force partners.

Gay positive and feminist issues related to family and personal relationships take center stage in both books. *The Lessons* focuses on the devastating effects of homophobia that include lesbian bashing. Everyone, including Tenny, learns lessons about the need to combat homophobia, racism, and other forms of prejudice. *The Search* sounds an alarm about the growing problem of child abduction. At the end of each book, when the criminals are brought down, the world *is* a better place—even if the future is uncertain.

JANET MCCLELLAN: *Tru North* (1997–1999)

Janet E. McClellan (1951–) spent twenty-seven years in law enforcement serving as a patrol officer, detective, juvenile officer, homicide and arson investigator, and police chief. McClellan writes mysteries, historical novels, romance, science fiction, and nonfiction. She's published nonfiction papers on criminal justice in scholarly journals, trade magazines and the popular press. She taught criminal justice at Southwestern Oregon Community College and in 2003 accepted an Associate Professor position in the Criminal Investigation program with SUNY at Canton.

Detective: Tru North, Detective Grade 2, Kansas City PD

Setting: Primarily Kansas City. Time period is contemporary with publication dates

Books: *Penn Valley Phoenix* (1997); *K.C. Bomber* (1998); *Chimney Rock Blues* (1998); *River Quay* (1999)

Publishers: iuniverse.com, The Naiad Press

Tru North is a young police detective trying to learn her craft. "The cases that I select come from my investigations. *Penn Valley Phoenix* is made up of several cases, including one involving a woman who robbed a bank and couldn't otherwise be identified. It's a real story. So is the story of a man with the car who was later found to be an inmate. That was a different case. In *K.C. Bomber,* Tru shot and killed a mirror. I did that in a burglary case at a clothing store. I try to pick parts of cases that will give Tru the people interaction, processes, complications, and other things I want to involve her in and evolve her through -plus having an interesting mystery....

"I was not trying to make a superwoman. I wanted a character that readers could relate to. She's someone who learns through experience, but she's a two-steps-forward-and-one-step-back kind of person." She's attractive and physically fit but not an outstanding physical specimen. "She wants to be competent and capable—and she thinks it would be nice if she were viewed that way. That's not always the case. Sometimes people see her as an irritant." North is a capable detective but she tends to rush into dangerous situations. At least once in each book a criminal gets behind her or surprises her. These miscalculations often result in hospital stays.

McClellan likes to give her characters lives beyond their work, but North's personal life is a mess. "Tru is much more attuned to the professional than the personal.... She ignores things or just lets them ride." At the start of the series she's despondent because her lover dumped her but almost immediately falls into the clutches of a controlling and emotionally abusive lover. While she is still living with that partner, she establishes a secret relationship with a more supportive lover. "She's still young enough to do that 'wishing' thing: wishing that she doesn't get caught, that she'll figure out what she wants to do, that it will work itself out.... She's not stupid, though. She can hear the sound of feet coming up behind her."

North generally works on "special evaluation"—code for being in trouble with her captain. McClellan uses North's organizational woes to expose the internal politics of police forces, including the old and new faces of sexism. "I remember a couple of reviewers who scoffed at my stories saying that Capt. Rhonn was made up. I didn't have to make him up. Capt. Rhonn is a kind of person I've seen a number of times. I've even seen him in female form—which I've yet to put into the series."

The series covers sexism, sexual abuse, abuse of power, and other issues that "run through women's lives. When you look at them more closely, all these themes boil down to interpersonal relationships." There's less coverage of homophobia, primarily because North is solidly in the closet. "It is reality oriented. In even major law enforcement agencies ... there is recognition, but there is not acceptance. It comes down to whether coming out would be a good thing careerwise—depending also on what you want in a career...."

CLAIRE MCNAB: *Carol Ashton* (1988–CURRENT)

Claire McNab (1940–; pseudonym for Claire Carmichael) was born in Melbourne, Australia. She's currently a citizen of the United States and Australia. She began writing fiction when she was teaching English in Sydney and soon became a full-time writer. She's published over forty books: mysteries, thrillers, children's books (under Claire Carmichael), lesbian romances, plays, and nonfiction. She's a past president of *Sisters in Crime* and speaks frequently at mystery writers' conferences. McNab lives in Los Angeles with her partner.

Detective: Detective Inspector Carol Ashton, Sydney, Australia PD

Setting: Primarily Sydney, Australia. Time period is contemporary with publication dates

Books: *Lessons in Murder* (1988); Finalist Lambda Award—Best Lesbian Mystery/Science Fiction (1988); *Fatal Reunion* (1989); *Death Down Under* (1990); *Cop Out* (1991); *Dead Certain* (1992); *Body Guard* (1994); *Double Bluff* (1995); *Inner Circle* (1996); *Chain Letter* (1997); *Past Due* (1998); Finalist Lambda Award—Best Lesbian Mystery (1998); *Set Up* (1999); *Under Suspicion* (2000); *Death Club* (2001); *Accidental Murder* (2002); Finalist Lambda Award—Best Lesbian Mystery (2002); *Blood Link* (2003)

Publisher: The Naiad Press

The Carol Ashton mysteries are police stories starring a beautiful but supremely flawed product of the Australian upper class. At the start of *Lessons in Murder* Ashton is on a meteoric career path fueled by her mentor, the police commissioner, and her exceptional investigative and communication skills. "She's driven to succeed by a strong sense of duty. She likes structure and enjoys power. She's also fair, just and motivated by a desire to set the world right—insofar as she can.... She doesn't indulge in self-examination, so the other reasons she enjoys her job (power, prestige) don't impinge on her consciousness."

Ashton works closely with Det. Sgt. Mark Bourke to dissect and debate evidence garnered from interviews, interrogations, observations, and forensic analysis. Otherwise, Carol is a solitary individual. "It is significant that she's kept very few close friends from her earlier life ... most she now knows through professional contacts. She needs people whom she can admire, who are in some sense her equals" but such people are a rarity. Furthermore, her long residence in the closet has taught her to insulate herself from everyone, including her son, David, and her lovers. "In her personal life she believes she wants a committed relationship, but has little time to work on it, as her job always comes first." Her ferocious need to remain closeted is so powerful that she comes out to

her son only after being compelled by others to do so. Her fears about coming out appear justified when she is outed and her career stalls.

Ashton's flaws arise from her personal life, in particular her lack of self-analysis and her overpowering sexual needs. "Although of course she doesn't analyze it, she's very self-protective. With lovers she's very happy to enjoy the physical side but wary of very close emotional involvement." Sexual urges cloud her judgment and threaten her career from the very first book. In the course of the series, she initiates a sexual liaison with the chief suspect in a murder case she's investigating, has an affair with a hit woman, and is almost murdered by an ex-lover about whom she admits "I loved her so much I was willing to put everything on the line for her, and in the end, that's what I lost—everything."[29]

"Carol investigates the cases that fate (and the author) give her, however there's always an underlying theme." Those themes include social, personal, and political issues as wide-ranging as pedophilia, willful spread of HIV, right-wing conspiracies, and abuse of power. "The most important themes are the operation of the media, violence against women, feminism, and casual, taken-for-granted homophobia." Abuse of power and privilege is a thread that runs through the series surfacing in both main and secondary plots. Investigations are often set in the homes and retreats of the rich and powerful who view Ashton as one of their own and admit her with the expectation she will protect them from scrutiny, do their bidding, or shield them from the consequences of their own criminal behavior. When all else fails, they have no compunction about resorting to threats, blackmail, and even murder.

MARY MORELL: *Lucia Ramos* (1991–1993)

Mary Morell (1945–) has written novels, poems, plays, political diatribes, and other pieces of fiction and nonfiction. She has had a remarkably diverse employment background. She has been an English teacher, counselor, travel agency manager, and bookstore owner. She and her partner owned and operated Full Circle Books, a feminist bookstore in Albuquerque, New Mexico.

Detective: Det. Lucia Ramos, San Antonio PD
Settings: San Antonio and Alabama. Time period is contemporary with publication dates
Books: *Final Session* (1991); winner Spinsters Ink Lesbian Fiction Contest (1991); *Final Rest* (1993)
Publisher: Spinsters Ink
Detective Lucia Ramos is the first lesbian Chicana (Mexican–Amer-

ican) main character in mystery fiction. Ramos is close to her Mexican heritage and her family, but they play virtually no role in the stories. These are feminist mysteries written in a traditional mystery format. Their aim is to highlight women's issues—in particular the lifelong damage created by incest and other forms of sexual abuse worsened by society's silence on the subjects.

Final Session begins not long after Lucia Ramos is promoted to the rank of homicide detective. Her first big case is the murder of a prominent lesbian therapist. Despite her lack of experience, Ramos investigates the case alone with virtually no supervision. Assisted by a psychologist who consults for the police department (who later becomes her lover), Ramos reveals how the victim exploited her power over clients to manipulate and sexually abuse them.

Ramos takes a leave of absence in *Final Rest* to travel to Alabama so she can help clear her lover's Aunt Meg of murder. Since she's out of her jurisdiction, Ramos is forced to operate as a private investigator employed by Aunt Meg's attorney. She complains about the constraints of that role but demonstrates she doesn't need a badge to solve the murder.

The lesbian community is portrayed as a powerful network willing to support its members. In *Final Rest,* Ramos' friend Freddie Christian brings to bear the power of her nationwide network of closeted lesbians to help Aunt Meg obtain the legal resources needed to clear her name. Christian and Aunt Meg are older lesbians whose appearance, lifestyle, and decency fly in the face of negative lesbian stereotypes and society's tendency to dismiss and demean older women.

Lesbian/gay-related themes play a secondary role to women's issues, but Morell makes it clear that they exist. Homophobia in the San Antonio PD keeps Ramos solidly in the closet at work—even though she's out of the closet with her family. Internalized homophobia extends to the larger lesbian community. In the following conversation Ramos and Freddie Christian, who is also deeply closeted, come out to each other in code.

> [Freddie Christian] My, my, my, Officer Ramos. Are there many like you on the force?
> [Ramos] Alas, I appear to be in a very small minority, shall we say one in ten, but my unique perspective does have its uses in police work.[30]

The lightheartedness of this exchange stands in stark contrast to the danger, fear, and mistrust that impel these characters to speak in code. The tone is, however, consistent with the presentation of the lesbian community as a source of positive energy. It's also an example of the humor that makes the novels good vessels for communicating feminist ideas.

TRACEY RICHARDSON: *Stevie Houston* (1997–1999)

Tracey Richardson (1964–) has worked as a journalist for daily newspapers since 1986 and now edits one in central Ontario. In addition to the Stevie Houston mysteries, she's published a lesbian romance and short stories for Naiad anthologies. Richardson grew up in Ontario and has a degree in journalism. She lives with her partner of more than twelve years (a police officer) and their two dogs.

Detective: Homicide Detective. Stephanie Elizabeth (Stevie) Houston, Toronto PD

Setting: Toronto, Ontario, Canada. Time period is contemporary with publication dates

Books: *Last Rites* (1997); *Over the Line* (1998); *Double Take Out* (1999)

Publisher: The Naiad Press

This series uses police stories to make feminist and gay positive social commentary. It pits the forces of good against entrenched evils, in particular homophobia, sexism, corruption, and abuse of power. "Homophobia is very much entrenched in our society's institutions, and I hope my novels help show how ridiculous, how 'false' the foundation of some of the institutions is." The triumph of good makes the world a better place. "It's really at the whole root of the Stevie character, i.e., she wouldn't continue to be a cop if she didn't inherently believe good can overcome evil. Also, pure and simple, it's for escapism purposes, so the reader has something uplifting to take from it."

The plots center on crimes involving closeted lesbians and gay men in environments with culturally sanctioned homophobia. "You could almost take the view that the characters in my novels who try to remain closeted are 'punished.' The priest who is murdered. The married lesbian who is falsely suspected of murder." And the lesbian police officers who are mercilessly harassed by their male colleagues. "This theme wasn't intentional, but perhaps shows some underlying 'dim' view I take of being closeted."

Last Rites begins shortly after Stevie is promoted to homicide detective at the tender age of thirty. She's worked hard to earn that rank but veteran detectives believe she was promoted solely because she's female. There's also talk she's a lesbian. "The development of the Stevie character illustrates some patience with her coming to terms with being out. She's tormented about it but realizes it's a process that's very personal." Stevie's butch persona also fits well in the police culture and is used as a source of humor. In *Double Take Out*, for example, Stevie gives another lesbian officer "a good butch-to-butch wallop on the arm."

The series also follows Stevie's relationship with forensic pathologist Dr. Jade Agawa-Garneau, a native Canadian, whose femininity contradicts stereotypes about lesbians. It's emotionally and sexually charged, in part because of Stevie's difficulties with intimacy. "I like to think that throughout the series she has gotten more in touch with her inner feelings, has become more understanding of the human condition and less a 'bulldozer' if you know what I mean. I think that comes with more confidence both on the job and in her relationship." By the end of the series Jade and Stevie clearly define their relationship as a marriage in every way except by law. Jade says "believe me, I'd be dragging her down the aisle if we could legally get married."*[31]

Richardson believes "character development is the most challenging part of writing for me and any writer– making the character believable, three-dimensional, so that every reader can recognize and identify with elements of the characters' personalities." Writing mysteries is also challenging for a romance writer. "The plot is a lot trickier. There are more developments the writer must keep track of and weave together. Also, with the romance, the characters' lesbianism is the whole purpose of the book, but with mysteries, the sexuality is more of a subplot or secondary theme...."

"It's liberating to write about the world in which you live every day of your life. Our sexuality is such a central part of who we are, though, speaking along that line, if the series were to continue, I would like less emphasis on the sexuality part of the characters, to reflect reality a little better."

LINDA KAY SILVA: *Delta Stevens* (1991–CURRENT)

Linda Kay Silva has a master's degree in English (emphasis in Eighteenth Century British Literature). In addition to the Delta Stevens series, she's written *Tory's Tuesday*, a fictionalized story about a Nazi holocaust survivor. She's currently writing modern and historical novels. Silva worked in law enforcement as a beat officer and did undercover work for a year and a half. Originally from northern California, she now lives, writes, and does home schooling in rural Oregon.

Detective: Officer Delta (Storm) Stevens, River Valley, California, PD

Setting: River Valley, California, and Costa Rica. Time period is contemporary with publication dates

Books: *Taken by Storm* (1991); *Storm Shelter* (1993); *Weathering the*

This series predates Ottawa's legislation supporting lesbian and gay marriage.

Storm (1994); *Storm Front* (1995); *Tropical Storm* (1997); *Storm Rising* (2000)

Publishers: Paradigm Publishing Company, Rising Tide Press

The first Delta Stevens novels are police stories set in California. They track Stevens' police work and professional relationships. The series changes to international intrigue and adventure in *Tropical Storm* after Delta leaves for Costa Rica to rescue her kidnapped lover, Megan Osbourne. Silva explains that "the nature of the series changed because I changed. It's related to my commitment to help save the rain forests." The Costa Rican books highlight the relationship between Delta and Megan. "Megan's connection with Delta is so deep that she's with Delta even though she may not be physically present."

Stevens is a supercop. She's a good-looking, strong, very physically fit, action-oriented champion of good over evil and a loyal friend willing to risk her life for others. "She is my white knight—my hero. I carry her around with me 24–7." Delta is guided by a strong sense of justice, ESP, and her "Merlin," Connie Rivera. "Connie was supposed to be a minor character, but it was like she grabbed the pen and said 'I'm going to have a big role.' She's also the sage that understands that the rough edges are part of Delta's charm." When the series shifts to Costa Rica, Connie's mystical side rises to the surface and Delta, although still a woman of action, becomes more vulnerable and sensitive.

Taken by Storm begins with the murder of Miles Brookman, Delta's partner and mentor, whose bond with Delta is so strong it transcends death. "That's the impetus for all of the things she does. She doesn't really get cleansed of that loss until she's in the rain forest and accepts the fact that she was a killer." Before then, she exposes official corruption in her own police department, breaks up a pornography ring preying on Native American children, and protects Connie from a serial killer. "The biggest theme of her world is doing what's right. It comes up in every book and is the moral/ethical part of her character." Her honesty extends to her sexual orientation. Delta is out of the closet and the object of homophobic abuse from heterosexual female and male colleagues.

For Silva, writing is a cathartic experience. "I can't imagine sitting down and trying to figure out a story for Delta. I know when a story is fermenting inside me. I don't think about it. When I was in Costa Rica I was feeling that way. One day I was walking by myself, and the next thing I knew the entire story was playing out from beginning to end. It always comes to me like that—all at once.... And then the next book came right at me. 'Boom!' Completely done. I was stunned.... The first draft is the emotions. I just go. My revisions are actually the writing craft—I put in all of the details and the things that pretty it up, so the revisions are usually longer."

The Delta Stevens series came into being when "a friend suggested I write a cop story because I'd been a cop. I decided to do it, and it led to an incredible part of my life. I have no regrets."

LARRY TOWNSEND: *Dr. Bruce MacLeod* (1991–1992)

Larry Townsend (1935–) is a BDSM activist known for his prodigious output of "leatherman" erotica that includes *The Leatherman's Handbook*, a book on SM philosophy and techniques. In 1995, he was awarded Man & Woman of the Year and Lifetime Achievement Awards from The National Leather Association. Townsend has a degree in psychology and served in the intelligence service of the United States Air Force during the Korean War. He lives in California with his lover of more than thirty-five years and runs his own press and mail-order service.

Detective: Dr. Bruce MacLeod, psychiatrist and consultant with the LAPD

Setting: Los Angeles. Time period is contemporary with publication dates

Books: *Masters' Counterpoint: A Suspense Novel* (1991); *One for the Master, Two for the Fool* (1992)

Publisher: Alyson Publications

Dr. Bruce MacLeod is a psychiatrist on retainer with the LAPD Criminal Profiling division. Although he's a consultant rather than a police officer, MacLeod is the quintessential supercop: he's handsome, athletic, sexually well-endowed, talented, intelligent, well-educated (M.D., Ph.D., computer scientist), wealthy, successful, and a highly respected authority on criminal profiling. MacLeod battles the forces of evil with the aid of powerful allies, such as the superintendent of the LAPD who is a good friend and a member of the BDSM community. Evil resides in individuals who appear to lack any sense of morality and whose perfidy permeates their environments. A kidnapper-rapist's house "with its disregard for aesthetic effect, was merely an extension of his own attitudes towards the rest of humanity"[32] and the house of the murderer in *One for the Master, Two for the Fool* has "a threatening aura about the place, an almost malevolent feeling."[33]

Like Townsend's other publications, the Bruce MacLeod series provides a view of the BDSM/leatherman subculture accompanied by a tremendous amount of BDSM sex. *Masters' Counterpoint* concerns two men who kidnap young men and subject them to repeated sexual attacks that are part of a BDSM power game. The game's rules require they be so "gentle" in their "play" (i.e., rapes and beatings) that they won't inflict permanent physical damage on their victims. The psychological damage also appears to be transient because the experience actually leads one victim to accept his homosexuality and embark upon a sexual relationship with his therapist, Bruce MacLeod. *One for the Master, Two for the Fool* describes the sexual activities of several young men involved in a double murder.

Masters' Counterpoint addresses the AIDS epidemic and counsels safe sex. Homophobia emanates from family members of gay characters, heterosexual victims of the kidnapper-rapists, and police officers. Internalized homophobia surfaces in the denials of hustlers who enjoy sex with men but pretend they do it for the money, in the confusion experienced by one of Bruce's clients who is grappling with his own sexual identity, and in a TV actor's fear of being outed.

Unlike some of his clients, MacLeod is completely out of the closet as a gay man. He is, however, closeted about his involvement in leather-sex and neither MacLeod nor his heterosexual friends in the BDSM underground appear to have any interest in breaking free of that restraint.

KIERAN YORK: *Royce Madison* (1993–1995)

Kieran York (1943–) lives in the foothills of the Rocky Mountains. In addition to the Royce Madison mysteries, she has written mainstream mysteries, police stories, and romances under another name.

Detective: Royce Madison, acting sheriff

Setting: Timber City, Colorado. Time period is contemporary with publication dates

Books: *Timber City Masks* (1993); *Crystal Mountain Veils* (1995)

Publisher: Third Side Press

In describing her objectives for this series, Kieran York wrote that "exposing the kindness and bravery of lesbians could give those struggling with self-worth a chance to believe in their own strength and fineness."[34] These feminist mysteries include a number of strong lesbians and non-lesbian female characters. These portrayals are counterbalanced by negative characterizations of women and men who value money above all else. Among them is Royce's lover in *Timber City Masks* who is an unabashed social climber.

Both books feature murders that are tied to homophobia, racism, and sexism as well as to ongoing criminal activities, such as drug running. In *Timber City Masks*, Royce comes face-to-face with entrenched racism when she questions the guilt of a Native American man accused of murder. Royce's campaign to be elected sheriff in *Crystal Mountain Veils* pits her against the homophobic and sexist religious right. She encounters all of those "-isms" in her personal life when she and a Native American woman become lovers.

According to York, "The soft spoken Sapphic enforcer confronts more than murder in each adventure. She comes away with inner-conflict resolved as well."[35] Her primary inner conflict stems from being in the closet. Although many of Timber City's residents suspect Royce is a lesbian, she remains closeted until the middle of *Crystal Mountain Veils* when she discovers that her opponent in the sheriff's election plans to "out" her. Although the series argues strongly for coming out, York neither dismisses nor minimizes Royce's concerns. Madison's constituents exhibit an array of homophobic behaviors, including insults, family rejection, outing threats, and murder. It is also clear that Royce is not alone in her fears about coming out. *Masks* and *veils* worn by others hide closeted lesbians and gay men, some of whom are married.

The mysteries are set in the western United States.

> I wanted to introduce the reader to the folks of the Rocky Mountain West. For while the plot may be the foundation of a mystery, I strongly believe that the structure's walls rely on the setting. The decorator fashion, texture, and flavor are found within the characters. Décor is displayed through colorful, solid prose and realistic dialogue.[36]

There are stock Western characters, including Faye, the busty, bighearted saloon owner; Laramie, the town drunk; Orson and Bonnie Laird, simple but good people who own the general store; and Dave Osborne, a drifter. These characters communicate in colorful, folksy dialogues, such as "I always said that Nick is a tad short of flour to make a full loaf"[37] and "I'm movin' slower than a three-legged mule goin' up Pikes Peak."[38] Madison's own favorite expression is "plenty amazing." As with traditional Westerns, Royce Madison always makes sure that the good guys (and gals) win.

MARK RICHARD ZUBRO: *Paul Turner* (1991–CURRENT)

Mark Richard Zubro is an openly gay junior high school teacher in a suburb south of Chicago. He has been writing gay mysteries since 1989. In addition to the Paul Turner series, he writes a Lambda-winning mystery series about Tom Mason and Scott Carpenter (see the section on partners). Zubro lectures frequently about the craft of mystery writing and about the problems inherent in being an openly gay school teacher.

Detective: Det. Paul Turner, homicide detective, Chicago PD

Setting: Chicago. Time period is contemporary with publication dates

Books: *Sorry Now?* (1991); *Political Poison* (1993); *Another Dead Teenager* (1995); *The Truth Can Get You Killed* (1997); *Drop Dead* (1999); Finalist Lambda Award—Best Gay Men's Mystery (1999); *Sex and Murder.com* (2001); *Dead Egotistical Morons* (2003)

Publisher: St. Martin's Press

According to Mark Zubro, "The entire spectrum of our lives needs to be portrayed—not just little bits and pieces.... I wanted to portray in my books fully developed, fully rounded characters. There could be a drag queen. There could be people dying of AIDS. There could be depressed people, but that's not all."

Families are central to this series. "The original concept of Turner was that he would be gay.... Also, I knew when I created him he was going to have children.... I wanted to explore another aspect of gay life: gay parenthood.... I wanted his family and his home life to be essential to what was going on.... I wanted him to be a good cop. I had read lots of police procedurals, and I knew he had to be smart, brave, etc., but I also wanted him to be a good father.... Plus, I gave his younger son a serious birth defect so that not only did he have to parent—which is tough enough—but parenting a child with that kind of serious defect requires even more from a parent. He couldn't just say, 'I think I will stay here at work and just investigate around the clock.' No. There was parenting that needed to be done, and I wanted that to be a part of the series."

By the time the series begins Paul Turner and his poetry-writing and show-tune-singing heterosexual partner, Buck Fenwick, have worked together for five years. Paul is out to Buck but not to the rest of the department. Like many gays and lesbians, Paul is "what I call 'gently out.' They don't talk about the date that they had the week before with anybody but their closest friends at work even though everybody might kind of know.... To create Paul as a totally out officer, I think, would not be entirely realistic. Plus, it's also part of his personality. In one of the books he says he is not a joiner. I think people with kids are less likely to join things. They have to get home to the kids rather than going to a political meeting of some sort. I think that comes closer to the reality of someone's life. It's not a statement about whether or not one should come out."

The fast-moving plots are laced with hidden agendas, power politics, and humor. Most of the humor comes from Paul's partner and the other detectives of Area Ten. Buck has a treasure trove of bad puns and "cute-corpse jokes" and the other detectives include a klutzy loudmouth and a hyper-competitive duo. ("If you had a crime with ten bodies, they had one with eleven.... If you'd solved a case in ten hours, they could have done it in nine."[39])

The stories are overlaid with political intrigues of a city still wrapped in the tendrils of machine politics and ethnic divisions. *Political Poison*, for example, has extensive information about political machinations in Chicago's Irish community and *Sex and Murder.com* looks at the politics of money. There are also treatments of gay themes and issues, such as AIDS, homophobia, gay bashing, and difficulties faced by gay youth. "If I use the books as kind of a commentary, it has to be secondary to the plot—because they are mysteries—but they are a venue for doing that. For example, you can create a villain, but you can't create a one-dimensional villain or you just have a cardboard character. If you create characters and situations around real issues in real life, then the commentary and theme follow."

—— PRIVATE INVESTIGATORS ——

> She's a PI.... That's why she seems competent. She can do ... everything.[40]

Private investigators (PIs) are professional detectives who probe into matters on behalf of their paying clients. Most of them are also trained and licensed. "Consulting detective" Sherlock Holmes (Arthur Conan Doyle), who began his career in 1878, is the first PI. Although he labored for the love of the detecting arts, he had set fees. In 1914, Holmes was joined by Violet Strange (Anna Katharine Greene), the first female PI. The number of PIs expanded during the Golden Age (1919–1939). The most well known is Agatha Christie's Hercule Poirot, who was joined by others including Rex Stout's Nero Wolfe, Nicholas Blake's Nigel Strangeways, and Hulbert Footner's Madame Rosika Storey who specialized in crimes involving women.

The number of fictional PIs swelled in the 1930s when the "private investigator" was supplanted by the hard-boiled "private eye." The first hard-boiled PI was probably John E. Bruce's African American Sadipe Okukeno. The best known from the classic hard-boiled era are Dashiell Hammett's Sam Spade, Raymond Chandler's Philip Marlowe, Mickey Spillane's Mike Hammer, and Ross Macdonald's Lew Archer. The 1970s brought hard-boiled female and ethnic PIs, including Sue Grafton's Kinsey Millhone and Walter Mosley's Easy Rawlins.*

Main Characters

PIs are as popular in gay/lesbian detective literature as in the mainstream. The first gay/lesbian PI was Francis Morley. Morley is a decidedly unboiled detective who appeared in the 1961 stand-alone pulp novel, *Gay Detective,* a parody of hard-boiled fiction. The first gay PI with his own series was Joseph Hansen's Dave Brandstetter.

> The idea for Dave Brandstetter came not from books or radio but from an actual insurance investigator I met in 1955 when he was looking into a swimming pool accident my daughter witnessed at school. This man was, however, nothing like Dave Brandstetter in appearance, manner, tastes, or habits of mind. It was his occupation that caught my imagination. And a dozen years passed before I put the idea to work in *Fadeout,* written in 1967, but not published until 1970....[41]

Hansen adds that Brandstetter's "forbears on the printed page were Sam Spade, Philip Marlowe, and Lew Archer—the California hard-boiled private eyes."† By the time Dave Brandstetter retired in 1991, he was featured in twelve novels and several short stories.

The first lesbian PI, Eve Zaremba's Helen Keremos, appeared in the 1978 novel *A Reason to Kill.* She's a self-employed gumshoe modeled on the classic hard-boiled detectives. Like Brandstetter, Keremos' series concludes with her retirement.

Table 1: Main characters

Character (and author)	Employment	Background
Helen Black (Pat Welch)	Self-employed	Police officer Berkeley, California, PD

See Part I for an overview of hard-boiled detective fiction.
†*All unattributed author quotes come from interviews for this book.*

Character (and author)	Employment	Background
Dave Brandstetter (Joseph Hansen)	Employed by Medallion Life Insurance Company	Not specified
Tor Cross (Penny Sumner)	Employed by a private investigation agency	Archivsit and document analyst
Meg Darcy (Jean Marcy)	Employed by Miller Security	Army MP
Poppy Dillworth (Dorothy Tell)	Self-employed	Clerk (retired) Calice County Sheriff's Dept
Brigid Donovan (Karen Saum)	Self-employed (unlicensed) Freelance writer	Freelance writer
Colleen Fitzgerald (Barbara Johnson)	Investigator at Sampson and Rhoades Investigations	911 dispatcher
Nell Fury (Elizabeth Pincus)	Owner Fury Investigations	Investigator Continent West detective agency
Maggie Garrett (Jean Taylor)	Owner Windsor & Garrett Investigations	Musician
Cassidy James (Kate Calloway)	Self-employed	Junior high school teacher
Helen Keremos (Eve Zaremba)	Self-employed	Navy intelligence officer
Micky Knight (J.M. Redmann)	Self-employed	Bartender, martial arts instructor
Lauren Laurano (Sandra Scoppettone)	Self-employed	FBI agent
Chanse MacLeod (Greg Herren)	Self-employed PI and security consultant	Police officer New Orleans PD
Saz Martin (Stella Duffy)	Self-employed	Not specified
Cal Meredith (Marsha Mildon)	Self-employed	Not specified
Robin Miller (Jaye Maiman)	Partner Serra Investigations	Romance writer
Frances Morley (Lou Rand)	Owner Morley Agency	Actor
Caitlin Reece (Lauren Wright Douglas)	Self-employed and investigator for Crown Prosecutor's office	Attorney for the Crown Prosecutor's office
Lil Ritchie (Phyllis Knight)	Owner Lillian Ritchie Detection Agency	Musician
Sue Slate (Lee Lynch)	Self-employed	Not specified

Character (and author)	Employment	Background
Sydney Sloane (Randye Lordon)	Partner Cabe Sloane Investigations	Police officer NYPD
Donald Strachey (Richard Stevenson)	Self-employed	Army intelligence officer and Investigator with detective agency
Aud Torvingen (Nicola Griffith)	Self-employed	Police officer Atlanta PD (elite Red Dog unit)
Emma Victor (Mary Wings)	Self-employed and investigator for Baynetta Security and attorney Wilhemina Rossini	Publicist and miscellaneous jobs

Table 1 reveals that virtually all gay/lesbian PIs are either self-employed, like Chandler's Philip Marlowe, or work in a partnership, like Hammett's Sam Spade. Hansen's Brandstetter and Marcy's Meg Darcy work in companies owned or run by their families. Two work for attorneys, like Perry Mason's investigator, Paul Drake. Wings' Emma Victor and Sumner's Tor Cross work for companies owned by friends. Cross is employed in her ex-lover's woman-only investigation agency. Only one, Colleen Fitzgerald, has no personal ties to her employer.

Hard-Boiled

Most gay/lesbian PIs are also hard-boiled. Orland Outland, whose series is described in the discussion of partners (pp. 195–233), explains:

> PIs in serious mysteries are hard-boiled because they are traditionally operating in an underworld where you'd better be able to watch your own back. You'd better be tough enough to defend yourself, and even if you can't, you'd better be tough enough to recover from a beating. That's part of the classic PI.

For some authors, inspiration lay closer to a fictional source. Elizabeth Pincus says she "was a little obsessed with the Hammett myth,"[42] Greg Herren sees his Chanse MacLeod as "Gaymond Chandler," and Mary Wings admires Raymond Chandler's writing. "I love the stylistics of Chandler. They were so good and so sparse a writing style."

Outland, Pincus, Rand, and Scoppettone play with the genre. Scoppettone describes *My Sweet Untraceable You* as a "takeoff on corny mystery novels. For instance, quite a few writers have used the ploy of twins, so I took that a step further and used triplets."

Some authors intentionally reshape the mold. Hansen's plan was to

> write a novel in the tradition of Chandler, Hammett, Ross Macdonald, but.... I would hand the toughest, most masculine job in fiction to a homosexual. Because whatever most of us believe, homosexuals ... work

in all kinds of jobs, from carpentry to stock brokerage, from auto mechanic to college professor.[43]

Rand's Francis Morley may look "un-masculine"[44] but he can deck an ex-football player in the boxing ring and he's as tough as any classical gumshoe when it comes to outsmarting crooks. Dorothy Tell created a tough (and not at all feisty) sixty-five year old PI, "Because real life lesbians often fade into the wallpaper, I want them to have a heroine (Wondercrone) to emulate." Barbara Johnson created a capable femme-identified PI, in part because

> the hard-boiled PI detective has historically been male-identified. Butches are generally seen as male-identified even if they are really not. The stereotype of the tough butch fits with the genre. For detective work you have to be stoic, strong, and tough. You can't show emotions when horrible things happen. To do that, people assume you have to be a butch character.

Randye Lordon adds

> I wanted to show that a lesbian, hard-boiled, hard-core PI can still know how to make love, make a gourmet meal, massage an ego, make herself vulnerable, do the ironing, carry a purse and wear makeup.

Police

Having a background in law enforcement is a PI tradition. Mainstream PIs as different as Agatha Christie's Hercule Poirot, Ross Macdonald's Lew Archer, Sue Grafton's Kinsey Millhone, and Robert B. Parker's Spenser are former police officers. Table 1 shows that many gay/lesbian PIs adhere to that tradition as well. Many of them have retained relationships with former colleagues and other members of the police. For example, in addition to being a source of information, NYPD Lieutenant Peter Cecchi is one of Sandra Scoppetone's Lauren Laurano's best friends. Randye Lordon's Sydney Sloane says

> Unlike some other private investigators, I work well with the police. Maybe that's because I spent seven years on the force myself…. Or maybe its because I trust the old adage that "many hands make light work."[45]

Cassidy James (Kate Calloway) and Micky Knight (J.M. Redmann) have no law-enforcement experience but have established friendships with lesbian police officers. James also has a good working relationship with Cedar Hills Sheriff Tom Booker.

> Sheriff Booker is one of my favorite characters in the series because he's a great example of how real friendship is based on mutual values more than outward similarities. Booker looks like the Marlboro Man, Stetson and

all.... In many ways, he's a mentor to Cass—even when they're on opposite sides of the law....

Relationships with the police are not always amicable. Zaremba's Keremos, a former intelligence officer, knows that "cops are trained to intimidate and mystify"[46] and has little patience with such posturing: "Let's cut the crap. We're on the same side."[47] The police don't always see it that way ("Cooperate with a dick?... When roaches are extinct."[48]). Many law-enforcement professionals who appear in these series view PIs as interfering pests—even those who have law-enforcement credentials: "We don't need your PI's expertise to catch this creep. We've got it wrapped."[49]

The police also exhibit sexism, homophobia, and other "-isms." Jean Hutchison (one half of the Jean Marcy collaboration) describes the problems faced by St. Louis PD Det. Sarah Lindstrom, a series character in the Meg Darcy series, who was

> forced out of the closet against her will. She has to deal with the prejudice against her. As we see it, her biggest problem in the police department is that she's a *woman* in the homicide squad.

Homophobia is one reason Greg Herren's PI Chanse MacLeod left the police. Homophobic police officers abound in Richard Stevenson's series, prompting Stevenson's PI Donald Strachey to remark, "law enforcement is not one of the nation's bastions of enlightened social thought."[50*]

Secondary PI Characters

In *Hangdog Hustle,* author Elizabeth Pincus, who worked as a PI herself, writes, "This business is a nonstop hustle of back-scratching and hunch playing...."[51] The "back-scratching" includes networking with and assisting other PIs. Most other PIs in gay/lesbian detective fiction are nameless operatives whose work is discussed in their absence.

Heterosexual

Pincus' PI Nell Fury belongs to a nationwide network of PIs who help each other with big and small favors. They include her mentor Tad Greenblatt and Darnelle Comey, an investigative novice whom Fury takes under her wing. Sydney Sloane (Randye Lordon) also takes charge of a young PI

For a more detailed examination of homophobia and sexism in police departments see the discussion of police, pp. 26–66.

in her series. Robin Miller (Jaye Maiman), Don Strachey (Richard Stevenson), and Helen Keremos (Eve Zaremba) all occasionally obtain assistance from other PIs. Most of these professional contacts are heterosexual.

Gay/lesbian PIs with heterosexual partners engage in brainstorming and other types of mutual assistance. Tor Cross (Penny Sumner) and her colleagues help each other on several cases. Max Cabe, Sydney Sloan's partner, plays an important role as her good friend and as her business partner.

> I wanted the yin and yang. I wanted him to be straight and wanted them to be very close friends. I also wanted to know that if I couldn't get Sydney out of a pickle there was someone else there to help her.

Tony Serra is Robin Miller's (Jaye Maiman) partner and mentor.

> Tony was one of the key father figures in Robin's life, though she never acknowledged this role. Professionally, he was a mentor to Robin.... His illness also acted as a prism for all her obsession with death and emotional abandonment. Despite an unyielding awareness that his death was slowly approaching, Robin allowed herself to grow closer to him and appreciate their friendship. This represented an enormous shift for Robin.

Some gay/lesbian detectives who are not PIs also have strongly positive experiences with heterosexual PIs. In *Wicked Games,* PI Earl Wilcox appeals to amateur sleuth Jane Lawless (Ellen Hart) for help investigating a suspicious death. "We're gonna be a great team, you and me. I could tell, right off."[52] Attorneys Henry Rios (Michael Nava) and Harriet Fordham Croft (Marion Foster) rely heavily upon investigators to help them build cases for the defense. PI Jim Bob Luke appears sporadically in Joe R. Lansdale's Hap Collins and Leonard Pine series. Luke is a skilled investigator with extensive contacts and a huge ego.

Not all experiences with heterosexual PIs are positive. Lesbian PI Helen Keremos (Eve Zaremba) and others encounter slimy and corrupt PIs. Amateur detective Cass Milam (Antoinette Azolakov) hires a PI to do a skip trace but when he's implicated in a murder he skips town; and an enterprising PI hired to get dirt on a businessman in Sharon Gilligan's *Danger! Cross Currents* extends his activities to blackmail. Some PIs are simply incompetent. One man who is hired by a worried father in Tony Fennelly's *Glory Hole Murders* is a ham-handed hack, and another in Jackie Manthorne's *Ghost Motel* "was incredibly incompetent and preferred to flirt with me rather than to conduct a serious investigation."[53]

Gay and Lesbian

There are very few gay or lesbian secondary PI characters, even in gay/lesbian PI series. Tor Cross' (Penny Sumner) colleagues, some of whom are lesbians, appear briefly in the series. Marcy Judy, novice PI Poppy Dillworth's equally green partner in Dorothy Tell's *Murder at Red Rook Ranch*, has a more substantive role. Judy uses her skills as a femme among butches to elicit information the others cannot get. Judy's discoveries in the book also include the realization that she's attracted to women.

In *Bourbon Street Blues,* Greg Herren's amateur detective Scotty Bradley is inspired by the plans of a gay FBI agent to become a PI. The subsequent books track Bradley's transformation. Jenny Roberts' amateur detective Cameron McGill follows a similar path. In *Breaking Point,* she's assisted by Beano (aka Beatrice Nolan), a lesbian PI who is initially described as an arrogant slob. By the end of the novel, the two women have found enough common ground to form a private-investigation partnership.

Themes

Many of the themes in gay/lesbian PI series arise directly from the reasons clients hire PIs. For example:

- find someone ("I want ya to find my mother."[54])
- clear someone's name ("They're railroading him, Meg. It's only been twenty-four hours, and the goddamned cops aren't doing anything but terrorizing my sister and Kyle."[55])
- find the perpetrator of a crime ("I want to hire you and Max to find out what happened to my grandniece."[56])
- dig up dirt on someone ("I would like to engage your services to investigate Dr. North."[57])
- prevent a crime and/or provide protection ("Even if you are not able to figure out who's trying to kill me, you can at least act as my bodyguard."[58])
- find out what's behind unsettling events or behavior ("[my sister] Cissy told me that Judy was murdered.... She's been acting real strange ever since. I think someone needs to get to the bottom of this."[59])

They also, no doubt, ask PIs to follow philandering spouses, serve summonses, and perform other tasks that are not generally included in detective novels.

A client's motives for seeking help from a PI intersect with the issues that prevent them from involving the police:

- there hasn't actually been a crime ("There's been an unexplained death. No more real than the ones I think up for my books ... it's mine."[60])
- the police don't or wouldn't take the problem seriously ("I went to the police. They wouldn't help me: they don't have the time to go chasing down every woman who leaves her boyfriend."[61])
- there's a need or wish to be discrete ("We can't let this thing get out; we'll have to play their game, for a while."[62])
- they have a criminal history ("I can't deal with the cops, Lil. It's a long story."[63])
- they want to keep things "in the family" ("One doesn't make a fuss. College handles its own problems."[64])
- the police aren't doing their job properly ("they've sort of thrown in the towel."[65])
- they don't trust the police ("neither the police nor the FBI have given me cause to believe in their competence."[66])
- the activity, itself, is illegal ("You mean the lying, cheating, and stealing? The breaking and entering? The intimidating? The clobbering and shooting?"[67])

Sometimes clients in gay/lesbian detective fiction also specifically seek the services of a gay or lesbian PI. ("I need someone who's, ah, partial to women."[68] "Jay has mentioned to us that you are a, ah, avowed homosexual...."[69]) Sometimes, the client is a lesbian or gay man who simply prefers to hire services from the lesbigay community. Other clients hire the PI to find a missing lesbian or gay man. In most cases, the wish to have a gay or lesbian PI is a by-product of blackmail or gay bashing and tied to the closet and outing.

Many of the examples accompanying the items on the foregoing lists reveal another central theme: family. The family unit and extended family relationships often lie at the heart of the problem that is set before the investigator. Randye Lordon, whose book titles refer to familial relationships (e.g., *Mother May I*), states, "The whole series is based on family and friendship that creates family." This is true for many of the other series as well.

Unfortunately, clients often conceal their real apprehensions and misrepresent their true motives. Stevenson's PI Don Strachey becomes suspicious, for example, when Mr. and Mrs. Blount hire him to find their missing son, a murder suspect, but not to help clear his name. ("I didn't trust them any farther than I could toss their walnut sideboard."[70]) He eventually learns they intend to commit their son to a mental institution for reprogramming to become heterosexual.

Strachey's experience is the norm which is why Stella Duffy uses her Saz Martin series to explore truth. "I think all four books are about truth and lies—everything else stems from that." Some, like Karen Saum's Brigid Donovan, see being lied to as part of the job, "I just looked gullible: fifties, grey, tennis shoes. Who could blame them...."[71] while others, including Douglas' Caitlin Reece, throw their hands up in dismay.

> They ask for my help—hell, they pay me for it—but they're never straight with me. At best they tell me something approximating the truth. At worst they just plain lie.[72]

KATE CALLOWAY—*Cassidy James* (1996–CURRENT)

Kate Calloway (1957–; pseudonym, real name undisclosed) is a teacher and education leader in southern California and has been instrumental in changing school-district policies on equity issues, such as health benefits for domestic partners. In addition to the Cassidy James series, Calloway has published several lesbian short stories. She's also a song writer and loves boating. She and her longtime partner split their time between southern California and the Pacific Northwest.

Detective: Cassidy James, private investigator

Setting: Cedar Hills, Oregon. Time period is contemporary with publication dates

Books: *1st Impressions* (1996); *2nd Fiddle* (1997); *3rd Degree* (1997); *4th Down* (1998); *5th Wheel* (1998); *6th Sense* (1999); *7th Heaven* (1999); *8th Day* (2001)

Publishers: Bella Books, The Naiad Press

This series blends mystery with romance in books set in the stunningly beautiful Pacific Northwest. "The small Oregon lake-side town is host to moneyed vacationers..., big city refugees..., colorful small-town eccentrics ... and other native Oregonians.... It's the interaction between the different types that sets the stage for the ensuing plots."

Book titles follow an ordinal sequence (*1st Impressions, 2nd Fiddle...*) that are as likely to refer to a facet of the romantic subplot as they are to elements of the main mystery. "Romance (or perhaps more importantly the development and maintenance of relationships) is a key element of the series.... Having said that, the romantic escapades do serve as a sort of red herring to the mystery plots. I seem to write parallel plots (the love interest, the unsolved crime, and the personal growth issues) and interweave them so that they simultaneously ... reach climax and achieve resolution together." Following the pattern of traditional mysteries, once Cassidy has identified the perpetrator and that person is taken into custody or killed, order is restored in the lives of the people involved and in the world as a whole. Often, the final chapter of a book takes place at a party or other celebration.

James' career as a PI begins with *1st Impressions* and her skill as an investigator improves as the series progresses. "I see Cass as a work in progress—not by me as the author so much as by herself as she faces challenges in both her work as a detective and her personal life. She is often brave, but just as often scared. She fears intimacy as much as she craves it, which is why she seems drawn to women who in one way or another are unobtainable. Cass is driven to make things right in the world—the reason for her chosen vocation. She is sometimes naïve in her faith in humanity, which can limit her as a detective but makes her a likable character.... The stories may be about the mysteries, but I think the series is really about Cass's growth as a human being."

When starting a book "I always start with a story I want to write about. I begin with the setting, the kinds of characters who inhabit that setting, the kinds of things they might do in that setting.... Cass's involvement is secondary, because without the crime, there'd be no reason for her to be involved in the first place.... While Cass's involvement is secondary, it is also crucial. I've set aside a number of intriguing plots and story ideas simply because I did not find a way to involve Cass to my liking....

"There is no doubt that this is a feminist mystery series.... Some of my favorite feminists in the series are kids: Jessie in *1st Impressions*, and especially Maddie in *8th Day*." Related to that, one of the strongest recurring themes is the physical, emotional, and sexual abuse of children. "It's a theme that interests me.... I've always been intrigued by the fact that some people emerge stronger than ever from painful experiences, while others crumble and deteriorate into hateful, pitiful beings.... In many of the stories the perp *thinks* they're righting wrongs ... so maybe an underlying theme is, no one ... ever thinks they're the bad guy....

"Probably the one common theme in the series is good vs. evil ... about how people handle adversity, about strengths and weaknesses and, ultimately, the potential for good and evil in all of us." Unlike hard-boiled and noir series, even though bad things happen, good triumphs both in the individual novels and in the series as a whole.

LAUREN WRIGHT DOUGLAS: *Caitlin Reece* (1987–1994)

Lambda award winner Lauren Wright Douglas (1947–) grew up in a military family. She was born in Canada and spent part of her childhood in Europe. As an adult, she's lived in the southwest desert of the

United States and in British Columbia. She now lives on the Oregon coast with her longtime partner. In addition to the Caitlin Reece mysteries, Douglas wrote a mystery series about Allison O'Neil and Kerry Owyhee (see the section on partners).

Detective: Caitlin Reece, private investigator

Setting: Victoria and Vancouver Island, British Columbia, Canada. Time period is contemporary with publication dates

Books: *The Always Anonymous Beast* (1987); *Ninth Life* (1990); Lambda Award—Best Lesbian Mystery (cowinner) (1990); *The Daughters of Artemis* (1991); *A Tiger's Heart* (1992); *Goblin Market* (1993); *A Rage of Maidens* (1994)

Publisher: The Naiad Press

This strongly themed series is filled with quirky characters. At the top of the character list is PI Caitlin Reece who is a blend of sophistication, feminism, and thuggery. She loves to read poetry (excerpts appear in the text) and listen to classical music; she's skilled in self defense; and "I walk softly and carry a big .357."[73] She's also inherited a rudimentary clairvoyance and other psychic gifts, along with a tendency towards insanity that her family calls "the Dark Lady." These abilities generally take the form of flashes of insight, foreboding, and out-of-body dreams.

A former prosecutor, Reece abandoned the legal system in frustration. "I had seen one too many leering rapists, grinning child molesters, and smirking muggers elude justice."[74] Although she claims that she's "discarded such meaningless notions as 'right' and 'justice' and 'fairness'"[75] she appears to be guided by a concept of justice that is clearly distinct from "law." Consequently, she's willing to break laws to achieve it.

Among the crimes included in these books are rape, illegal experimentation on animals, and spouse abuse. The perpetrators, most of whom are men, are evil. "I don't think we have the luxury to be merciful in the presence of evil. Instead, I think we have an obligation. I don't think evil can be unmade. So I think we have to stop it."[76]

The method for stopping evil is a subject of debate in several of the novels. The focus is on the specific theme (e.g., rape, blackmail). Two sides are represented with Reece taking a clear stand on one side of the equation. The subsequent progression of the story line provides an exemplar of why the position Reece adopts is better.

Reece is assisted by a heterogeneous collection of recurring characters. Among the most noteworthy are a woman who can communicate with animals and a prickly computer hacker who likes to dig up information about the people Reece is investigating. ("Dirt....You know, Caitlin, that's my favorite kind of job."[77])

STELLA DUFFY: *Saz Martin* (1996–CURRENT)

Stella Duffy (1963–) was born in the UK and grew up in New Zealand. She's written eight novels (including four Saz Martin novels) and adapted one for the UK National Youth Theatre Company. She coedited the anthology *Tart Noir* from which her story "Martha Grace" won the 2002 Crime Writers' Association Short Story Dagger. Stella's an actor, comedian and improviser. For over fifteen years she's performed with the Spontaneous Combustion Company and tours extensively with the Improbable Theatre's Lifegame Company.

Detective: Saz Martin, self-employed private investigator

Setting: Primarily London. Time period is contemporary with publication dates

Books: *Calendar Girl* (1994); *Wave Walker* (1996); *Beneath the Blonde* (1997); *Fresh Flesh* (1999)

Publishers: Mask Noir, Serpent's Tail

"I think all four books are about truth and lies—everything else stems from that."

The concept of truth is somewhat more relative than is usually the case in detective fiction. "I'm really not at all interested in whodunits. I'm far more interested in WHYdunnit—reasons and excuses and explanations and circumstances that force unexpected/unwanted/unintended change—all these things are SO MUCH more interesting to me than following the traditional detective." This psychological "whydunnit" component is sometimes represented by combining the third-person narrator that usually follows Saz with a first-person voice, generally belonging to someone with a marked fixation, such as the person stalking rock-and-roll star Siobhan Forrester in *Beneath the Blonde*.

"I never intended to write a crime novel. Maggie is the protagonist of *Calendar Girl*; Saz was only there as a device to find out about the 'Woman with the Kelly McGillis Body.'... Saz has become a more rounded character through four books, but I think that's as much to do with having four books of history now as anything else."

The rounding includes "her class (lower middle in UK parlance), her education (not great), her relationship with Molly (who is Indian as well as being gay)." Saz and Molly, who is a physician, are devoted to each other and in *Fresh Flesh*, the fourth book, they are going to have a baby through artificial insemination.

"Saz is brave to the point of foolhardiness—a bravery that comes from a certain degree of stupidity I think. She runs—literally and metaphorically—into danger without thought. She's driven by a quest for truth above all else. She's so morally driven by this desire for truth that she'd generally rather have truth than an easy life. She couldn't work successfully without help from her girlfriend and many other friends—and anyway, I don't really think she does work successfully. She's not a very good PI!! She tends to find stuff out but not in time to stop whatever awful consequences may be waiting.

"I'm aware that when I talk about writing these books that it can sound like I don't care for Saz at all—that she's simply a cipher for my ideas. That isn't the case at all. I'm very fond and proud of the character, and I'm interested in her. But it is true that I don't think she lives outside of myself and that ... the character is secondary to what I'm trying to say. I'm aware THIS sounds as if I look for a theme or issue to tie the story into. I don't. I look for a STORY I want to write. When I have a good STORY that involves Saz—I write it!...

"She's not a character independent of my desire to tell a story. I'm always a little suspicious of writers who say their characters live on outside of them. Saz doesn't. She's totally my fiction and only used when I have a story to tell that involves her. She enables me to tell a different kind of story—usually one involving my own personal obsession of truth vs. lies. (See—it's my obsession, hence hers!!) That's not to say that I don't feel she's a strong, vivid character, but that I'm very aware she doesn't exist beyond me. She's driven purely by my need to tell another story and my awareness that she's the best vehicle to do so."

NICOLA GRIFFITH: *Aud Torvingen* (1998–CURRENT)

Award-winning author Nicola Griffith (1960–) was born in Yorkshire, England. Before she began writing, Griffith taught women's self-defense and sang with a band. Since then, she's published both nonfiction and fiction and coedits the *Bending the Landscape* series of original short fiction. She's won three science fiction awards and five Lambdas. In 1993, Griffith was diagnosed with multiple sclerosis. She lives with her partner of more than fifteen years in Seattle, Washington.

Detective: Aud Torvingen, independently wealthy, part-time security consultant

Setting: Norway and various U.S. locations. Time period is contemporary with publication dates

Books: *The Blue Place* (1998); Lambda Award—Best Lesbian Mystery (cowinner) (1998); *Stay* (2002)

Publishers: Avon Books, Doubleday

These books chart the evolution of the main character, Aud Torvingen, from an insular killing machine into a human being. The investigations in which she's involved form the backdrop for that metamorphosis.

Aud enjoys watching animals in her back yard stalk and kill their prey. When she's with other humans, she considers how she could kill (or be killed by) them, as in this example:

> It would be so easy—a step, a smile, swift whirl and grab, and snap: done. I even knew how she would fall, what a tiny sound her last sigh would be, how she would fold onto the pavement. Eight seconds.[78]

Superior martial-arts skills and experience as a member of the Atlanta PD's elite officer unit give her the tools to execute such observations. Like the animal predators she admires, she's tuned to sensory stimuli and she can adjust her own appearance and behavior to achieve her objectives. ("My face is my most useful tool. I made it smile."[79]) She calls these changes "wearing a mask." Nothing has penetrated her carapace except the realization that the pleasure she derives from stalking and killing is dangerously seductive, a Blue Place from which she might never return.

"*The Blue Place* was about Aud discovering that she was human...."[80] This process begins when Julia Lyons-Bennet hires her to find out who murdered her friend Jim Lusk. In the process of solving the case she falls in love with Julia. Then she loses her. "Grief changes everything. It's a brutal metamorphosis."[81]

In *Stay*, Aud's friend Dornan interrupts her grief-induced seclusion and beseeches her to help find his missing girlfriend. Her investigation is sloppy and dangerously out of control, in part because "I had forgotten how to wear a mask."[82] According to Griffith,

> Loving and then losing Julia leads to Aud's emotional understanding of the effect of her violence on the people upon whom she unleashes it. In *Stay*, when she commits violence in the full knowledge of the hurt she is causing, she loses her particular innocence. To some extent, the novel is about her reaction to her fall from grace, the acknowledgement that the world has changed irrevocably.[83]

Aud's next step, according to Griffith, is finding her place in the world and reconciling the gap between Aud, the killing machine, and Aud, the human being.

> My goal for Aud is pretty ambitious. I want to talk about what makes a human being a human being, what causes change in a human being.... It's about juxtaposition. I want her to be a canvas.[84]

JOSEPH HANSEN: *Dave Brandstetter* (1970–1991)

Award-winning author Joseph Hansen (1923–) was born in Aberdeen, South Dakota. He was married to artist and teacher Jane Bancroft for fifty years (until her death), and they had one child. Hansen has published poetry collections, short stories, and 35 novels. He also founded the pioneering gay journal *Tangents*. He's won a Creative Writing Grant from the National Endowment for the Arts, two Lambdas (1994 for his stand-alone novel *Living Upstairs*) and a Lifetime Achievement Shamus award. Hansen lives and writes in Laguna Beach, California.

Detective: Dave Brandstetter, insurance death-claims investigator

Setting: Primarily Los Angeles, California. Time period is contemporary with publication dates

Books: *Fadeout* (1970); *Death Claims* (1973); *Troublemaker* (1975); *The Man Everybody Was Afraid Of* (1978); *Skinflick* (1979); *Gravedigger* (1982); Finalist Private Eye Writers of America—Best PI, hardcover (1983); *Nightwork* (1984); *The Little Dog Laughed* (1986); *Early Graves* (1987); *Obedience* (1988); Finalist Lambda Award—Best Gay Men's Mystery (1988); *The Boy Who Was Buried This Morning* (1990); *A Country of Old Men* (1991); Lambda Award—Best Gay Men's Mystery (1991)

Publishers: Harper, Holt, Mysterious Press, Viking (rereleases by No Exit)

The publication of the first Dave Brandstetter novel in 1970 marked an important change in the portrayal of gay characters in fiction.

> In *Fadeout* I wanted to tell a rattling good mystery yarn, but I also wanted to turn a few more common beliefs about homosexuals inside out and upside down, as many as I could in a space of fifty thousand words.[85]

"The earlier Brandstetter novels centered around homosexuality. But as the series ran on, I began to explore other areas so far as the mystery plots went. When I saw a likely plot in a news story or heard one in something said by a friend (or a stranger), I developed a novel from it. Homosexuality continued as a subtheme in all the books; that had to happen given Dave's own homosexuality and that of many of his friends who keep cropping up in book after book. A good theme (like the respect for traditional Asian ways in *Obedience*) was enough for me. I can't imagine ever bypassing a good story because Dave couldn't handle it. I may have done so—but not that I'm aware of."

Brandstetter's "forebears on the printed page were Sam Spade, Philip Marlowe, and Lew Archer—the California hard-boiled private eyes.... When we meet him in *Fadeout*, he has just lost Rod Fleming, his lover of two decades, to cancer. And by the time the novel ends, he has joined his life with that of Doug Sawyer. Both these lovers were ... of Dave's age. Not until years later, when Doug leaves him, does he link up with a very young lover, Cecil Harris, who is the instigator of the pairing."

Hansen used a number of methods to keep the Brandstetter series fresh. "One of my methods was to let my detective age, which brought changes in his life and in the lives of those he cared about. He grew old as I grew old. This furnished grist for the mill. Also I didn't rush the series. I took time out to write other sorts of novels, and after 1982, to write a series of mystery short stories featuring a totally different kind of hero, Hack Bohannon, a horse rancher who is not gay (though he is not a bigot, either)....

"When you are secure in a fundamental decency of character, and your life work is dependent upon your approach to moral problems, you don't change a lot as you age. In his last decade, he became uneasy not just at slowing down physically but at making mistakes of judgment in his work. I recorded these misgivings with regret. After all, Dave and I were almost exactly the same age; he was born in Pasadena, California, February 2, 1923....

"By the time of Dave Brandstetter's heart attack at the end of *A Country of Old Men*, I had written 800,000 words that describe how I see him. After finishing twelve books about him, I found I had nothing more to say. That still feels right to me."

GREG HERREN: *Chanse MacLeod* (2002–CURRENT)

Greg Herren is the former editor of *Lambda Book Report*. He's published articles in numerous gay magazines, including the *Harvard Gay and Lesbian Review*, *A&U*, and *Genre and Instinct*. He also writes gay erotica and the Scotty Bradley series (see the section on amateur sleuths). Herren lives with his partner of eight years in New Orleans where he writes and works as a personal trainer.

Detective: Chanse MacLeod, self-employed private investigator and security consultant

Setting: New Orleans. Time period is contemporary with publication dates

Books: *Murder in the Rue Dauphine* (2002); Finalist Lambda Award—Best Gay Men's Mystery (2003); *Murder in the Rue St. Ann* (2004)

Publisher: Alyson Publications

"I see the Chanse series as definitely hard-boiled—my vision for him was 'Gaymond Chandler.'" Like those classic hard-boiled novels, the series has "a cynical smartass" main character who doesn't trust anyone. "There's been a lot of pain in his past—the pain of not being accepted, of not being loved by his family, of being an outsider"—because of his sexual orientation and his working-class, "white trash" origins.

He's accepted his sexual orientation and is out of the closet, but he views being gay "as a cosmic joke played on him by God, and wishes he weren't." Before he came out of the closet he "yearned to be open about himself, thinking it would solve all of his problems, but it didn't—and he feels somewhat cheated by that....

"Chanse has a lot to learn about life and his own identity—so every case he gets involved with also involves a life lesson for him. I know what lesson I want him to learn in the book. The first one was about shedding his preconceived ideas of how relationships work.... I get impatient with Chanse sometimes ... but I have to recognize that no one learns and changes overnight ... and the readers wouldn't buy it. I certainly wouldn't."

Paige Tourneur is a top-notch crime reporter with a local newspaper and Chanse's best friend. "I see Paige primarily as comic relief as well as emotional support for Chanse. Chanse's worldview is so dark, I needed someone to relieve the tension in the book. If Chanse didn't have Paige, I don't think I could have written about him." Paige is heterosexual (created before the Will and Grace series) and constructed from three women "who shone a bright light of joy and laughter into my life.... They were a lifeline for me, and I wanted Chanse to have that as well. Paige is a strong woman who is not afraid to speak her mind—and Chanse needs someone to tell him when he's being an asshole....

"The most fun thing for me is creating characters. I love creating characters—and describing the way they interact.... The most challenging thing about writing a mystery is coming up with a motive for the crime that is understandable for the reader and not contrived. Plotting is a nightmare for me, and I agonize over it.... I start with the crime—who is the victim, who is the killer, and why—and then comes the really hard part: the other suspects. It's really hard trying to figure out different motives that are unrelated, yet compelling enough to drive someone to want to kill. It's hard making the victim so completely awful that everyone wants to see him/her dead.... Most people just aren't that evil. But then again, most people don't wind up being murdered either!"

The themes Herren addresses include relationships, preconceived notions about monogamy, homophobia, and criminal behavior within the gay community. "We all have a tendency to think gay is good—if someone is gay, they can't be a criminal ... so I wanted to definitely show that gay people can be criminals just as easily as straight people. We automatically confer trust on gay people, and gay organizations—and I wanted to show that such blind trust can frequently be misplaced."

Herren has considered doing a crossover book with his two main characters, Chanse MacLeod and Scotty Bradley, "but I really don't see how I could make it work. There are crossover characters between the two series ... because I didn't think it made sense to create two completely different New Orleans universes ... but I doubt Chanse and Scotty will ever have an adventure together."

BARBARA JOHNSON: *Colleen Fitzgerald* (1995–1998)

Barbara Johnson (1955–) was born in Germany. When she was three, she and her German mother immigrated to the United States to join her American father. Her first publication, at age eight, was an award-winning essay. Johnson writes lesbian romances, mysteries, and short stories. She's also a technical editor at Johns Hopkins University. She lives in Maryland with her partner of thirty years. They are both very active in the lesbian and gay community.

Detective: Colleen Fitzgerald, investigator with Sampson and Rhoades Investigations

Settings: Washington, D.C., and Rehoboth Beach, Delaware. Time period is contemporary with publication dates

Books: *The Beach Affair* (1995); *Bad Moon Rising* (1998)

Publisher: The Naiad Press

The Colleen Fitzgerald mysteries blend romance and humor with traditional detective fiction. This series also features one of the few femme-identified lesbian sleuths.

The Beach Affair, the first book of the series, "was intended to be a romance with Colleen as an insurance investigator whose case involved possible insurance fraud because of a suspicious death.... As the story evolved from a romance to a mystery, it seemed I had an opportunity to do something new.... With an insurance investigator, I can focus on motivation and personalities, on psychology rather than on police procedures.... I don't have to talk about the details of tests that were done and how they collected the evidence."

The transition from romance to mystery was not automatic. "When you write a romance you have two women who meet and fall in love. End of story. When you write a mystery it has to be believable. To do that you have to do a lot more research because you need to know what you're talking about. Otherwise, readers won't finish the book."

On the other hand, Johnson believes that sex scenes do cross literary genres. "Sex scenes are essential to lesbian literature—especially fluff literature. Women want it and you need to put it in, but it needs to be in a way that doesn't seem contrived. It has to flow with the story.... Sex is so intensely personal to me that no matter how hard I try to keep myself out of it I'm right there. So I have to work hard to relax and let the characters bring their own sexuality in."

The choice of a more traditional mystery fit Johnson's selection of a femme-identified sleuth. "The hard-boiled PI detective has historically been male-identified. Butches are generally seen as male-identified even if they are really not. The stereotype of the tough butch fits with the genre. For detective work you have to be stoic, strong, and tough.... To do that, people assume you have to be a butch character.

"I'm a self-identified femme, and I wanted to give femme readers someone they could identify with as a character rather than someone they wanted to sleep with. Having her be a femme character also gave me an opportunity to expand on people's comprehension of the butch-femme dynamic and to challenge their assumptions. The general stereotype of femmes is that they need to be taken care of, but here is somebody who ends up being very strong and can take care herself."

In addition to exploring the butch-femme dynamic, the series touches on lesbigay themes and more general issues. "My books are very feminist and gay positive, but I try not to compartmentalize people. There are bad women and bad gay people just like there are good men and good straight people.... I wanted to include positive gay male characters because I thought they were lacking in most lesbian literature."

One of the themes that flows through this series is family. Colleen's biological family appears sporadically. She's not out to most of them. In contrast, her "chosen" family is a constant in her life. "The positive aspect of choosing your own family is that you can surround yourself with the people who love and accept you. You have the common bond of shared experiences. That goes beyond gay people to anyone on the fringes of society in any way. It's nice if you can merge the two families. Some people do."

PHYLLIS KNIGHT: *Lil Ritchie* (1988–1991)

Phyllis Knight grew up in central Virginia where she played guitar and sang in the family band. She moved to Austin, Texas, in the mid 1970s with her band, Possum Delight. Since then, she's lived in San Francisco, New Mexico, Quebec, and Maine. In the mid 1990s she returned to the Charlottesville area of Virginia. A guitar player since the age of eleven, she has been a founding member of several bands and still writes and performs original music with like-minded friends.

Detective: Lillian (Lil) Ritchie, owner, Lillian Ritchie Detection Agency

Settings: Montreal, Canada, and various locations in the U.S. Time period is contemporary with publication dates

Books: *Switching the Odds* (1993); Finalist Shamus—Best First Novel (1993); *Shattered Rhythms* (1995)

Publisher: St. Martin's Press

This series centers on music. Hard-boiled PI Lil Ritchie is a former professional rock guitarist who discovered her gift for detecting when she solved the murder of another musician in her band. *Switching the Odds* includes lyrics of songs that reflect Ritchie's feelings, and *Shattered Rhythms* is about the murder of a famous (in the story) jazz musician.

The series begins seventeen years later when music is still very much in her life, but it has become an avocation. "Private detectives spend a fair amount of time in motels, and it's nice to have something other than the all-pervasive tube for entertainment."[86]

As a self-employed PI running a one-person agency, Ritchie works on a variety of cases. The ones that constitute the main plots fall into her specialty: missing persons. "I find people who're missing, usually. Other times I solve crimes the police have given up on or aren't too interested in, for one reason or another."[87] In addition to the cases that comprise the primary story line, the books show her following a philandering husband and catching shoplifters red handed.

The central cases in these books require Ritchie to do a great deal of traveling, mostly by car. While driving she not only listens to music, she reflects on the familiar and unfamiliar scenery she's passing.

> Tennessee is always disconcerting to me.... We drove through old farm-land and quiet, green parts of the Smoky Mountains, where nothing much had changed, to the naked eye at least, for many a year. Then we hit the stretch of highway between Knoxville and Nashville where huge stinking trucks threaten to swallow you whole and then puke you back out. I felt bad-tempered and vile through most of that stretch.[88]

The crimes Ritchie uncovers include murder, snuff films, drug trafficking, rape, and intimidation. Her efforts expose the perpetrators and prevent them from reaping greater gain from their crimes.

RANDYE LORDON: *Sydney Sloane* (1993–CURRENT)

Award-winning author Randye Lordon (1954–; pseudonym, real name undisclosed) was born in Chicago. Lordon is the youngest of three children. She moved to New York City after high school to attend the American Academy of Dramatic Arts. Since then, she's been an actor, director, playwright, chef, and author. She started writing in her mid-twenties. Lordon lives and works in Amagansett, New York.

Detective: Sydney Jessica Sloane, co-owner, Cabe Sloane Investigations (CSI)

Setting: Manhattan. Time period is contemporary with publication dates

Books: *Brotherly Love* (1993); Finalist Shamus—Best First Novel (1994); *Sister's Keeper* (1994); *Father Forgive Me* (1997); Lambda Award— Best Lesbian Mystery (1997); Finalist Shamus—Best PI, Paperback (1998); *Mother May I* (1998); Finalist Lambda Award—Best Lesbian Mystery (1998); *Say Uncle* (1999); *East of Niece* (2001); *Son of a Gun* (2003)

Publisher: St. Martin's Press

Sydney Sloane is a savvy gumshoe whose mysteries have book titles that refer to family relationships (e.g., *Brotherly Love*). By the time the series begins, Sloane has spent seven years as an officer in the NYPD followed by ten years as a PI at CSI. "When I started the Sydney Sloane series, my intention was to bridge the gap between the gay and straight community—a very lofty goal and unattainable, I might add. I also was tired of reading PI series—lesbian and straight—where the female PI was hard-edged and hard-core. They didn't have relationships. I wanted to show that a lesbian, hard-boiled, hard-core PI can still know how to make love, make a gourmet meal, massage an ego, make herself vulnerable, do the ironing, carry a purse and wear makeup…. I've watched her grow as I've watched myself grow over the years. If there's been any development, for both Sydney and me, it's that she's less afraid to confront and be honest with her feelings."

Sloane has an easy, collaborative relationship with her partner Max Cabe. "I wanted the yin and yang. I wanted him to be straight and wanted them to be very close friends. I also wanted to know that if I couldn't get Sydney out of a pickle there was someone else there to help her." Together, they've built a business that includes a crack office assistant (part-time actress Kerry Norman) and a growing number of operatives and contacts.

"People like Max Cabe and Kerry Norman are bits and pieces of people that I know and love. I always start with a clean slate, but every now and then I'll develop a character and notice that they remind me of someone I know…. So, when I am stumped at knowing what Kerry might say in a given situation, I get into the mindset of the person I know that she reminds me of. It keeps me on target for the character and, most importantly, makes her voice completely different from mine. Different voices and dialogue are hard to keep alive and fresh, but I enjoy the challenge…. When I'm writing, I read out loud. Sometimes, it sounds like there's three or four people in my office….

"The whole series is based on family and friendship that creates family.... I think families are boundless. I don't think that family is the DNA yet that's what I've used in the series." Sydney uncovers incest, bigamy, spousal abuse, homophobia, and other ills in her clients' families, her own family, and the family of her devoted lover, interior designer Leslie Washburn. They produce multiple crimes leading to multiple denouements that embroil Sydney in high-speed chases, gun fights, and brawls. "I deliberately figure out these plots and subplots, and they all have to work at their own pace. There are different threads, like colors on a white board: green, blue, and red all coming together as purple."

Other core themes are loyalty and "having the courage of your convictions. In all of the books you'll find a moment when Sydney has to stand up for what she believes in—even if she could get hurt by doing it or compromising herself in some way."

The violence and disturbing themes are counterbalanced by humor emanating from wisecracking Sydney ("You know me. What's on my lung is on my tongue.")[89] and the antics of Sydney's octogenarian Aunt Minnie (who communes equally well with dead and living relatives) and other colorful characters. The novels are also peppered (and salted) with gourmet meals and delicious homemade desserts. "My taste buds were jumping for joy."[90]

LEE LYNCH: *Sue Slate* (1989)

Lee Lynch (1945–) has written lesbian short stories, nonfiction, and eleven novels (including *The Swashbuckler* and the *Morton River Valley Trilogy*). Her column "Amazon Trail" appears in numerous magazines, and she's had one of her novels appear in serialized form in *Girlfriends Magazine*. Originally from New England, Lynch now lives and works on the Oregon coast.

Detective: Sue Slate, feline private investigator
Setting: San Francisco. Time period is contemporary with publication date
Book: *Sue Slate: Private Eye* (1989)
Publisher: The Naiad Press

This parody of hard-boiled detective fiction features Sue Slate, a feline lesbian detective, who is hired by a calico torch singer named Tallulah Mimosa to find three kitnapped kittens. The investigation leads directly to an underworld filled with alley cats trading in illegal catnip and a human scheme to rid the world of gays. Slate must rely on her keen sense of smell, feline curiosity, and nine lives to rescue both kittens and humans from four- and two-legged predators.

Like her human counterparts, Slate is as tough as they make 'em. Her dialogue with the other cats sounds like Sam Spade on catnip: "In this business, Sweet Lips, something can mean nothing, but nothing always means something."[91] The first-person narrator sprays the book with Spillane-like observations: "This judy steps out of a dream I never even know I'm having."[92] Overlaid on this is a "cat" language that only has present tense and translates human terms into cat concepts (e.g., "return to the matter at paw"[93]).

Most of the other cats are characters one expects to find in a hard-boiled mystery. Mimosa, Slate's client, is a sex kitten who "wears Roemance, the ritzy scent sold exclusively at Cats Fifth Avenue"[94] and captures Slate's heart. There are also a slick and too-handsome tomcatting tom, a bighearted kitty of the evening ("You come on back Sue Shamus!... And next time not on business!"[95]), catnip abusers, and scruffy alley cats. Less typical characters, including a howling queen cat who loves bad jokes, a guard parrot, and a collection of human cat owners, also litter the story.

As one might expect, the humans are not as smart as the cats. Most of them are also either good or evil. The gay men and lesbians are involved in a global research network working to develop a cure for AIDS. The evil characters are members of an antigay church intent on destroying the queer menace. Both groups exploit the link between AIDS and feline leukemia virus to achieve their goals. That is, until Sue Slate pounces on the case.

JAYE MAIMAN: *Robin Miller* (1991–CURRENT)

Lambda award-winning author Jaye Maiman (1957–; real name undisclosed) grew up in a Coney Island housing project and has lived most of her life in the New York City metropolitan area. She attended Brooklyn College and the University of Virginia, where she studied creative writing. She's worked in public relations, on Wall Street, for a university, and for a national professional association. She lives in Brooklyn with her partner and their two children.

Detective: Robin Miller, private investigator with Serra Investigation Agency

Setting: Primarily New York City. Time period is contemporary with publication dates

Books: *I Left My Heart* (1991); *Crazy For Loving* (1992); Lambda Award—Best Lesbian Mystery (cowinner) (1992); *Under My Skin* (1993); *Someone to Watch* (1995); *Baby It's Cold* (1996); *Old Black Magic* (1997);

Finalist Lambda Award—Best Lesbian Mystery (1998); *Every Time We Say Goodbye* (1999)

Publisher: The Naiad Press

This series charts the evolution of a charming but emotionally damaged main character. "The nexus of Robin's unresolved conflicts is her father's extreme rejection and disgust with her after the accidental death of her sister.... She is also driven by a desperate need to seek justice, to correct the damages inflicted on those she encounters."

Despite the serious nature of Robin's personal problems, the series is filled with humor. The books' titles are taken from popular songs, such as *Old Black Magic* and *Baby It's Cold*, and Robin often finds herself in humorous situations. For example, Robin is greeted by a proud dog owner who exclaims, "She loves you, Rob. Kiss her."

> I complied reluctantly, receiving a healthy dose of wet dog breath in return, then tried to climb the stairs with eighty pounds of dog humping my right calf.[96]

Robin Miller begins the series a successful writer of romance novels and travelogues. "The romance writer angle intrigued me because it played against stereotypes.... I liked demonstrating that Robin's sexuality did not prohibit her from understanding and recognizing sexual tensions between men and women. A more prosaic reason for her prior career was that I wanted Robin to be free of financial worries, and romance writing is about the only type of writing that can be extremely lucrative."

Robin changes careers after being outed by a vindictive adversary.

> ... on the gossip page was a six-line blurb revealing that Laurel Carter, the famous romance writer, had recently been uncovered as an "active lesbian." I hadn't been as active as I would have liked, but I figured that could easily be remedied.[97]

She apprentices herself to PI Tony Serra. "These two would never have hooked up or seen the connections between them if Tony hadn't contracted AIDS and been forced into an unexpected role of social outcast. His illness also acted as a prism for all her obsession with death and emotional abandonment. Despite an unyielding awareness that his death was slowly approaching, Robin allowed herself to grow closer to him and appreciate their friendship. This represented an enormous shift for Robin."

The other major figure in Robin's transformation is her lover, internationally-acclaimed chef K.T. Bellflower. "I love K.T. She is a rock, an anchor. And the perfect foil for Robin.... She is a no-nonsense woman, with a strong sense of self and direction. A romantic and a dreamer who will never allow herself to be victimized.... Where Robin is alienated from her family and uncomfortable with even the concept of family ties, K.T. is immersed and surrounded by a large, mostly loving, quirky family....

"Family is a pretty deep drumbeat throughout the series. In many ways, this theme reflects my conviction that our environment and childhood experiences shape our sense of self, values, and approaches to 'others.'"

Maiman describes the primary themes of the series as "the untold truths in relationships. The shattering of personal mythology surrounding family relationships and roles. The quest for a world that makes sense, in which good prevails. The fact that the richness of our lives, our communities is born in an awareness of everything that makes us unique and different, in the context of all the forces and life events that tie us all together."

JEAN MARCY: *Meg Darcy* (1997–CURRENT)

Lambda award-winning Jean Marcy is the pen name of Jean Hutchison (1940–) and Marcy Jacobs (1959–) who have been partners for seventeen years. The Meg Darcy mysteries are their first novels, although Jacobs published a short story in *Sinister Wisdom*. They began writing when Hutchison retired after teaching high school English for twenty-nine years. Jacobs continues to work in a shelter for battered women. They live and write in Godfrey, Illinois.

Detective: Margaret Ann (Meg) Darcy, investigator, Miller Security

Setting: St. Louis, Missouri. Time period is contemporary with publication dates

Books: *Cemetery Murders* (1997); *Dead and Blonde* (1998); *Mommy Deadest* (2000); Lambda Award—Best Lesbian Mystery (2001); *A Cold Case of Murder* (2003)

Publisher: New Victoria Publishers

Meg Darcy is "courageous, smart but not intellectual, romantic, somewhat immature, loyal, and self-reliant." She's also a personable woman with a good sense of humor and a skilled investigator whose background includes military police and familiarity with security systems. These qualities contribute to Meg's effectiveness at Miller Security, a firm owned by Meg's Uncle Walter, where her responsibilities include evaluating security systems, investigating employee theft, and training recruits.

Unlike typical Miller Security assignments, the central investigations in this series arise from Meg's contacts in the gay community and involve murder rather than security breaches. Although some Miller resources are occasionally available, Meg performs much of the work alone or assisted by her friend and neighbor, Patrick Healy. Patrick's friendship is a cornerstone in Meg's life. "He brings out Meg's loyalty, and he shows that *she* is worthy of loyalty.…

"We are not trying to write characters who are always perfect in every way. We are trying to create a world in which ordinary people live and struggle with big issues." Meg's big issue is her unrequited love for Det. Sarah Lindstrom of the St. Louis PD. Actually, she loves the image of womanly perfection that she's fabricated for Lindstrom. "Meg is a flawed character and one of her flaws is that she's too romantic. She doesn't see Lindstrom, the person. What she sees is the woman she wants to love. So, she exaggerates Lindstrom's flaws and her more desirable character-istics." Meg's unrealistic expectations also lead her to dramatize Lind-strom's perceived shoddy treatment of her. "That's why it's interesting readers hate Lindstrom—especially after reading the first two books. It's because they see her only through Meg's eyes."

In addition to being Meg's "Watson," Patrick "also throws light on what is real and what isn't in Meg's relationship with Lindstrom. A cou-ple of times he explains Lindstrom's behavior to Meg.… We use him to get those kinds of things out through someone other than Meg who, much as we love her, is an unreliable narrator."

The biased viewpoint of Meg's first-person narrative is part of a larger theme of appearance vs. reality. "It's not only Meg's perception that differs from other people's reality but the perceptions of some of the villains as well. The way the guy who was stalking Lindstrom in *Dead and Blonde* saw the world determined how he behaved. It didn't matter whether his view was accurate or not. The same thing applies to the adopted boy in *Mommy Deadest* who had his own version of what his mother had done to him."

This is not a comic series, but the humor emanating from the char-acters and their confrontations infuses the stories with lightness. "One of our most favorite things in the world is to get an outloud laugh from each other." Beyond that, writing a series collaboratively demands rules and mutual respect. "We write the first draft separately, and we have a rule that the first time we hear what's been written no criticism is allowed. There have been times when, under the pressure of a deadline, that rule has been hard to keep. Sometimes, one of us is sitting there rolling her eyes and waiting until we get past that first-draft rule. Then, we go into the revision. From that point we go back and forth.… We've had dra-matic moments where we've said things like 'Not in MY book you don't!'

but, overall, it's been a good thing for our relationship. It's made it richer and has made it possible for us to keep growing and having fun together."

MARSHA MILDON: *Cal Meredith* (1995–1999)

Marsha Mildon (1946–) lives in Canada where she teaches scuba diving. In addition to the Cal Meredith mystery series, she writes poetry and plays and has taught composition at the University of Victoria.

Detective: Calliope (Cal) Meredith, self-employed private investigator

Setting: Canada's Gulf Islands (Pacific coast) off Vancouver Island, BC. Time period is contemporary with publication dates

Books: *Fighting for Air* (1995); *Stalking the Goddess Ship* (1999)

Publisher: New Victoria Publishers

This series is immersed in the worlds of scuba diving and underwater archeology. The Canadian landscape that leads to these underwater domains is equally beautiful but, for Cal Meredith, "something felt dark and ugly.... I felt there were things down on this beautiful coastline that I didn't want to know."[98]

Meredith is one of the rare full-figured lesbian main characters. She's almost six feet tall and tips the scales at 195 pounds. Despite her imposing size, she's a vulnerable character who, at the start of the series, is struggling to recover from her lover's recent violent death.

Meredith is also a skilled and experienced investigator.

> I've made finding my specialty: finding kids, long lost relatives, family heirlooms, even championship dogs and cats on occasion. This kind of business often results in happy reunions and doesn't usually involve danger or hassles with the local police, both of which I like to avoid.[99]

Both Meredith stories entangle Cal in cases in which lesbian friends and acquaintances are accused (and sometimes convicted of) serious crimes. She's hired to prove their innocence, but her clients do little to help themselves. They are debilitated by depression and overcome with remorse for irresponsible things they *have* done.

Meredith is also hampered by schools of red herrings and by the strong and volatile emotions that course through the stories. Explosive anger, jealousy, hatred, and desire swirl and eddy everywhere. "Everybody's got grudges."[100] And there's an undercurrent of racial and ethnic hatred. Even Cal is not immune, and she's accused of mishandling one investigation: "You're just all emotionally wrapped up in this one. Too emotionally wrapped up. You're darting off in all directions. Not thinking with your usual clarity."[101]

The series includes a number of strong, centered women. One establishes a research site for underwater archeologists called the "Goddess Ship." Another establishes a safe house for troubled Native American girls. At the same time, many of the characters in the series are flawed, including Meredith. Some women have been damaged by abusive childhoods or emotional trauma; most of the men are selfish, grasping, and violent; and the murder victims are venal. The women accused of the crimes begin their stories strong and confident, but they are badly shaken by their experiences. Even though Cal clears them of all misdeeds, her success can't repair the emotional trauma they've experienced. Nor does finding the truth produce entirely happy endings for others, either.

ELIZABETH PINCUS: *Nell Fury* (1992–1995)

Lambda award winner Elizabeth Pincus (1957–) was an investigator for Pinkerton (the same firm that employed Dashiell Hammett). She has been a film critic for *Harper's Bazaar* magazine, film editor of *LA Weekly,* and has contributed articles to the *San Francisco Chronicle* and other publications.

Detective: Nell Fury, self-employed private investigator

Setting: San Francisco. Time period is contemporary with publication dates

Books: *The Two-Bit Tango* (1992); Lambda Award—Best Lesbian Mystery (cowinner) (1992); *The Solitary Twist* (1993); *The Hangdog Hustle* (1995); Finalist Benjamin Franklin Award, Gay/Lesbian (1996); Finalist Lambda Award—Best Lesbian Mystery (1996)

Publisher: Spinsters Ink

The stories in this series, particularly *The Two-Bit Tango*, are parodies of classic hard-boiled mysteries, particularly the writing of Dashiell Hammett. "I first walked those mean streets with Hammett, Chandler and James M. Cain. In fact, I was a little obsessed with the Hammett myth...."[102]

There was also no question that PI Nell Fury would be a lesbian. "I had no doubt I would create a lesbian protagonist for my series. I was a lesbian, out of the closet, and political. I wanted my private eye, Nell Fury, to be a lesbian, too. For one thing, it was second nature to write from my own experience. But I also wanted to bring lesbian concerns front and center, and develop a series that would be funny, sexy and contemporary."[103] Furthermore, "Nell's lesbianism is both matter-of-fact and a perspective that informs her first-person point of view."[104]

Pincus uses her series to reverse the detective-fiction tradition of having few lesbian and gay characters. "Books that did include us usually made being gay an indication of a character's pathology, or as a twisted secret that was revealed in the unraveling of a perverse plot complication."[105] The stories are set primarily in San Francisco's lesbian community and populated with lesbian characters (and a sprinkling of gay men). Following the conventions of hard-boiled mysteries, the criminals are greedy rich people (heterosexuals and lesbians) and corporations engaged in dirty tricks. Some antiestablishment themes have a feminist and/or lesbigay flavor, such as the argument in favor of unionizing sex workers.

Pincus also recasts Hammett's heterosexual husband-and-wife relationship of *The Thin Man* into a lesbian mother-and-daughter relationship. Nell is the proud parent of teenager and nascent poet Madeline (Pinky) Fury.

> Her poems—full of beat angst and youthful outrage—were evolving well, but I couldn't possibly categorize them. All I knew was that her poetry made my eyes tear up. And the only other writing that affects me that way was the front page of the daily newspaper.[106]

Pinky is a delightfully normal teenager. In the course of *The Solitary Twist*, for example, Pinky develops a sudden and inexplicable interest in the local malls, listens to blasting music, attends a "rave" ("a new-fangled kind of event—all peace, love, and flower-power"[107]), and may be sexually active. Those rapid developmental shifts are a source of angst to her loving mother. ("Damn, I was hopelessly confused."[108])

The writing is full of street slang and imagery, like this description of a potential client: "She was lanky, a scared-looking brunette, but tough too, like a pool room hustler with innocent eyes and a couple of tricks up her sleeve."[109] Analogies and other linguistic curlicues are also a primary source of humor (e.g., "He balked. I balked back. We kept it up for a while..."[110]). Like other fictional PIs, Nell is a tough-talking straight shooter. For example, when a nervous client says, "Forgive me, I don't mean to be indiscrete," Nell spits out, "Go right ahead. Indiscretion's my middle name."[111] As with everything else, it molds hard-boiled tradition into the lesbian perspective. "China Basin was as deserted as the men's room in a k.d. lang concert."[112]

LOU RAND: *Francis Morley* (1961)

Lou Rand (~1900–1975; pseudonym for Lou Rand Hogan) was born in the Los Angeles area and moved to San Francisco in the 1920s. He was a talented chef who worked on ocean liners, in exclusive restaurants, and as a private chef for millionaires. Rand wrote food columns for *Sun-*

set and *Gourmet* magazines. His 1965 book *The Gay Cookbook,* contained recipes for "swish stakes" and similar treats. He also wrote a cooking column for *The Advocate* under his real name.

Detective: Francis Morley, Morley Agency

Setting: Bay City, California. Time period is contemporary with publication date

Book: *Gay Detective* (1964 rereleased as *Rough Trade*)

Publisher: Saber Books (rereleased by Argyle, Alyson Publications)

Gay Detective is probably the first published gay or lesbian detective novel. It's an outrageous parody of classic, hard-boiled detective fiction set in a thinly-veiled San Francisco. It includes many of the standard characters: a beautiful, but duplicitous, femme-fatale client; the loyal secretary; corrupt police; underworld figures; and genre-linked language (e.g., "big lug").

In the main story, beautiful Vivian Holden hires the Morley Agency to find her beloved missing brother, a young gay man. ("Mr. Morley, I've been just frantic—just crazy with anxiety since Arthur's disappearance."[113]) Like Sam Spade and Philip Marlowe, Francis discovers that Vivian has not been entirely honest, but neither has anyone else. He quickly ascertains that Vivian's brother is dead and that his murder points to a larger pattern of criminal activity. These discoveries lead him to a cabal of city leaders and mobsters running illegal operations from the back rooms of gay bars and baths.

The book surrounds the hard-boiled formulae and story line with a gay context. The importance of the gay theme is established on the first page of the book when Hattie Campbell, Francis' uncle's loyal secretary admits, "she knew only too well that the simple old classifications of 'men and women' simply didn't cover the situation any longer."[114]

Francis Morley, the new owner of the Morley Agency, has "an unconsciously un-masculine air"[115] at work, but he can be screamingly conscious about his air when he wants to. ("My Gawd, dearies! There's nothing like this in Philadelphia!"[116]) Many of the other men squeal and banter ("Oh, Bessie!"[117]), and puns abound. For example, during a city council debate about increasing the number of ferries on the bay "someone loudly remarked that he would like to see more ferries on the streets."[118] Even Tiger Olsen, a heterosexual football player and war hero, exhibits a talent for interior decorating that wows the diesel dyke who was hired to redecorate Francis' office. ("You can come work for me ... anytime ya' want to."[119])

Interleaved among these fey sounds and scenes are strong gay positive images that go beyond Francis' ability to be an effective investigator.

For example, Francis takes Tiger to a local gay "ballet school" which turns out to be a working-class gym; and when Francis and Tiger go a couple two-minute boxing rounds, Tiger spends most of the time on the mat.

"That, Mr. Olsen, was to knock one idea out of your mind."[120]

J.M. REDMANN: *Micky Knight* (1990–CURRENT)

Award-winning novelist J.M. (Jean Marie) Redmann (1955–) grew up in Ocean Springs, Mississippi, a small town on the Gulf of Mexico. At eighteen, determined to escape the South, she headed north. After earning a degree in drama from Vassar College, Redmann went to New York City where she embarked on a career in theatrical lighting that included a stint as lighting director of the New York Playboy Club. In 1988, she began writing the book that became *Death by the Riverside*. She moved to New Orleans in the 1990s and now works as the Director of Education at NO/AIDS Task Force, the largest AIDS service organization in Louisiana.

Detective: Michele (Micky) Knight, self-employed private investigator

Setting: New Orleans, Louisiana. Time period is contemporary with publication dates

Books: *Death by the Riverside* (1990); *Deaths of Jocasta* (1992); *The Intersection of Law and Desire* (1995); Lambda Award—Best Lesbian Mystery (1995); *Lost Daughters* (1999); Finalist Lambda Award—Best Lesbian Mystery (1999)

Publishers: Avon Books, New Victoria Publishers, W.W. Norton

In this series, New Orleans lives down to its name as "the city that God forgot." The stories address dark themes, such as child molestation, and are imbued with a menacing quality that is accentuated by demons from Micky Knight's past. "Micky didn't get justice as a kid; her cousin got away with molesting her; her aunt, save for the final scene in *Lost Daughters*, ... has had no retribution for how she treated Micky as a child. Micky is trying to make things okay for that haunted little girl by seeking and sometimes finding justice for others. But her childhood is gone, fixed in the past and unchangeable, so she will always be searching."

These events are tempered by memories of a devoted father and a loving, if absent, mother. Taken together, they have produced a complex adult with a hard shell and a fragile, still evolving, sense of self. "She's smart and funny, with a mixture of self-confidence and bravado that covers someone who is never sure she's good enough. It is that 'not good enough' part of her that pushes her—sometimes to do the right thing and sometimes not."

Micky is supported (and sometimes stymied) in her quests for justice by a tight-knit group of equally complex friends, who include her on-and-off lover, Cordelia James, and her ex-lover, Danielle (Danny) Clayton. "While I want to attempt to show the effects of the damage in Micky's, as well as some of the other characters', lives, I also want to show how some of them struggle to overcome the damage, to contain it so it doesn't strike out at others. I'm interested in characters who struggle, who stumble and fall, yet they still try to do the right thing." Their lives intersect with other flawed characters whose needs bring additional pain to Micky and her friends. Among them is Micky's friend Barbara Shelby, whose response to the molestation of her daughter is to descend into homophobia and evict Micky from their lives. "You might hurt her even more.... Because if the only place you look is the queer part of town, you'll miss the real child molesters."[121]

The most unsavory characters in the series often present the most benign appearance. "Often the damage is from evil or at least weakness, and often there is little difference between them. Evil, as Hannah Arendt famously noted, is often banal, a smiling face instead of a monster." For example, the child-porn mastermind in *The Intersection of Law and Desire* is a mild-mannered gentleman whose social position suggests he's nothing other than an upstanding citizen.

The mysteries are equally complex and layered. "In the last two books, I was more deliberate about having a structure in which the mystery plot echoed what was going on in Micky's life.... While I've wanted resolution, justice and some measure of happiness for my characters, I didn't want to write books with a perfect happy ending. Life just isn't that way. I don't know anyone who just gets over something as haunting as child abuse, even with all the therapy, love and support, there is still a place that is damaged. Nothing is ever as if it didn't happen."

KAREN SAUM: *Brigid Donovan* (1990–1994)

Karen Saum (1935–) is a social activist. She's helped organize women who were on welfare and has run an experimental college program for rural low-income people in Maine. In addition to the Brigid Donovan mysteries, Saum wrote a stand-alone mystery featuring Alex Adler who appears in the Brigid Donovan mystery *Murder Is Germane*.

Detective: Brigid Donovan, freelance writer, unlicensed private investigator

Setting: Primarily coastal Maine. Time period is contemporary with publication dates

Books: *Murder Is Relative* (1990); *Murder Is Germane* (1991); *Murder Is Material* (1994)

Publishers: The Naiad Press, New Victoria Publishers

These mysteries revolve around complex, shifting relationships within and between families. Virtually all of the characters have hidden agendas and some of them go to considerable trouble to confound and mislead the main character, Brigid Donovan.

Donovan is an unlicensed private detective who, because of financial constraints, accepts assignments that tax her sleuthing skills and abuse her goodwill. Her employers claim they want to hire her to solve a murder or locate a missing person. They actually want to use her to help them pin the murder on someone other than the real killer, to help them raid the missing person's bank accounts, or to simply find out what other people know. "I just looked gullible: fifties, grey, tennis shoes. Who could blame them, I conceded...."[122]

Much of the misdirection involves families. Patriarchs and matriarchs are especially manipulative and controlling, but virtually everyone misrepresents their lineage or familial antipathies. Lovers turn out to be grandfathers or siblings, siblings are actually unrelated, landladies are found to be aunts, and aunts are really mothers.

Sisters and brothers of a different stripe are also involved in the chicanery. They range from an incestuous Buddhist monk to an unbalanced young woman claiming to have stigmata. Nuns and ex-nuns are by far the most populous. They include a deeply disturbed novice with multiple personality syndrome, a blackmailer who insists the money she brings in comes from God, and an ex-nun named Santa Clara who operates a faith-healing scam.

All these shenanigans would drive Donovan to drink if she weren't already in Alcoholics Anonymous (AA). Whenever possible she bolsters her resolve by attending AA meetings or invoking AA mantras. This commitment to AA sets her apart from the other characters in these books, some of whom exhibit behaviors associated with alcoholism. "She wasn't sober, but she was lucid. Sort of lucid. She was entertaining the television, talking to it anyway."[123]

Despite these odds, Brigid succeeds in unraveling the family ties and sews up the mysteries.

SANDRA SCOPPETTONE: *Lauren Laurano* (1991–1998)

Award-winning author Sandra Scoppettone (1936–) received a

Shamus award and an Edgar nomination for *A Creative Kind of Killer*, one of three crime novels written under the pseudonym Jack Early. Her young adult novel, *Playing Murder*, received an Edgar nomination. *The Late Great Me*, a young adult novel about alcoholism, became an Emmy-winning television program. Scoppettone lives in New York state with her long-time partner, novelist Linda Crawford.

Detective: Lauren Laurano, self-employed private investigator

Setting: Manhattan. Time period is contemporary with publication dates

Books: *Everything You Have Is Mine* (1991); *I'll Be Leaving You Always* (1993); *My Sweet Untraceable You* (1994); *Let's Face the Music and Die* (1996); *Gonna Take a Homicidal Journey* (1998)

Publisher: Ballantine Books

This was the first series with a lesbian detective published by a mainstream publishing house and reviewed by *The New York Times*. "I wasn't sure anyone would publish the first novel [*Everything You Have Is Mine*], which by the way was the only novel about Laurano that I intended to write.... I was delighted to be the first mystery writer with a lesbian detective that a mainstream house accepted and published."

Laurano is an engaging character whose resilience enables her to survive the mayhem that surrounds her. "She's a no-nonsense person who says what she feels, sometimes when she shouldn't. She's a good friend, a loving person who isn't afraid to let her vulnerability show.... She's smart and eager to learn new things. She takes pride in her loyalty and her honesty. Lauren is not fearless, but she will risk doing what must be done on the job."

Her FBI background combined with the violent death and trauma she's endured in her personal life have given Lauren the tools to do her job well. Her persistence and creative thinking enable her to expose wily criminals even when they adopt false identities. In *My Sweet Untraceable You* not only does the perpetrator assume multiple guises, but what initially appears to be a single victim turns out to be triplets, which produces multiple headaches for Laurano. "I was doing a takeoff on corny mystery novels. For instance, quite a few writers have used the ploy of twins, so I took that a step further and used triplets."

The two anchors in her life are her friend, NYPD Lt. Peter Cecchi, and her long-term lover Kip Adams. Cecchi is a kindred spirit who serves as a sounding board and resource for Laurano in her work. "Kip is her lover and best friend. She keeps Lauren balanced as Kip is the more pragmatic one. Although she's in no way a mother figure, she does take care of her."

Lauren's relationship with Kip is a core element of the series. "The only thing I set out to do was to show that a lesbian couple's relationship is essentially no different from that of a heterosexual couple. Lauren's profession is unusual; otherwise, Kip and Lauren lead an average middle-class American life together." It is beset by financial problems, Lauren's addiction to Internet chat rooms, the painful decline and death of Kip's brother, and Lauren's infidelity. "I allowed Lauren to be unpredictable in her personal life by allowing her to step outside of her relationship with Kip, something Lauren thought she would never do."

The series is filled with humor. "There is a tremendous amount of humor in life and people. That's simply a given for me. It interests me to juxtapose the comic and the frightening; the laugh and the shriek of violence." That humor emanates from the characters, the plots, the language, and from the city of New York itself. "When fictional characters live and work in New York, the city unavoidably becomes a distinct character as well. Its reality is bigger than all of us and cannot help but impose on plots and characters. I spent most of my adult life in Manhattan; its problems, personalities, complications, and idiosyncrasies are in my blood. The city is also a plot unto itself. It cannot help but impose on plot and characters. A car alarm going off can lead to violence. There are a thousand ways to get murdered in New York City every day-nasty for the victims, great for a crime writer. "

RICHARD STEVENSON: *Don Strachey* (1981–CURRENT)

Richard Stevenson (1938–; pseudonym for Richard Stevenson Lipez) is a novelist, journalist, and freelance writer for numerous publications. After earning a BS in English, he joined the Peace Corps where he taught English, evaluated programs, and gave volunteers cross-cultural training. He later became executive director of Action for Opportunity, an antipoverty agency. He has two children from his twenty-two year marriage, and now he lives in Massachusetts with his partner of thirteen years.

Detective: Don Strachey, private investigator

Setting: Primarily Albany, New York. Time period is contemporary with publication dates

Books: *Death Trick* (1981); *On the Other Hand, Death* (1984); *Ice Blues* (1986); *Third Man Out* (1992); *Shock to the System* (1995); *Chain of Fools* (1996); *Strachey's Folly* (1998); Finalist Lambda Award—Best Gay Men's Mystery (1998); *Tongue Tied* (2003)

Publishers: Alyson, St. Martin's Press

"I see Strachey as the star—or sometimes the costar with Timmy, his boyfriend—in a series of social comedies. I try to give readers a funny take on a moral stance on gay life in America and American society more generally."

For Stevenson, Strachey is "a likable-rogue detective.... Part of the fun of writing the Strachey books is having a character who will just go ahead and do things to crooks and small-bore creeps for the rest of us. Strachey is being roguish and sometimes rude and unmannerly—where appropriate—on behalf of the rest of us.... Some people think that Strachey is my mouthpiece. Anybody who knows me well knows that there's as much of Timmy in me as there is of Strachey. A lot of the warring of different moralities that goes on between the two of them mirrors the warring of different moralities that goes on inside my head....

"The great dividing line between *Death Trick*, which was written in 1979, and the next book is the arrival of AIDS. *Death Trick* is about the Golden Age of 'anything goes' in the seventies ... when the sexual revolution and the gay rights revolution were fresh and energetic and fun.... It couldn't have lasted even without AIDS. Eventually, people have to settle down and have more orderly lives in order to get fulfillment...."

Political satire is a core element of the series. "Some people say 'forget the politics and just tell the human story.' I don't think they are mutually exclusive at all. I think politics is about individual people and their individual stories.... As long as you give the reader his or her money's worth of interesting characters, good writing, and an entertaining story, what's the problem with the people being politically aware and politically pointed?...

"The big theme in all of the books—the overarching theme—in one way or another is that the villain is always homophobia. That includes irrational fears of homosexuality, misunderstanding of homosexuality, attempts to stamp out homosexuality. I hate what homophobia does to everybody—straight and gay—and to families.... Everything that happens is some variation on that theme. Shock jocks, for example, they didn't exist earlier, but their thoughts and expressions on homosexuality are basically the same thoughts and expressions that appear in the schoolyard in their crudest forms. They're just making money from it.

"I use the humor in the book to make some of the uglier facets of gay life in America—the crassness, intolerance, and stupidity—easier to take.... Sometimes reviewers say there's a hard satirical edge to a lot of what I do. I hope that's true when I'm doing people like the shock jocks.... *Tongue Tied* is a kind of revenge fantasy about those kinds of awful people. Strachey is my mechanism for that. I put him in the center of a revenge fantasy....

"Usually I know exactly how a book will begin and pretty much how it will end. I have a good idea of who the main people are in a story. I've got the What Ifs: *what if certain circumstances turned up with certain people in it? What might the consequences be? What would it lead to? How might it all turn out?...* Then I have very brief sketches of these characters and even briefer sketches of minor characters....

"I find that just finishing a book is deeply pleasing—having something that didn't exist at all and giving it a life. Taking that terrifying blank page and having it become a thing with a story full of people that are real to you."

PENNY SUMNER: *Tor Cross* (1992–1994)

Penny Sumner (1955–; pseudonym for Penny Smith) was born in Australia and moved to Britain to do postgraduate studies at Oxford University. In addition to the Tor Cross series, she's written short stories, one of which was shortlisted for a Crime Writers' Association Dagger Award. She has been an editor of the feminist creative-writing magazine, *Writing Women*, and has taught creative writing and contemporary literature at the University of Northumbria.

Detective: Victoria (Tor) Cross, archivist and investigator for a private investigation firm

Setting: Southeastern England. Time period is contemporary with publication dates

Books: *The End of April* (1992); *Crosswords* (1994)

Publishers: The Naiad Press, The Women's Press

These mysteries are equal parts romances and crime stories. Tor Cross is an expert in forgeries and a skilled archivist whose expert testimony has put people behind bars. ("I did my training as a questioned document analyst at Scotland Yard."[124]) In her work, she's a pro; but when it comes to love, she behaves like a bewildered novice.

The series begins when Tor returns to England to assist her great aunt Rosemary, an Oxford University professor. Rosemary's project entails analyzing the writings of a nineteenth-century English pornographer. As with most of Tor's cases in this series, her client has misrepresented the true nature of the work she wants Tor to perform ("I'm used to my clients lying to me."[125]). She really wants Tor to use her skills as a PI to determine who has been sending intimidating letters to a student, April Tate. Unfortunately, Tor breaks one of the cardinal rules of private detection: "Don't get emotionally involved."[126] Tor falls in love with April and her subsequent judgment errors and inattention allow the threats to escalate to murder. It's only after Tor adopts a professional attitude that the case begins to gel.

By the start of *Crosswords*, Tor has begun working in her friend Alicia's all-female detective agency. Tor and her colleagues work well together and help each other on stakeouts, surveillance, and other tasks. In one case, Tor easily interprets the clues in two writing samples that tell her that, despite an attempt to disguise her handwriting, both were written by the same person. After Tor is almost killed on the job, however, she misinterprets the clues in April's cross words about private detection as a rejection of the profession rather than as April's actual fear of losing her. ("Could it be that, deep down, she found my being a private detective, a gumshoe, embarrassing?"[127])

The books also contain examples of lesbians and gay men competently raising children, of feminist politics in action, of racism, sexual harassment, and homophobia. For example, April admits that "I got pregnant because I was sleeping with a man, and I was sleeping with a man because anything else was unthinkable."[128]

The day-to-day work of an agency-based investigator is woven into *Crosswords*. For the main-plot cases, Tor systematically follows leads, does legwork, and calls on her extensive array of contacts. She also works on other cases that require validating documents, analyzing handwriting, taking formal statements from witnesses, participating in stakeouts, and serving summonses.

JEAN TAYLOR: *Maggie Garrett* (1995–1996)

Jean Taylor works as a proofreader at a San Francisco law firm and has worked as a secretary, kitchen helper, interviewer for cultural anthropologists, volunteer coordinator, emergency room clerk, and Marxist party functionary. She lives in San Francisco.

Detective: Maggie Garrett, sole proprietor, Windsor and Garrett Investigations

Setting: San Francisco. Time period is contemporary with publication dates

Books: *We Know Where You Live* (1995); *The Last of Her Lies* (1996)

Publisher: Seal Press

Most of Maggie Garrett's clients are gay or lesbian, and the cases she's hired to investigate involve people in San Francisco's lesbigay community. Each book exposes the nefarious activities of multiple criminals, and the stories about them are rich in gay- and lesbian-related themes.

In *We Know Where You Live*, the newly-elected executive committee of the Pride Lesbian and Gay Democratic Club (aka Gay Pride Club) becomes concerned about editorials about the club in one of the sleazier gay newspapers. The articles suggest that the Gay Pride leadership has been engaged in fiscal sleight-of-hand. Even though the publication is known to disseminate gossip and innuendo, they are concerned. ("Believe me, by this time tomorrow, it'll be all over town that the Pride leadership is about to be hauled off to jail."[129])

Maggie's investigation uncovers a network of fraud and misman-agement along with a program of blackmail for keeping former treasur-ers in line. The novel also highlights some of the personal and philosophical conflicts that swirl around activist organizations like the Gay Pride Club. One former treasurer provides the following historical analysis of the Club's leadership:

> Geoffrey ran Pride as the "gravy train club." He and a few other guys used it to get jobs for themselves. Now there's the "purity" club. They always have to be on the absolutely correct side of every issue. Before Geoffrey there was the "assimilation" club. They thought if they acted like straight people, then straight people would tolerate them. Even before that, before AIDS, there was the "get naked and do it in the streets" club. They built *fabulous* floats for Gay Pride....[130]

In *The Last of Her Lies*, Maggie investigates a case in which a lesbian therapist has been charged with sexual exploitation of a client. "This isn't about having sex with a client. This is about telling a woman that she can't get well unless she gets into the therapist's bed."[131] Actually, it's about characters other than the therapist looking for sex with all the wrong peo-ple. They include sexual harassment of employees, child prostitution, and heterosexual marital infidelity. It's also about families and the power of parents to destroy and damage their children through rabid homophobia and misogyny. ("I believe Mr. Simmons used the Bible and God as an excuse for hating women. Those girls were fighting for their self worth.")[132]

Maggie's clients are as unruly as the perpetrators—and sometimes the two groups overlap. She slogs her way through morasses, misdirec-tions, and muggings fortified by persistence, a strong ego, an uncrackable head, and a sense of humor.

> "Thank you," I replied, willing him to get the subliminal message that "Thank" was not my verb of choice.[133]

DOROTHY TELL: *Poppy Dillworth* (1990–1991)

Dorothy Tell (1939–; pseudonym for Dorothy I. Toopes) was born in San Francisco and brought to Dallas in an orange crate at the age of six weeks. Her writing spans the late 1980s and early 1990s. In addition to the Poppy Dillworth mysteries, she wrote lesbian short stories and romance novels and is writing a novel under the pseudonym Dorothy Lee Harper. Now retired, she lives in San Miguel de Allende, Guanajuato, Mexico, with her partner of thirty-two years.

Detective: Papillon Audobon (Poppy) Dillworth, self-employed private investigator

Setting: Rural Texas. Time period is contemporary with publication dates

Books: *Murder at Red Rook Ranch* (1990); *Hallelujah Murders* (1991)

Publisher: The Naiad Press

At sixty-five, Poppy Dillworth is the oldest lesbian or gay detective to begin a series. "I needed a role model for growing old ... so I imagined Poppy Dillworth." Dillworth first appeared in the lesbian romance novel *Wilderness Trek,* and the romance, humor, and feminist themes of that earlier book are carried into the mysteries. "Romance and sex exist in the real lives of old lesbians—it should play as it is. White-haired, wrinkled and fun."

Unlike most other older female sleuths, Dillworth isn't modeled on Agatha Christie's amateur detective, Jane Marple. She's a trained and licensed private investigator who is "scrappy, in pain, but DOING WHAT HAS TO BE DONE with as much humor as possible." Plus, "Poppy was always willing to laugh at herself."

Poppy and her age peers suffer from arthritis, hearing loss, and other afflictions associated with ageing. "It's important to tell it like it is. Stuff that was fun and felt good twenty years ago now necessitates visits to chiropractors." Ageing is also a source of humor. In *The Hallelujah Murders*, for example, Poppy quickly determines why one friend is hard to understand over the telephone. "'Have you got your teeth in?'... After a pause punctuated by wet-sounding clacks, the voice began anew, the words more distinct now."[134]

Problems linked to ageing are secondary to the images of strong, older women leading active (and sexually active) independent lives. For example, midway through *The Hallelujah Murders*, the first book of the series, Belle Stoner announces to Poppy that after having "served her time in the patriarchy"[135] by marrying a man and raising children, Belle is ready to embrace a new, lesbian life with Poppy. "I'm free now—and I've been waiting a long time to meet someone like you."[136] The sexually-charged romance between Poppy and Belle flows through the rest of the series. These women also prepare for the future with projects like Cronesnest, a retirement home for women. "My fictional characters work their way through difficulties and reveal to me models for self-growth."

Most of the lesbian couples, including Poppy and Belle, are butch-femme pairs. "One half of every couple I know (gay or hetero) does some things better than the other half. To me it's just the way people fit together and negotiate the shit work. In our culture (maybe because females have babies and males don't?) some of the tasks are easier to perform while wearing jeans and ballcaps." Since Poppy is a butch, the series adopts a butch perspective that includes irony and other elements. For example, Poppy bridles at being called "little lady" by a man but refers to Belle as her "little woman." In one scene, Marcie, a young investigator assisting Poppy, begins a report on her findings: "Marcie sucked in a big lungful of air.... Her large breasts swelled out like rapidly rising dough.... *Forty-four doubled, or I've lost my eye completely,* Poppy registered mentally.... Marcie continued her story, unaware of the unanimous appreciation of her anatomy."[137]

Poppy's mysteries follow a traditional puzzle format embellished with romance and lighthearted humor. There's minimal violence, a few red herrings, and exposure of the perpetrators that makes the world a better place for Poppy and her friends.

PAT WELCH: *Helen Black* (1990–CURRENT)

Pat Welch (1957–) was born in Japan and grew up in an assortment of small towns in the southern United States. She relocated to southern California to attend college and remained there until 1986 when she moved to the San Francisco Bay Area. She now lives and writes in Oakland, California. Welch writes short stories as well as mysteries.

Detective: Helen Black, self-employed private investigator

Settings: San Francisco and Mississippi. Time period is contemporary with publication dates

Books: *Murder by the Book* (1990); *Still Waters* (1991); *A Proper Burial* (1993); *Open House* (1995); *Smoke and Mirrors* (1996); *Fallen from Grace* (1998); *Snake Eyes* (1999); *Moving Targets* (2001); *A Day Too Long* (2003)

Publishers: The Naiad Press, Bella Books

This series begins shortly after Helen Black leaves the Berkeley, California, Police Department to establish her own private investigation firm. It tracks her growing alienation and self-destructiveness until, at the end of *Moving Targets*, she hits bottom. The series could have ended there. Instead, it reconnects with Helen two years later, after she's emerged from an even deeper plunge and is beginning to construct a new life. She still seems to thrive on violent, life-threatening situations, but she's making tentative connections with the lesbian community in Mississippi and reasserting her identity as an investigator.

Helen is a deeply flawed character cast from the noir/hard-boiled mold. She grapples with ingrained self-hatred arising, in part, from the homophobia and sexism of her fundamentalist Christian upbringing in rural Mississippi. Restless, unhappy, and alienated, Helen is driven to find truth and justice in a world where those two goals are, at minimum, separate and often incompatible.

The stories are populated by a myriad of characters who follow hidden and open agendas—sometimes with little concern about their own welfare or that of others. Their behavior contributes complex plotting and numerous red herrings. Added to the mix are Helen's lovers, friends, and family who do their utmost to save Helen from herself and others. Ultimately, the incompatibilities between their needs and Helen's internal demons drive them away.

The series addresses social as well as personal issues. Helen's cases involve racist and homophobic hate crimes, antiabortion violence, political refugees from Latin America, abuse of the homeless, police corruption, and exploitation of foreign workers by U.S. corporations. "People with a lot of money, big companies with power—what's so strange about those kinds of people equating human life with dollar signs?"[138]

Family, a theme that runs throughout the series, assumes many guises including biological family and the lesbian community/family. Although there are examples of loving families, some of the biological families are the worst incarnations of the concept. They include a father who allows his teenaged lesbian daughter to die in a fire because she's "a sick pervert"[139] and a mother who willingly accepts hush money to drop an investigation into her daughter's death. In contrast, the lesbian family is supportive and inclusive, but it remains in the background throughout most of the series. Although Helen appears to have good friends in the San Francisco Bay Area community, she remains isolated. Not until *A Day Too Late*, when she's back in Mississippi, does she appear to actively seek greater involvement in the community.

MARY WINGS: *Emma Victor* (1987–1999)

Award-winning author Mary Wings (1949–) was born in Chicago and now lives in San Francisco. She has published several lesbian comic books and several short stories. She did graphic design and book production work for feminist research projects in Amsterdam. In 1992, she won the Lambda Award for best lesbian mystery for *Divine Victim**. Wings recently converted *Divine Victim* into a play.

---

*Divine Victim *is not included in this book because it is a stand-alone novel rather than a series.

Detective: Emma Victor, self-employed private investigator

Settings: Boston and San Francisco. Time period is contemporary with publication dates

Books: *She Came Too Late* (1987); *She Came in a Flash* (1988); *She Came by the Book* (1996); *She Came to the Castro* (1997); *She Came in Drag* (1999); Finalist Lambda Award—Best Lesbian Mystery (1999)

Publishers: The Women's Press, The Berkley Publishing Group

This series is one of the few that is immersed in the lesbian and gay community. "I didn't want to put the detective into heterosexual world situations. The crimes that Emma Victor investigates are perpetrated within the lesbian-feminist activist community of Boston and, in the later books, within San Francisco's gay community. "I wanted her to be in the lesbian and gay community because no one was writing about that. I wanted to do something new under the sun, and no one was looking at our community and satirizing it." Furthermore, writing about the community "meant I could have a book where everyone was gay."

Politics, infighting, funding battles, dogma, and exuberance of the community not only form the backdrop for the main plots, they are often the impetus for murder and other criminal activities. Emma Victor stands at the center of these activities. She's smart, courageous, and tough, but she has lost her way in life. She begins her series working at a woman's crisis hotline in Boston. In *She Came in a Flash,* she moves to California and briefly resumes an earlier career as a publicist. By the start of *She Came by the Book,* she's settled into San Francisco (which she calls "Gaylandia") and has found her calling as a private investigator.

In the final two books she hones her technical skills (including forensic technology) and solidifies her relationship with a security company owned by a disabled lesbian. "Emma is not me, but part of me is Emma. I'm always doing a lot of things at once—multitasking. When I was writing, I had to sit in a chair all the time, so I created a character that was very active. Also, she did things I wish I had done."

Virtually everyone in these books is flawed in some way. "In mystery novels everything has to be logical and everyone has to be suspicious. That's one of the many forms it can take. If everyone has to be suspicious, then everyone has to have a dark side. So, people in the books tended to be dark, although when I put friends in, they were good."

Wings began writing *She Came Too Late* while she was still living in Holland. "I had no idea it could get published. I wasn't aiming to publish at all. I did it for fun.... In terms of the writing, I love the stylistics of Chandler. They were so good and so sparse a writing style. That was my initial inspiration. It was a big discovery for me to view the world like that. So, in *She Came Too Late* I was readopting the genre—with a kind of awareness of it—almost tongue-in-cheek. You could call it a parody of hard-boiled novels…. The second book, *She Came in a Flash*, was more like an Angela Lansbury story,* and I put Emma in a different setting…. The third one, *Divine Victim*, was absolutely no problem because it was a gothic, psychological novel. *She Came to the Castro* and *She Came by the Book* are *romans a clef*…. It was great fun."

Eve Zaremba: *Helen Keremos* (1978–1997)

Eve Zaremba was born in Poland and immigrated to Canada in 1952. After graduating from the University of Toronto, she worked in a variety of industries, owned a used bookstore, and operated a publishing enterprise. Her first book, *Privilege of Sex, A Century of Canadian Women*, appeared in 1972. She was a founding member of *Broadside, A Feminist Review* and wrote articles for the review. Zaremba lives in Toronto with her partner of more than twenty years.

Detective: Helen Keremos, self-employed private investigator

Settings: Various locations in Canada, the United States, and Japan. Time period is contemporary
with publication dates

Books: *A Reason to Kill* (1978); *Work for a Million* (1986); *Beyond Hope* (1987); *Uneasy Lies* (1990); *The Butterfly Effect* (1994); *White Noise* (1997)

Publishers: Amanita Enterprises, Second Story Press, Virago Press

In an introduction to the 1989 rerelease of *A Reason to Kill*, the first Helen Keremos mystery, Eve Zaremba wrote "Helen Keremos … is a middle-aged dyke, an anomaly in the seventies when any of us over 27 were definitely 'older.' She was one of the very first of her kind."[140] When *A Reason to Kill* was first released in 1978, Keremos was not only the first middle-aged lesbian main character, she was the first lesbian PI, the first gay Canadian detective, and the first lesbian or gay detective with Native American heritage.

Helen is tough, savvy, and action-oriented. "I'm not what you might call a cerebral type of investigator. Action is more my strong point."[141] Following hard-boiled tradition, she's a loner with a hard-knocks background who is more comfortable with criminals than with corporate boards of directors, although neither group intimidates her.

> My protagonist was to be a hard-nosed, street-wise, professional private investigator. With just one small difference: the protagonist would be lesbian.[142]

Angela Lansbury was the star of a television show called Murder She Wrote *about an elder amateur sleuth who is also a mystery writer.*

Her specialties are finding missing persons and recovering lost goods. Consequently, her work involves a great deal of travel. In the novels, she crisscrosses Canada and makes excursions into the U.S. and Japan. Those assignments also lead to murder and sometimes involve international crime and terrorism. Fortunately, Helen is not only a seasoned investigator, she's a former intelligence operative for Canada and the United States.

The story lines of the novels are complex and often include multiple, but related, criminal activities. In *Work for a Million,* for example, she exposes a murderer, a blackmailer, a duo of miscreants involved in a harassment campaign, and a firm of attorneys engaged in contractual chicanery.

The series has a gay positive, feminist, and leftist political perspective that is strongly influenced by the traditions of hard-boiled detective fiction.

> Helen Keremos doesn't fit the profile of a lesbian/feminist hero. She isn't a middle-class boomer. Life experience has lowered her belief in the perfectability of the world and the people in it, including herself.... Yet she is by no means a cynic.[143]

In *A Reason to Kill,* gay issues take center stage. "*A Reason to Kill* ain't romantic.... It's about homophobia, coming-out, gay self-hatred, betrayal, murder, all manifested exclusively through the lives of a couple of young gay men—yet written by a lesbian!"[144] *Work for a Million* addresses child sexual abuse while *The Butterfly Effect* looks at sexism in Japanese society. The other books have at least one lesbian or gay subplot or plot element. *Uneasy Lies* includes an extramarital lesbian affair; part of the action in *Beyond Hope* takes place on lesbian-separatist land; in *White Noise,* Helen is hired by a gay man who believes he's being pursued by mobsters; and when Helen retires at the end of *White Noise,* she chooses to live in a lesbian community.

—— PROFESSIONAL SLEUTHS ——

The term "professional sleuth" applies to trained investigators that police detectives and PIs are likely to encounter in the course of a typical investigation, primarily journalists and attorneys. They differ from amateur detectives because they are trained to investigate criminal activities and because doing so is part of their jobs. As Lisa Haddock explains, "It's smart to have someone who is already involved in criminal investigations."* According to Val McDermid, this applies to journalists because

> The journalist detective is in many ways the bridge between the professional investigator and the amateur sleuth. It's a journalist's job to be professionally curious and to learn how to develop investigative and interviewing skills such as those possessed by a professional detective.

The same can be said about attorney-sleuths. On the other hand, neither reporters nor attorneys are hired to solve criminal cases. Rather, the object of their efforts is to generate a good story or to win a legal case. In detective fiction, of course, their probing does unmask the perpetrators.

Journalists

> [Journalism] is full of lying, cheating, drunken, cocaine-sniffing, unethical people. It's a wonderful profession.
> *Piers Morgan, editor, Daily Mirror*

Journalists were among the earliest fictional detectives, and they continue to be popular in both gay/lesbian and mainstream fiction. The first journalist sleuth was Joseph Rouetabille, who appeared in Gaston Leroux's 1908 novel *The Mystery of the Yellow Room*. He was modeled on Poe's Dupin and had a Watson-like assistant (an attorney rather than a physician) who dutifully recorded and reported his exploits. Rouetabille's mainstream descendants include George Harmon Coxe's hard-boiled newspaperman Flashgun Casey, Frederick Nebel's 1930s "female reporter" Torchy Blaine, Edna Buchanan's crime reporter Britt Montero, Lillian Jackson Braun's columnist Jim Qwilleran (and his cat), Crabbe Evers' sports reporter Duffy House, Michael Connelly's Jack McEvoy, Barbara D'Amato's freelancer Cat Marsala, John Sanford's TV video news team, and Sparkle Hayter's TV journalist Robin Hudson.

In 1977, M.F. Beal's stand-alone novel *Angel Dance* introduced the first lesbian sleuth to appear in a novel, Maria Katerina Lorca Guerrera Alcazar (Kat Guerrera). She's also the first Latina gay/lesbian detective. Guerrera is not a trained journalist, but when *Angel Dance* begins she's the primary contributor to the four-page, leftist news weekly published by her antiestablishment collective. Within the first fifteen pages of the book she's forced out of her collective and abandons her fleeting career

---

*All unattributed author quotes come from interviews for this book.

in journalism. Consequently, the analysis of *Angel Dance* appears in this chapter's discussion of amateur sleuths (pp. 150–195).

In 1982, Vicki P. McConnell's *Mrs. Porter's Letter* introduced lesbian reporter Nyla Wade. She was featured in two subsequent mysteries. Gay entertainment feature writer Sam Bone appeared as the main character in W. Stephen Gilbert's 1991 novel *Spiked*. Five years later two novels marked the beginning of the first series with gay main characters: John Morgan Wilson's *Simple Justice* and R.D. Zimmerman's *Closet*.

Professional Involvement

Journalism is a core element of some series; for others, it is purely background. For example, crime reporter Hollis Carpenter (Deborah Powell) quits her job at the start of the first book in her series and engages in no journalistic activity from that point forward. Nevertheless her reputation as a top-notch investigative reporter and her claim to be investigating certain suspicious activities precipitate the events in the books.

In contrast, Mark Manning's (Michael Craft) activities are inextricably bound to journalism. Manning and his staff continually generate articles that comment on events that synthesize information and move the stories forward. Furthermore, Manning is intended to represent a journalistic ideal.

> Mark Manning is my literary embodiment of the objectivist philosophy. He is a rationalist, a humanist, and by extension, an atheist. These are the basic values I hope to convey to my readers, and indeed, I chose an investigative reporter as my hero because these values are, or should be, important to his profession (just the facts, ma'am).

John Morgan Wilson's Benjamin Justice's investigations are always tied to an assignment. He probes sources, bullies unwilling informants, and sometimes behaves like the sleaziest of his ilk. "You work in a cesspool profession and still manage to make all the other turds smell like chocolate kisses."[145]

Mimi Patterson, Penny Mickelbury's* investigative reporter, works for a newspaper but can choose some of her own assignments. She enjoys bringing down officials who have violated the public trust. In the novels, she focuses on murders and disappearances that slip through official cracks. "Like most good investigative reporters, she is highly instinctive," says Mickelbury. "She can be very focused and directed when in pursuit of a story." Her work is always directed at getting a story although the investigations she pursues have personal ramifications.

The analysis of Mickelbury's series appears in the discussion of partners, pp. 195–233.

Sometimes, a novel revolves around internal politics or the journalistic "culture" of an organization. Carmen Ramirez (Lisa Haddock), Mark Manning (Michael Craft), and Lexy Hyatt (Carlene Miller) all investigate crimes that are linked to politics in their own newspapers. Lindsay Gordon (Val McDermid) does the same for her journalism union. R.D. Zimmerman's novels present a world of broadcast journalism where the truth is barely considered because reporters and stations are engaged in brutal competition for hot stories that will boost ratings. Those TV news rooms exhibit a callous disregard for human dignity that is marked by manipulation of viewers' fears and prejudices. "People want dirt and they're going to get it somewhere, so they might as well get it from us."[146]

Even when journalism is not a focus of a series, an author's background in journalism influences the style, structure, and content of the stories. According to veteran reporter Elizabeth Sims

> ... if you're serious about reporting, ... you're constantly looking for one good word to do the job of three or four half-assed words, you're constantly challenging yourself to keep the reader's attention....

For journalist Lisa Haddock

> Journalism is the foundation: keep it short, keep it moving, learn about what you are writing about and punch it out. I want them to be factually-based and believable.

Personal Development

> There's no question the entire Nyla Wade series gives the main character the opportunity to share her journey to greater self-realization and maturity.

Vicki P. McConnell, Nyla Wade's creator, is not the only author to adopt this stance regarding their main characters. In fact, the transformations that some gay/lesbian journalists undergo are among the most dramatic in the literature. Craft's Manning experiences a series of cataclysms that parallel Wade's journey: recognition of his gay sexual orientation, finding a life partner, and transplanting himself from a large city to a small town.

> I think of these ongoing lifestyle upheavals as the "serial subplot" of the books. The primary plot of each story deals with a distinct whodunit, but it's Manning's ongoing struggle for self-definition as a happy, complete, mature gay man that provides the series with its "serial" flavor.

The murder of Todd Mills' lover at the beginning of Zimmerman's *Closet* hurls Mills out of his closet and turns his life upside down. According to Zimmerman, from that point on he's no longer "presenting the world as a two-dimensional self and hiding that third aspect behind himself." By the time Stephen Gilbert's Sam Bone writes his "manuscript," his professional world has imploded and Bone has become a man willing to put his life on the line for a greater truth—knowing that it could lead to his death. Each of Mickelbury's novels has dramatic effects on Mimi Patterson. At the conclusion of *Night Songs*, for example, when she looks at pictures of the murder victims

> it suddenly struck Mimi that they were all Black. Black like her. And she allowed herself to feel fully the pain of knowing that there were people who believed her life had no value because of her race.[147]

Some journeys are more gradual. Characters learn hard lessons and emerge with greater self-understanding, but they are not immediately transformed. For example, in *Damn Straight*, Elizabeth Sims says

> I wanted Lillian [Byrd] to learn about disappointment. I wanted her to learn about betrayal, and I wanted her to be horrified at the lengths someone will go to protect a selfish interest.

Byrd is "sadder but wiser," but the foundations of her life have not been shaken. Likewise, in her series, Lexy Hyatt (Carlene Miller) is on a "journey wherein she will become more comfortable in her own skin."

> I see Lexy as a developing person who is learning more about herself through relationships with others, which is both satisfying and disturbing. Her habit of compartmentalizing elements of her life is being challenged by new experiences. I view her not so much as changing as growing and evolving through encounters with events and individuals.

By the time her series ends, Lisa Haddock's Carmen Ramirez was also more comfortable in her own skin. She's learned to appreciate her family, her lover, and her own courage.

Themes

Abuse of Power

The triad of wealth, power, and corruption is a natural object of interest for journalists. Abuse of power and privilege forms the background for Wilson's noir landscapes, Powell's hard-boiled spoofs, McDermid's social activism, and the feminism of Drury and other authors. Novels by Haddock, McDermid, Mickelbury, Wilson, and other authors show individuals exploiting their personal or class-related power to perpetrate violent crimes against women, children, lesbians, and gay men. In *Night Songs*, for example, Mickelbury quickly sets the stage for the serial killings that will take place by having Mimi Patterson observe that "poor people, and especially poor people of color, believed they got short shrift from an overburdened justice system, and they quite often were correct."[148] The perpetrators in these novels are rich, white, male and heterosexual (although wealthy gay men number among the worst offenders in Wilson's noir series). The crimes they engage in range from gun smuggling to murder.

Feminist mysteries, such as the Tyler Jones (Joan Drury) and Nyla Wade (Vicki P. McConnell) trilogies and Claudia McKay's Lynn Evans series, tie abuse of power to patriarchy. Drury's series "is about *all* the ways in which women have been silenced by patriarchal power and privilege." Jones fights back by using her newspaper column to expose these silences and by establishing solidarity with other women. McConnell addresses homophobia and sexism. Wade turns to political activism, and her solidarity extends to gay men. McKay makes the view global.

> I think that most people in the U.S. are uneducated about the rest of the world. I wanted to bring other interesting places into the consciousness of my audience. I wanted to show how Lynn, by traveling and with Marta's influence, begins to look at her prejudices, in this case about religion and ethnicity, with new eyes.

Authors also address manipulation of the media for personal gain or to control public opinion. Influential criminals induce Hollis Carpenter's (Deborah Powell) newspaper to reassign her to the society page in an attempt to short-circuit her investigation of police corruption. A senior reporter at Ramirez' (Lisa Haddock) newspaper suppresses and distorts the truth about a lesbian teacher's suicide, and his version inflames an already homophobic public. Wealthy extremists infiltrate Hyatt's newspaper and similar forces are already in power at Manning's and Bone's publications. Bone decries the activities of his own publisher.

> Here was a press baron who would go so far as to hire killers to prevent it getting about that he was gay. And yet the press, of which he was part owner, did more than any other British institution to pillory people for being gay. Somewhere it must make sense. But not to me.[149]

Homophobia

All gay/lesbian journalist series to date attack homophobia. One of their favorite targets is homophobia in families. Tyler Jones' (Joan Drury) father and sister reject her (although her mother doesn't), and her extended family has tried to obliterate the memory of a lesbian foremother. When Mark Manning (Michael Craft) becomes the guardian of his teenaged nephew, he's almost immediately confronted with the young man's homophobia. Haddock's Carmen Ramirez lives with her Baptist grandmother who "pronounced me a 'hell-bound reprobate' … when I told her I was a lesbian."[150] Furthermore, her best friend's brother participates in gay bashings, and her lover's family blames Carmen for perverting their beloved daughter ("You're the creature who's dragged her into a life of sin"[151]).

Secondary characters are forced into unwanted marriages, disowned, disinherited, and "when someone queer dies, the family pretends they never had any friends."[152] Nyla Wade's friend Pat becomes a "double daughter" (a daughter lost and found) after she's attacked and put into a coma. Her mother, who had disowned her, realizes how much she loves her lesbian daughter, but another family in Wilson's *Justice at Risk* willingly loses both a daughter and a son when they renounce their transsexual child.

Gay and lesbian children quickly learn how to hide and deny their sexual orientation and to hate themselves for it. Benjamin Justice explains to his heterosexual friend Harry Brofsky, "Some of those kids would rather die than face the truth about themselves or reveal it to someone else."[153] Charley, a teenager in Miller's *Mayhem at the Marina*, believes she must hide her lesbianism or risk rejection by her friends at the marina. A gay teenager in Craft's *Boy Toy* mocks Mark Manning's nephew, but his taunts are really "accusing someone else of being what he hated in himself."[154] Elliott, an AIDS activist in Zimmerman's *Hostage*, learned self-hatred after being systematically harassed by his high school classmates. Todd Mills admits that those feelings are carried into adulthood.

> For so long he'd fought his sexuality, did everything he could do to deny it, prove he wasn't a fag and therefore a despicable deviant, an incompetent ninny unworthy of love, a fairy who couldn't do anything but swish about.[155]

The burden of internalized homophobia in gay/lesbian journalist series is borne almost entirely by secondary characters. The reason is that the three main characters who begin their series in the closet (Todd Mills, Sam Bone, and Carmen Ramirez) are outed. Ironically, both Bone and Ramirez are outed as a result of their work on stories.

Some secondary characters cower in the closet, even if they are power brokers or Hollywood glitterati. Some gay men pretend to be womanizers. Other closeted gay men and lesbians enter marriages of convenience. These people are ideal victims for the blackmailers and "outers" who appear in books by Craft, McConnell, McDermid, Powell, Wilson, and Zimmerman and for the serial killers in novels by Mickelbury and Sims. Others project their self-hatred onto others instead. One lesbian in a McDermid novel becomes a blackmailer herself and preys on her ex-lovers. An angry ex-cop in Wilson's series enjoys raping and beating other gay men. A closeted lesbian in a Sims' novel attacks other lesbians because "Deep down she'd rather destroy herself, but doesn't have the guts to do it."

Elizabeth Sims' response is

> ... it makes me sick that so many lesbians and gays consider themselves victims by definition. In my work I strive against such self-defeating ideological bullshit.

Other authors agree with sims. This is one reason they strive to present the positive role models described earlier in this chapter. They also offer new definitions of "family." Drury says, "It's about how we create 'family' if we don't have family. I wanted to look at other ways of having family." Similarly, Zimmerman describes his novel *Tribe* as being "about how you form a family in a different way—in a family-of-choice kind of way." Their main characters forge families that are comprised of friends from their youth.

Gay and lesbian couples in long-term relationships also figure among the family models. Lexy Hyatt joins a family of new friends whose lives intersect at a women's bar and at the marina in *Mayhem at the Marina*. Among them are life partners Donna and Fran. Benjamin Justice's family also includes life partners.

> Fred and Maurice ... have been together more than forty years.... I like them both immensely, and I'm not sure I could live in Justice's world ... if Maurice and Fred were not there. Justice learns a lot from them, Maurice in particular.... They constitute Justice's family, nest and support system in a harsh, cold world.

Michael Craft describes a similar bond between his main character Mark Manning and Mark's lover Neil Waite.

> In a word, it's bedrock.... It was indeed my intention to create a model relationship that demonstrates the rewards of living a life based on Mark's values.

Secondary Characters—Heterosexual Journalists

> During my years at the *Eye*, I'd come to understand that a successful journalist possesses two important characteristics. One is the ability to be an asshole at will; the other is having the killer instinct.[156]

Journalists stampede through all of gay/lesbian detective literature like cattle at feeding time. They mass, swarm, hover, lurk, and pursue as they brandish microphones and shout questions, accusations, and headlines. Even when individual reporters separate briefly from the herd they retain clonelike non-identities that ooze sleaze ("he looked the type: seedy, greedy, and all those -eedy words"[157]), vacuous gloss ("She was being questioned by a young woman wearing the obligatory TV newswoman's scarf around her neck"[158]), or rapaciousness ("The woman had a manic glint in her eye"[159]).

With few exceptions, the media are portrayed as strongly homophobic. A sportswriter in Orland Outland's series declares that, "Regardless of his talent, Mark Bowers must leave the game of baseball.... Our national pastime is more than a game, it is a moral beacon to youth...."[160] After reporter Ramirez is outed "Most of my coworkers avoided me; others, hoping to convert me, invited me to church...."[161] A German official tells Sam Bone that he must remain in the closet because "The public does not really care. But the press cares, as you know better than most."[162] Todd Mills knows better, too. When his lover is murdered, Mills' own coworkers happily sacrifice him to get good ratings.

> A killer always fascinates viewers.... But don't forget to keep sex and sexuality right up there too. Everyone finds that interesting. Particularly famous queers who've buried themselves deep in the closet.... In the South you could get more mileage out of homosexuality, but ... on the other hand AIDS has everyone afraid of homos, and a murdering fag is an entirely different beast.[163]

They are also sexist. Rose Beecham's Detective Inspector Amanda Valentine fields a never-ending stream of questions about how her male subordinates respond to having a female boss, Reporter Lillian Byrd (Elizabeth Sims) is sexually harassed by a male colleague, and the shock jocks in Richard Stevenson's *Tongue Tied* treat the women on their staff (and in their lives) like slaves.

Authors of gay/lesbian detective novels also recognize the power of the media to shape opinions. For example,

> Cops and reporters coexisted peacefully to the extent they could help each other. Sometimes it was a news story that broke a case for the cops, a carefully worded, well-planted news story.[164]

Activists and criminals are equally adept at using media to manipulate public opinion. AIDS activists in Zimmerman's *Hostage* require the media to play videos about their lives in exchange for not harming their prominent anti-AIDS hostage. A vandal in Keith Hartman's *The Gumshoe, the Witch, and the Virtual Corpse* alerts the media to his "artistic" activities. Hartman also projects the power of the press into a future world where

> ... if you're a Southern Baptist, you get all your news from the Christian News Network, you send your kids to Southern Baptist private schools, and watch only Southern Baptist entertainment programming. So you have an extreme world view that isn't challenged by any outside voices.

> And Wiccans do the same thing, and Mormons, and gay men, and all these other little subcultures.

He then asks "How do we know what's true?" and "When do you believe what people tell you, and when do you break from the pack and decide on things for yourself"?

Secondary Characters—Lesbian and Gay Journalists

PI Kate Brannigan's (Val McDermid) friend Alexis Lee is one of the few lesbian or gay journalists to appear in a mainstream series. They are far more common in gay/lesbian detective series. Some of them exhibit the same undesirable behaviors as their heterosexual colleagues. One gay reporter seduces Jack Caleb (Michael Allen Dymmoch) in the hope of getting access to an AIDS hospice where Caleb works. Another tries to trick and bully Det. Kate Delafield (Katherine V. Forrest) into divulging information about a list of closeted LAPD officers. A few are sleazy gossip columnists. Others have built their reputations on outing, including a lesbian in Nikki Baker's *The Lavender House Murder* who, when asked what happens to the people she's outed, says she doesn't care.

Such behavior contributes to the suspicion often shown by the lesbigay community—and the general population—towards reporters. Miller's main character, Lexy Hyatt, discovers that such reticence can even be exhibited by friends. "I could read behind her eyes that she was adjusting her relationship to me."[165]

Most lesbian and gay journalists are portrayed as thoughtful professionals who battle the same biases that face gay/lesbian journalist main characters. For example, Rudolph Sharpe, an openly gay reporter working for a mainstream newspaper in Mary Wings' *She Came by the Book*, covered the riots following Harvey Milk's murder.

> Rudolph Sharpe ... had covered the riots well, even though his bosses were initially worried that his reporting would be biased, as if they would be objective.[166]

Many journalists are lovers and friends of main characters. Cecil Harris is a long-term lover of insurance claims investigator Dave Brandstetter (Joseph Hansen). Det. Inspector Amanda Valentine (Rose Beecham), Lt. Gianna Maglione (Penny Mickelbury), and PI/partner Doan McCandler (Orland Outland) develop greater respect for journalism after they fall in love with top-notch reporters. In the process of defending lesbian journalist Leslie Taylor, attorney Harriet Fordham Croft (Marion Foster) acknowledges her own lesbianism and falls in love with her former client. Reporter Ian Hume is a friend and former lover of Det.

Paul Turner (Mark Zubro) and journalist Gwen Ives is a friend of Sheriff Royce Madison's (Kieran York) family.

Attorneys

> The first thing we do. Let's kill all the lawyers.
>   William Shakespeare
>   *Henry VI*, Part 2 act 4, sc. 2, 1

Attorney/sleuths have been popular in mainstream literature since 1896 when the wiley Mason appeared in a series of short stories by Melville Davisson Post. Wiley Mason did little to dispel the negative image of attorneys except to inspire Earle Stanley Gardner to create another fictional detective with the same surname. Since the 1933 publication of *The Case of the Velvet Claws*, Perry Mason has starred in eighty mystery novels and stories, a popular television series, and a series of made-for-TV movies. The Perry Mason mysteries introduced many elements that became standard features of legal mysteries and courtroom dramas, including details about legal procedures, a confrontational (rather than disdainful) attitude toward police and prosecutors, and romance with a worthy partner (Della Street).

In 1978, John Mortimer's *Rumpole of the Bailey* featured a disheveled, cigar-chomping London barrister named Horace Rumpole whose popularity now rivals Perry Mason's. Although he defends his sleazy clients with poetry and circumlocution, Rumpole seems to subscribe to the philosophy that the "glory of the advocate is to be opinionated, brash, fearless, partisan, hectoring, rude, cunning and unfair."[167]

Other popular attorney/sleuths include Sara Woods' Anthony Maitland, Lia Matera's Willa Jansson, and Jean Hager's Molly Bearpaw (a Cherokee tribal-advocacy attorney). Legal fiction also includes non-series mysteries, such as Scott Turow's *Presumed Innocent*; legal thrillers by John Grisham; and courtroom dramas, such as Agatha Christie's "Witness for the Prosecution," Robert Traver's *Anatomy of a Murder*, and Meyer Levin's *Compulsion*.

To date, there are only three gay/lesbian series featuring attorneys: Michael Nava's Henry Rios, Marion Foster's Harriet Fordham Croft, and Elizabeth Woodcraft's Frankie Richmond.* All are seasoned defense attor-

---

*Lauren Maddison's Connor Hawthorne and Tony Fennelly's Matty Sinclair are former district attorneys and Nathan Aldyne's Clarisse Lovelace completes a law degree at the end of the series. They aren't considered here because their legal expertise plays no role in their series.

neys whose practices tilt towards the disenfranchised. They also reveal some of the inner workings of the judicial systems in which their main characters operate. For Woodcraft, that is an important goal.

> I wanted to reflect what happens to people when they go to court, how the judicial system affects them. I think the judicial process is very important and necessary for people as an indication that society as a whole sees their troubles as important....

Otherwise, these three series are markedly different.

Rios is a dark-skinned Mexican American from a family of modest means whose noir series focuses on social and personal issues. Even as a child he was aware of his homosexuality although he didn't come out to his parents before they died. By the start of the series he's living an openly gay life and he's been active in the gay rights movement. His sexual orientation is a major source of Rios' alienation from his family and the Hispanic community. "I wondered whether my father would have hated me more because I was homosexual or a lawyer."[168]

Croft is a beautiful, wealthy, and self-confident member of Toronto's high society. She operates a small but successful law firm. Her cordial relationship with her ex-husband becomes strained after she recognizes her lesbianism at the conclusion of *The Monarchs Are Flying*. That book is a courtroom drama with a classic Perry Mason-like conclusion.

Richmond comes from a working-class English family and grew up in public housing. Like her creator, Richmond is a barrister working in barrister's chambers in London ("firms are where solicitors work"). She's out of the closet as a lesbian and as a feminist and has many ties with the lesbian community. "Frankie is at ease with her sexuality, as are her friends and family." Her hard-boiled, comic mysteries are filled with wine, women, and song—Motown, that is.

Themes

Homophobia surfaces in all three series. It titillates Richmond's colleagues, it haunts Rios," and it's the linchpin of Croft's defense of accused murderer Leslie Taylor. "If it weren't for Miss Taylor's sexual orientation, she would never have been charged in the first place."[169] Croft attacks the homophobia of police, prosecutors, and witnesses who portray Taylor as a monstrous predator. Rios contends that "Whatever their other disagreements, the races all united in their contempt for people of my kind."[170] Homophobia is also melded with fear of AIDS, a specter that dominates Nava's series from *How Town* through *The Death of Friends*.

> I'm gong to die, Henry.... Not just because of AIDS but also because the

lives of queers are expendable.... They hate us, Henry, and they just as soon we all died.[171]

Homophobia surfaces in families as well. Croft's ex-husband accuses her of cheating on him. "So goddamn high and mighty, and all the time you were screwing women behind my back."[172] Rios is rejected by his sister whom he believes to be a closeted lesbian. Frankie Richmond is more fortunate than Croft and Rios, although her clients are not. One client's husband is infuriated. "It hit him right in his manhood. He blamed everything on Saskia, me becoming a lesbian, his bad luck, losing his job."[173]

Although Croft and Rios are comfortable with their sexual orientation, both series address internalized homophobia. Many of Rios' clients and associates hide behind marriages of convenience or cower in the closet. One client "told me that he wasn't gay with the desperation of someone who could not allow himself to believe anything else."[174] Other attorneys are deeply closeted. Rios knows that "It takes incredible strength to withstand hatred without internalizing some of it."[175] Croft's client Leslie Taylor would agree. Having hid in the closet most of her life, she faces her worst fears when she's outed following the murder of her lover.

All three series describe families made dysfunctional by spousal abuse. In Foster's series, investigative reporter Leslie Taylor has done stories on spousal abuse and later runs a workshop on violence against women. Both Croft and Richmond defend clients who have risen up against their abusive husbands. Child molestation is a central theme of Nava's *How Town* and of Woodcraft's *Babyface*. A prominent Mexican American politician in Nava's *The Hidden Law* is revealed to be an alcoholic and a wife batterer. Woodcraft also describes the inherent sexism in the legal system related to such cases.

> Sometimes that judicial process can be part of the problem—the way men can cross-examine their wives, the way judges try to make men feel better when they have breached an order, the way women have to sit in waiting rooms, physically close to their abusing men.

Strong female characters appear in all series. Rios' friend, Inez Montoya, is a skilled attorney and savvy politician. Leslie Taylor's mother

> had encouraged her daughter to make her own decisions, to set her own goals, and to work towards them.... Even if women's rights were given short shrift in a male-oriented mining town like Spruce Falls, there was a whole wide world out there and Leslie was entitled to it.[176]

Frankie Richmond's friend Lena is a women's rights activist. Frankie herself is a feminist.

> She is conscious of herself as a woman and a lesbian and aware of the impact her gender and sexuality have in the world. And I wanted to show that feminists can be funny, likeable, have a sense of style.

Secondary Characters—Heterosexual Attorneys

> There was a snakelike quality to Paul I'd never noticed before.[177]

That's Sydney Sloane's (Randye Lordon) assessment of her cousin-in-law Paul, an attorney. It captures the most persistent, negative perception of attorneys in gay/lesbian detective literature and beyond: they're sleazy, money-grubbing crooks. These "criminal" attorneys appear throughout gay/lesbian detective fiction. They consort with drug dealers, engage in real estate scams, and participate in blackmail schemes. They also rob, rape, and commit both incest and murder. Like Paul, these attorneys are almost invariably heterosexual. PI Robin Miller (Jaye Maiman) and police consultant Bruce MacLeod (Larry Townsend) encounter attorneys involved in illegal drug operations. Vicki P. McConnell's reporter Nyla Wade and Grant Michael's amateur detective Stanley Kraychik expose real estate scams run by attorneys. Gay attorney Henry Rios (Michael Nava) learns that two high-powered LA law firms are involved in a blackmail scheme and girl-detective Nancy Clue (Mabel Maney) reveals that her father, respected attorney Carson Clue, is a child molester.

Some attorneys are actively racist, sexist, and homophobic and willingly manipulate those biases in the courtroom. In Foster's series, the prosecutor working for Leslie Taylor's conviction uses inflammatory language to paint her as a predatory lesbian. The attorney defending a murderous gay basher in Forrest's *Murder by Tradition* builds a "gay panic" defense by invoking the same stereotype for the victim—adding fear of AIDS to the mix. He expands upon the theme by outing police detective Kate Delafield because he knows the inevitable judicial rebuke can never remove the doubt about her objectivity that he's planted in the jurors' minds.

Heterosexual attorneys are also portrayed as honest advocates who work hard for their clients. One example is Jane Lawless' (Ellen Hart) father Raymond Lawless. He believes everyone deserves good representation, but he "readily agreed that most of his clients were guilty.... He took each case as a challenge, as one of the most sacred obligations of his profession."[178] Aaron Gold assures fellow attorney Henry Rios (Michael Nava), "I won't be an instrument of crime.... I either have to clear my client of this murder or urge him to turn himself in. That's my obligation."[179] Unfortunately, Gold is killed before he can meet it. Similarly,

Florida Grange, solicitor for Leonard Pine's (Joe Lansdale) uncle (and, briefly, Hap Collins' lover), is murdered while investigating the suspicious suicide of an African American prisoner.

Secondary Characters—Lesbian and Gay Attorneys

Nearly all the gay and lesbian attorneys who appear in gay/lesbian detective novels are portrayed as honest, ethical individuals. Some are lovers or ex-lovers of the main character, including Timmy Callahan, the lover of PI Donald Strachey (Richard Stevenson) but most of them are good friends of their main characters. The friendship between PI Micky Knight (J.M. Redmann) and Assistant District Attorney Danielle Clayton began in college as did that between Corporate attorney Grant Hancock and Henry Rios (Michael Nava), and Janice Grey and Todd Mills (R.D. Zimmerman). Grey and Mills served as each other's "beards"* while students at Northwestern University.

Some of these attorneys use their practices to help disenfranchised groups and individuals. Lindsay Gordon's (Val McDermid) lover Francis Collier was an early advocate for lesbian mothers. Amateur sleuth Scotty Bradley's (Greg Herren) landlady Millie Breen specializes in criminal law "but her passion was environmental law ... and was known to strike terror in the heart of the corporate CEO."[180] Feminist attorney Jenna Bolden, Colleen Fitzgerald's (Barbara Johnson) friend, devotes her practice to fight for women's rights, and Pam Nilsen's (Barbara Wilson) friend Janis Glover uses her work to make a feminist statement.

> I need to prove to myself and the rest of the world that women have a right to win. And the only way I see for establishing that is through legal means, through case after case of precedents.[181]

A mob litigator in Keith Hartman's *Gumshoe Gorilla* is one of the rare corrupt gay attorneys. Another is Naomi Weiss, amateur sleuth Ginni Kelly's (Nikki Baker) friend. Weiss is a swaggering political animal with virtually no moral fiber. For example, in *In the Game*, Naomi hands Ginni a completed change-of-address form saying

> Drop the postcard in the mail and Kelsey won't figure out that she's not getting her mail for at least one billing cycle—maybe longer. By that time you'd have all her bills and anything else you need....[182]

Fortunately, Naomi Weiss is the exception rather than the rule.

A "beard" is a member of the opposite sex who dates, attends social functions with, or otherwise knowingly helps the lesbian/gay man present a public image of heterosexuality.

MICHAEL CRAFT: *Mark Manning* (1997–CURRENT)

Michael Craft (1950–; pseudonym for Michael Craft Johnson) began writing fiction while working as a graphic designer for the *Chicago Tribune*. His first book, *Rehearsing*, was an Adult Fiction Award finalist (Society of Midland Authors). In addition to his Mark Manning series, Craft writes a series about a heterosexual female theatrical director. He lives in Kenosha with his partner of twenty years and is VP of communications for his lover's family-owned company.

Detective: Mark Manning, investigative journalist

Settings: Chicago and Dumont, Wisconsin. Time period is contemporary with publication dates

Books: *Flight Dreams* (1997); *Eye Contact* (1998); *Body Language* (1999); *Name Games* (2000) Finalist Lambda Award—Best Gay Men's Mystery (2000); *Boy Toy* (2001); Finalist Lambda Award—Best Gay Mystery (2001); *Hot Spot* (2002); Finalist Lambda Award—Best Gay Mystery (2002)

Publishers: Kensington Books, St. Martin's Press

Mark Manning begins the series as a successful, heterosexual reporter in Chicago. By the fourth book he's burst out of the closet, leapt into a marriage-like relationship, acquired a newspaper, relocated to Wisconsin, and become guardian to a teenager. "I think of these ongoing lifestyle upheavals as the 'serial subplot' of the books. The primary plot of each story deals with a distinct whodunit, but it's Manning's ongoing struggle for self-definition as a happy, complete, mature gay man that provides the series with its 'serial' flavor." Newspaper articles reprinted in the novels reinforce the series' journalistic flavor.

"From the beginning, I have viewed Mark as conventionally heroic ... because he embodies certain ideals that I find important and worth promoting. Mark Manning is my literary embodiment of the objectivist philosophy. He is a rationalist, a humanist, and by extension, an atheist. These are the basic values I hope to convey to my readers....

"I chose an investigative reporter as my hero because these values are, or should be, important to his profession (just the facts, ma'am).... He has struggled ... to arrive at his mind set, and he is now unwavering and unapologetic when it comes to his respect for reason and his disdain for faith, superstition, or other forms of illogic." Those failings are embodied in evil or buffoonish characters who are lampooned and ultimately brought down.

At least one subplot of each novel is erotic. "Though it would be a grave mistake to say that sex is what gay people are 'about,' at some level, the sexual act (or the fantasy of it) is indeed what defines the crucial difference between gays and everyone else. In a novel told by a first-person narrator…. I find it inconceivable that the narrative would not occasionally veer toward the erotic."

Craft calls Mark's relationship with his lover the "bedrock" of the series. "Mark and Neil's relationship is just about 'perfect,' and some readers have criticized that as impossibly Leave-it-to-Beaver. It was not my intention to depict a real, everyday relationship…. It was indeed my intention to create a model relationship that demonstrates the rewards of living a life based on Mark's values."

Craft acknowledges Agatha Christie's influence on his work. "Though I'm unblushing about the erotic content of my stories (I doubt that Mrs. Christie would approve), I have no taste whatever for violence or, as it translates into pop culture, 'action.' So my mysteries most closely resemble the cozy genre, but with an erotic twist." Other Christie-like features are puzzle plots, red herrings, and perpetrators who are the least likely suspects.

The books contain considerable word play, including numerous alliterative names (e.g., Mark Manning). "I can attribute this to nothing more than the sheer joy of writing…. The trick, of course, is not to distract (not *too* much) from the artificial reality that the writer is attempting to construct for the reader…. I suppose I do, at times, overindulge … but that's a risk I'm willing to take." Book titles also have multiple meanings. "At a deeper or thematic level, there's the 'name game' of identity crisis or labeling. This is a thread that runs throughout the series, most clearly in the earlier books."

Craft sees plotting as "the most crucial stage of each story. Everything has to mesh—it has to be a plot that Manning could conceivably solve, and Manning has to be brought up to the task of solving it…. That's always the great, looming uncertainty for me as I approach each new project. Once I have that primary question nailed, there's still plenty of work ahead—detailed plotting, drafting, and revision—but the hurdle of uncertainty has been crossed."

JOAN M. DRURY: *Tyler Jones* (1993–1998)

Award-winning novelist Joan Drury (1945–) has spent most of her life working against violence towards women. For ten years, she was the publisher/editor of Spinsters Ink, a feminist publishing company. Drury lives in northern Minnesota where she owns a bookstore and is Executive Director of Norcroft: A Writing Retreat for Women. She also coproduces and/or cohosts local radio shows, coproduces the annual Shakespeare Festival, and is the developer of an affordable housing project. In 1998 the Lambda Literary Foundation gave her a Publisher's Service Award.

Detective: Tyler Jones, newspaper columnist and author of feminist nonfiction books

Settings: U.S. West coast and northern Minnesota. Time period is contemporary with publication dates

Books: *The Other Side of Silence* (1993); Finalist Minnesota Book Award—Mystery & Detective (1994); *Silent Words* (1996); Benjamin Franklin Award, Fiction/Drama (1996); Minnesota Book Award, Mystery & Detective (1997); PMA Benjamin Franklin Award Winner, Gay/Lesbian (1997); Northeastern Minnesota Book Award (1997); Midwest Independent Publishers Association Award of Merit Fiction (1997); Finalist Edgar Award—Best Paperback Original (1997); Small Press Book Award Finalist, Gay/Lesbian (1997); *Closed in Silence* (1998); Midwest Independent Publishers Association Award of Merit Fiction (1997–1998); Finalist Minnesota Book Award, Mystery & Detective (1999); PMA Benjamin Franklin Award Winner, Gay/Lesbian (1999)

Publisher: Spinsters Ink

These novels are murder mysteries designed to expose readers to feminist ideals and concerns. "Mystery readers enjoy getting information as well as a good story, so I knew that people who knew none of the statistics about violence against women would be reading my books if I wrote them as mysteries. It was true. *Silent Words* was nominated for an Edgar.... It went to audiences that would never have gotten exposure to those feminist issues. That was very exciting."

Tyler Jones is a newspaper columnist and author of award-winning books on women's social issues. Although each novel begins with a column providing background for the stories, Tyler's subsequent investigations are purely personal and linked to feminist values and issues. "My tendency is to always look for characters who could be role models, rather than characters who are in flux. Tyler's like that; she's a very strong character.... I wrote it as if being a lesbian would be treated as if it were normal. Again, it's about role modeling.... I think her being a feminist is much more descriptive and far more important to the series than being a lesbian....

"Feminism is always going to be big in my books because it's a big thing in my life.... Every single one of the books has a great deal in it about friendship: the friendship between Mary Sharon and Tyler is a constant in the first book. The second book explores the idea of community.

The third book is about the friendship of six women that has survived 20 years.... Friendship/family/community is what I think love is all about.... It's about how we create 'family' if we don't have family."

The word "silence" in the titles refers to silence about violence against women. "The series is about *all* the ways in which women have been silenced. They've been silenced from childhood on about things that have happened to them that shouldn't, like incest or rape. That silence is '*don't tell because I'm going to....*' Then there's silence about economic and psychological violence, like harassment. That silence is '*you'll be fired if you complain about....*' It even goes beyond that to everyday silence...." In the series, that includes incest in "respectable" families, spouse abuse, and murder. The "other side" of silence is women's response to silence. "Often it is to turn against our own bodies, such as breast and uterine cancer. Or, to create an organization like F.U.C.K, which appears in the first book—to get some kind of justice that this society is not going to give them.... I see the women in this organization as desperate and damaged." Each book concludes with a victory of exposure of individual perpetrators accompanied by realization that the silences still remain.

Writing required balancing the major components of each novel: characters, themes, and plot. "Before I wrote a word, I thought a great deal about the story and about the characters. I wanted to write about violence against women. I also knew that what makes people come back to a series is the characters so I knew that in some ways characters come first." Balancing also meant ensuring that the political issues didn't overwhelm the story line, distinguishing herself from her characters, and allowing the story to flow. "Tyler is a feminist like me and a lesbian, but she is still different, and I had to think about what she would do in a situation— not what I would do.... Finally, it was a challenge to trust my instincts— to let the story happen without trying to control it."

MARION FOSTER: *Harriet Fordham Croft* (1987–1992)

Marion Foster (1925–1990s) was born in Canada and lived in and around Toronto. The Harriet Fordham Croft legal mysteries are the only novels she is known to have published. Ms. Foster passed away in the 1990s.

Detective: Harriet Fordham Croft, attorney at law

Settings: Toronto, Ontario, Canada, and nearby towns. Time period is contemporary with publication dates

Books: *The Monarchs Are Flying* (1987); *Legal Tender* (1992)

Publisher: Firebrand Books (rereleases from Second Story Press)

Harriet Fordham Croft has a privileged background, arrogant demeanor, and self-confident attitude. Combined with her agile mind and knowledge of the law, these attributes make her a dynamic and successful trial lawyer. *The Monarchs Are Flying*, the first novel in the two-book series, is about Leslie Taylor, a closeted TV news anchor accused of murdering her ex-lover. It has all the elements of a good courtroom drama: a sympathetic defendant, legal strategizing, savvy jury selection, a prosecutor who is a worthy opponent, overzealous (and homophobic) police, a tearful family, a calculating killer, and a courtroom dénouement worthy of Perry Mason. Croft sails through as the brilliant defense attorney who is aided by her devoted staff: a Della Street-like receptionist/secretary and a Paul Drake-like PI. *Legal Tender*, the second book, has a dramatic courtroom scene in it, but the main plot revolves around the possible source of a personal threat to Croft.

This series is both feminist and gay positive. Among the feminist themes are violence against women including spousal battery and rape. The series also addresses some of the social conventions of sexism, such as the behavior of Harriet's ex-husband that suggests she "belongs to" him.

The gay-positive messages are directed at exploding homophobic myths. In *The Monarchs Are Flying* prosecution witnesses and experts raise homophobic fallacies and stereotypes that are dismantled on-the-spot by Croft's adroit questioning or by the testimony of defense witnesses and experts. When, for example, Detective Sergeant Moore testifies he didn't have to be told Taylor was a lesbian—he just knew—Croft says, "What you are telling this court is that you can identify a homosexual by some sixth sense you happen to have.... Based on your knowledge of the subject, Sergeant, I would like you to indicate the thirty persons in this room who are exclusively homosexual."[183] That novel also describes homophobic activities by the police (including entrapment), internalized homophobia (e.g., the closet, fear of family rejection), and what one character terms "compulsory heterosexuality." Except for the characterization of bars as popular places to socialize, however, there is little sense of a gay or lesbian community.

From the perspective of the two central characters, Croft and Taylor, the first book is about coming out and the second is about coming together. Taylor's trial for murder in *The Monarchs Are Flying* forces her out of the closet and makes her confront her fear of family rejection. Her attraction to Taylor coalesces Harriet's unformulated awareness into a clearly defined recognition of her own lesbianism. The physical danger they face in *Legal Tender* makes them realize how important they are to each other.

W. STEPHEN GILBERT: *Sam Bone* (1991)

W. Stephen Gilbert worked for many years as a playwright and television critic. His book, *The Life and Work of Dennis Potter*, about the famous British dramatist, won wide acclaim. Gilbert now works as a television producer, critic, and journalist and regularly contributes articles to *The Independent, The Observer,* and *Time Out.* He lives and works in London.

Detective: Sam Bone, entertainment columnist for *The Globe*

Setting: London. Events take place several years prior to publication date

Book: *Spiked* (1991)

Publisher: Gay Men's Press

The stand-alone novel *Spiked* was the first mystery to feature a gay man journalist/sleuth. The story uses a parody of classic, hard-boiled mysteries to attack abuse of power and internalized homophobia.

Sam Bone is a mediocre reporter who writes entertainment feature stories for a London tabloid that are sometimes "spiked" (killed/not printed). When the novel begins, he's established in his job and in a long-term relationship with an American man who does a great deal of traveling. His world is filled with daydreams of himself as a no-nonsense champion of truth; his models for this imagined self are Humphrey Bogart's Sam Spade and Philip Marlowe.

The story line is well suited to a hard-boiled mystery. The beautiful American actress that Bone interviews for a story commits suicide the following day. Her death escalates the journalistic value of Bone's article even though the writing was originally declared "absolute crap" by Bone's boss and spiked. Bone wonders about the timing of her death, but only begins to probe in earnest when a mysterious caller suggests that her death may not have been suicide.

A great deal of the language, including character names, was inspired by hard-boiled mysteries, primarily Dashiell Hammett's *The Maltese Falcon.* The actress whose death precipitates Bone's investigation shares both her names (Bridget Wonderly and Bridget O'Shaunessy) with Sam Spade's femme-fatale client. Tom Polhaus is Bone's boss and trusted colleague. He gets his name from Det. Tom Polhaus, Spade's friendly contact in the police department. Kasper Gutman is a powerful and corrupt "fat man" in both books, and both main characters are named Sam.

Slang-laden dialogues mimic the underworld jargon that permeates classic hard-boiled novels. Examples include "I clamped my trilby square on my bounce and clicked off the anglepoise"[184] (translation: "I put my hat on and hung up the telephone"), and "Me, I like to shoot them a couple under the ribs to see if the house of cards goes down"[185] (translation: "I like to ask hard questions in interviews"). They are accompanied by the expected picturesque similes "His other hand clung grimly to my shoulder, like a dead twig on an April branch. I wriggled in the grip like a cat going under a fence."[186] Gilbert adds other word play to the mix, such as "the blond's face remained dark"[187] (translation: he was still angry) and "my ears pricked down"[188] (translation: I lost interest).

Bone's investigation sparks the anger of a group of high-ranking, closeted gay men who dispatch a legion of thugs and killers to stop him. His escape routes wind through London's gay bars, private clubs, and trysting spots, leaving a trail of dead bodies and satisfied sex partners. In the end, Bone learns how easily powerful people can dispense death and destruction and how effortless it is for them to cover it all up. These and other revelations transform Bone from a naïve romantic into the hero of his daydreams.

LISA HADDOCK: *Carmen Ramirez* (1994–1995)

Lisa Haddock (1960–) was born in Tulsa, Oklahoma. She has a bachelor of arts in mass media news and a master of arts in modern letters, both from the University of Tulsa. Like Carmen Ramirez, she is of Puerto Rican and Irish heritage. She works as a journalist in New Jersey.

Detective: Carmen Ramirez, copy editor, *Frontier City Times*

Setting: Frontier City, Oklahoma. Events take place in the early 1980s

Books: *Edited Out* (1994); *Final Cut* (1995)

Publisher: The Naiad Press

"What I tried to write was a story about a character and the issues she faced in her life." The character is Carmen Ramirez, a young, naïve, and idealistic copy editor working the night shift at a newspaper in a small Oklahoma town. Carmen wants to prove herself at her new job and forge a relationship with Julia Nichols, an intern at the newspaper who is starting to reexamine her sexual orientation. Carmen also contends with socially sanctioned sexism, homophobia, and racism. She confronts these challenges with youthful optimism and a passion for truth and justice. "She's very young and idealistic—way too idealistic. She's sweet—way too sweet." Haddock adds humor to the mixture which pro-

II. *The Authors and Their Characters*   133

vides an upbeat feeling that belies the seriousness of the underlying social commentary.

Carmen lives with her maternal grandmother who loves her but makes frequent snide remarks about Carmen's dark-skinned, Puerto Rican father. "Writing this series was partly an exercise in imagining what my life would have been like if ... I'd been more identifiably Hispanic. That's why I gave her an ethnic name. I also wanted to divorce her from that ethnicity by having a white mother-figure raise her. So, I wanted to show the tension between having this ethnicity and having no connection to it."

The greatest tension between the two women is tied to Carmen's lesbianism. "Oklahoma is very conservative and evangelical Christian. That's a much more oppressive environment for gays. The Baptist church condemns homosexuality. It's a fixation of theirs.... It was OK—it was actually sanctioned to be homophobic. There was no penalty or price to be paid."

Combating homophobia also motivates Carmen to embark upon her investigations. In *Edited Out,* she's assigned to a story about a lesbian teacher accused of child molestation. "There was a notorious case in Oklahoma in the late seventies involving three girl scouts who were murdered at a sleepover camp. At first, the police speculated that a female scout leader had murdered them. I wondered what would have happened if one of the scout leaders had been a lesbian and she became a convenient target.... I changed her to a teacher because the idea of gays teaching is still a touchy issue." Carmen thwarts the newspaper's plans to use the story to validate homophobia when she uncovers the truth and exonerates the teacher.

In *Final Cut* "I wanted to do something about the gay bashings I knew about in Tulsa. Some guys were pretending to be gay, picking up guys, and beating them up. I knew they were just getting slapped on the wrist.... I was also obsessed with fraternities because we had a series of rapes at frat houses when I was in college.... There's a group mentality—a pack mentality—that allows people to surrender the idea they are morally responsible for what is going on."

In the process Carmen "learned about her courage and her strength and how much she loved her grandmother and how important her family was to her. How important it was to stand up to a system that didn't want to listen and wasn't interested in the truth. She learned that an individual with some integrity can make a difference, which I no longer believe."

Haddock sees considerable overlap between journalism and writing mystery novels. "Journalism is the foundation: keep it short, keep it moving, learn about what you are writing about and punch it out. I want them to be factually based and believable.... The main difference is scale. You spend weeks or months rather than hours or days. Also, in journalistic writing you have a structure to hang things on."

VICKI P. MCCONNELL: *Nyla Wade* (1982–1988)

Vicki P. McConnell (1947–) has had a diverse career as a writer and editor. She's written poetry, lesbian-feminist mysteries, a feminist coming-of-age novel, and technical nonfiction. Her recent technical writing has garnered multiple awards. McConnell's editorial experience includes freelance editing for New Victoria Press, Spinsters Ink, and Rising Tide Press. Currently, she's editor of "Fuel Cell Industry Report" and technology editor of "Aviation Maintenance." McConnell lives and writes in Denver, Colorado.

Detective: Nyla Wade, journalist

Settings: Denver, Colorado, and Burnton, Oregon. Time frame is contemporary with publication dates

Books: *Mrs. Porter's Letter* (1982); *The Burnton Widows* (1984); *Double Daughter* (1988)

Publisher: The Naiad Press

The Nyla Wade series is the first gay or lesbian journalist series. These feminist mysteries follow the personal and professional evolution of investigative reporter Nyla Wade. "I consider the Nyla Wade mysteries feminist because while males are part of the plot as men are in the world, the stories are first and foremost about the evolution and empowerment of the female characters. And showing these characters with multiple dimensions, as womyn are in the world....

"I chose to write about Nyla Wade as an investigative journalist because I believe investigative journalists can take risks that could cost them their lives (witness Daniel Pearl). This is important for creating situations that work in mystery fiction." Those situations involve following the trail of a missing person, exposing a conspiracy involving fraud and multiple murders, and tracking down gay bashers.

"Nyla Wade is my own *sheroe*. She's a 'power adventurer' in the way that men expect to be and she pursues solutions to problems and injustices that would probably intimidate me sufficiently to stop me in my tracks. She has a fearless quality that I admire and aspire to." These qualities lead Wade to recognition and acceptance of her own lesbianism, her bond with the community of women, and true love. "Nyla's relationship with Lucy reflects my integration of the 'personal is political' philosophy. Their love with its flaws and challenges demonstrates the positive and dimensional elements of lesbian partnerships."

In *The Burnton Widows*, solidarity is extended to the gay community. "We're not just separate individuals.... With each mystery plot Nyla affirms that she cannot fight for any important cause alone. Intelligence and passion are only part of the arsenal one needs to fight violence and injustice.... For all the progress made by the gay community, there's always the possibility of violent backlash." Indeed, each novel gives a different face to those threats, ranging from hate-filled individuals to colluding power brokers.

"Within my books, I think these themes are resilient:

- balance in one's life of self-actualization and effort to create a supportive community
- the importance of language—both in actual words said, and that which is literally unspoken but 'speaks' just as loudly

"Feminism is not a separate theme, it infuses the other two organically." The unspoken includes symbols, such as the images of gloxinia in *Mrs. Porter's Letter*, that haunt Wade until she comes to terms with her lesbianism. Those and other images are captured by Janet Fons' illustrations.

"I consider the act of writing to be a combination of spiritual openness and technical alertness. The act of spiritual openness is twofold: my own (to avenues I might investigate that reveal a conflict within me), and my characters (to pursuing the ideas that interest me). I ask my characters their permission and hope they give it to me....

"Technical alertness comes in keeping the 'critical editor's' voice out of the first writing efforts as much as possible, so I can enjoy the character dialogues and not interrupt them with the rules of English. This critique voice can return in rewrites where that is appropriate. Ultimately, I want readers to walk a path with the characters, so technical alertness helps clear the brush from that path....

"And I would be remiss if I didn't mention the sheer bliss brought by moments with the Muse, an unexplainable phenomena. The Muse brings the pure blaze of creativity. She lets me hear the Siren Song of Inspiration, as well as whole pages of character exchange whether in dialogue or monologue."

VAL MCDERMID: *Lindsay Gordon* (1987–CURRENT)

Award-winning author Val McDermid (1955–) is from a Scottish mining community. She read English at Oxford and after graduating from St. Hilda's College, Oxford, she trained as a journalist. McDermid worked in journalism for sixteen years, including as the weekly crime critic for the Manchester Evening News. She currently reviews for several national newspapers and is a regular broadcaster on BBC radio. In addition to her Lindsay Gordon series, she writes mysteries about PI Kate Brannigan, psychological thrillers featuring forensic psychologist Tony Hill and police detective Carol Jordan, non-series novels, and short stories. She also wrote a nonfiction book about real-life female private eyes called *A Suitable Job for a Woman*. Her work has been adapted for radio. McDermid writes full-time and lives with her partner and their son in south Manchester.

Detective: Lindsay Gordon, investigative journalist and college professor

Settings: Primarily Glasgow and London. Books include flashbacks but, overall, the time frame is contemporary with publication dates

Books: *Report for Murder* (1987); *Common Murder* (1989); *Deadline for Murder* and *Open and Shut* (U.S. titles for *Final Edition*) (1991); *Conferences are Murder* (U.S. title for *Union Jack*) (1993); *Booked for Murder* (1995); Finalist Lambda Award—Best Lesbian Mystery (2000)

Publisher: Spinsters Ink, The Women's Press

The Lindsay Gordon series is the earliest British gay/lesbian journalist mystery series and quite likely the earliest British gay/lesbian detective series as well. It's strongly feminist and left-leaning politically, as is its author. "To some extent, Lindsay is an alter ego. Like most writers, when I began, I lacked the confidence or the technique to move very far from my own experience. So, like me, Lindsay was Scottish, lesbian, feminist, broadly left in her politics and a journalist. While the superficial facts of our lives have much in common—working class, Oxford-educated, etc.—in terms of personality, we are very different. She is far more foolhardy than I am; more brave, more ingenious, more stubborn. She's also good fun, I think, although there are times when I think if I had to deal with her in real life I would want to give her a good shake!…

"There is a further dimension to Lindsay. I was conscious growing up of the complete lack of any sort of lesbian role model, anything out there that would make young women growing up gay feel less like a freak, so I wanted Lindsay to be a kind of Everydyke. This is one reason why she's never physically described—I want the reader to make her in their own fantasy image. Also, I didn't want to write books that only dealt with the lesbian community. Most lesbians live in the wider world, and that's what I wanted to reflect in my books. I wanted them to speak to straight readers as well as to lesbians. So although Lindsay lives an out lesbian life, she also lives very much in the world....

"She's also grown up—hardly surprising, given that the books span nearly ten years. I'm working on a new Lindsay Gordon, and she's nearly forty now. The concerns of a woman of 39 are inevitably different from those of a woman in her mid twenties, and the books reflect that shift, I think. She's probably less radical than in her youth, and maybe a bit more inclined to value her relationships a little more....

"I never start off a novel with the idea of having a particular theme or agenda. With me, the story is always what comes first, and it is paramount throughout. I suppose with Lindsay I tend to think about the kind of environments where she would be comfortable, where she would be able to feel her way with confidence, and take it from there. Because I'm a political animal, and because Lindsay is close to me, inevitably she takes on a lot of my own political concerns, but that's not where I start out from." The hardest part of writing these stories is "getting the tone right. Finding a story that works for Lindsay. Figuring out where she's moved forward to in terms of her own life."

This is a feminist series in which lesbian issues are important because "there wouldn't be much point in writing a series with a lesbian detective if she didn't confront the things in her own life and the lives of those around her along the way. So, while there will be other themes in the books, the lesbian element will always have a strong contribution to make."

CLAUDIA MCKAY: *Lynn Evans* (1994–1997)

Claudia McKay was born in Idaho, grew up on the west coast, and has lived in Vermont for thirty-five years. In 1976, she founded (and still runs) the feminist/lesbian New Victoria Publishers. She edited and designed most of the eighty books published by New Victoria over the years and has written two mysteries and two fantasy novels herself. She lives in an old farmhouse with her partner of twenty-six years and enjoys gardening, pottery and playing with her five granddaughters.

Detective: Lynn Evans, investigative reporter, *Hartford Chronicle*

Settings: New England, Nepal, and Belize. Time period is contemporary with publication dates

Books: *The Kali Connection* (1994); *Twist of Lime* (1997)

Publisher: New Victoria Publishers

This series uses exotic settings to illuminate social problems and feminist issues. The stories include a romantic subplot because, according to McKay, love and romance are "almost always present in books for and about women."

Lynn Evans is a seasoned investigative reporter with an American newspaper. She travels to Nepal on assignment in *The Kali Connection* and vacations at a Mayan archeological dig in Belize in *Twist of Lime*. Both excursions involve love and romance as well as a range of crimes, including murder. "Lynn and her love affairs are an important part of her character" but the books are "about her and her adventures....

"I am what some writers call an unconscious writer. My plots and characters write themselves for the most part. I set out to write a mystery, of course, and intended a lesbian-feminist consciousness and character, but Lynn Evans just appeared one day as I began to write. I am a writer and editor and have never been a detective, so it was easiest to write from experience. Although I have never worked for a newspaper, I have friends who do."

The Kali Connection shows Evans in her role as a working journalist. She writes a favorable article about a cult she wants to investigate in order to coax them into giving her a personal interview with their leader. As soon as she arrives in Nepal, she submits a travel piece to her paper. Once she learns about the woman-led people's movement in Nepal, she offers to become part of if it—not only because she wants to help restore order but because "It would be the news story of my life. Not only would I have an exclusive world-wide, but I would get to tell the story, first person. It will be the making of my career."[189]

Evans is attracted to dangerous women who may be involved in murder. "Lynn Evans is smart conscientious and honest, but rather naïve. It makes it possible for her to fall in love with the wrong person and to get into situations that are dangerous and get out of them too." In *The Kali Connection* she becomes so emotionally involved with a Nepalese cult member/murder suspect that other journalists question her ability to be objective. "People in love always seem to have their judgment clouded. I suppose that is why there is so little romance in most detective novels. I prefer my characters to be fully human with all their faults as well as their strengths....

"She becomes more realistic in her goals and loves, and accepting of her vulnerabilities as well as more competent in her profession and more global in her thinking." Part of that global thinking is to become sensitive to damage being done on a global scale by greed and acquisitiveness. "I think that most people in the U.S. are uneducated about the rest of the world. I wanted to bring other interesting places into the consciousness of my audience. I wanted to show how Lynn, by traveling and with Marta's influence, begins to look at her prejudices, in this case about religion and ethnicity, with new eyes....

"Since my stories more or less write themselves, thinking about them and watching them unfold is very exciting. It's as if someone else is telling me a wonderful story. Discovering the story bit by bit and thinking of alternative versions is easy. Choosing the right one and getting the details right is hard."

CARLENE MILLER: *Lexy Hyatt* (1998–2001)

Carlene Miller (1935–) was drawn to the east coast of Florida by the need for teachers created by the burgeoning space industry of the 1960s, and she retired after thirty years to help ease her partner's journey through Alzheimer's to her death. Miller has begun two other mystery series with lesbian main characters. She lives and writes in a small town on the east coast of Florida.

Detective: Alexis (Lexy) Hyatt, investigative reporter, *The Ledger*

Settings: Central and northern Florida. Time period is contemporary with publication dates

Books: *Killing at the Cat* (1998); *Mayhem at the Marina* (1999); *Reporter on the Run* (2001)

Publisher: New Victoria Publishers

This series possesses many defining characteristics of traditional mysteries: victims are nasty people with enough enemies to generate a plethora of red herrings; there's very little violence; clues are deposited in strategic places; killers are often the least likely suspect; and the dénouement restores a sense of order. "Although I keep track of characters' traits and the planting of clues, I do not plan or outline plot development or general content. Some idea or activity prompts the start of each book. For instance, an article in the Sunday paper on orienteering was the impetus for *Reporter on the Run*.... I am as much an observer of what happens as the creator. Sometimes I am not certain who the murderer is going to be when I start. In *Killing at the Cat* I put a comment in a character's mouth a few chapters into the book and suddenly realized that person was the murderer and the comment embodied the reason."

Lexy Hyatt is an energetic and inquisitive woman who is making a transition from teaching to reporting. "Lexy is a reporter because I wanted her in a job that let her move about and encounter a variety of happenings and people. Her profession is not exceptionally important to the series, more a device for that variety." That variety includes changes in location, people, activities, and even the way people talk. The military terms used at a bar for women veterans, for example, differs markedly from the nautical jargon Lexy encounters at a marina.

"I see Lexy as a developing person who is learning more about herself through relationships with others which is both satisfying and disturbing. Her habit of compartmentalizing elements of her life is being challenged by new experiences. I view her not so much as changing as growing and evolving through encounters with events and individuals.... Perhaps, I want to take her on a journey wherein she will become more comfortable in her own skin." Helping her in that effort are her friends and her lover, Wren. "I don't know where Wren came from—she just flowed onto the paper, her quiet assuredness and composure a natural counterpart of Lexy's occasional unrest and edginess. I was surprised to discover that many readers took to her very protectively. They were adamant in demanding that I keep Lexy faithful to her."

The series tackles racism, homophobia, sexism, and other social issues. Also addressed is the danger a free press faces when extremists gain control of the media. "No good teacher ever ceases to be an interpreter and guide or desires to cease instructing and elevating. I want to do those things while developing an interesting plot filled with unique and believable characters, and hopefully with satisfying language and images.... I do not consciously determine themes in advance. They seem to happen naturally as the plot unfolds—or because I see a place for something I have recently encountered in conversation or in my reading and observing." Stories often contain parallel threads that reinforce a particular theme. *Mayhem at the Marina*, for example, presents the concept of "family" in a variety of guises, including a committed lesbian relationship, the family that consists of a network of friends, and even the bond formed between lesbians when they first meet outside of their home communities.

"Most challenging for me is wrapping everything up in the final two or three chapters. That is when I procrastinate. I get impatient toward the end of a book and want to get on to the new one that has started simmering in my mind."

MICHAEL NAVA: *Henry Rios* (1986–2001)

Award-winning author Michael Nava (1954–) grew up in Stockton, California, and received a law degree from Stanford University in 1981. He has been practicing law ever since. Nava has a private law practice in San Francisco. In addition to the Henry Rios mysteries, Nava has edited anthologies and written nonfiction. In 2001, The Publishing Triangle Association of Lesbian and Gay Men in Publishing awarded Nava the Bill Whitehead Award for Lifetime Achievement.

Detective: Henry Rios, defense attorney

Setting: San Francisco Bay Area and Los Angeles, California. Time period is contemporary with publication dates

Books: *The Little Death* (1986); *Goldenboy* (1988); Lambda Award—Best Gay Men's Sci-fi/Mystery (1988); *How Town* (1990); Lambda Award—Best Gay Men's Mystery (1990); *The Hidden Law* (1992); Lambda Award—Best Gay Men's Mystery (1992); *The Death of Friends* (1996); Lambda Award—Best Gay Men's Mystery (1996); *The Burning Plain* (1997); Finalist Lambda Award—Best Gay Men's Mystery (1997); *Rag and Bone* (2001); Lambda Award—Best Gay Men's Mystery (2001)

Publishers: Alyson Publications, HarperCollins, Penguin and Putnam

This dark and somber series chronicles the evolution of Mexican-American attorney Henry Rios from the San Francisco Public Defender's office into a private practice that moves between San Francisco and Los Angeles.

Henry Rios is an angry, alienated workaholic and recovering alcoholic. He's estranged from his family, ostracized by a homophobic Hispanic community, and too dark-skinned to find ready acceptance in the white community. When the series begins, Henry has worked as a public defender for ten years and manifests a cynical attitude towards life. "People are basically screwed-up and often the best you can do for them is listen, hear the worst and then tell them it's not so bad."[190]

Like other hard-boiled heroes, Rios adheres to a high moral code, and he's driven to seek the truth—no matter how ugly it might be. For his clients, the truth includes child molestation, spouse abuse, exploitation, betrayal, and murder. For gay men like Henry, the truth encompasses homophobia, violence, fear, and self-hatred. "… people who inspire such homicidal hatred in others can come to believe they deserve it, subliminally if not consciously."[191]

The specter of AIDS clouds Nava's series from the first chapter of *Golden Boy*, the first book in the series. AIDS is not only horrific by itself, but is also a symbol of society's ingrained homophobia. Henry loses several friends and his lover Josh to the disease and sees a deeply closeted friend communicate HIV to his unsuspecting wife and his lover. The series also shows the discord that can develop between lovers when one is dying of AIDS and the other is HIV-negative. The following example describes the deteriorating relationship between Henry, who is HIV-negative, and his lover Josh.

Just that morning, bickering again over the wisdom of outing closeted gay politicians, he'd snapped "Spoken like a true neggie," as if being negative for the virus was a defect of character.[192]

Conflict leads to rupture. When Josh says he's leaving because he loves another man Henry retorts, "Are you sure it's not because you're in love with his diagnosis?"[193]

Nava incorporates literary references, including poetry by gay authors, into the novels. He also utilizes the physical setting of the stories to reinforce Henry's mental state. In *The Death of Friends*, for example, the shock of Josh's death is echoed by an earthquake that awakens Henry and gives him the feeling that someone is in the room with him. The Los Angeles of *The Burning Plain* is a purgatory with searing heat, "poisonous air," and "smoky sky." Later, rain accompanies one character's account of the devastation in his life.

The series ends with more hope than at any other point. Henry, felled by a massive heart attack at the start of *Rag and Bone*, feels world weary and welcomes death. He initiates reconciliation with his sister Elena whose daughter needs his legal expertise and whose grandson Angel looks like Henry did as a child. Henry's outlook changes as the bond with his grandnephew grows, his relationship with a potential lover deepens, and as he considers leaving law practice to become a judge.

DEBORAH POWELL: *Hollis Carpenter* (1991–1992)

Deborah Powell (1951–) was born and grew up in Sunflower, Mississippi. She lived for a while in Houston, Texas, where the Hollis Carpenter novels are set, and then relocated to Denver, Colorado. The Hollis Carpenter novels are Powell's only publications.

Detective: Hollis Carpenter, investigative journalist
Setting: Houston, Texas. Time period is 1936–37
Books: *Bayou City Secrets* (1991); *Houston Town* (1992)
Publisher: The Naiad Press

The mysteries in this series parody the hard-boiled style. They are written with sardonic humor that becomes more cutting in the second novel, *Houston Town*.

Hollis Carpenter is a seasoned crime reporter who lives in a world of violence and corruption populated by gangsters, con artists, crooked cops, and unprincipled rich people. Carpenter is a large, imposing woman who wears slacks, saddle shoes, a sharp tongue, and a large chip on her shoulder. Despite her masculine dress and size, she encounters far more sexual harassment than overt homophobia.

Carpenter is always after a story, even when crime hits close to home, as it does in both books. Like the hard-boiled male reporters she's modeled on, she has a network of informants that come from both sides of the law. Lt. Frank Brumfield, her most reliable police contact, trades information that sometimes includes the activities of crooked cops. Her ties to the criminal element include Houston's most powerful mobster, a Godfather-like figure who thinks of Hollis as his daughter. In *Bayou City Secrets* he deploys western-garbed enforcers to ensure her safety. She's also protected by her reputation as a reporter, a willingness to resort to violence, her uncrackable head, and a cache of guns that always seems to be near at hand.

Hollis' sidekick is her beloved schnauzer, Anice. She's the one Hollis consults about her investigations and who accompanies Hollis to sinister assignations. Anice is a source of humor in both novels. She knows she's beautiful and likes to be the center of attention. She's also credited with humanlike thought and behavior, including a recurring nightmare about a large cat and artistic preferences. "Anice cut her eyes at me and grinned. She loved a western theme."[194]

The beautiful woman who captures Hollis' heart is Lily Delacroix. She's the wife (soon to be widow) of the owner of the *Houston Times*, the newspaper that employs Hollis. Lily first appears in *Bayou City Secrets* as the ultrafeminine scion of Houston's wealthy high society who believes she's frigid—until she kisses Hollis, that is. Then, much to Hollis' horror, she decides to tell her husband and family the wonderful news which, as Hollis anticipates, is a mistake that leads to Lily's banishment to Europe. When Lily resurfaces towards the end of *Houston Town* it is as a reincarnation of the wealthy Nora Charles in Dashiell Hammett's *The Thin Man* who wants to be in on the excitement of tracking a killer. "You're not going to go out and get yourself killed without my being there to help."[195]

Hollis' relationship with Lily is intriguing in view of one of the series major themes: abuse of power and privilege. This strong bias against the upper class is in keeping with the hard-boiled style as is the corruption that emanates from wealthy and powerful men who twist the system to suit their own interests. Hollis and Lily also encounter homophobia and the blatant sexism that provokes Hollis to resign from her job of fifteen years and strike out on her own.

ELIZABETH SIMS: *Lillian Byrd* (2002–CURRENT)

Elizabeth Sims (1957–) grew up in the Detroit metropolitan area. She holds degrees from Michigan State University and Wayne State University, where she won the Tompkins Award for Fiction. She's a veteran reporter, photographer, and bookseller, and has written about bookselling for the quarterly *LOGOS: Journal of the World Book Community*. In addition to her Lillian Byrd series, she's written short fiction and poetry that appeared in *Moving Out* and *The Smudge*, as well as stories for the anthologies *A Woman's Touch* (2003) and *Best Lesbian Love Stories 2004*. Sims now lives and writes in northwestern Washington.

Detective: Lillian Byrd, freelance reporter

Settings: Detroit and other locations. Time period is contemporary with publication dates

Books: *Holy Hell* (2002); *Damn Straight* (2003); Lamba Award— Best Lesbian Mystery (2004)

Publisher: Alyson Publications

Elizabeth Sims defines her Lillian Byrd series as "deadpan comic noir." "Deadpan comic noir is writing that is dark and funny, but delivered straight, not flagged for the reader as comedy. Because it is delivered straight—that is, deadpan—it demands that the reader be on her toes. If you're not on your toes, you're not going to get it. You're going to be bored or confused.... I expect my readers to work a little bit....

"With *Holy Hell*, one of my goals was to spoof the detective genre while at the same time delivering on it.... Some readers and reviewers picked up on that, and understood *Holy Hell* to be absurd and far out, and they got the funny stuff. Others totally missed the comedy of it.... In *Damn Straight*, I smoothed things out, developed a plot that more readers would find 'plausible,' and continued to supply Lillian with a deadpan wit. I keep resisting clichés, I keep trying to give readers something other than what they've been conditioned to expect."

Investigative reporter Lillian Byrd leads the parade of outlandish characters who hurtle through these stories leaving trails of death and absurdity behind them. "Starting in *Holy Hell*, I wanted to build a character who was flawed but lovable." She's guided by her "fearlessness: her willingness to risk trouble to do the right thing. This boldness is fueled by her curiosity and sense of right and wrong.... Lillian doesn't take herself too seriously, she doesn't feel entitled to much of anything—happiness, money.... She doesn't let other people get away with anything and doesn't let herself off the hook, either."

The stories are set in places where lesbians congregate: a popular lesbian bar and the Dinah Shore Invitational Championship Golf Tournament. "Lesbian culture offers a great many set pieces for Lillian to explore in future books, such as the softball culture, the music festival culture, the separatist-commune culture, the activist culture. The list goes on...."

"The great question of life to me is, *Why do people do what they do?* And I explore that in my fiction. Why and how do people rationalize immoral acts? Why and how do people select and apply standards to their own and others' behavior?...

"In *Holy Hell* I specifically wanted to explore how self-loathing can lead to violence and diseased rationalization. It's unfortunate that so many gay people despise themselves for being what they are, although I think we can all agree that being openly gay is generally easier today than it used to be. In *Damn Straight* I wanted to celebrate women's athletic achievement, as well as the singular lesbian festival of the Dinah....

"Social issues are so much more complicated than most of us want them to be. I try to acknowledge that in my work. I try to give the reader a neglected point of view." Social issues are important but "most important of all, is that I work hard to deliver fun to my readers. I want them to be entertained. I want them to experience that satisfying brainfeel you get when you read something good and provocative and entertaining. That is my goal. I strive for excellence, so that readers will say, 'Hey, I'm surprised! This little book in this little niche in this little bookstore is pretty good! And it made me laugh!'"

JOHN MORGAN WILSON:
Benjamin Justice (1996–CURRENT)

John Morgan Wilson (1945–) has a degree in journalism, was a news editor on Fox TV, an *LA Times* editor, and an award-winning reporter. He's written more than one hundred documentary and reality episodes for television and two guidebooks for writers. Wilson lives in West Hollywood, California where he writes fact-based television episodes (e.g., *Anatomy of Crime* documentary series on Court TV) and writes two mystery series.

Detective: Benjamin Justice, freelance writer and journalist

Setting: Primarily Los Angeles, California. Time period is contemporary with publication dates

Books: *Simple Justice* (1996); Edgar Award—Best First Novel by an American Author (1996); Finalist Lambda Award—Best Gay Men's Mystery (1996); *Revision of Justice* (1997); Finalist Lambda Award—Best Gay Men's Mystery (1997); *Justice at Risk* (1999); Lambda Award—Best Gay Men's Mystery (1999); *Limits of Justice* (2000); Lambda Award—Best Gay Men's Mystery (2000); *Blind Eye* (2003); Lambda Award—Best Gay Men's Mystery (2004)

Publishers: Doubleday/Bantam, St. Martin's Press

Hollywood, with all its excesses, is the true context for this noir series;

and the image of the "Hollywood" sign, a potent symbol of the power of the rich, is woven into the stories.

Benjamin Justice is a talented journalist who is best known for the fact he won a Pulitzer prize for a story on AIDS and lost the prize after it was revealed he'd falsified information in the story. The crimes he exposes include child molestation, willful transmission of HIV, rape, and murder. The perpetrators are rich, famous white men who often commit those crimes simply because they can.

"I see Justice as a deeply flawed human being, burdened heavily with guilt and a savior complex, forever trying to redeem himself for having let others down, particularly his little sister, who suffered sexual abuse at the hands of their father. Justice can be arrogant, unreasonably tough, even violent, but in the end, he tries to do the right thing. He's a man looking for a reason to hope in a world he sees as basically unjust and hopeless."

The series begins shortly after Justice has lost his lover to AIDS. He's rescued from a descent into alcoholism by Fred and Maurice. "Fred and Maurice, Justice's elderly landlords, who have been together more than forty years, provide some relief and goodness, I hope, from the darkness and depravity Justice tends to be drawn to. They are there for a very specific purpose. I like them both immensely, and I'm not sure I could live in Justice's world as I write these books if Maurice and Fred were not there.... They constitute Justice's family, nest and support system in a harsh, cold world."

Harry Brofsky, Justice's former editor at the *LA Times*, drags Justice back into journalism and pairs him with a savvy young African American reporter, Alexandra Templeton, who assists Justice on some of his assignments. "I felt Justice needed a 'partner' who was more stable and professionally driven to keep him on course and help him out when he needs it. At the same time, I wanted some conflict there.... Templeton is strong and doesn't take a lot of crap from Justice....

"I created a world for Justice and put him in situations that come out of my own life. I've worked in print journalism, TV documentary writing, film writing, and celebrity writing, which provide the backdrops for the first four books." The series shows how journalists think and work. In *Simple Justice*, for example, Justice alternately threatens and interrogates a potential source of information until the man breaks down. Afterwards Justice thinks, "I went out remembering why, too many times, I'd hated being a reporter."[196]

"I really found my voice as a writer when I began writing fiction in the first person with *Simple Justice*. It's changed my writing and my life profoundly. It's enabled me to write more personally and honestly.... I write for a living, but also to express myself to the world, to make my voice heard, to say to the world: this is who I am, good or bad. Writing has been a wonderful trade and vehicle of expression for me, and I'm eternally grateful to the readers who have let me tell my stories and been there as an audience."

ELIZABETH WOODCRAFT:
Frankie Richmond (2000–CURRENT)

Award-winning author Elizabeth Woodcraft (1950–) has been practicing as a barrister in London since 1980. She has represented the Greenham Common women, striking miners, animal-rights demonstrators, and victims of domestic violence and sexual abuse. *Good Bad Woman* is her first published work of fiction.

Detective: Frances (Frankie) Richmond, barrister

Settings: London and central England. Time period is contemporary with publication dates

Books: *Good Bad Woman* (2000); Short-listed CWA John Creasey Memorial Dagger (2001); Lambda Award—Best Lesbian Mystery (cowinner) (2002); *Babyface* (2001)

Publisher: Kensington Publishing

Frankie Richmond is a London barrister with working-class roots who usually represents working-class women in a system that's biased towards men from privileged classes. "Frankie is someone who is trying hard, to represent her clients well, not to compromise, to be true to what she believes in. She's a loyal friend, a bad cook, a fan of Tamla Motown, and someone who is looking for love. Perhaps she drinks too much....

"I wanted to reflect what happens to people when they go to court, how the judicial system affects them. I think the judicial process is very important and necessary for people as an indication that society as a whole sees their troubles as important, but sometimes that judicial process can be part of the problem—the way men can cross examine their wives, the way judges try to make men feel better when they have breached an order, the way women have to sit in waiting rooms, physically close to their abusing men....

"*Good Bad Woman* is sometimes described as 'hard-boiled.' That would possibly be because of the air of cynicism—particularly concerning the judicial system. Frankie is a flawed heroine, but has a strong personal code, and of course the humor—the use of irony, the wise-cracking badinage.... Humor is a way of defusing the embarrassment and the anguish.... So the humor in the books is telling it how it really feels.

What I did not want to do was make fun of Frankie's clients, since that would not be fair."

Frankie has been a barrister for ten years and is out of the closet. "Frankie is at ease with her sexuality as are her friends and family," but her sexual orientation feeds the fantasies of her firm's partners. In *Good Bad Woman,* for example, when Frankie calls her firm to report her arrest for murder one partner exclaims, "Was it some terrible lesbian brawl, with torn clothing and scratching with long red nails?"[197]

"In *Good Bad Woman,* of course, the subplots revolve around who is and isn't a lesbian and the reactions people have to that, which are issues I wanted people to think about" including issues related to being butch or femme ("My partner is often faintly amused at my attempts at portraying butch women"), which leads one character to declare that "the headings Butch and Femme are merely a shorthand and superficial description of the myriad ways women express their sexuality."[198]

When starting a new project, Woodcraft uses Frankie as her starting point. "I write scenes with Frankie in them and usually a theme emerges and then the plot comes.... I don't usually find out what the book is actually about until I reach the very end of the second draft.... The most fun is the dialogue—the badinage between Frankie and the other characters.... It's all the things you ever wanted to say to people but couldn't think quickly enough, or didn't dare because there really would have been hell to pay....

"I would describe the series as feminist, because that's what I'd like to think it is. Frankie would describe herself as a feminist (and if she didn't, her friend Lena would make sure she did). She is conscious of herself as a woman and a lesbian, and aware of the impact her gender and sexuality have in the world. And I wanted to show that feminists can be funny, likeable, have a sense of style."

R.D. (Robert) Zimmerman:
Todd Mills (1996–current)

Award-winning author R.D. Zimmerman (1952–) has written children's books, best-selling historical fiction (under pseudonym Robert Alexander), and mysteries—including mysteries for the back of Total cereal boxes. He studied Russian in college and worked as a translator in the Soviet Union for U.S. Information Service (with a security clearance). Born in Chicago, he now lives and works in the Minneapolis area with his lover of almost twenty-five years.

Detective: Todd Mills, Emmy award-winning TV news reporter

Setting: Minneapolis, Minnesota. Time period is contemporary with publication dates

Books: *Closet* (1995); Lambda Award—Best Gay Men's Mystery (1995); Finalist Anthony Award (1995); *Tribe* (1996); Finalist Lambda Award—Best Gay Men's Mystery (1996); Finalist Edgar Award—Best Paperback Novel (1997); *Hostage* (1997); Finalist Lambda Award—Best Gay Men's Mystery (1997); *Outburst* (1998); Lambda Award—Best Gay Men's Mystery (1998); *Innuendo* (1999); Finalist Lambda Award—Best Gay Men's Mystery (1999)

Publisher: Dell Publishing Group

Todd Mills is the son of Polish immigrants who settled in Chicago, anglicized their last name, and worked to achieve the American dream. Todd did his best to fulfill his parents' expectations by completing a journalism degree at Northwestern University, marrying a physician, and earning two Emmys for investigative reporting. But "for almost twenty years ... he'd worked like a secret agent to hide his sexuality, lying, conniving, twisting until he'd nearly lost his mind."[199] All that is demolished when, upon learning of his lover's murder, Todd blurts out, "Michael Carter was my lover!"[200]

"I see Todd as someone who's always known the difference between the spoken truth and the unspoken truth but who only in his forties was able to bring those two into unison as one ultimate truth.... I wanted that disparity between the personal self and the projected self.... I use television as a metaphor for that disparity....

"The closet represents the two truths.... Interestingly enough, of course, those are the very aspects of any good mystery: the disparity between one truth and a different truth or a truth and a lie. In a mystery we try to bring those two into focus until we form the ultimate truth: the solution.... That's why I think mysteries work so well for gay fiction. As gay people, we all know not only the difference between truth and lie, we know when it's appropriate to tell the truth and when it's not appropriate—how to guard the truth. That's a sad thing to say."

In writing this series "I was trying to make heroes out of people that I've known and issues that I've seen.... When I talk about them as heroes, I talk about them as people who know right from wrong. My gay friends know right from wrong. My transgendered friends know right from wrong, and furthermore they have a picture of the world and a grasp of humanity that is far superior to many people who haven't had to do a self-accounting ... there is a self-accounting that pushes us towards the ultimate truth of who we are: the self-acceptance and appreciation and self-admiration of that...."

"I believe in a good story…. That's the ultimate goal. If I can weave a theme into a story and if the theme propels the story along that much faster and that much more dynamically, I'll use it. If it bogs down the story, it's not appropriate for that book." The result is fast-paced stories that radiate emotion. Threatening one-word titles are set in large print on grainy blue-and-black book jackets. The characters don't drive, they race. They don't run, they storm. When they're not speechless they mutter, shout, and erupt. They are "electrocuted with fear" and "overwhelmed with shock and confusion." It's not surprising that one character finally exclaims, "Sorry, I'm having a meltdown."[201]

AMATEUR SLEUTHS

What's a detective except someone who wants to find out what happened?[202]

This is really a definition of "amateur detective" which is a catchall name for a diverse group of unpaid sleuths. It makes no claims about their skill (or lack of skill). The first fictional sleuth, August Dupin who appeared in Edgar Allan Poe's "Murders in the Rue Morgue" (1841), was a highly skilled amateur whose mental agility put the police to shame.

Unlike Dupin, most amateur sleuths aren't experts in detection and most are fully employed in one of a vast spectrum of professions. For example, Bernie Rhodenbarr, Lawrence Block's amateur detective, is a bookseller and a burglar. His best friend and confidant, Carolyn Kaiser, is one of the few lesbian supporting characters in a mainstream amateur-detective series.

Mainstream amateurs belong to all races and come from a variety of ethnic and religious backgrounds. They range in age from Laura Lee Hope's youthful Bobbsey twins to Agatha Christie's Miss Jane Marple. They also include celebrities, such as Elliott Roosevelt's series about first lady Eleanor Roosevelt, and Steve Allen's books starring himself and his wife Jayne Meadows. This category is not restricted to humans, either. Nonhuman amateur detectives include cats (e.g., Rita Mae Brown's Sneaky Pie Brown), dogs (e.g., Virginia Lanier's bloodhounds), vampires (e.g., Lee Killough's Garreth Mikaelian), and aliens from outer space (e.g., Mike Resnick's *Whatdunits*), but only one dinosaur: Eric Garcia's Vince Rubio.

Main Characters

The first gay/lesbian amateur sleuth was lesbian Maria Katerina Lorca Guerrera Alcazar (Kat Guerrera), the main character of Mary F. Beal's 1977 *Angel Dance*. Guerrera was also the first lesbian detective and the first gay/lesbian Latina. "Guerrera" is Spanish for "female warrior," which is emblematic because the book is an antiestablishment manifesto. Barbara Wilson/Sjoholm's lesbian sleuth Pam Nilsen was the first amateur in a series. She was introduced in the 1984 feminist mystery *Murder in the Collective* and starred in two subsequent novels. The following year, Tony Fennelly's first Matty Sinclair mystery was published. Sinclair, a wealthy antique store owner, was the first gay male amateur and also the first to have his own series.

Gay/lesbian amateurs are almost as diverse as their mainstream counterparts. As table 2 reveals, they range in age from sixteen to the midfifties, and they hail from Canada, England, Scotland, and all regions of the United States. Most are white, but there are also an African American, a Native American, and a Latina. Their work ranges from bar dancing to physician, and there is one lesbian PE teacher and one gay hairdresser. Many of them are entrepreneurs, a few are involved in the arts, several are counselors or therapists, and some are engaged in more than one occupation. Their religious affiliations include Christianity, Judaism, Ojibwe traditionalism, Goddess worship, and atheism. None of them is a celebrity outside of her/his series, although in their own worlds a few have achieved notoriety. Taken together, they reflect the larger lesbigay community—with the possible exception of Dean James' vampire.

Table 2: Main characters

Character (and author)	Profession	Race/Ethnicity/ Religion* and Nationality	Age range
Nikki Barnes (Joan Albarella)	Episcopal priest University professor	White, American Episcopalian	Late 30s
Scotty Bradley (Greg Herren)	Bar dancer Personal trainer	White, American Goddess worshipper	29
Letty Campbell (Alma Fritchley)	Chicken farmer	White, English	30s
Mitchell Draper (Warren Dunford)	Freelance screenwriter	White, Canadian	28
Kat Guerrera (M.F. Beal)	Activist with no fixed profession	Latina, American Atheist anarchist	29

Character (and author)	Profession	Race/Ethnicity/ Religion* and Nationality	Age range
Nick Hoffman (Lev Raphael)	University professor	Jewish, American	Late 30s
Harriet Hubbley (Jackie Manthorne)	High school PE teacher Owner, bed and breakfast	White, Canadian	Late 40s to 50s
Virginia(Ginny) Kelly (Nikki Baker)	Financial analyst	African American	Late 20s to 35
Simon Kirby-Jones (Dean James)	Historian Romance writer	White, American vampire	Ageless
Stan Kraychik (Grant Michaels)	Hairdresser	White, American	30s
Renee LaRoche (Carol laFavor)	Artist Art instructor	Native American Ojibwe traditional religion	Around 40
Jane Lawless (Ellen Hart)	Restaurateur	White, American	30s and 40s
Cameron McGill (Jenny Roberts)	Drug and alcohol counselor	White, English	Mid-30s
Stoner McTavish (Sarah Dreher)	Coowner, travel agency	White, American	30s
Cass Milam (Antoinette Azolakov)	Owner, lawn care company	White, American	Late 30s
Alix Nicholson (Sharon Gilligan)	Art photographer Art instructor	White, American	Early 40s
Pam Nilsen (Barbara Wilson)	Member, printing collective	White, American	29 to early 30s
Cassandra Reilly (Barbara Wilson)	Translator	White American	Late 40s
T.D. Renfro (Antoinette Azolakov)	Psychotherapist	White, American	Mid-30s
Laney Samms (Carol Schmidt)	Owner, lesbian bar Publicist	White, American	48 to 50
Cynthia Chenery Scott (Pele Plante)	Psychologist (retired)	White, American	Mid-50s
Sean (no last name) (Mark A. Roeder)	High school student	White, American	16
Matty Sinclair (Tony Fennelly)	Owner, antique store	White, American	Late 30s
Dr. Kellen Stewart (Manda Scott)	Physician	White, Scottish	Late 30s to 40s

* Religion is not always specified

Their mysteries range in spirit from light spoofs to bleak noir landscapes, with occasional excursions into the supernatural. The majority are traditional mysteries and many focus on personal development of the main character, romantic liaisons, and friendship. Carol Schmidt selected story lines designed to promote the evolution of her main character, Laney Samms. "I asked myself, where would Laney go now? What story line would help her grow in ways I saw her growing?"* Manda Scott's main character, Kellen Stewart, "became a great deal more emotionally stable through the series and developed her own personality, distinct from mine." Nikki Baker's Virginia Kelly evolved in less positive ways.

> I think she has become less hapless, and her view has become darker over the series. In the first book, she was a cheerful dupe.... Just as the world is getting worse, she is also more capable of creating harm, and we see more of a perverse turn in her state of mind.

These and other authors would likely agree with Jenny Roberts who, in talking about her character Cameron McGill, stated, "to leave her unchanged would make the job of writing about her considerably less interesting and less challenging."

Why They Investigate

Since investigating crimes isn't part of an amateur detective's job, the reason an amateur begins snooping is personal. Dean James' Simon Kirby-Jones "is an exaggeration of the nosey amateur detective, a throwback to the days when gifted amateurs aided the police in tracking down the murderer." This is appropriate for James' mysteries because they spoof Golden Age traditional mysteries.† Other amateurs need a more compelling reason to investigate—what Patricia Boehnhardt (whose pseudonym is Ellen Hart) calls a high degree of involvement. "For Jane and Cordelia, I try to develop a scenario that really pulls them into the story—gives them a reason to become personally involved."

Direct Involvement

Amateurs are motivated to investigate when they become suspects. One way this can happen is to find a dead body. According to Lev Raphael this is not something to be taken lightly.

All unattributed author quotes come from interviews for this book.
†*For more information on Golden Age tradition mysteries see Part I.*

> Imagine going by a really gory traffic accident. Imagine how shaken you would be. That's just seeing somebody strapped on a stretcher and put into an ambulance. Multiply that many times to see what it would be like if you were to find a dead body.

Finding a body quickly transforms a main character into a suspect—if the victim is someone they knew. Their suspect status rises significantly if the deceased is found on the main character's property, which happens to Stan Kraychik (Grant Michaels) and Scotty Bradley (Greg Herren). Similarly, the untimely death of Letty Campbell's (Alma Fritchley) best laying hen from a drug overdose causes the local veterinarian to eye Campbell with suspicion.

A sleuth's suspect-rank skyrockets if they've had a recent disagreement with the victim or if they benefit from the death. In *Last Resort*, the police believe Harriet Hubbley (Jackie Manthorne) tried to kill her friend Barbara Fenton to inherit Fenton's sizeable estate. Simon Kirby-Jones (Dean James) admits that, shortly before her murder, he verbally attacked a woman claiming to be Dorinda Darlington. ("Had I just put myself at the head of the list of suspects?"[203]) Hubbley and Kirby-Jones would concur with Stan Kraychik's (Grant Michaels) belief that "If I don't try to get myself off the hook, who's going to do it?"[204]

Amateur detectives also initiate investigations when a lover, friend, or relative becomes a victim or suspect. Nick Hoffman (Lev Raphael) leaps to the defense of his lover Stefan and several good friends as does Kellen Stewart (Manda Scott). They and other amateur sleuths likely would agree with Virginia Kelly's (Nikki Baker) justification for sleuthing: "You can't let a friend go to jail to keep your name out of the papers—well, I couldn't, anyway."[205]

Sometimes amateur detectives become entangled in the machinations of others. Fritchley's Letty Campbell becomes embroiled in the money-making schemes of her friend Julia. Unfortunately, they are invariably exposed as fronts for illegal operations. In *Murder in the Rue Dauphine*, bar dancer Scotty Bradley's (Greg Herren) troubles "all stemmed from someone slipping something in his boot besides money." Mitchell Draper (Warren Dunford) is possessed by a ghost who wants his killer apprehended, and Stoner McTavish (Sarah Dreher) is hurtled into the nineteenth century by powerful spirits who won't allow her to leave until she's exposed the perpetrators of a series of crimes.

Appeals for Help

Amateur detectives find it difficult to refuse when someone asks for help. Usually, the plea comes from friends, lovers, or relatives although in

Breaking Point, Cameron McGill (Jenny Roberts) responds to a cry for help from a dying stranger. For example, Renee LaRoche's (Carole laFavor) grandmother expects LaRoche to investigate a series of thefts because "It's traditional for younger ones to protect the tribe's honor."[206]

Occasionally, they seek help from an amateur as part of a police investigation. Matty Sinclair (Tony Fennelly) is deputized, but Virginia Kelly (Nikki Baker) cooperates because her firm's buyout will be stalled until the murder is solved. Boston PD Detective Vito Branco asks Stan Kraychik to do an unofficial investigation into the murder of a gay forest ranger because "from what I can see so far, this whole case is likely to vanish without an answer."[207]

Police Replacement

Wrongheaded and blatantly biased police investigations are guaranteed to provoke an amateur into investigating. Some amateurs, like Pam Nilsen (Barbara Wilson/Sjoholm) proceed because "We know for sure the police are going to make a botch-up job of the whole thing."[208] Others, including Roberts' McGill, Manthorne's Hubbley, and Roeder's Sean know there's been a mistake or that the police investigation has been tainted by homophobia. Homophobic police also goad Hart's Lawless and Raphael's Hoffman into their first investigations.

Once amateur detectives have a taste or two of detecting, many of them become addicted. This is clearly the case for Hart's Jane Lawless whose detecting has already produced about a dozen books.

> The funny thing is, when I work these ... investigations.... I feel engaged in a way I used to feel at the restaurant. And occasionally, it's even gone beyond that. I'm *consumed* by the chase. I used to think it was just simple curiosity, but it goes way beyond that.[209]

Themes

Mysteries with amateur sleuths share many themes with other categories of detectives. Some include romance, heartbreak, and sexual interludes. The detectives themselves are open or closeted about their sexual orientation. They encounter homophobia, sexism, and racism, and they have friends and relatives who have been struck down by AIDS or cancer. As Patricia Boehnhardt (aka Ellen Hart) says, "Quite often the stories come directly from their lives." The themes that emerge from those stories arise directly from their lives as well.

Families

Families, including those of the main characters, play a central role in many series. According to Barbara Sjoholm (formerly known as Barbara Wilson):

> The Pam novels are about family, of course, but the Cassandra novels are mainly about family. There are a lot of orphans and mother-daughter combos in all of them. I was exploring all of those things.

Among those mother-daughter combos is Cassandra and her mother "who said she never wanted to see me again if I persisted in my unnatural desires. That was almost thirty years ago, and I still miss her."[210] Stoner McTavish's (Sarah Dreher) parents had a similar reaction. "When your mother repeatedly tells you you make her sick, you either give in, get out, or learn to ignore it."[211] Stoner "gets out." She moves in with her maternal aunt Hermione Moore who becomes Stoner's protector, advocate, role model, and a source of humor in the series. Protecting Hermione is also the subject of *Shaman's Moon*. The homophobia of Gwen's (Stoner's lover) grandmother precipitates the events in *Gray Magic*.

Cameron McGill (Jenny Roberts) is estranged from her parents for reasons that extend beyond homophobia, but she has a close bond with her older sister "who acted almost as a surrogate mother" which is why, in *Needlepoint*, McGill is determined to uncover the truth about her sister's death. According to Baker, Virginia Kelly "was carefully bred and socialized by her family and community to marry a nice black dentist (they make as much money as doctors, but they keep better hours)." Kelly's parents hold onto their dreams by denying their daughter's sexual orientation. Their behavior provides the context for the events in *Long Goodbyes*.

Renee LaRoche's (Carole laFavor) family includes her daughter, lover, clan, and tribe. The series focuses on these various family segments, including LaRoche's relationship with her white lover. Although LaRoche's mother is homophobic, her traditional grandmother and aunt have no issue with Renee's lesbianism (two spirit). "Creator made you and we don't question the work of our Creator.... Two Spirits have always been part of our community."[212] Her mother has adopted white attitudes. According to Greg Herren, Scotty Bradley's extended family forms a protective shield around him.

> Their closeness is something I think every family should aspire to—what everyone wants from their family. Imagine having parents who are delighted when a child comes out to them, rather than going through the *Sturm und Drang* that so many of us have to face. The family is what

made Scotty who he is.... In the future the whole family dynamic will be explored.

The Jane Lawless (Ellen Hart) series tracks changes in Lawless' family relationships. The events in *Immaculate Midnight*, for example, are directly tied to one of Jane's father's (attorney Raymond Lawless) cases. Patricia Boehnhardt (aka Ellen Hart) explains, "Well, for me I suppose it always comes back to family and relationships. This is very much the territory of the traditional mystery." Alma Fritchley's *Chicken Out* and *Chicken Shack* are partly about Letty Campell's mother and her Aunt Cynthia. Campbell's extended family plays an important role in all of the novels. They include Letty's ex-lover's niece AnnaMaria and her expanding family, all of whom live with Letty.

Work, School, and Community

Work and academic environments are not always friendly to gay/lesbian detectives. Rev. Doctor Nikki Barnes (Joan Albarella) has "worked on integrating being a lesbian with other aspects of her life, like being a priest,"[213] but when she came out to her vicar, "he asked her to please not share that information about herself with anyone else."[214] Untenured professor Nick Hoffman (Lev Raphael) is out of the closet but

> I still felt somewhat unwelcome in the department after a year. And then I also wondered how much of it was my being openly gay and proudly Jewish ... in a department with few Jewish professors and some apparent closet queens.[215]

Openly gay high school student Sean (Mark A. Roeder) not only endures homophobia from his classmates, he learns that students are involved in gay bashings. Cynthia Chenery Scott's (Pele Plante) lover Barbara is fired by her high school district when they are informed she's a lesbian, and Alix Nicholson's (Sharon Gilligan) high school declines to renew her teaching contract after learning that two of her female students took nude pictures of each other. "No one said it out loud, but it was obvious they suspected me of 'recruiting' baby dykes."[216]

Virginia Kelly (Nikki Baker) is one of the few amateur detectives working in the corporate world. She conceals her lesbianism, but she can't disguise her race, sex, and social background. According to Baker, "As overarching themes, I guess all issues of race and sexual orientation are important to me." Virginia Kelly encounters them everywhere she goes—including in the lesbigay community.

When the crimes occur in the lesbigay community, the author can present the reader with images of the community and its culture. Baker's

Kelly vacations in Provincetown and Manthorne's Harriet Hubbley travels to several lesbigay environments. This example is from Manthorne's *Last Resort*, which is set in Key West:

> Gay and lesbian couples sauntered hand-in-hand, singles cruised on skateboards or on in-line skates, while others loitered under the tropical sun as it moved slowly toward the horizon. It was wonderful, Harry thought as she took a sip of white wine which had been perfectly chilled before being served.[217]

Fritchley's Campbell presents a far different view of lesbian culture when well-to-do lesbians flock to a classic car auction being held on Campbell's farm. They form a cliquish community that accepts Campbell's sophisticated friend Julia but shuns the less affluent Campbell.

Some amateur sleuths live or work in a lesbigay community. Greg Herren's Scotty Bradley is a bar dancer and personal trainer, and his first mystery, *Bourbon Street Blues*, takes place during New Orleans' Southern Decadence (an annual circuit event/giant "block party" held Labor Day weekend). Schmidt's Laney Samms owns a lesbian bar, and *Silverlake Heat* describes lesbian bar culture and butch-femme dynamics from the 1990s and pre-Stonewall times. "Remember how it used to be in the old days, when all our bars had some sort of bird name so we could tell?"[218] As its name suggests, Antoinette Azolakov's *Cass and the Stone Butch* includes a considerable amount of information about butch-femme roles. Fennelly's Matty Sinclair is part of a society of wealthy gay men who belong to an exclusive gay men's club.

> There are two intractable requirements for membership in Kitt's Club: The first is money. Initiation alone is twenty-five grand. The second is the matter of sexual preference. No straights were allowed inside the club, even as guests. Even as *employees*.[219]

Fennelly's books describe the club's social ambiance as well as other facets of gay culture.

Gilligan's *Danger! Cross Currents* provides details about living in an idyllic lesbian-separatist community called The Spread. Wilson/Sjoholm's Pam Nilsen is introduced to various aspects of the lesbian community in *Murder in the Collective*, and *The Dog Collar Murders* offers insights into a lesbian community that is sharply divided along political lines.

> I thought it was interesting to put up the different viewpoints and give them to people. Then, in the guise of a murder mystery, you not only say, "Where were you on the night of August 5th?" but also "What are your opinions on prostitution?"

JOAN ALBARELLA: *Nikki Barnes* (1999–CURRENT)

Joan Albarella (1944–) is an Associate Professor in the University of Buffalo Educational Opportunity Center. In addition to the Nikki Barnes mysteries, she's written four books of poetry, including the bilingual *Mujeres, Flores, Fantasía.* She is a member of Sisters in Crime, Mystery Writers of America, and the Italian American Writers Association.

Detective: Reverand Father Nikki Barnes, Episcopalian priest and professor and counselor at St. David University

Setting: Sheridan, New York (upstate near Buffalo). Time period is generally contemporary with publication dates

Books: *Agenda for Murder* (1999); *Called to Kill* (2000); *Close to You* (2003)

Publisher: Rising Tide Press, iUniverse

Reverend Father Nikki Barnes is a courageous and compassionate woman who has spent her life bringing peace of mind to others but who has little peace within herself. "I see Nikki as a lesbian, priest, Vietnam vet, professor and counselor. A complex woman, who is constantly integrating all these aspects of her life." Added to that is Nikki's relationship with her lover Dr. Virginia Clayton. "Nikki's relationship with Ginni is an ongoing courtship which does end in marriage. It unfortunately, but quite often, puts Ginni in harm's way, but that's what makes a good detective story...."

"The Vietnam War is probably the catalyst for the creation of Nikki Barnes." Albarella read firsthand accounts by women who served in that war "and realized that their experience was different than the men who served and very little has been done to relate that experience to others, especially in fiction. So Nikki created herself as an amateur detective who happened to be a Vietnam vet with all the bravery and baggage that went with that." Trang, Nikki's Vietnamese "Mama san" from the war era, is "a symbol of the duality of the war. She is the beauty and charm of the country being pillaged and also the danger and distrust that may be buried within that beauty...."

"Nikki Barnes is a feminist. She has overcome the odds against women to become one of the first female priests in the country. She served in a war that is mostly defined by the men who were there, and she is very women oriented and lives in a women-driven world.... Her choice of Episcopalian had to do with the fact that I had researched the underground ordination groups of the seventies and eighties. Nikki's ordination was historically correct. I just made her one of the first women ordained by the Episcopalian Church."

Agenda for Murder and *Called to Kill* "were concerned with Nikki's life in and after Vietnam and her becoming a priest. These were character-driven books. They seemed to be something Nikki had to create herself." The third book in the series, *Close to You*, "was influenced by a local serial killer and the epidemic in ecstasy deaths." That book also addresses "some of the nature of good and evil, in the sense of the personification of evil and if that really does exist....

"Gay and lesbian issues are very important to the series, but I hope they are presented in a subtle way.... I want readers to see that what makes a person gay is not the only thing that defines him or her.... I also want readers to see that gays come in all shapes, sizes, economic conditions, and even physical conditions. It was very important for me to include a wealthy, successful, flirtatious, sexy, almost obnoxious, wheelchair-bound lesbian amputee in *Close to You*."

Albarella's primary goals for the series are very clear. "I want to communicate the damage that war does to the individuals involved. I want readers to believe that good does triumph over evil, and that heroes need a sense of humor."

ANTOINETTE AZOLAKOV: *Cass Milam* (1987–1988)

Antoinette Azolakov (1944–) grew up in Lufkin, Texas, and moved to Austin as an adult. In addition to the Cass Milam novels, she wrote a short series about a lesbian psychotherapist, T.D. Renfro. She's taught high school English and Latin, worked in an explosives plant, owned a welding shop, and done lawn care work.

Detective: Cassandra (Cass) Milam, owner of Milam Lawn and Landscaping

Setting: Southern Texas. Time period is contemporary with publication dates

Books: *Cass and the Stone Butch* (1987); *Skiptrace* (1988); Lambda Award—Best Lesbian Mystery/Sci-fi (1988)

Publisher: Banned Books

This two-book series is strongly character focused. Cass Milam's investigation into the deaths that occur is a secondary outcome and a byproduct of the steps taken towards personal healing and growth.

Cass Milam is a successful entrepreneur with good friends, a nice house, and few pretensions. "Getting home after a day at work can almost always make me smile."[220] She's happy with her "comfortable routine," but she's always felt the need to reconnect with her first lover, Claudia.

She was the love of my life. She was my friend, my wife, my fantasy lover made real ... and she lived with me and she loved me, and I was a lucky, lucky young dyke."[221]

Milam hires a private detective to find Claudia but takes over the skiptrace herself when he's implicated in the murder of Sandy Marigold, a woman in the Austin lesbian community. Unfortunately, Milam's efforts to find Claudia set her on a collision course with Marigold's murderer. The outcome not only solves the murder but allows Milam to let the past go.

In *Cass and the Stone Butch,* Milam helps investigate the death of a lesbian that the police have called an accident. Milam guides the woman's lover Lester (aka Celeste) as she delves into the events surrounding the woman's death as a way of helping Lester deal with her grief. At the same time Milam teaches the young stone butch about loving and being loved.

Milam guides Lester through the larger lesbian culture as well, using the butch-femme dichotomy as a starting point. ("Lisa's not butch.... She's a lesbian-feminist. They're a different animal from butches and fluffs."[222]) The series also addresses lesbian-bashing homophobia in families, and the sense of community.

Azolakov allows her characters to express their views and their personalities through dialogues. Sometimes, she runs a thread of humor through them. For example, the following interaction occurs when Lester decides she wants to have a butch-to-butch talk about sex:

"Cass? Are you awake?"

"Yeah."

"You sure?"

I grinned to myself. "Yeah. I'm about as sure as I can be. Why?"

"You were snoring."

"Well, I'm sorry. Next time just push on me or roll me over or something and I'll probably stop."

"It doesn't bother me. I just meant, were you sure you were awake, since you were snoring."

I rolled onto my side to face her and propped myself on an elbow. "I'm awake, anyway, so what do you need?"

"Nothing."[223]

ANTOINETTE AZOLAKOV: *T.D. Renfro* (1989–1993)

Antoinette Azolakov (1944–) grew up in Lufkin, Texas, and moved to Austin as an adult. In addition to the T.D. Renfro mysteries, she wrote a two-book series about working-class lesbian Cass Milam. Milam is mentioned as Renfro's gardener. Azolakov has taught high school English and Latin, worked in an explosives plant, owned a welding shop, and done lawn care work.

Detective: Tahoka Daisy (T.D.) Renfro, psychotherapist

Settings: Austin and east Texas. Time period is generally contemporary with publication dates

Books: *The Contactees Die Young* (1989); *Blood Lavender* (1993)

Publisher: Banned Books

Although the first T.D. Renfro mystery, *The Contactees Die Young*, was published only one year after *Cass and the Stone Butch*, it is markedly different from the Cass Milam series. Milam is a working-class entrepreneur whereas Renfro is a middle-class, highly educated psychotherapist; Milam is actively involved in the lesbian community while Renfro shies away from social involvement in a community that supplies many of her clients; Milam's identity is strongly butch but Renfro is not at all butchy: "butch isn't bad! But, well, it's just that I'm not ... well, not that much of a stereotype."[224] She is, however, attracted to butch women, and Milam's weekly service of T.D.'s yard could foreshadow a future romance.

The tendency to reflect Renfro's analytic thinking is different from the emphasis on dialogue in the Milam series. Although Milam comes across some lovely gardens, her adventures are entirely personal. In contrast, Renfro's stories are tied to her profession, either directly through a client or indirectly, by encountering issues she usually works on with her clients. In both series men are responsible for all murders and murder attempts.

The most notable theme in the Renfro series is internalized homophobia, which emerges in the form of self-hatred, fear, and residence in the closet. The "glass closet" is a phenomenon in both Renfro books.

> It was as if the person involved were on the reflecting side of a one-way mirror, basking in an imagined safety from the gaze of others while everyone outside could see right through his walls. What amazed me was not so much that the closeted one was unaware of how conspicuous he was, but that most of the time those on the outside were willing to play along with the charade, and though they might discuss the person's sexual orientation freely among themselves, they rarely would mention it to the one most concerned.[225]

The series includes a personal subplot involving T.D.'s relationship with her lover June Leland. They have been together for several years, but the bond between the two women has become strained. June's pursuit of a graduate degree in forestry and her relocation to east Texas adds an extra burden. Those issues are resolved in *Blood Lavender* after T.D. helps identify the man who murdered June's friend Guy Pearson.

NIKKI BAKER: *Virginia Kelly* (1991–2001)

Nikki Baker (1962–; pseudonym, real name undisclosed) is originally from Ohio but lived in Chicago for several years before moving to San Francisco. In addition to the Virginia Kelly series, Baker writes short stories and has begun a mystery series about Cassandra Hope, an African American police detective.

Detective: Virginia (Ginny) Kelly, financial analyst
Settings: Chicago, downstate Illinois, Provincetown. Time period is contemporary with publication dates
Books: *In the Game* (1991); *The Lavender House Murder* (1992); *Long Goodbyes* (1993); *The Ultimate Exit Strategy* (2001)
Publishers: Bella Books, The Naiad Press
This series about an African American lesbian contains sharp, biting humor and examines social issues that are rarely treated in gay/lesbian detective fiction, such as homophobia and classism in the African American community, racism among lesbians, and child abuse in the middle class.

Ginny Kelly is "a square peg, but one desperately trying to conform and failing at every turn.... Kelly was carefully bred and socialized by her family and community to marry a nice black dentist.... The fact of her lesbianism has precluded the expectations of her family and peer group— as well as her own ... and her internal class bigotries further alienate Kelly from the greater set of black folk. Being black alienates her from the larger American cultural mainstream. So, she is pretty much out in the cold and pissed off about it."

Ginny's alienation increases as the series progresses. "In the first book, she was a cheerful dupe. She happened into situations, which invariably went bad, but Virginia just rolled with it. There was some anger, but she was a pretty ineffectual (if mean spirited) creature—and always sort of surprised by the ugly turn of events. By *Long Goodbyes*, Virginia is expecting the worst from people and getting it." Her own behavior deteriorates as well. "Just as the world is getting worse, she is also more capable of creating harm, and we see more of a perverse turn in her state of mind.... She steals some clothing from a trick she picks up in *The Lavender House Murder* and by *Long Goodbyes* she is committing what amounts to some weird coercive acquaintance rape on an old high school crush." In *The Ultimate Exit Strategy*, however, she's corrected her moral compass, become a junior partner, and is looking forward to a profitable exit from her company.

For Baker, themes are the most important element of her fiction writing. "I am always interested … in why people do things—what was their thinking…. My interest is in finding the internally consistent logic in different points of view than my own. What spin could you put on the world to be able to justify murder or rape, abuse, whatever…. As over-reaching themes I guess all issues of race and sexual orientation are impor-tant to me…. Race is sort of immutable to me—you are part of the tribe or not….

"Virginia Kelly is an exploration vehicle, and the mystery story form really just gives me a box to work in…. Since I really care most about themes and episodes, it is hard for me to get a beginning, middle and end, which are essential for a good mystery story."

Baker describes the humor in the books as "all pretty nasty" adding that "I think it is interesting that people always find the Virginia Kelly series very funny. They must be, although I have never found them really quite as funny as people say. I think, rather, that the books are a little absurd (an effect that is completely intentional) and very dark (although, I don't really experience them as such), and it's a case choosing between laughing and crying. Most people choose to disassociate from the really pretty awful things that befall Virginia, so I guess the humor has been a counterbalance."

MARY F. BEAL: *Kat Guerrera* (1977)

Mary F. Beal (1937–) wrote numerous stories in the 1970s that were published in *Fiction International, New American Review,* and other mag-azines. Her first book was *Amazon One*, which follows a group of fictional revolutionary activists for one month and warns of abuses by those in power. She and her husband, David Schetzline, are known for their espousal of a humanized, sentient earth—what is currently called the Gaia philosophy.

Detective: Maria Katerina Lorca Guerrera Alcazar (Kat Guerrera), no fixed profession

Settings: Various locations in the United States and Canada. Time period is contemporary with publication date

Book: *Angel Dance* (1977)

Publisher: Daughters Publishing Co.

Angel Dance marks the beginning of the lesbian side of gay/lesbian detective mysteries. The book is an anti-imperialist call to arms with a lesbian main character.

Kat Guerrera (feminine variant of the Spanish word for "warrior") is a radical feminist who has carved out a lifestyle that is designed to challenge and ultimately defeat the devastating power of imperialism. Guerrera begins the book working as a reporter for a leftist weekly newsletter published by her collective, work she enjoys but for which she has no formal training or other experience. She leaves when the collective becomes concerned that warrants for her arrest will attract unwanted attention from federal authorities.

Kat accepts a job working for Michael Tarleton that entails both assisting his wife, feminist Angel Stone, in her work and gathering information about his wife's grandmother. When Tarleton is murdered, it becomes evident that Angel's life is in danger as well. Guerrera discovers that both Angel and her husband know that Angel's father is part of an international conspiracy to use drugs to tranquilize the masses. Both women vow to continue the fight. "I wanted to say ... everything would be okay, *but* the truth was *la luta continua* so I said that and she brought her fist to her heart. That was the last time I saw Angel Stone in the flesh."[226]

SARAH DREHER: *Stoner McTavish* (1985–CURRENT)

Award-winning author Sarah Dreher (1937–) was born in Hanover, Pennsylvania, and has lived in Amherst, Massachusetts, since 1965. Despite being diagnosed with adult attention deficit disorder, she writes plays (including the award-winning *8×10 Glossy*), novels, and the Stoner McTavish mystery/fantasy series. Dreher uses her master's degree in psychology in clinical psychologist practice where she specializes in women's issues and dream analysis. She has also taken up the practice of Core Shamanism.

Detective: Stoner McTavish, co-owner of Kesselbaum and McTavish Travel

Settings: Various locations. Except for *A Captive in Time*, time period is contemporary with publication dates

Books: *Stoner McTavish* (1985); *Something Shady* (1986); *Gray Magic* (1987); *A Captive in Time* (1990); *Otherworld* (1993); *Bad Company* (1995); *Shaman's Moon* (1998); Lambda Award—Best Lesbian Mystery (cowinner) (1998)

Publisher: New Victoria Publishers

This series melds mystery with fantasy in stories that include cosmic battles between good and evil. The chief combatant for the forces of good is Stoner McTavish, an unwilling warrior who co-owns a small travel agency in Boston.

"Stoner first came to me as Nancy Drew grown up.... Insecure down to the roots of her fingernails, wearing her heart on her sleeve, and prone to untimely blushing. Stoner is one of the last truly honorable people left in the world.... Stoner is always respectful, kind, and considerate. I hoped she would become a role model for other lesbians....

"With Gwen in her life, ... she's grown into a woman when she started out a girl. Life in ordinary reality no longer scares her quite as much. Unfortunately, at the same time, she begins to see non-ordinary reality, which scares her twice as much as ordinary reality did....

"Shortly after *Stoner McTavish* was published, Stoner became her own person. I lost the ability to shape her. If I wanted to have her do or feel something and she didn't feel it 'expressed her,' I might as well go weed the garden, because I wasn't going to write another word until I did it the way it was supposed to be." At that point, Stoner changed "from being someone I 'made up' to a real, living person with her own needs and attitudes and loves. This usually happens at some point when I'm writing. It's then that I know we're flying....

"I don't take a cognitive/analytical position on my work. It would drain my spontaneity and bore me to tears. I create characters, I put them in a series of situations, and I watch what they do. If they convey some kind of Truth along the way, great, but I don't set out with anything as heady as 'themes.'...

"I usually start with a place. Then I ask myself what kind of a crime could take place there, and how would Stoner go about solving it in that setting?... All of the settings in my books (so far) are places I've loved. I've been blessed with the imagination to put myself back into those places, to relive the sights and smells and sounds of a place. Even the way the air feels in different places, and the rain, the texture of the dust. These sensory experiences feed my Soul. Once I'm 'back there,' I only have to describe what I see and feel."

Humor flows through the stories, emerging in characters, situations, and language. Sometimes Stoner stumbles into linguistic or cultural tangles as in the following exchange with a Hopi woman:

"My name is Stoner McTavish," she repeated.
"That's okay." The woman went on staring.
"What's.... I mean ... do you have a name?"
"Plenty."
"That's nice. Plenty. That's a nice name...."
The old woman grunted. "I have plenty of names."
"Oh. Well ... uh ... what should I call you?"
"Why you want to call me? I'm here."[227]

The manifestation of evil varies from novel to novel and, with it, the fiction genre. *Something Shady* is a gothic horror story/mystery with a haunted house, *A Captive in Time* is a western set in 1871, and *Otherworld* is a farcical romp through tunnels beneath Disney World.

"I really don't know what the future holds for Stoner and company. I usually wait for something to occur to me, or get a plot idea or see a place I'd like to write about. It all happens unexpectedly."

WARREN DUNFORD: *Mitchell Draper* (1998–CURRENT)

Warren Dunford (1963–) is a Toronto native. In addition to the Mitchell Draper series, he has published short pieces in *Quickies 2, Queer Fear 2*, and *AWOL: Tales for Travel-Inspired Minds*. He works as a freelance copywriter in Toronto.

Detective: Mitchell Draper, screenwriter

Setting: Toronto, Canada. Time period is contemporary with publication dates

Books: *Soon to Be a Major Motion Picture* (1998); *Making a Killing* (2001)

Publisher: Alyson Publications

All screenwriter Mitchell Draper wants is success ... and fame ... and fortune ... and love. "For me the books are really about the pursuit of success, looking at the balance between hard reality and fantasy expectations. Mitchell is constantly struggling between his dreams (the movie world) and what's actually good for him (the substance of his everyday life)...

"Because my main character is a screenwriter, I came up with the gimmick of having each book be a send-up of a different movie genre.... As I'm working, I read a lot of books and see a lot of movies in those specific genres, trying to pick up all the clichés, so I can throw them into my stories and have fun with them." The use of the screenplay format also helps to highlight the disparity between Mitchell's ideal, exciting fantasy world and the world he lives in, which is not as drab as he thinks. "In *Soon to Be a Major Motion Picture*, he's hired by a rather questionable movie producer to write the script for a crime thriller, and then his life turns into a crime thriller." In *Making a Killing*, his investigation into a twenty-year-old murder becomes a gothic horror story. "He then fears he's been possessed by the ghost of a schizophrenic dead teenager."

Despite the dramatic elements, this series remains focused on its main character. "I usually come up with a situation first, then I figure out how Mitchell would handle it. The original kernel is usually very small, so Mitchell's point of view is crucial to the plot and character development. I like to bounce him against very strong personalities, because that's when his neuroses are at their peak, and thus, at their most amusing."

Mitchell gets help from his friends, struggling artists Ingrid and Ramir, whose own efforts to achieve fame and fortune enhance the drama and occasionally conflict with Mitchell's investigations. In *Soon to Be a Major Motion Picture*, for example, Ramir uses confidential information in his one-man show thinking it's merely a screenplay Mitchell is writing. "In a technical writing sense, they're foils—ways to liven up the drama and bring in subplots—but they also represent the two sides of Mitchell's personality. Ingrid has a grounded sensitivity, while Ramir has unbridled ambition. Mitchell is always swaying between the two. In the end, I think it's the friendship of the three of them that really holds the books together...."

"In addition to being mystery stories, the novels are my way of capturing the world as I see it—as a gay man living in a big city in the twenty-first century. I make sure the books have a balance of straight and gay characters, male and female, people of various ages, ethnic and financial backgrounds. Portraying that diversity is very important to me." In the process he touches on issues related to diversity, such as sexism, racism, and homophobia. For example, racism in the entertainment industry limits Ramir's acting opportunities to portraying Puerto Rican gang members who die in scene one.

"All my study of the screenwriting form has definitely influenced the shape of the books. They're built in three acts, according to traditional dramatic structure. I think that helps give me a good backbone for the stories, ensuring that the plots stay entertaining.... The style of the books in general is highly visual and cinematic. For me, that's how everyone actually experiences the world—from a first-person, immediate perspective that's based on visceral sights and sensations. That style seems like the most authentic way to tell a story.... I like to think my books show how real, contemporary people would cope if they were confronted with a traditional mystery situation. There's less blind courage, and more neurotic fear, mixed with constant ironic questioning—'Could this really be happening to us?'"

TONY FENNELLY: *Matty Sinclair* (1985–1987)

Tony Fennelly (1945–; pseudonym for Antonia Fennelly Catoire) grew up in New Jersey and moved to New Orleans in 1969. After completing a B.A. in drama from the University of New Orleans, she began writing full time. In addition to the Matty Sinclair series, she writes a series about a heterosexual former stripper/society columnist. Fennelly lives in New Orleans with her husband of thirty years.

Detective: Matthew Arthur (Matty) Sinclair, antique store owner

Setting: New Orleans. Time period is contemporary with publication dates

Books: *The Glory Hole Murders* (1985); Finalist Edgar—Best First Novel by an American Author (1986); *The Closet Hanging* (1987); *Kiss Yourself Goodbye* (2003)

Publishers: Arlington Books, Carroll & Graf Publishers

This campy and catty series communicates some of the flavor of the Crescent City through descriptions of its older neighborhoods and with offbeat characters. The books also include some descriptions of the high-society world in which Matty Sinclair lives.

Sinclair is the scion of one of New Orleans' oldest high-society families. Despite his wealth, he chooses to operate an exclusive antique boutique. He also has a law degree and worked briefly as a district attorney. "I see him as a suave modern-day Noel Coward."

Matty is an unwilling sleuth. He investigates one case because he's a potential suspect and is dragged into another by New Orleans PD Lt. Frank Washington who knew Matty when he was a DA. In addition to extremely gruesome murders, Matty encounters extortion, child molestation, and rape.

The series is dominated by Matty's campy repartee and observations (e.g., "I'm a winter and look scrumptious in purple"[228]). "It may take me weeks to come up with a one-liner that Matt delivers in a split second, so he comes off as very witty." Sinclair's wit is combined with stereotypic characterizations that are sometimes cutting.

Despite the importance of the Matty Sinclair character to the tone and content of the stories, the series did not originate with him. The first book, *The Glory Hole Murders*, "started with the concept. I wrote a story around an urban legend about a glory hole murder. Then Matt Sinclair came along to solve it." Once she began writing the series, however, Fennelly had the most fun writing about her sleuth "because he was a fantasy figure, a well-to-do aristocrat who is sophisticated, charming and generous."

Robin, Matty's sex partner ("it would be romanticizing our association to call him my lover"[229]), is a misogynistic eighteen-year-old ("At least that's what he swore to. And if he was any younger, I didn't want to know it"[230]) who calls women "fish." Robin may have cause for his distaste for women because in the books Matty has sexual liaisons with women. "I knew gay men who occasionally went with a woman, even married them and were happy with them for a while. I don't think that's a false note for the character.... I think he is more attractive to women because they know they have a chance to be with him, if only briefly. He will always go back to men, Robin in particular."

Fennelly says, "I guess I don't want to communicate anything except tolerance for gays," adding that "living in New Orleans, I am surrounded by wonderful gay men. It isn't difficult to write about them."

ALMA FRITCHLEY: *Letty Campbell* (1997–CURRENT)

Alma Fritchley (1954–) is from a small mining town in Nottinghamshire, England. Since leaving school at age sixteen, she's held various office jobs, including her current job in the tax office. A one-year stint in a bird sanctuary introduced Fritchley to chicken rearing. "I never looked back. So, at age forty when I first put pen to paper, these enigmatic creatures had to be central to the series." Fritchley began writing for pure entertainment and says, "While it still entertains, I will continue to write."

Detective: Letitia (Letty) Campbell, chicken farmer

Setting: Calderton, West Yorkshire, England (near Manchester). Time period is contemporary with publication dates

Books: *Chicken Run* (1997); *Chicken Feed* (1998); *Chicken Out* (1999); *Chicken Shack* (2000)

Publisher: The Women's Press

Letty Campbell, chicken farmer, is a reluctant sleuth whose farm is part of a nest egg inherited from her Aunt Cynthia. "Letty is, at the start of *Chicken Run*, a thirty-something dyke new to country living and fairly fresh from life in the big city. She's spicy and likes to think of herself as dynamic though in fact she's every lesbian's best pal. [She's a] good listener and supportive but [she's] looking for that extra something or someone in her life. Which, of course, I make sure she finds!... and some of the stuff I'm most proud of concerns affairs of the heart.... I felt I needed to keep it real though. Love comes hand in hand with loss....Over the course of the series she evolves, ... and with love in her life she blossoms though manages to retain ... her friendships."

These fast-paced stories are peppered with British slang, such as *gobsmacked* (shocked) and *dosh* (money), and overrun with bad eggs engaged in nefarious activities ranging from a drugs-for-weapons conspiracy to the premeditated murder of Campbell's best egg-laying hen. Opposing them are the befuddled local police (who do little more than scramble) and Campbell's selfish and foul-tempered friends and neighbors who include Letty's librarian/Babylonian-researcher lover and her sharp-tongued auto-mechanic niece; a conspiracy-theorist/town gossip and her story-crazed journalist niece; money-grubbing (and grabbing) teenaged hooligans; and a brood of hungry chickens. Together, they generate maelstroms that produce dramatic, feather-flying conclusions.

Letty's troubles often result from the romantic escapades and bird-brained financial schemes of her best friend and onetime lover, Julia Rossi. "Well heeled and wealthy, her rich Italian heritage and upbringing is a million miles away from our heroine's working-class, financially insecure past. Somehow their friendship transcends these polar opposites." Julia's well-to-do and social-climbing associates make no such effort. They are greedy, arrogant, and self-absorbed.

At the core of the series lies its humor. "Humor crosses all boundaries and trips over quite a lot of them! Though classism was an accidental theme, Julia's unstinting, but somehow loveable, snobbishness causes several belly laughs.... She sees herself in riding boots, strutting across farming land being very much To the Manor Born. Her reality—vile weather, uncooperative chickens and mud from September to March was too much to bear.... Homophobia, while far from humorous, can be seen to be ridiculous, and people's farcical reasons for holding the views they do can be sniped at, ridiculed and eventually shot down.

"The most challenging aspect of the writing is making all the disparate pieces fit into place. I remember killing off one of my characters ... only to bring him back to life in Chapter 8. A sharp-eyed editor spotted that catastrophic mistake. I suppose the most fun I have is with the development of the characters—watching them grow older and not necessarily wiser. Sylvia Buckham, the elderly owner of the village's corner shop must be one of my favorite characters.... Her eccentricity knows no bounds. I wish I had a neighbor exactly like her.

"I sometimes think my books are written by accident. I avoid planning like the plague and never have the remotest idea where the plot is going, usually until well into the book. Hence the nervous breakdowns suffered by my editors and proofreaders. It's a bit like reading a book, I never know what's going to happen until it happens. It's an exciting if convoluted approach to my novels."

SHARON GILLIGAN: *Alix Nicholson* (1993–1994)

Sharon Gilligan (1943–) is originally from the midwestern United States and subsequently moved to northern California. In addition to the Alix Nicholson series, Gilligan wrote one novel, *Faces of Love* (1992). In the early 1990s she joined Women of Mendocino Bay (WOMB) and began writing for their newsletter *WOMB with a View.*

Detective: Alix Nicholson, art photographer and teacher

Settings: Northern California and Washington, D.C. Time period is contemporary with publication dates

Books: *Danger in High Places* (1993); *Danger! Cross Currents* (1994)

Publisher: Rising Tide Press

These mysteries are about a gifted art photographer who is trying to find her emotional and physical home. Her experiences along the way highlight a variety of issues and themes. The stories adopt a feminist viewpoint that becomes more pronounced in *Danger! Cross Currents,* the second book of the two-book series.

Alix Nicholson is a wanderer who drifts from relationship to relationship and from place to place. Her mother died from cervical cancer when Alix was twelve, and she's alienated from her homophobic father and stepmother. One of the few people she allowed to penetrate her protective shell is Brian Bellamy, her talented darkroom assistant whom she met when he took a photography class she was teaching. "From the first day he walked into my class, I knew he was gay. Probably before he did."[231] Brian dies from complications related to AIDS shortly before the start of the series. His death leaves Alix isolated and rootless.

The two books take her to Washington, D.C., and the Pacific coast and involve Alix in murder investigations. Each book examines a different facet of political involvement. *Danger in High Places* looks at politics as it is generally understood. While in Washington to photograph the AIDS quilt, Alix becomes embroiled in a battle for Federal funding that pits advocates for AIDS research against women seeking funding for research on breast, uterine, and cervical cancer. The political shenanigans she encounters teach Alix that some of the most dangerous high places in Washington, D.C., are the apexes of organizations and seats of political power where people lie, connive, and manipulate false images of themselves and their goals.

Danger! Cross Currents is set in a small, scenic area of northern California. Some of the cross currents in the book are generated by conflicts between land developers interested in boosting the local economy through tourism and longtime residents who want to maintain the pristine landscape of the area. Among those whose existence is threatened by aggressive development are the women who reside in a women-only community called The Spread. The Spread was endowed by a grieving father whose daughter was raped and killed, and it represents the feminist philosophy that the personal is political. Other dangerous cross currents include blackmail, infidelity, spouse abuse, and greed.

Both books end on a strongly positive tone. In *Danger in High Places,* not only is the murderer exposed but the political forces move to support funding for both AIDS and cancer. Both *Danger! Cross Currents* and the series end with Alix finding the true love she's been seeking and recognizing that her spiritual home lies with the women living on The Spread— "women who shared not only their space, but their energies, their meager resources and their impressive talents."[232]

ELLEN HART: *Jane Lawless* (1989–CURRENT)

Award-winning author Ellen Hart (1949–; pseudonym for Patricia Boehnhardt) is from Minneapolis. She has a BA in theology and was active in a fundamentalist church until her feminism led her to leave the church. In addition to the Jane Lawless series, she writes mysteries about Sophie Greenway and her husband. Hart lives in Minneapolis with her partner of over twenty-five years, their children, and grandchildren.

Detective: Jane Lawless, restaurateur

Setting: Primarily, St. Paul/Minneapolis metropolitan area. Stories begin with flashbacks. Otherwise, time period is contemporary with publication dates.

Books: *Hallowed Murder* (1989); Finalist Lambda Award—Best Lesbian Mystery (1989); Finalist Minnesota Book Awards—Best Crime Fiction (1990); Golden Earphones Award (Audio World)—Best Unabridged Book (1996); to Carol Jordan Stewart—Best Reader of an Unabridged Work (books on tape) (1996); *Vital Lies* (1991); *Stage Fright* (1992); Finalist Lambda Award—Best Lesbian Mystery (1992); *A Killing Cure* (1993); Finalist Lambda Award—Best Lesbian Mystery (1993); Finalist Minnesota Book Awards—Best Crime Fiction (1994); *A Small Sacrifice* (1994); Lambda Award—Best Lesbian Mystery (1994); Minnesota Book Award— Best Crime Fiction (1995); *Faint Praise* (1995); Finalist American Library Association Gay, Lesbian & Bisexual Book Award (1996); Minnesota Book Award—Best Crime Fiction (1996); *Robber's Wine* (1996); Lambda Award—Best Lesbian Mystery (1996); *Wicked Games* (1998); Finalist Lambda Award—Best Lesbian Mystery (1998); *Hunting the Witch* (1999); Lambda Award—Best Lesbian Mystery (1999); *The Merchant of Venus* (2001); Finalist Lambda Award—Best Lesbian Mystery (2002); Finalist Minnesota Book Award—Best Popular Fiction (2002); *Immaculate Midnight* (2002); Lambda Award—Best Lesbian Mystery (cowinner) (2003)

Publishers: Seal Press, Ballantine Books, St. Martin's Press

"When I started my first mystery.... I decided to follow the prescription: write what you know. At the time, I was a kitchen manager at a sorority at the University of Minnesota.... Jane came about because I needed a sleuth. She was an alumna of the sorority, and as the book begins, she's signed on to become an alumna advisor.... Essentially, Jane was someone who was stuck into the story, someone I needed to fit the plot I'd devised. I gave her character a personal history, an English mother, a lawyer father, etc.. After the book was published, I realized that I had to live with what I'd written—and I had to build on it. Fortunately, I liked the world I'd created."

Lawless is a serious woman who watches and listens before acting. "Mysteries tend to develop characters in incremental doses, so as I've learned about Jane, the books have reflected that knowledge. Actually, Jane really took a leap forward in my thinking after Seal Press decided that ... they needed to focus on publishing nonfiction. That meant, after they'd published seven books of mine, that my series was dropped.... Because I came so close to losing Jane forever, I found myself thinking more deeply about her. She opened up to me in a way she never had before."

Cordelia Thorne "is Jane's sidekick. Watson to her Sherlock.... From the very first, I thought of Cordelia as the salt in the books. Jane seems more visible when Cordelia is around. Opposite character types help form each other. Jane and Cordelia feel like real people to me. I walk the halls with them at night when I can't sleep."

The series has a feminist perspective and the primary themes are "family and relationships. This is very much the territory of the traditional mystery.... What feels real to me are the tensions and stresses that come from human relationships.

"The closet is also a very important theme. It's clearly one of the primary issues all gays and lesbians have to come to terms with. Coming out is painful, and yet staying in the closet—indeed, living a life there—surely destroys something fundamental in our souls....

"In my early books.... I'd find a story line that interested me, and Jane's major contribution to the book would be that of sleuth. Now, it's more a matter of a plot evolving from the characters. Quite often the stories come directly from their lives....

"For Jane and Cordelia, I try to develop a scenario that really pulls them into the story—gives them a reason to become personally involved.... I guess the bottom line is, Jane's sidekick and sleuthing pal will always be Cordelia—and only Cordelia. Jane may become romantically attached again in the future, but it will need to be part of the plot of a specific book, or books. Either that, or the lover will have to be somebody who travels a lot!"

GREG HERREN: *Scotty Bradley* (2003–CURRENT)

Greg Herren is the former editor of *Lambda Book Report*. He's published articles in numerous gay magazines, including the *Harvard Gay and Lesbian Review*, *A&U*, and *Genre and Instinct*. He also writes gay erotica and a lambda-nominated hard-boiled mystery series about gay PI Chanse MacLeod (see the section on private investigators). Herren lives with his partner of eight years in New Orleans where he writes and works as a personal trainer.

Detective: Milton (Scotty) Bradley, personal trainer and part-time bar dancer

Setting: New Orleans. Time period is contemporary with publication dates

Books: *Bourbon Street Blues* (2003); *Jackson Square Jazz* (2004)

Publisher: Kensington Publishing Corp.

"I didn't originally plan to do a second series with a gay main character, actually." Then, a call for stories arrived in which city streets figured prominently. "Since I live in New Orleans, naturally I thought of Bourbon Street—and then I thought of the title *Bourbon Street Blues*—I almost always start with a title. I had a basic premise—I wanted to tell the story from the perspective of a gay male stripper dancing on a bar who one night gets caught up in something Alfred Hitchcockian." It grew into a novel and then a series.

Scotty Bradley is a highly buffed "hottie" who lives beyond the trust-fund allowance established for him by his grandparents. He's also the apple of his counterculture parents' eyes. "The Bradley family is a large part of who Scotty is … and the other characters in his world who aren't family by blood are definitely family by choice." This includes his elderly lesbian landladies. "Millie and Velma never had children of their own, and so they kind of adopted the Bradley children, and of course, they would be closest to the gay child. Again, Millie and Velma are a strong piece of who Scotty is as a person....

"I love Scotty! I love his sense of himself, his sense of humor, his zest for life and determination to enjoy it as much as he can … he is very honest, doesn't care what other people think, and is a genuinely kind person. Scotty is the kind of person that you want to dislike because he is so perfect in so many ways, but he's just so darned sweet you can't....

"When I'm writing about Scotty, it's more a 'what kind of mess would he get into next?' so I guess it's a matter of fitting the stories to him rather than fitting him to the story." Consequently, the first two novels of the series are "wrong place at the wrong time" stories. *Bourbon Street Blues* romps through the New Orleans gay party scene during the ultimate party extravaganza: Southern Decadence. "In the second book, Scotty has already taken his private investigator licensing course and is waiting to complete an internship to get his license and become an official private eye, when he stumbles over another body."

Herren wanted to write about Southern Decadence in the first book because "there is this perception—fueled by the media—that these so-called 'circuit events' are really all about the drugs, the body conscious-ness, the casual sex and the drinking. What people don't realize is that for many people, this is the only time where they ever feel like they are part of a community.... I wanted to make it clear that these kinds of weekends aren't restricted to the young and beautiful, which is one of the biggest misconceptions about them." Chapter titles and subtitles based on tarot cards highlight Bradley's emerging psychic powers. (e.g., "Chapter Seven—The Moon—*Bad luck for an acquaintance.*"[233])

The series is laced with humor, much of which emanates from Scotty. For example, his reaction to seeing a film of himself being carried away on a stretcher is "I had no idea lime green picked up so well on television. It made my package look *huge.*"[234] Needless to say, "Scotty's world was an enormous amount of fun for me to create; the family and friends who inhabit his world are really fun people, the kind I'd like to know."

DEAN JAMES: *Simon Kirby-Jones* (2003–CURRENT)

Dean James (1959–) was born in Mississippi and lived half his life in Texas. He has a doctoral degree in medieval history from Rice University and manages Houston's venerable Murder by the Book bookstore. In addition to the Simon Kirby-Jones series, James writes short stories, mystery novels, and nonfiction collaborations with Jean Swanson, that include the Agatha Award-winning *By a Woman's Hand.* James lives and writes in Houston.

Detective: Dr. Simon Kirby-Jones, historian, romance writer, and mystery writer

Setting: Snupperton Mumsley, England. Time period is contempo-rary with publication dates

Books: *Faked to Death* (2003); *Posted to Death* (2003)

Publisher: Kensington Publishing Corp.

"The Vicar doesn't know I'm a vampire. Nor does he know I'm gay."[235]

"I had to write the book to figure out whose voice it was that I heard." James goes on to say that the voice belongs to Dr. Simon Kirby-Jones, and his words set the tone for the series. "The Simon Kirby-Jones books are, on the whole, intended as affectionate spoofs of the classic traditional mystery. Devout Anglophile that I am, I adore the Golden Age English mystery novel.... I thought I might have some fun with the Simon books by taking a recognized form, exploiting the conventions which everyone recognizes, and twisting them about a bit." Those conventions include a quaint English village, a colonel who cries "Good show!," a school of red herrings, the least likely suspect as murderer, and a tremendous amount of tea.

The humor in the first two books, *Posted to Death* and *Faked to Death*, is directed primarily at mystery literature and authors. "Many people read mysteries to escape, and I want to provide that opportunity for them, keep their attention for a few hours and give them a few laughs." Not all the targets of James' humor are pure escapism. *Faked to Death* also attacks plagiarism. "I dislike any kind of intellectual theft, and I thought it would make a good theme for a book about writers and writing. The rather predatory agent in the book is simply an exaggeration, the result of thinking 'what if?' What if an agent took extraordinary measures to help her clients sell books? Everything is exaggerated for the purposes of comedy and the mystery plot."

Planned Kirby-Jones mysteries target culinary and locked-room mysteries and more romance. "From the beginning I wanted there to be some sort of romantic 'possibility' for Simon. He has a very healthy libido, and he loves to flirt. I wanted that to be a part of his character, but I didn't want it to overwhelm the plots of the books." Simon's relationship with his secretary, Sir Giles Blitherington, generates considerable sexual tension but "by the third book, things begin to heat up between Simon and Giles."

James' approach to writing is character centered. "I start with the characters and a basic situation and work from there. I know who the murder victim (or victims) will be, but I don't always know 'whodunit' until I get to the end.... The stories have to fit into the world I've created for Simon, and they also have to fit into the framework, loosely, at least, of the classic traditional mystery.... The most fun is getting so deeply involved in the process that the characters show me what's going to happen next. To me it's the most fascinating part of the whole writing process, letting the subconscious have its head, so to speak, and seeing where it takes me...."

"Being able to write from the point of view of a gay male character was a fundamental step forward for me in the coming-out process. In my first attempts at writing mysteries, I included gay minor characters, but I shied away from committing to a gay protagonist because that would have been too revealing. But as I became more comfortable with myself and more open about my sexuality, telling stories through a gay protagonist allowed me to find my own voice."

CAROLE LAFAVOR: *Renee LaRoche* (1996–1997)

Carole laFavor (1948–) is an Ojibwe activist, mother, registered nurse and person with AIDS. She served on the Presidential Advisory Council on HIV/AIDS from 1995 to 1997. *Her Giveaway* (1988) and *Interruption in the Journey* (1992) are movie/video portraits by Mona Smith that relate how laFavor came to terms with AIDS by combining Native beliefs and healing practices with western medicine. The Renee LaRoche series is laFavor's only fiction writing. laFavor lives and works in Minneapolis.

Detective: Renee LaRoche, traditional artist and part-time art teacher

Setting: Red Earth reservation, Minnesota. Time period is contemporary with publication dates

Books: *Along the Journey River* (1996); *Evil Dead Center* (1997); Finalist Lambda Award—Best Lesbian Mystery (1997)

Publisher: Firebrand Books

This two-book series is filled with traditional Ojibwe stories, beliefs, and practices although the crimes are invariably tied to white racism. "Ojibwe traditions are essential to the series. I also wanted to help the reader understand there are many tribes in Native America so it isn't Native American traditions—it's Ojibwe traditions. I wanted people to see how Ojibwe people can live in two cultures—the dominant one and the Ojibwe one—honoring traditions of old, but live in modern times."

Some of those traditions, such as morning prayers and carrying a medicine bag, appear in the books as do Ojibwe language and commonly used terms such as "Boozho" (greetings/hello), and "Megwetch" (thank you), as well as designations like "chimook" (white person).

"My initial inspiration to write the Renee LaRoche mysteries had to do with my belief that Native Americans write the best books about Native Americans (except for Tony Hillerman of course). For too long the stories about native people were written by non-natives, with a distinctly non-native perspective." She also wanted to show that "Ojibwe people come in all forms.... Too often it seems non-natives see two types of Indians: the drunken Indian or the spiritual Indian who sits cross-legged before a fire dispensing advice."

This world is seen primarily through the eyes of Renee LaRoche, a two-spirit (lesbian or gay) Ojibwe artist and teacher. "I tried to write the

Renee LaRoche character as a strong Ojibwe woman who is full of quirks and shortcomings. To portray parts of her that weren't any different than most other women. I wanted the reader to see a lesbian who, except for being a lesbian, was like many other women: a single mom, committed partner, and good friend, respectful of all living things. I also wanted the reader to see how traditional Ojibwe ways can be side by side with modern ways.

"I wanted the reader to have to deal with the fact that Renee and Samantha are lesbians.... I also wanted the reader to see how regular a lesbian lifestyle can be. There isn't much difference between a lesbian and non-lesbian mother for example. I also wanted the chance to relay the traditional Ojibwe view of 'two-spirits' which is expressed by Renee's traditionalist grandmother as 'Creator made you and we don't question the work of our Creator.... Two Spirits have always been part of our community.'"[236]

"I think it makes the series more interesting if the reader sees the reservation as a character in the story.... The 'rez' has a personality and a sacred spiritual role to play in the people's lives. It is a part of Mother Earth and therefore honored and respected, but it is also the family's 'step child' or 'black sheep' and therefore can be ignored, abused and disrespected. Whether you're a 'rez Indian' or a 'city liver' the rez is your home. A person could have been living in the city for ten years, but if asked where they live they'll say: 'I'm stayin' in the city for awhile. I live up on Red Earth.' When people go back to the rez from the city, they aren't just going to visit family, they're going to visit 'the rez.'"

JACKIE MANTHORNE:
Harriet Hubbley (1994–CURRENT)

Jackie Manthorne (1946–) is from Nova Scotia and lived in Montreal before moving to Ottawa where she and her partner currently live. She writes both fiction and nonfiction, and her work has been published in literary journals and magazines. She's taught junior high school, worked for feminist and literary organizations, and was Executive Director of PEN Canada. She's currently Executive Director of the Canadian Breast Cancer Institute. Manthorne and her partner of over thirty years recently married.

Detective: Harriet Hubbley, high school physical education teacher

Settings: Various Canadian and U.S. locations. Time period is contemporary with publication dates

Books: *Ghost Motel* (1994); American Library Association—Gay and

Lesbian Book Award (1994); *Deadly Reunion* (1995); *Last Resort* (1995); *Final Take* (1996); Finalist Lambda Award—Best Lesbian Mystery (1996); *Sudden Death* (1997) Finalist Lambda Award—Best Lesbian Mystery (1997)

Publisher: Gynergy Books

These humorous, puzzle mysteries document the sleuthing activities of a lesbian PE teacher as she vacations in popular lesbigay communities in Canada and the United States. "So many lesbians had crushes on their PE teachers. I think it was because PE teachers were seen to be more independent, assertive, sporty and physically active, and young lesbians were often attracted to those characteristics in women, or thought they might be gay.... I wanted to take the myth and explore it.... It didn't drive the series....

"Harriet is a person in evolution.... She is good-natured but can be very jealous; she procrastinates; she sees the humor in sex; she can be obtuse; she cares about other people. She is often passive, and ... she isn't finished growing emotionally....

"I knew from the beginning that I wanted to write as much about relationships as about solving the murder. This has been a constant throughout the series.... At the time I was writing most of the books, many of the women I knew were in flawed and failing relationships, including a lot of faithlessness and short-term serial monogamy. Perhaps also I can write about flawed relationships because I am very secure in my own relationship.... Harriet is more comfortable in a relationship than in being alone.... Sex is also important to her.... While the murder mystery is solved, her relationship issues are not—they continue from book to book."

Hubbley would like nothing more than to spend the rest of her days living in quiet obscurity with one woman. Instead, she's beleaguered by friends and acquaintances engaged in complex and deadly games of musical beds ("It's all so incestuous"[237]). Harriet, herself, invariably attracts the attention of an alluring siren whose intentions are almost always dishonorable. Of course, emotions flare and fingers point when someone is murdered.

"Harriet isn't a detective by profession or by nature—she is an accidental detective. She stumbles on bodies, usually someone she knows. I think she doesn't see things because she is shocked when someone she knows meets a violent death. She solves mysteries because of her curiosity and her knowledge of the people involved, not because she is good at following clues. This is how the murder mystery and the relationship story relate and mesh."

She's not a terribly good sleuth, but neither is anyone else. For example, one police officer summoned to Harriet's apartment following a break-in asks, "Are you in the habit of leaving messages for yourself on the bathroom mirror?... It's written with lipstick and says 'Stop asking questions.'"[238] He then hands Harriet a pile of report forms to complete. ("Not that you're likely to get your stuff back, you understand. But, we do our best."[239]) Unfortunately, those bumbling professionals often view Hubbley as the prime murder suspect. That, plus the need to leave for home or some other destination, gives Harriet greater incentive to conclude the investigation quickly.

Humor is an inherent part of the situations in which Harriet finds herself. "It's important not to take ourselves too seriously. Relationships can be fantastic, or disastrous and soul-destroying. Sex also can be fantastic or a flop. Many women are insecure about their bodies, and I think a little bit of humor in bed is helpful in getting through the stressful bits."

GRANT MICHAELS: *Stan Kraychik* (1991–CURRENT)

Grant Michaels (1947–; pseudonym for Michael Mesrobian) was born in Lawrence, Massachusetts. He's had a varied career that has generally focused on the arts: music, classical dance, theater, and writing (novels and plays)—but not hairdressing. He even taught ballet to a National Guard tank commander. In addition to the Stan Kraychik series, he writes novels under the pseudonym Mike Munro. He lives, writes, and works in Boston.

Detective: Stanley (Stan) Kraychik, hairdresser at Snips Salon

Setting: Primarily Boston. Time period is contemporary with publication dates

Books: *A Body to Dye For* (1991); *Love You to Death* (1992); *Dead on Your Feet* (1993); *Mask for a Diva* (1994); *Time to Check Out* (1997); *Dead as a Doornail* (1998); Finalist Lambda Award-Best Gay Men's Mystery (1998)

Publisher: St. Martin's Press

Try to imagine the most unlikely profession for an amateur sleuth and you could easily arrive at Stan Kraychik, hairdresser extraordinaire. Kraychik (aka Vannos) is an "artiste" who works his magic on the tresses of rich and famous customers of Boston's Snips Salon. In *A Body to Dye For*, which begins the series, Stan initiates his investigative career because he's a suspect in a murder. He quickly discovers he has a talent for detective work—and a penchant for stumbling over dead bodies. As the series progresses Stan shifts his focus from hairdressing to detection, a transition that is facilitated by a sizable insurance settlement related to the death of his lover.

Many of the mysteries have unusual contexts, such as opera, modern dance, and the retail candy industry. The stories contain breezy dialogues; campy humor; outlandish characters, such as a hefty drag-queen-like torch singer named Cozy Dinette; and outrageous situations. While at the police academy, for example, Stan discovers a limp-wrist method of holding a gun that results in superior marksmanship. "Then some of my toughest colleagues asked me to teach them my 'soft-hand' technique."[240] Each book has an older woman (or drag queen) who befriends Stan and becomes his confidant, including Nicole, the owner of Snips Salon; and at least one stunningly handsome, sex-fantasy man who has eyes for Stan. "Suddenly I was Queen for a Day and the three valley men I'd met all had sex on their mind."[241]

Early on, Stan establishes a love-hate relationship with sexy Vito Branco, a gruff police detective who alternately insults Stan and asks for his help with cases. Det. Branco has an opportunity to observe the strengths and weaknesses of Kraychik's investigative technique which leads him to recommend Stan for the police academy towards the end of the series. Stan's relationship with Branco also involves longing for the seemingly unattainable man, a theme which is repeated as part of the main plot of one mystery.

Homophobia is manifested in a variety of ways, including Det. Branco's facile assumption that Stan has sexually molested a young boy ("I can't figure out why the boy would say that unless you tried to do something to him."[242]), religious condemnations, an attorney's belief that Stan will turn a child gay, and a gay-bashing murder ("He thought I was a fag, and that's when I flipped out.... But what are you supposed to do when a fag comes on to you, just because you look good and have your shirt open?"[243]).

Stan's friends, customers, and associates range from drag queens to gym queens, and he's keenly aware of his own effeminacy. Sometimes he acknowledges it with humor as when he responds with "Hardly me, doll" to his employer/friend Nicole's contention that his reliance on logic is "typically masculine."[244] Other situations reveal that as a plump, effeminate man he feels shunned by a gay culture that demands "chisel-bodied" beauty.

PELE PLANTE: *Cynthia Chenery Scott* (1991–1993)

Pele Plante grew up in southern California. Her sensitivity to the disparity between the "haves" and "have-nots" whom she witnessed as a young child engendered a strong social consciousness which later embraced feminism. In 1994, after retiring from her work as a psychotherapist, Plante and her longtime lover established Blue Iris Books in Waldport, Oregon.

Detective: Cynthia Chenery (CC) Scott, retired therapist

Settings: Small towns in California. Time period is contemporary with publication dates

Books: *Getting Away with Murder* (1991); *Dirty Money* (1993)

Publisher: Clothespin Fever Press

"I had conjured up a lesbian protagonist, CC Scott ... and her partner, Barbara ... because who we really are was missing from the genre. We were invisible."[245] Visibility entails presenting lesbians and gay men who are teachers, artists, congresswomen, professional opera singers, therapists, librarians, and attorneys. "We are your own family members, your sister and your mother and your aunt."[246]

Stylistically, the CC Scott mysteries share many traits with traditional mysteries: there is no overt sex or violence; the murders and other crimes occur within small, well-defined communities; and the amateur detective is an older woman who understands human nature. "In creating CC Scott I wanted to get away from the classic hard-boiled detective and create a softer, more compassionate sleuth."[247] Sometimes, however, the compassion and understanding are couched in clinical terminology.

> The emotional abuse by his alcoholic father had contributed to a rigid need for order to compensate for a childhood of chaos and confusion. Thus today he was obsessed with protocol and rules to avoid unexpected events.[248]

Like other feminist mysteries of the late 1980s and early 1990s, these stories concern themselves with the lives of women of all ages and the issues they face. CC and Barbara are middle-class professionals who have been together twenty years and are adjusting to partial retirement. In contrast, Mickey and Angela, a couple they meet in *Dirty Money*, are young, working-class lesbians. *Dirty Money* also contains subplots dealing with child abuse, incest, and domestic violence. Both books address drug and alcohol abuse. CC, for example, is a recovering alcoholic but other characters are practicing alcoholics. *Getting Away with Murder* is about a scam to defraud and murder elderly people, primarily women.

The transgressions in these books are perpetrated by clever criminals who victimize groups of individuals. Order is restored only when their schemes are exposed and they are removed from society. The solutions of the mysteries also lead to the resolution of personal issues facing CC and other characters.

LEV RAPHAEL: *Nick Hoffman* (1996–CURRENT)

Award-winning author Lev Raphael (1954–) is the son of Holocaust survivors. He has a master of fine arts and a doctoral degree. He won the Harvey Swados Fiction Prize for a story that was later published in *Redbook*. His short-story collection, *Dancing on Tisha B'Av*, won a Lambda Award. His novels include *Winter Eyes* and *German Money*. Raphael is an Edith Wharton scholar who wrote *Edith Wharton's Prisoners of Shame: A New Perspective on Her Neglected Fiction*. In collaboration with Gershen Kaufman, he has written a number of works, including *Stick Up for Yourself: Every Kid's Guide to Personal Power and Self Esteem*. He lives with his partner in Okemos, Michigan.

    Detective: Nick Hoffman, Professor at State University of Michigan

    Setting: Michiganapolis, Michigan. Time period is contemporary with publication dates

    Books: *Let's Get Criminal* (1996); *The Edith Wharton Murders* (1997); *The Death of a Constant Lover* (1999); Finalist Lambda Award—Best Gay Men's Mystery (1999); *Little Miss Evil* (2000); *Burning Down the House* (2001)

    Publisher: St. Martin's Press

    "This series is a protest against abuse of power that's cloaked and is happening in an environment where it shouldn't be happening." That is, on a university campus. "You know, academia is the real world, despite talk of 'the ivory tower.' It's frequently cruel, authoritarian, inhumane, but it has this surface rhetoric of a shared community of knowledge and responsibility to students. Nowadays, most universities talk about 'customer satisfaction.' They think in terms of business and bottom line, and the disjunction between reality and rhetoric makes it a great environment for satire."

    At the center of these scathing academic satires is untenured professor Nick Hoffman. Hoffman is "a man with a strong sense of justice and injustice—and a strong sense of the ridiculous connected to that. So, of course, he wound up in the wrong career. He's a decent, loving, thoughtful person, very comfortable with his Jewishness, who's wound up in situations that are pushing him past his own perceived limits—both the crimes in the series and the academic unfairness. Nick is very much an outsider. He's Jewish, he's gay, he's from New York and that creates a lot of possibilities for conflict and observation...."

    "When I started this series one thing that was very clear in my mind was that Nick was going to be affected by what happens to him—within the limitations of having a satirical voice. He's been physically attacked; he's been terrorized into thinking about buying a gun for protection. So he's changed in a lot of ways and a lot of things are coming undone for him. That's also partly why Juno is in there—to shake his sense of himself. Nick is in midlife crisis and consequently he's been pulled away from his center."

Part of his center is his relationship with his lover Stefan which, until "sex bomb" Professor Juno Dramgoole appears, "was a given—not taken for granted but was the bedrock of the series. Like Mr. and Mrs. North. They're married and that's the center of the books.... Beyond the physical, Juno has carte blanche to say what she wants. In a situation where power is wielded so brutally and people can't say the truth, for Nick it's kind of dazzling to have someone who can speak the truth whenever she wants to. To tell people they are full of shit."

The series also lambastes the homophobia, anti-Semitism, sexism, and racism in our culture. Raphael establishes linguistic correspondences among these prejudices. He describes Stefan's father as "coming out" as a Jew, and he shows Nick and Juno "passing" as a straight couple. "These are the baggage that society has. It is implicit in the cultural viewpoint, in language, and in the sense of what's acceptable and what's not. It's also what's taken for granted: everybody's straight. Whites are better than nonwhites. Straights are better than gays, men better than women. There's no question a gay man would be considered a lesser man...."

"For me, the environment of the series is fascinating. It's great to go back to that wacky campus.... I'm always going back to the same set of characters. They're old friends.... It's always a pleasure to come back to their world. "

JENNY ROBERTS: *Cameron McGill* (2000–CURRENT)

Jenny Roberts (1948–) was born in Bridlington, England, and now lives in York where she owns and runs the Libertas women's bookshop. She's a transsexual lesbian with grown children. In 1999, she was nominated for the Yorkshire Women of Achievement Awards. Roberts has a published short story in addition to the Cameron McGill mysteries.

Detective: Cameron McGill, drug and alcohol counselor
Settings: Amsterdam and Yorkshire. Time period is contemporary with publication dates
Books: *Needlepoint* (2000); *Breaking Point* (2001)
Publisher: Diva
These stories blend social consciousness with intrigue, and they are per-

vaded by a menacing atmosphere. Despite obvious dangers, Cameron McGill hurtles into investigations—barreling past the objections of friends and the threats of foes—with "an impetuosity that isn't tempered by the will to live....

"Cameron brings events on herself and so, by definition, she will not have an easy time.... I see her progressing rather than healing. I see her learning how to cope more as the series progresses. And I see her developing more of an insight into her own flawed character, even though she may ultimately always remain a prisoner to her past....

"At the opening of *Needlepoint*, she is a 34-year-old lesbian who displays in turns anger, sensitivity, despair, self-confidence, neediness and a tendency to reject anything in her life which may help to heal her." She dislikes authority—especially male authority. "She is a committed outsider and is very proud of her lesbian identity and her differences to mainstream society. She is comfortable with other 'outcasts'—squatters, hippies, travelers and drug addicts—which eventually led her into a career of drug counseling." By the end of *Breaking Point*, the second book in the series, she's left drug counseling to become a private investigator.

"Cameron can be out of order at times and, sometimes, downright unpleasant. This is also useful in discussing some of the social issues." Those issues include violence against women, exploitation of illegal immigrants, homelessness, and the use of animals for scientific experimentation. "Cameron changes other characters' views—of her as a lesbian, say. But other characters ... change Cameron's sometimes ill-informed views on other issues." This is an important theme in the series because, according to Roberts, "it is vital to remember that life is not drawn in clear lines. Issues, whatever they are, are complex and often there is no easy right or wrong."

When Roberts starts on a new book, she begins "with a general theme and plot which fits both the character and the subject I want to write about.... The real story comes with the writing.... I generally give Cameron her head. She leads me through the story. I'm mostly guided by what happens to her on her journey and what her reactions are—and that's what I write down. The downside is that sometimes she can go off at tangents and, if I let her, I may ultimately have to dump maybe weeks of work because that particular direction simply doesn't work. On the other hand, she often leads me into places where I would never have imagined going and introduces me to extraordinary people who are very often a complete surprise to me."

Roberts' primary goal in writing the series is to entertain and "the theme that most epitomizes my writing is *respect*. And I hope that the violence and the overcoming of violence helps to underline the message that we should all respect each other and the different views and outlook that we all hold. If we all treated each other with respect, then there would be no violence. I suppose if I have a message in my books then that may be it."

MARK A. ROEDER: *Sean** (2000)

Mark A. Roeder writes juvenile fiction for gay readers. Most of his books are part of a series called the *Gay Youth Chronicles* which focuses on gay youth growing up in a small town. There are currently nine books published in the series plus a stand-alone novel and several more novels to appear. He has lived almost all of his life in small Indiana towns.

Detective: Sean, high school student

Setting: Verona, Indiana. Time period is contemporary with publication date

Book: *Someone Is Killing the Gay Boys of Verona* (2000)

Publisher: iUniverse/Writers Club Press

Someone Is Killing the Gay Boys of Verona is the third book in Roeder's *Gay Youth Chronicles* series. Each novel has a different main character. "There is a little bit of mystery and romance in most of my novels, and some of them delve into the supernatural too. Most don't fit into a specific genre, however....."[249]

Like the other books in the series, *Someone Is Killing the Gay Boys of Verona* bundles gay-positive messages into an action-packed story. Its dedication reads:

> This book is dedicated to all the gay boys that have died because others do not understand, to those that must struggle against the prejudice and hate of others, and to those wise and courageous enough to help them.[250]

Sean is an openly gay, sixteen-year-old high school student whose family recently moved into a house that is said to be haunted. "Sean is an average teen-aged boy. He's not a jock and he doesn't look like a model. He's a little pudgy around the middle and he's not happy about that. He's like most of us and I think that makes him someone who most readers can identify with.... Sean is comfortable with being gay from the beginning of the novel. He doesn't announce it, but he doesn't hide it either."[251] He's also helped other gay boys handle the coming-out process. Despite

---

In an email message to the author on November 27, 2003, Roeder says, "Of course Sean has a last name, but I don't know what it is. Sometimes I assign a character a last name right away and sometimes I leave it open. This is something that just hasn't been defined with Sean."

his apparent popularity among his classmates, Sean struggles with self-image and dreams of having a real boyfriend. "I think any book dealing with teenagers is a coming of age book. It's a time of life with many changes and new realizations."[252]

When the story opens, Sean's friend, Marty Crawford, has just come out to his classmates. Marty's death shortly thereafter comes as a shock which is magnified when the official cause of death is listed as suicide. Sean obtains a copy of Marty's autopsy report and determines that the adult professionals have made serious errors. When other gay boys are killed in gay bashings, he's convinced Marty's death was murder.

Sean's investigation leads him to the ghosts of two gay high school students (who are among the many ghosts inhabiting Sean's house) who help protect him against the gay-bashing murderers.

The teenaged ghosts are also used to make a strong statement against suicide. They both committed suicide twenty years earlier and regret their actions. "By ending our lives we cheated ourselves of the lives we could have led."[253] Roeder says that "Many of my books touch on gay teen suicide. The suicide rate of gay youth is obscene, and religious intolerance and bigotry are to blame. I've always been astounded that some who claim to be Christians speak out so vehemently against gays. Their words and actions cause great pain and lead to death."

Sean also deepens his relationship with an adult gay couple, Nathan and Ethan. The men provide a compelling, positive model of gay life that contradicts the homophobic material included in a pamphlet distributed by a group whose mantra is "God hates queers." "Sean comes face-to-face with evil in the form of religious prejudice and hatred. This forces him to grow in order to be able to combat it."

The book presents powerful gay-positive arguments and images (living and dead). The absence of Sean's parents—a common feature of juvenile fiction—enables Sean and his classmates to pursue their investigations and to participate in rollicking adventures with spirits from beyond.

CAROL SCHMIDT: *Laney Samms* (1993–1995)

Carol Schmidt (1942–) has been a reporter, editor, PR director, entrepreneur, and full-time novelist. Her articles garnered three first-place awards from the National Gay and Lesbian Press Association. She has been active in civil rights and antiwar activities (since the sixties), in lesbian-feminist and gay communities, and in a women's RV retirement community. She now lives in an art colony in central Mexico (where she's "exploring her artistic side") with her lover of twenty-five years.

Detective: Laney Samms, owner of Samms lesbian bar
Settings: Los Angeles area and Michigan. Time period is contemporary with publication dates
Books: *Silverlake Heat* (1993); *Sweet Cherry Wine* (1994); *Cabin Fever* (1995)
Publisher: The Naiad Press

These mysteries have complex plots with twists that throw into question the nature of the crime that has been committed. There are also final twists at the ends of stories that are life's wry jokes.

"*Silverlake Heat* grew out of my fascination with the movie *Body Heat*, and I wanted a kind of well-meaning, bumbling but likeable fool like the William Hurt character in the movie, who is shellacked by Kathleen Turner.... I also wanted her to be sexy in her own way, so the love scenes could be fun to write and easily accessible.... Laney also is a bit like a gorgeous white-haired butch who hung around the Ms. Fitz bar in Culver City.... That kind of barfly butch was also in the back of my mind as I developed Laney."

The selection of an older lesbian "was a deliberate statement of the value of older lesbians who are almost as invisible in the lesbian community (except for the few token allowable sheroes) as older women are in the larger community."

Despite her chronological age, Samms has a lot of growing up to do. "In *Silverlake Heat*, she's immature, self-centered, and not fully sober even after all those years. She's just sort of hanging around the bar that her longtime lover has bought for her as a way to give her some purpose in life, and she has never explored her talents or appreciated what business sense she does have.... The next two books were driven by Laney's character development. I asked myself, where would Laney go now? What story line would help her grow in ways I saw her growing?" By the end of *Cabin Fever* she realizes how much she's changed. "I felt as if I'd grown a lot in the last few months—and if you don't grow up at age fifty, when the hell are you going to get around to it?"[254]

The series expresses a feminist perspective, in part, by looking at issues of concern to women, such as child molestation, sexism, and "lookism." Sometimes she creates minor characters, such as Tess, who are designed to challenge such stereotypes. "I deliberately made Tess fat and spirited, a bit antagonistic and vengeful, proud, aggressive, and attractive." Added to those themes are obstacles many lesbians face: homophobia, family rejection, the closet, and alcoholism. Alcoholism is examined, in part, through Laney's acceptance of AA compared with her friend Haley's continued addiction. Racism ("Racism awareness creeps up every-

where in my writing."), anti-Semitism, and animal rights are also represented, as is mental illness. "Hayley crosses over from 'mere' alcoholism
at times, and her persecutor is definitely trying to drive her mad....

"I have a broad understanding of feminism, and it encompasses all
of the themes mentioned above. To me a feminist integrates all issues of
discrimination, stereotyping and social limitations, not just 'women's
issues.'"

MANDA SCOTT: *Kellen Stewart* (1997–CURRENT)

Manda Scott was born and brought up in Scotland. She trained at
the Glasgow Veterinary School and specialized in horses as a surgeon and
later as an anesthetist. Scott began writing veterinary and animal series
for television. She published her first novel, *Hen's Teeth*, in 1997. In addition to the Kellen Stewart series, Scott has a second series about a police
detective and a novel of historical fiction. Scott describes herself as a
writer, climber, and increasingly less a veterinary surgeon. She lives and
works in Glasgow.

Detective: Kellen Stewart, consulting physician/psychiatrist
Setting: Glasgow. Time period is contemporary with publication
dates
Books: *Hens Teeth* (1997); Short-listed Orange Prize (1997); *Night
Mares* (1998); *Stronger Than Death* (1999); Finalist Saltire Scottish Book
of the Year (1999)
Publishers: Bantam Books, Headline, The Women's Press

These medical mysteries overflow with ominous menace because the
villains are medical professionals—people we usually trust with our lives.
They dispense disease and death to colleagues and anyone else who stands
in the way of their greed, revenge, or hatred. Their medical knowledge and
skill further enable them to make murders look like accidents or suicides.
"Who ever is doing this, why ever they are doing it, they have to be a
medic. No one else could have put this all together."[255] "I try to anchor
each novel in a relevant present with which the reader can identify but
beyond that, I'm not certain what mood or atmosphere is invoked. Kellen's
a fairly driven individual so perhaps that gives the sense of impending
doom. I think, more, that there's a sense of emotional fluidity...."

Dr. Kellen Stewart, a consulting physician/therapist and horse-farm
owner, is an unlikely combatant. Honest, ethical, and loyal, she's more of
a follower than a leader. She's sucked into the roiling miasma when her
friends, lovers, and clients are terrorized and killed. She labors to extract
herself and them through collaboration with trusted medical colleagues

and other, less reliable, guides. Cast as the first-person narrator, Stewart's emotions, observations, and internal dialogues exacerbate the disquieting plots. The following example is her reaction to the death of a friend.

> The back door opens. Someone puts the kettle on the Rayburn. The dog takes the stairs in three strides and lands on the bed with the fourth. I roll over to give her room. Keep rolling. There's more space in the bed than there was. I hadn't realized I was alone. Nina has gone. She was never here. The world has ended.[256]

"The prose is written in first person and part of the choice for that was to give me the opportunity to explore the boundary between what people say and what they think. Without seeing both sides of that, then there is no visible dichotomy. In first person prose, there's a tendency to see inside the head as well as out of it, which is its great strength. Its great weakness, of course, is only being able to see one individual view point on what may be a complex subject. Readers have a tendency to believe everything Kellen thinks and says, which never fails to astonish me."

Lesbian- and gay-related themes, such as homophobia and coming out, are secondary to more personal concerns. "I'm not particularly interested in themes or issues, more in what makes people tick and what happens when they're pushed to the limits of their own emotional envelope.... I think I am more concerned with death and the impact of death, or the proximity of death, or the wish for death, than greed or abuse of power or drugs....

"Every book I write is driven by the need/desire to push the central character to and beyond the margins of her/his own emotional envelope. In those books in which Kellen is the primary character, she is therefore pushed as far as is reasonable and then a little more. Her emotional curve is what drives the narrative. To me, this is what makes fiction interesting, certainly as a writer, but also as a reader."

BARBARA WILSON/SJOHOLM: *Pam Nilsen* (1984–1989)

Award-winning author Barbara Sjoholm (1950–; formerly Barbara Wilson) grew up in Long Beach, California, and then lived in Europe. She cofounded Seal Press, a feminist press which was recently sold to Avalon Publishing Group. She's written two mystery series, novels and short stories, and fiction for juveniles. Her memoir, *Blue Windows: A Christian Science Childhood*, won a Lambda and was nominated for a PEN award. Wilson lives in Seattle and writes essays and travel narratives.

Detective: Pam Nilsen, member of a printing collective

Setting: Seattle, Washington. Time period is contemporary with publication dates

Books: *Murder in the Collective* (1984); *Sisters of the Road* (1987); *The Dog Collar Murders* (1989)

Publisher: Seal Press

This is the first gay or lesbian detective series with an amateur detective. "It had a lighthearted beginning. I'd run into a friend on a bus who was telling me about a merger between a grain collective and a fruit-and-vegetable collective. Some people didn't want to merge. One day, one of the women in the grain collective found her desk covered with molasses. We were laughing about that. I think I just came home from that and wrote *Murder in the Collective* on my old typewriter.

"When I wrote *Murder in the Collective*, I'd never read a lesbian mystery because we were all writing our first ones at that time. I loved reading mysteries, and I thought it would be fun to write one. I also belonged to a newspaper collective and was in contact with people from a variety of other collectives, including printing collectives. I'd never read anything about that either. I thought that some of the things that went on behind the scenes in a collective would be suitable for a mystery."

Murder in the Collective is also a coming-out story. "Like any emerging literature, lesbian literature had forms that you followed—often without realizing it. There was a great interest in coming out because it had a great deal of metaphysical baggage: It was freeing yourself in some way and finding your true self. I wouldn't describe it that way now. We weren't conscious of it, but you almost had to have coming out in your books.

"I was also interested in figuring out how you brought a political consciousness to fiction. I thought the mystery—with its format of question-asking, issues of social justice and crime, and its accusations and vengeance—was well suited for that. I wanted to see what a mystery could do in terms of tackling social issues."

The stories also present opposing viewpoints on topics that were highly emotional at the time. "I was using a Hegelian dialectic: thesis, antithesis, and synthesis. It suits the mystery genre, and I liked doing it because there was so much tension in the feminist movement about issues like prostitution, the 'porn wars,' and the SM stuff…. I thought it was interesting to put up the different viewpoints and give them to people. Then, in the guise of a murder mystery, you not only say, 'Where were you on the night of August 5th?' but also 'What are your opinions on prostitution?'

"The books, especially *Dog Collar Murders*, were used a lot in women's studies classes because teachers wanted a way of communicating with students about such topics. A lot of older women have told me they first read them in women's studies classes as discussion assignments. That's probably different from what a lot of other mystery writers experience.

"There was a huge amount of excitement when those first mysteries came out. It was very heady. I don't think I would have written so much if I hadn't gotten so much attention—not only in the States but in England and Germany as well. Suddenly, people took note of feminist mysteries and lesbian mysteries. This was something new and it was a way to talk about issues and to create heroines who were hard, tough, and streetwise. Katherine* had a cop, and I had an amateur detective.

"That was a very political period for me....We had a Messianic feeling. We planned to publish the voices of all those women who hadn't been able to speak before. We were going to change the world."

BARBARA WILSON/SJOHOLM:
Cassandra Reilly (1990–2000)

Award-winning author Barbara Sjoholm (1950–; formerly Barbara Wilson) grew up in southern California, lived in Norway and other European countries, and settled in Seattle, Washington. Wilson cofounded Women in Translation, a nonprofit company that translates women's fiction into English. She wrote another lesbian mystery series, other fiction, and a Lambda-winning memoir. She won the Columbia Translation Prize for her translations of the works of Norwegian writer Cora Sandel. The Cassandra Reilly mystery *Gaudi Afternoon* was made into a motion picture. At age fifty, Barbara Wilson formally changed her name to Barbara Sjoholm and now writes essays and travel narratives.

Detective: Cassandra Reilly, translator

Settings: Various locations. Time period is contemporary with publication dates

Books: *Gaudi Afternoon* (1990); Lambda Award—Best Lesbian Mystery (cowinner) (1990); Crime Writers' Association Award—Best Mystery Set in Europe (1991); *Trouble in Transylvania* (1993); *The Case of the Orphaned Bassoonists* (2000); Finalist Lambda Award—Best Lesbian Mystery (2000)

Publishers: Seal Press, Virago

Gaudi Afternoon, the first Cassandra Reilly novel, appeared one year after the final Pam Nilsen mystery. "I wanted to do something completely different.... I wanted to create a character who traveled extensively and

Katherine Forrest, whose main character is police detective Kate Delafield; see "Police," pp. 26–66.

was at home in many places and who had friends all over the world.... With the Cassandra books, I definitely wanted to create a sense of the place she was in.

"I invented a lesbian network for her. I also liked the idea that she was so rakish. She had lovers but no partner, and she was butch in a very friendly way. Cassandra really likes women especially big, curvaceous, feminine women. Actually, she pretty much likes all women—even men who have changed into women. She can't tell that they are transsexuals. Plus, in *Gaudi Afternoon*, Frankie intrigues her.... She's hard to identify with. She's so swashbuckling and cynical whereas Pam* is the girl next door."

Age is a crucial part of who Cassandra is. "Once again, we are talking about writing in a vacuum.... Most novels, and certainly most mysteries, have younger women. That's probably because they were being written by younger women. I thought it would be interesting to have an older detective who, at the same time, was not Miss Marple. I liked the idea of a sexually active older woman who had a roving eye and who was attractive as well.... When I first started writing her, she was older than I was. I used her to explore some aging issues I was wondering about."

Like the Pam Nilsen books, these mysteries grow out of themes. "As I worked out a plot that would illuminate the themes, lots of other things came up so that the characters and plot developed together." One of those themes is families. "There are a lot of orphans and mother-daughter combos in all of them." Cassandra is estranged from her own family, and "Nicky, her friend, is really her closest family."

Another important theme is language. "By then, I was deeply involved in translation.... As a translator and as a detective, you work through what people actually say to you and look for what they might mean.... There are lots of misunderstandings based on language that I have fun with. For example, the jokes about bassoons (fagottos) and liver (fegato) in *The Case of the Orphaned Bassoonists*. It gives the dialogue a kind of vigor as well as creating misunderstandings. There is humor and sometimes the plot is advanced.

"I also think that language intersects in some ways with other things, like sexual identity. For example, Hungarian and Finnish don't have gender-related pronouns. So you wonder, 'How could they possibly talk about gender?' They say they know what they're talking about." Gender identity is a major theme of *Gaudi Afternoon*, which is set in Barcelona where the native languages (Spanish and Catalan) do have gender-related pronouns.

"I've been ambitious. I've wanted to write books with a range of emotions. I wanted to make them sad, poignant, and I wanted to make people laugh." Sjoholm gets great joy from "succeeding in meeting the challenges I set for myself.... Carrying it off in some way and hearing others say that they laughed or thought it worked."

PARTNERS

From the very beginning, fictional detectives have had assistants who help them when needed, serve as sounding boards for their theories, and trumpet their genius to the world. An unnamed admirer champions Poe's Dupin, Watson serves Holmes, Hastings aids Poirot, and Charlie Chan can always count on his number one son. Some, like Watson, are obtuse—by design—so that the detective can expound upon her/his logic to an enthralled listener. Even those who are intelligent and insightful retain their supportive role in the detection process.

Gay/lesbian detectives are no different. Ellen Hart's amateur detective, Jane Lawless, relies on her best friend Cordelia Thorne for support (and drama). Richard Stevenson's PI, Donald Strachey, involves his lover, Timmy Callahan, in some of his cases as does Sandra Scoppettone's PI Lauren Laurano. Randye Lordon's PI Sydney Sloane and her business partner, Max Cabe, brainstorm about cases and clients. Lordon adds that "I also wanted to know that if I couldn't get Sydney out of a pickle there was someone else there to help her."[*]

None of these sidekicks and lovers ever unravels a mystery. Furthermore, no matter how important they are to the detective and the series, they never lose their status as secondary characters.

The twosomes and teams that populate this chapter have more equitable roles. These partners work together or in parallel to solve their mysteries, each contributing her or his special skills or perspective.

Gay/lesbian partnerships began in 1980 when collaborators Michael McDowell and Dennis Schuetz authored *Vermillion* under the pseudonym Nathan Aldyne. They paired a gay bartender, Daniel Valentine, with his best friend, Clarisse Lovelace, a heterosexual woman-about-town. Five years later, Samuel Steward's *Murder Is Murder Is Murder* appeared featuring the lesbian duo, Gertrude Stein and Alice B. Toklas. Table 3 reveals that, since then, gay/lesbian partner mysteries have developed a tremendous amount of variability.

---

[*]*All unattributed author quotes come from interviews for this book.*

Table 3: Gay/Lesbian Partners

Author	Characters (*focal partner)	Relationship	Sexual Orientation	Type of Detective
Nathan Aldyne	*Daniel Valentine	Friends	Gay	Amateurs
	Clarisse Lovelace		Heterosexual	
Stan Cutler	Mark Bradley	Business	Gay	Amateur
	Rayford Goodman	associates	Heterosexual	Private investigator
Lauren Wright Douglas	*Allison O'Neil	Business associates		Amateur
	Kerry Owyhee	and friends	Lesbian	Private investigator
Michael Allen Dymmoch	Jack Caleb	Business	Gay	Amateur
	John Thinnes	associates	Heterosexual	Police
Keith Hartman	*Drew Parker	Business	Gay	Private investigators
	Jennifer Grey	associates	Heterosexual	
Fred Hunter	*Alex Reynolds	Lovers	Gay	Amateurs
	Peter Livesay			
	Jean Reynolds	Alex' mother	Heterosexual	
Bett Reece Johnson	Cordelia Morgan	Transient friendships	Incipient lesbian	Private Investigator
	*Anna Lee Stone		Heterosexual	Amateurs
	*S.J. Symkin			
	*Grace Lee DeWitte		Lesbian	
Joe R. Lansdale	Leonard Pine	Friends	Gay	Amateurs
	*Hap Collins		Heterosexual	
Josh Lanyon	*Adrien English	Lovers	Gay	Amateur
	Jake Riordan			Police
Lauren Maddison	*Connor Hawthorne	Lovers	Lesbian	Amateurs
	Laura Nez			
	Benjamin Hawthorne	Connor's father	Heterosexual	
	Gwendolyn Broadhurst	Connor's grandmother		
	Malcolm Jefferson	Connor's friend		Police
Mabel Maney	Nancy Clue			Private investigator
	*Cherry Aimless	Lovers	Lesbian	Amateurs
	Midge Fontaine	Lovers		
	Velma Pierce			
	Jackie Jones	Friend, Cherry's lover		Police
	Frank Hardly	Brothers	Gay	Amateurs
	Joe Hardly			
Penny Mickelbury	Mimi Patterson	Lovers	Lesbian	Reporter
	Gianna Maglione			Police
Orland Outland	*Doan McCandler	Friends	Gay	Private investigators

Author	Characters (*focal partner)	Relationship	Sexual Orientation	Type of Detective
	Binky Van de Kamp		Heterosexual	
Abigail Padgett	*Blue McCarron Roxie Bouchie	Lovers and business associates	Lesbian	Amateurs
Nancy Sanra	*Tally McGinnis Cid Cameron	business associates	Lesbian	Private investigators
Samuel Steward	Gertrude Stein Alice B. Toklas	Lovers	Lesbian	Amateurs
David Stukas	*Robert Willsop Michael Stark Monette O'Reilley	Friends	Gay Lesbian	Amateurs
Therese Szymanski	*Brett Higgins Allison Sullivan	Lovers	Lesbian	Amateur Police
Mark Richard Zubro	*Tom Mason Scott Carpenter	Lovers	Gay	Amateurs

Relationships

Many series (but not all of them) have a primary or focal partner (see Table 3). That individual will be the first-person narrator or the character whose perspective dominates a third-person narration. Cherry Aimless is the focal partner of Maney's series even though the titles suggest Nancy Clue would have that role. According to Maney

> Cherry Ames, unfairly, does not have the name recognition Nancy Drew has. George notwithstanding, the Cherry Ames books are much queerer than the Nancy Drews. Cherry is self-effacing, hard working, and proud of her profession. You'd think her passionate attachment to good hygiene, detective work, and attractive nurses would have earned her a bigger audience, wouldn't you?

Some authors aim for greater parity by allocating chapters to each partner. Dymmoch and Mickelbury use third-person narrators that alternately follow one or the other of their partners. Dymmoch changes the primary partner from novel to novel as well. Some stories center on Jack Caleb and others on John Thinnes. Cutler and Johnson use a comparable approach with first-person narrators. In Johnson's novels, Cordelia Morgan and the other first-person narrator advance the story in fundamentally different ways. "The main protagonist in each book leans more to the 'genre mystery' tone and action. It's in the Morgan sections that I can get the 'poetry' in." Hartman not only changes first-person narrators, he allows any of a number of characters involved in the story to become the narrator.

One of the major themes of the books is how different people in different subcultures see the world in different ways. One of the more interesting ways to explore that was to have several people hunting for the truth, and show how their preconceptions shape what they see.

Lovers and Spouses

Lovers are the most common detecting partners in both mainstream and gay/lesbian literature (see Table 3). Some gay/lesbian lovers meet and fall in love in the first book of their series. Szymanski's Brett Higgins and Allie Sullivan encounter each other at a women's rap group. Maddison's Laura Nez is assigned to protect Conner Hawthorne while she attends a conference. Mickelbury's Mimi Patterson and Gianna Maglione see each other across a crowded gym and are immediately drawn to each other. Maney's Cherry Aimless and Nancy Clue meet while traveling to Illinois on a mission of mercy. Lanyon's Adrien English and Homicide Det. Jake Riordan meet on a case.

This pattern of meeting, sleuthing, and falling in love is a long-standing trend in mainstream literature as well. In M. McDonnell Bodkin's 1909 mystery, *The Capture of Paul Beck*, a friendly competition between "lady detective" Dora Myrl and "rule-of-thumb detective" Paul Beck (won by Mryl) ends in love, marriage, and offspring novels. At the beginning of Agatha Christie's first Tommy and Tuppence mystery, *The Secret Adversary*, the two are hardly more than acquaintances. Between that 1922 publication and 1928, when *Partners in Crime* appeared, they tie the knot and start a detective agency. A more recent team, Carolyn Hart's Annie Laurence and Max Darling, don't marry until their fourth book.

Gay/lesbian lovers whose relationships predate the onset of their series are all depicted as very happy which can be easily viewed as a political, gay-positive, statement. In *Caravaggio Shawl*, Steward (who knew Gertrude Stein and Alice Toklas personally) has Stein describe Toklas as "she's my dear sweet Pussy and I love her."[257] Although his partners both must deal with coming out of the closet, Zubro says he always knew Tom and Scott "were, no doubt, going to be a happy gay couple. In fact, the first couple of books it turned into a problem because they were always happy and loving." They eventually marry. Hunter's Alex and Peter aren't married but they call each other "husband."

> I told a friend that I couldn't understand why people referred to the book as "political." She said, "Fred, if one teenaged gay boy picks up these books, reads them, and goes 'I can have a stable marriage' that's political." It had never dawned on me that I was doing anything like that. What's

strange is that the next day I got a letter from someone saying, "Reading your Alex Reynolds books helped me come out of the closet."

Such happiness does not come as easily to couples who meet during their series. Lanyon's English must overcome Riordan's overwhelming internalized homophobia. "I refused to do something so self-destructive as love a man who hated himself for being homosexual...."[258] Mickelbury's Patterson and Maglione must overcome both racial and professional differences.

> I paired the reporter and the cop *because* they are natural enemies. All the better to explore different angles of the same issues and subjects; but also it provides a natural tension to the interpersonal relationship that exists between the two women.

Maney's Nancy Clue is intensely private and "will ... always take care of her needs first, which makes her a perfectly hellish match for Cherry, the codependent poster girl of 1958." Nancy's behavior finally drives Cherry into the arms of a far better partner, Jackie Jones. Similarly, the problems faced by Szymanski's Brett Higgins and Allie Sullivan include Higgins' womanizing.

> Right from the get-go I thought that some day Allie would tell Brett, "If you want to be nonmonogamous, let's be nonmonogamous." I don't think Brett would do well with the idea of Allie being with other women.... Brett doesn't have a good grip on the idea that what's good for the goose is good for the gander.

Friends and Business Partners

Although unrelated partners can be as similar as Nancy Drew (and her lesbian correlate, Nancy Clue) and her teenage buddies, most partnerships are comprised of individuals who vary in age, profession, race, sex, and/or financial status. In mainstream literature, examples include Robert Parker's Spenser and Hawk (race, profession, and social background), Fred Hunter's Det. Jeremy Ransom and Emily Charters (sex, age, and profession), and S.J. Rozan's Lydia Chin and Bill Smith (sex, race, and ethnicity). In gay and lesbian mysteries, partners almost always differ in sexual orientation as well.

Some authors actively seek to represent different perspectives. Maney added African American Jackie Jones to her Nancy Clue parody because "The originals are so white the pages are practically transparent. I love the idea of giving a black woman in the 1950s official authority." Maddison argues, "Why not have a richer palette of beliefs and social customs and attitudes from which to draw? And why not show how they can blend with each other?" Lauren Wright Douglas pairs Native American and PI Kerry Owyhee with white, amateur detective Allison O'Neil.

Differences also create conflict and thereby enhance the stories. Cutler forced older, working-class and heterosexual Rayford Goodman to collaborate with a gay yuppie because "I personally thought the Bradley character was simply a good 'mismatch' ... to generate conflict and humor." Dymmoch agrees, "Traditional cops didn't have any use for 'faggots' or shrinks. So a gay shrink provides twice the conflict. A rich, gay shrink is gravy." By adding the lesbian Monette to the mix, Stukas knew, "I could have the characters play off each other and even touch on the taboo of gay versus lesbian culture. More tension, more jokes, more poking fun." Hartman sums it up:

> Two people who get along all the time wouldn't be that interesting to hang out with. But two people with radically different ways of looking at things, who are always getting on each other's nerves, who are competitive with each other, and yet who still manage to work together and like each other—now that can be fun.

Family

Among the most famous mainstream gumshoe relatives are the youthful Hardy boys and Bobbsey twins. They are joined by sleuthing teams comprised of adult siblings, a parent or grandparent and child, and entire families. To date, the gay/lesbian literature has only three sets of detecting relatives, all of whom are part of larger investigative teams. In Maddison's series, Connor Hawthorne, her father, and maternal grandmother form the core of their team of partners. Maney's youthful sleuths include brothers Joe and Frank Hardly, who parody the Hardy boys. Hunter's trio of detectives includes Alex Reynolds and his mother, Jean, who "were the basis for the series. Giving Alex a partner was a later decision." The partner, Peter Livesay, completes the threesome.

Themes

Gay/lesbian partnerships include philosophical odysseys, outrageous satires, and a great deal of social commentary. Sex, race, sexual-orientation, and social differences that exist between partners promote exploration of homophobia, sexism, racism, and other social issues.

Homophobia

Partnerships between heterosexual and gay men always force the heterosexual man to confront his homophobia. This is not the case for heterosexual women. Dymmoch's Thinnes, Cutler's Goodman, and Lansdale's Collins all find they need to make adjustments. Collins, for example, considers Leonard his best friend but

> I see two guys hugging up ... it makes me uncomfortable.... I know there isn't anything wrong with it. But I was taught one way all my life, that homos are perverts.[259]

Goodman's homophobia (and his many other prejudices) is couched in humor.

> I'm not one of those people goes around saying he's got no prejudices. What I will say, I've got considerably less since meeting Bradley. In a lot of ways he was a stand-up guy, no pun intended. But he was a you-know-what. And I've got to also say that while I no longer think gays should be tarred and feathered—definitely not feathered—I don't exactly understand all this pride stuff.... Anyway, I'm a lot more tolerant, you can see that.[260]

Adrien English's lover Jack Riordan (Josh Lanyon) isn't heterosexual but he might as well be. His internalized homophobia is so powerful that he can't even bring himself to kiss English.

Most homophobia is external to the main characters and emanates from police departments, families, the surrounding heterosexual community, and even hypothetical heterosexual readers of these books. It is an undercurrent running through a number of series. In Lansdale's series it sometimes surfaces as gay bashing; it keeps Mickelbury's Maglione in the closet; it feeds off fear of AIDS in Dymmoch's series; and in Hartman's future United States, the discovery of a test for the "gay gene" results in widespread abortions—even within pro-life groups. "The Southern Baptist Convention doesn't like abortions. But it *really* doesn't like homosexuals."[261]

Authors counteract homophobia through strong gay- and lesbian-positive images. Zubro, Hunter, and several others emphasize the positive elements in their partners/lovers' relationships. Taking a different tack, Johnson has been slowly increasing the level of intimacy between Morgan and her "main character" partners as a means of attenuating homophobia in the reader.

> I suppose if I write with any kind of agenda at all, that would be it ... to make a scene between two women together a perfectly natural occurrence—nothing to be screamed about, or whispered about either. It just simply Is.

Sexism

Like homophobia, most sexism emanates from secondary characters —although a few male main characters express and/or confront their own sexism (e.g., Dymmoch's Thinnes, Cutler's Goodman).

Sexism generally surfaces as violent acts against women, which is a series-level theme for Johnson, Maney, and Padgett and appears in individual novels by most of the other writers. Dymmoch's *Feline Friendship*, for example, "explores the battle lines in the war between the sexes." Those battle lines include child prostitution, rape, spousal abuse, and incest. Cutler's *The Face on the Cutting Room Floor*, Lansdale's *Bad Chili*, and Zubro's *A Simple Suburban Murder* all include spouse abuse. Mickelbury's *Night Songs* combines sexism with racism when serial killers target African American prostitutes.

Although few of these authors describe their series as feminist, many of them exhibit a feminist viewpoint designed to counteract damage caused by violence against women and other forms of sexism. Mickelbury, Maddison, Johnson, and Padgett underscore the strength and dynamism of older women. Hartman's Jennifer Grey is not only a skilled detective, she's a Wiccan warrior-witch and a leader of her coven. Maddison's series is "focused on aspects of worship centered on the Divine Feminine" as a way of righting a spiritual imbalance in Christianity. Although she admits she's not politically correct, Szymanski creates forceful women characters because "I like seeing women kicking butt and in control and making their own decisions."

Race and Racism

Even when partners are of different races, racism rarely becomes a source of friction between them. One striking exception is Padgett's Bouchie and McCarron. Bouchie is strongly black-identified and more sensitive to cultural differences between the races than McCarron, who is white. For Douglas' Kerry Owyhee, a mixed-race woman who was raised white and denied information about her Native American culture, racial and ethnic identity are issues.

Usually, racism is portrayed as a societal flaw. Mickelbury's Maglione, who speaks about hate crimes to groups across Washington, D.C., reflects that

> people were never prepared for the truth of hate in America…. Black people, Hispanic people, Jewish people, gay people, people of all colors— all the people so familiar with hate.[262]

Race and racism are series themes for Lansdale, Mickelbury, and Padgett whose partners include African Americans and for Douglas whose mixed-race Owyhee is paired with a white woman. They are also strong, recurring themes in Hartman's series, even though his partners are both white. Other authors address racism in individual books. Cutler deals specifically with prejudice against Palestinians in *Shot on Location*. Lanyon touches on the treatment of Chinese in *A Dangerous Thing* and Johnson highlights the exploitation of Mexicans—particularly illegal aliens, in *The Woman Who Found Grace*.

As with homophobia and sexism, the negative racist images are countered by positive characterizations. Padgett's Roxie Bouchie is a dynamic forensic psychiatrist, Mickelbury's Patterson is a top-notch reporter, Maney's Jones is a fine police detective, Douglas' Kerry Owyhee is good at almost everything she does, and Lansdale's Pine is sometimes larger than life. Hap describes Pine after he has torched a neighborhood crack house:

> Leonard standing on the front porch, smoke boiling out behind him.... He was like some kind of backwoods honky nightmare vision of the Devil—a nigger with a bad attitude and the power of fire.[263]

Humor

According to Hartman, humor is

> one of the best ways to define character: The things that a character finds funny, the wry observations he makes about the world, will tell a reader more about him than almost anything else.

Humor is a tradition in partnered detectives that began with Christie's Tommy and Tuppence Beresford. It was carried into hard-boiled literature by Hammett's *The Thin Man* and continues today in both mainstream and gay/lesbian partnership series.

Characters and Situations

Since the release of Aldyne's *Vermillion*, comic characters and situations have been a staple in gay/lesbian partnership series. Most of them are secondary characters, but main characters don't escape the skewer. The parade of wacky leading ladies and gentlemen includes Cutler's Rayford Goodman, Lansdale's Collins and Pine, Maney's Cherry Aimless, Outland's McCandler and Van de Kamp, and Stukas' Michael Stark and Monette O'Reilley.

These and other characters often find themselves in bizarre situations. An angry squirrel turns the tables on Lansdale's squirrel hunting. Hap reports that

> the sound of an angry squirrel is not to be forgotten. It is high-pitched and shrill enough to twist your jockeys up your crack.[264]

Aldyne's partners become involved in several outrageous and campy stage productions. On her first day working as a perfume demonstrator at a department store, Outland's Binky Van de Kamp finds herself in the midst of a protest. When a police officer asks Binky if she knows Kenny and other protesters

> Kenny, looking at her, nodded once. Binky nodded back. "Nodding acquaintances," she said truthfully.[265]

Language Play

Authors play with language in a variety of ways. Steward's series is filled with snappy banter involving sex, puns, or both.

> "You smelled as if you'd fallen into the lickerish barrel," Gertrude said. "I mean licorice, I always pronounce them the same."
> "It was both barrels," said Johnny. "Lickerish and licorice. Or maybe you could even combine the two, lust and anise, and come up with liquor-ish."[266]

Sexual allusions also swirl around Maney's oblivious Cherry Aimless.

Aldyne plays with surnames starting with those of his partners (Lovelace and Valentine) and Maney's primary partner is Cherry Aimless. Steward has a secondary character named Vain; Rev. Stonewall is a homophobic Baptist minister in Hartman's *The Gumshoe, the Witch, and the Virtual Corpse*; and in Dymmoch's series Officers Noir (French for *black*) and Azul (Spanish for *blue*) are partners.

Both Outland and Hunter have humorous book titles. Hunter admits that "I chose the titles so there would be no question about what the books were: funny and gay."

Padgett's McCarron notes funny sociolinguistic patterns, including her own.

> "You surprise me, Dr. McCarron."
> "In what way, Dr. Nugent?" I replied. We were playing doctor.[267]

Stukas, whose series satirizes everything in sight, could be speaking for other authors when he observes

> First, I need to make people laugh.... I mean, many of the issues that wander into the crosshairs of my satiric eye could make you jump off a ledge if you thought about them enough. That's not me. I deal with these issues with humor—it's the only way I can handle them.

NATHAN ALDYNE: *Daniel Valentine and Clarisse Lovelace* (1980–1986)

Nathan Aldyne is the pseudonym for the collaboration of Michael McDowell and Dennis Schuetz. These are the only mysteries by Schuetz, who died of complications from AIDS in 1989. McDowell (1950–2000) was a novelist whose *Blackwater* serial novels assured him a place in horror-fiction history, and a screenwriter whose works include *Beetlejuice* and *The Nightmare Before Christmas*. In addition to the Lovelace-Valentine series, McDowell and Schuetz cowrote other novels under the pseudonym Axel Young.

Detectives: Daniel Valentine, bartender and manager of the Slate bar (gay); Clarisse Lovelace, various jobs and law student (heterosexual)

Setting: Boston. Time period is contemporary with publication dates

Books: *Vermilion* (1980); *Cobalt* (1982); *Slate* (1984); *Canary* (1986)

Publishers: Ballentine Press, Alyson Publications

This is the first gay/lesbian partnership series. Its partners are a gay bartender and a heterosexual woman-about-town who develop a powerful and lasting friendship that includes solving the murders of gay men. Aldyne's four novels blazed a trail for other gay writers, including Orland Outland, creator of the Doan McCandler–Binky Van de Kamp series described later in this chapter.

> My inspiration for writing the series at all was the Nathan Aldyne books. I loved them. I loved Clarissa Lovelace, obviously. But Dan Valentine was very butch.

The series is immersed in the gay community of the 1980s and gives readers a good look at the pre-AIDS gay bar and party scene. Most of the action takes place in gay bars, in part, because Daniel Valentine is a bartender and later, manages a gay bar owned by Lovelace's uncle.

Valentine is a good-looking man who enjoys short-term sexual liaisons. Unfortunately, he often finds himself fending off equally handsome, marriage-minded suitors. He is serious, savvy, and a hard worker who began tending bar to supplement his income as a counselor in a prison. His integrity led him to blow the whistle on his boss for illegal activities. That ended Valentine's career in corrections.

Lovelace is Valentine's best friend and equal partner in sleuthing. She's a beautiful, somewhat narcissistic woman whose forceful personality balances Daniel's quiet pragmatism. Her intelligence pushes her to seek challenges, but she flounders professionally until she begins law school. By the start of *Canary*, the final book in the series, she's received her degree and plans to begin her law career.

The two are virtually inseparable—except when they are in the arms of their many transient lovers. The bond between them is so strong that at one point, Valentine tells a would-be husband that "Clarisse ... is the love of my life."[268] Clarisse would no doubt describe him in the same way.

The mysteries have clever plot lines that are filled with red herrings and other diversionary techniques, such as parties and extravaganzas. Dan and Clarisse are surrounded by a host of stereotypic and oddball characters who add both humor and threat to the stories. In *Cobalt*, for example, a wacky lesbian server in a Provincetown restaurant who calls herself the "Swiss Miss" yodels as she wheels the dessert cart through the restaurant. At the other end of the spectrum is the violent and homophobic police detective in *Vermillion* who is investigating the murder of a gay hustler.

The book titles are one-word color terms that figure into the stories: *Vermillion* is the color of the lipstick found on the murder victim's handkerchief, *Cobalt* is the color of a murdered man's eyes, *Slate* is the color of the walls inside Noah Lovelace's bar, and *Canary* is the color of the canary who becomes the bar's mascot.

Despite its pre-AIDS setting, the series addresses a number of issues that still face the gay community. They include drug- and alcohol-dependence, the closet, and, of course, homophobia.

STAN CUTLER: *Mark Bradley and Rayford Goodman* (1991–1994)

Stan Cutler is a veteran television screenwriter. The first two books in the Goodman-Bradley series were nominated for Lambda awards, and Cutler has also been nominated for the P.I. Writers of America Shamus Award. He lives in Los Angeles with his artist wife.

Detectives: Mark Bradley, ghost-writer (gay); Rayford Goodman, private investigator (heterosexual)

Setting: Los Angeles. Time period is contemporary with publication dates

Books: *Best Performance by a Patsy* (1991); Finalist Shamus Award—Best First Novel (1992); *The Face on the Cutting Room Floor* (1991); *Shot on Location* (1993); *Rough Cut* (1994)

Publisher: Dutton Books

This series lampoons everyone and everything in sight, including the two main characters and the mystery genre. The humor begins with the pairing of retired PI Rayford "fixer to the stars" Goodman and ghost writer Mark Bradley. The men are as ill-suited a pair as one could possibly imagine. "I personally thought the Bradley character was simply a good 'mismatch' ... to generate conflict and humor." The mismatch comes from a variety of sources: "the fact that one is gay and one is straight is extremely important and the basis for the character conflict. One is also liberal and one is not; one is alcoholic and one is not; one smokes pot and one does not."

Initially, they are obliged to work together so that Bradley can ghost write Goodman's autobiography. The success of that book forces them into further collaborations. The books in this series are also collaborative. They are written in the first person with Rayford as narrator in one chapter and Mark as narrator in the next.

Both Bradley and Goodman are intentionally drawn as cliché characters. "Goodman, as a reactionary, right-wing semi-alcoholic is a familiar character and one people recognize and are comfortable with (from early movies, W.C. Fields, for example), even in his prejudices and biases." His moniker "fixer to the stars" comes from "Goodman's halcyon days in service to the studios. That was often political, bagman stuff for the powers that be.... If there was trouble, he would fix it. If there was scandal, he would squelch it." In contrast, Bradley is a yuppy gay man. "Bradley is/was to the nineties a near-paragon in the way Sidney Poitier was in the sixties and seventies, and that, too, is comfortable for the reader." Each man is also a skilled professional. "Rayford is really quite good at his job, more intuitive than even he might realize, and actually the one who wraps up the cases and makes the final connections that lead to a solution. (Conversely, Mark does practically all the 'writing' for the team.)"

The series is rooted in the movie world of Hollywood. The book titles refer to aspects of film making (e.g., *Best Performance by a Patsy*, *Shot on Location*), the stories are populated by Hollywood stereotypes, and the crimes are motivated by fear of exposure, greed, abuse of power, and the battle against aging. "I truly do not know what the themes are in this series, except as they naturally occur in the storytelling." This is true for gay themes, as well, which are by-products of the main characters and events in the stories.

Cutler began each book with a story idea "then crafted it for my two characters. I seldom get a bolt of lighting IDEA! I sit down and plot and plod." To some extent, his approach to writing grew out of his experience in television. "Because I wrote so much TV, I was used to short scenes ... and so came to write very short chapters, each of which end with a rising action." There are, however, important differences between the two kinds of writing. "Book writing is an especial delight—being able to work over an extended period of time on the same project, rather than the short intensive work on a TV show episode, then starting all over on another so soon. TV, too, has so many time constraints, it must be so many pages per half hour, almost exactly—so many pages for an hour show. It must contain a specific number of act breaks for commercials, which affects your construction.... Whereas a book can be almost whatever you want— or require—to tell your story your own way."

LAUREN WRIGHT DOUGLAS:
Allison O'Neil and Kerry Owyhee (1996–1997)

Lambda award winner Lauren Wright Douglas (1947–) was born in Canada in 1947 and grew up in an itinerant military family. Before settling in coastal Oregon, she lived in Europe, British Columbia, and the southwestern United States. In addition to the Allison O'Neil and Kerry Owyhee series, she's written a second (award-winning) mystery series about lesbian PI Caitlin Reece (see the section on private investigators), short stories, and stand-alone novels, including one under the pseudonym Zenobia Vole.

Detectives: Allison O'Neil, owner of a mail-order book distributorship and bed and breakfast hotel (lesbian); Kerry Owyhee, private investigator (lesbian)

Setting: Lavner Bay, Oregon. Time period is contemporary with publication dates

Books: *Death at Lavender Bay* (1996); *Swimming Cat Cove* (1997)

Publisher: The Naiad Press

It would seem that a white book distributor and a mixed-race (Native American and white) private investigator would have little in common. Ironically, the lives of Allison O'Neil and Kerry Owyhee have striking parallels. Neither completed her college degree (dropped out and kicked out for Indian activism); they both recently moved to Oregon from their home states (California and Alaska) and are starting new lives; they each have just come into money (an inheritance and insurance payment); they've both lost their parents; and neither feels she belongs anywhere.

O'Neil's alienation comes from her sexual orientation. "Is this what it means to be a lesbian? Never to have a family?"[269] And Owyhee's comes primarily from being raised white and prevented from learning about her Native American background. "To say I'm ambivalent about being an Indian would be an understatement."[270] Much later, the "gaydar" of a tourist staying at O'Neil's newly inherited bed and breakfast alerts O'Neil to another layer of Owyhee's alienation that is not addressed in the series.

The two meet in *Death at Lavender Bay*, the first novel in the two-book series, when O'Neil begins to view the drowning death of her Aunt Grace as suspicious and hires Owyhee to find out. They collaborate on the investigation because Owyhee was injured in an arson fire and cannot do "leg work." In the process of uncovering the true nature of Aunt Grace's demise, O'Neil helps Owyhee reconcile with her Native American family and her tribe.

Owyhee's status as a licensed investigator and her experience working as an investigative researcher for Pinkerton enable the pair to access official documents and handle dangerous situations. She also harbors a well-reasoned disdain for Lavender Bay's sexist and racist police department. O'Neil's contributions to the partnership include an ability to mingle with the largely white and lesbian community and her aptitude for gleaning information from seemingly casual conversations.

By the end of *Swimming Cat Cove* both women have matured and become more integrated in their respective communities. Both of them still have much to learn.

MICHAEL ALLEN DYMMOCH: *Jack Caleb and John Thinnes* (1993–CURRENT)

Michael Allen Dymmoch (pseudonym, real name undisclosed) is a professional driver who lives and works in the Chicago metropolitan area. She has degrees in chemistry and law enforcement. In addition to the Caleb-Thinnes series, she's written short stories and a stand-alone romance. She was president and secretary of the Midwest Chapter of Mystery Writers of America and served five years as newsletter editor for the Chicagoland chapter of Sister in Crime.

Detectives: Dr. James Caleb, psychologist, North Michigan Avenue Associates, consultant to the Chicago PD (gay); Homicide Detective John Thinnes, Chicago PD (heterosexual)

Setting: Chicago. Time period is contemporary with publication dates

Books: *The Man Who Understood Cats* (1993); Malice Domestic Award—Best First Traditional Mystery (1993); *The Death of Blue Mountain Cat* (1996); *Incendiary Designs* (1998); *Feline Friendship* (2003)

Publisher: St. Martin's Press

Jack Caleb and John Thinnes meet in *The Man Who Understood Cats* when one of Caleb's patients is murdered and Caleb becomes Thinnes' chief suspect. "*The Man Who Understood Cats* was originally intended to be the screenplay for a cop-buddy film. So at least one character had to be a cop.... According to the formula, the cop's 'buddy' has to be someone he starts the story hating or suspecting. Traditional cops didn't have any use for 'faggots' or shrinks. So a gay shrink provides twice the conflict. A rich, gay shrink is gravy." By the end of the book Caleb accepts a position as the department's psychological consultant.

When the series begins, Caleb is in deep mourning over his dead lover and Thinnes has become a workaholic and has shut down emotionally. By the end of *Feline Friendship*, Caleb has broken out of his depression and taken a new lover. "Jack is almost too good to be true—intelligent, self-aware, curious, civilized, disciplined, compassionate, and rich enough to indulge his whims.... The fact that he is gay is not a particular issue. He was born that way and accepts it as he accepts that he has blue eyes and is right-handed. Since he is a shrink, he understands and is not thrown by other people's homophobia."

Thinnes is emerging from his shell as well. "John is loyal, faithful, and obsessive. He is probably not a great husband—too wedded to his job. He has no ambition beyond being a detective. Left to himself, he would probably work for free on his vacations. His homophobia is not consciously chosen or deeply held. He is not liberal by choice, but by nature is a good detective—which requires an open mind." For example, "meeting Caleb made him abandon any stereotype Thinnes may have had about homosexuals."

Themes are very important in this series. "Each book has one or more different (I hope universally important) theme(s). In book one I tried to explore loss/depression, homophobia, and rage. In book two it was art; book three deals with arson, passion, and religious fanaticism; book four explores battle lines in the war between the sexes." One of those battle lines is rape, which assumes a prominent place in book four, *Feline Friendship*.

"I start with the question: 'What would happen if...?' Collectively the characters embody my positions on different subjects (Thinnes's ideas about the average driver, the death penalty, or art, for instance; Caleb's love of cats, reading, and music). For the most part, though, I try to tell a story that satisfies me (so at least one person will enjoy it). I agree with Stephen King that often you have to finish the book to discover the theme—which is what it's really about."

The cat/feline theme flows through the stories. In particular, human behavior is clarified by references to comparable cat behavior. In *Feline Friendship*, for example, Caleb likens the animosity between Thinnes and his new partner to bringing a new cat into a household.

> At first, there's usually a good deal of hissing and growling. And once in a while the fur flies. But if you make it clear that fighting won't be toler-

ated, the hissing ought to diminish over time. They might even become friends.[271]

"If I live long enough, I could write at least ten more books in this series. I have story ideas about gay bashing, hydrophobia, repressed memory syndrome, art counterfeiting, jazz, baseball, the war on drugs."

KEITH HARTMAN: *Drew Parker and Jennifer Grey* (1998–CURRENT)

Keith Hartman (1966–) grew up in Huntsville, Alabama. After graduating from Princeton University, he studied finance but realized he preferred writing. His first book, the Lambda-nominated *Congregations in Conflict*, examined how nine different churches dealt with homosexuality. *The Gumshoe, the Witch, and the Virtual Corpse* was Hartman's first published novel. He's written a collection of horror stories featuring gay men and lesbians, a play, and short films.

Detectives: Drew Parker, PI (gay); Jennifer (Jen) Grey, PI (heterosexual)

Setting: Atlanta, Georgia. Starts in 2024

Books: *The Gumshoe, the Witch, and the Virtual Corpse* (1998); Drood Review of Mysteries One of the Eight Best Mystery Novels of the Year (1999); Finalist Lambda Award—Best Gay Men's Mystery (1999); *Gumshoe Gorilla* (2001)

Publisher: Meisha Merlin Publishing, Inc.

This series blends numerous genres. "Personally I classify it as a noir sci-fi mystery with elements of dark fantasy and a strong undercurrent of social satire.... I wanted to write a science fiction series, because I grew up reading science fiction and I love the way that you can use it for social commentary. I wanted to write a mystery series, because I love the idea of a search for the truth. And I decided to go with the multiple narrator structure because it would be fun and let me explore the truth from multiple points of view."

The series begins in 2024 when the United States is sharply polarized along racial, religious, and sexual-orientation lines. Homophobia and racism are rampant, and a test for the "gay gene" has led to widespread use of abortion (except by Catholics). "Keeping the story in the near future, say only twenty years away, keeps me honest. I have to explain why the world has come to be this way, and I have to convince the reader that this could reasonably happen."

Drew Parker and Jen Grey, the main characters, co-own three private-investigation firms: one (headed by Drew) works on cases in the gay community; one (headed by Jen) does psychic detection, and Fortress Security serves corporate clients.

"Jen is just this force of nature that goes blowing through the world damning the consequences. So when she hits a big life change, it takes her by surprise...." She's a Wiccan warrior-witch with psychic abilities. "Drew is the kind of cool character that I wish I could be.... Drew analyzes everything going on in his life, and questions his own motives, and wrestles with some really difficult ethical decisions.... Drew pretty much gave up on religion after his Baptist father kicked him out of the house because he tested positive for the gay gene. And Drew wasn't really looking for a new religion." So he's not thrilled when he starts having visions following an encounter with a Cherokee shaman.

They are joined by a plethora of amateur and professional detectives. "One of the major themes of the books is how different people in different subcultures see the world in different ways. One of the more interesting ways to explore that was to have several people hunting for the truth, and show how their preconceptions shape what they see....

"So if you're a Southern Baptist, you get all your news from the Christian News Network, you send your kids to Southern Baptist private schools, and watch only Southern Baptist entertainment programming. So you have an extreme world view that isn't challenged by any outside voices. And Wiccans do the same thing, and Mormons, and gay men, and all these other little subcultures.

"So, in order to show how those different subcultures view the world in radically different ways, I had to have narrators from each of those subcultures telling the story." Which leads to another core theme: "the question, '*How do we know what's true?*' That's one of the core problems of the human condition—when to believe what everyone else tells you, and when to strike out on your own."

Hartman begins work on a book by reading through a file of "ideas" that he maintains. "As I read, I'll start to see how certain ideas can fit together. So, the decisions about theme, character, and plot are all kind of made at the same time. And hopefully in a way where they all reinforce each other."

FRED HUNTER: *Alex Reynolds, Peter Livesay, and Jean Reynolds* (1997–CURRENT)

Fred Hunter (1954–) is a lifelong Chicagoan. In addition to the Alex Reynolds series, he writes a mystery series about heterosexual homicide detective Jeremy Ransom who is assisted by an elderly woman. He's published short stories, nonfiction articles, and reviews. Hunter works part-time for a private investigation firm in Chicago.

Detectives: Alex Reynolds, self-employed commercial artist (gay); Peter Livesay, retail sales employee (gay); Jean Reynolds, independently wealthy (heterosexual)

Setting: Primarily Chicago. Time period is contemporary with publication dates

Books: *Government Gay* (1997); *Federal Fag* (1998); Finalist Lambda Award—Best Gay Men's Mystery (1998); *Capital Queers* (1999); *National Nancys* (2000); *The Chicken Asylum* (2001)

Publisher: St. Martin's Press

These comedies follow the adventures of an investigative trio. Alex Reynolds, the first-person narrator, is "exuberant and enthusiastic in a way that's almost childlike." Peter Livesay, Alex' husband, "is the more intelligent of the two. He is the sane member of the duo, Alex's anchor." Jean Reynolds, Alex' mother, is a widow whose inheritance enabled her to buy the home they all live in. "She's based on my oldest friend in the world, Joan Edwards. She's a magical type of person. Magic follows wherever she goes, like Mary Poppins....

"Alex's relationship to his mother and his relationship to Peter are incredibly symbiotic. I wanted these people to be extremely close.... Alex and Peter's relationship was a definite, conscious decision on my part. I wanted their relationship to be a given. There would be no question about the fact they are simply a very happily married couple."

At the start of *Government Gay*, the first book in the series, they live a quiet, comfortable life—until a foreign agent passes Alex secret information in a gay bar. That brief encounter plunges them into a world of murder and international intrigue. Alex launches himself and the others into these adventures with visions of classic movies dancing in his head. "I suddenly felt like Olivia de Havilland in the movie *Government Girl*— ready to bypass the system, take on the big boys, and fight for what was right. All right, so in my case it was '*Government Gay*.'"[272]

In the process of solving crimes, the trio exposes government agents and political figures who are corrupt, corruptible, or incompetent. "I got flak from gay people because I didn't do gay issues. There are some in the later books, but that's not what the books are about—it's just what they run into. For example, they face homophobia in the police.... I *will* admit that I chose the titles so there would be no question about what the books were: funny and gay. But the politicizing of everything is agonizing. I've even been accused of using the term 'husband' for political reasons....

"The most important political thing in the Alex Reynolds books is that their sexuality is not an issue. That was an absolutely conscious decision on my part. It is treated as normal—just like everybody else." And, even though the stories are not embedded in gay culture, Alex and Peter encounter segments of the community, including political "queers," barflies, stereotypic queens, and gay-porn stars.

"Since this series is supposed to be fun, it can go off in pretty wild directions. I play a lot of 'What if this happened?' or 'Wouldn't it be funny if....' I really enjoy that, and I don't do it with the other series." Humor also arises from the personalities of the characters and situations. For example, when Jean becomes emotional, her proper British accent begins to lose its 'aitches. So, when she discovered the size of the inheritance from her dead husband, she exclaimed, "that bloody bastard was insured up to his bloomin' arse!"[273] And, at a party in *Federal Fag* "Most of the talk that flitted our way consisted of 'fuck this' and 'fuck that' and 'fucking something else,'.... Basically it was like riding the bus in Chicago."[274]

These elements combine to form entertaining stories that touch on issues, relationships, and, in some cases, moral dilemmas that are part of the fabric of everyday life.

BETT REECE JOHNSON: *Cordelia Morgan and partners* (1998–CURRENT)

Bett Reece Johnson (1945–) was born in Fountainhead, Tennessee. She has a Ph.D. in English and taught full-time before leaving in 1996 to write fiction full-time. She has a daughter who lives in San Francisco, and she presently lives in rural New Mexico with seven cats, one dog, one parrot, two koi, and four horses.

Detectives: Cordelia (Cord) Morgan, fugitive and former spy/research specialist; Various women partners

Settings: Various U.S. locations. Time period is contemporary with publication dates

Books: *The Woman Who Knew Too Much* (1998); *The Woman Who Rode to the Moon* (1999); *The Woman Who Found Grace* (2003)

Publisher: Cleis Press Inc.

When the series begins, Morgan is a highly skilled agent of The Company, "an organization that will do anything, literally *anything*, for a price." She's "autonomy personified. Every independent woman's dream, every macho man's nightmare. A woman with a serious Attitude." She can probe into people's psyches, sense events before they happen, and she has a remarkable affinity with animals, possibly because she's somewhat feral herself.

The series tracks Morgan's personal odyssey, which begins after her break with The Company, in combination with mysteries surrounding the women whose lives intersect with Morgan's. "Anna Lee/Jet, Sym, Gracie—they're all strong women, of course, with enough Attitude of their own to tweak Morgan. They are all weighted down by some form of guilt.... At the same time, they're also the 'walking wounded,' victims of some injustice in their pasts.... Being mired in the past, they're not really quite alive in the present. Morgan comes along and sets them free." They, in turn, teach Morgan about pieces of her own identity.

"In various ways, all the characters—even Morgan—have gaping dark abysses in their understanding of themselves and what's happened to them. Part of what Morgan does for all three protagonists is to shine some light into those spaces. On the narrative surface, it's a matter of Morgan digging up evidence ... and solving the crime, but beyond the trappings of the mystery novel, what she really provides are the pieces that each character needs in order to make sense of her life and bring her out into the world again.... But Morgan is the real central character, and all the books are really one book when it comes to following her on her route to self-knowledge....

"Each book begins with a character under pressure, less than a situation. I'm sure it's no secret that my novels are 'character driven' rather than 'plot driven.' I'm interested in people more than in finding the murderer, more in pursuing questions than in proscribing answers...." One of those questions involves "the central conflict between morality and justice, and how they're related. That is, if a horrifying crime has been committed and the means of justice are not available, how can justice be found?... As Morgan says in book one, 'If we live in an accidental universe, as opposed to one created by god, it's all guesswork, right? You can do anything, and it's okay.' I think all of the books to date have been about Morgan working out some kind of morality system of her own making." That system can be harsh and is not always shared by the main protagonist: the woman who is embroiled in a mystery.

The stories are told in the first person by Morgan and the main protagonist. "The main protagonist in each book leans more to the 'genre mystery' tone and action. It's in the Morgan sections that I can get the 'poetry' in." For example, "Dark angry clouds filled the space between his words"[275] and

> On the topside of the earth, there is no such thing as true darkness. You can only get that if you go down under, into the caves. The same is true for people.[276]

JOE R. LANSDALE: *Hap Collins and Leonard Pine* (1990–CURRENT)

Award-winning author Joe R. Lansdale (1951–) is from Texas. He holds belts in several martial arts, he's a two-time inductee into the International Martial Arts Hall of Fame, and he founded the Shen Chuan Martial Science. He owns and teaches at Lansdale's Self Defense Systems martial-arts studio. Lansdale has written numerous short stories and over twenty books which have earned him awards in fantasy, horror, and mystery. Lansdale lives with his wife in Nacogdoches, Texas.

Detectives: Leonard Pine (gay) and Hap Collins (heterosexual), intermittently employed laborers

Setting: LaBorde, Texas. Time period is contemporary with publication dates

Books: *Savage Season* (1990); Finalist Bram Stoker Horror Award (1990); *Mucho Mojo* (1994); *The Two-Bear Mambo* (1995); *Bad Chili* (1997); *Rumble Tumble* (1998); *Captains Outrageous* (2001)

Publisher: Warner Books

Leonard Pine is a violent and angry Vietnam vet with a superman complex and remarkable combat skills. He's also African American and gay and proud. "Leonard standing on the front porch, smoke boiling out behind him.... He was like some kind of backwoods honky nightmare vision of the Devil—a nigger with a bad attitude and the power of fire."[277] Hap Collins, the first-person narrator of the series, is a romantic but rudderless Vietnam War draft dodger with a college degree and a prison record. He's also white and heterosexual. "I know you, a good-lookin' woman comes along and plays the right tune, you dance."[278]

Pine and Collins are an unlikely pair of vigilantes. Nevertheless, the crimes they battle include child molestation, white slavery, gay snuff films, and drug pushing. The scalawags who burn in the fires of their indignation range from chiefs of police and captains of industry to crack-house residents and renegade bikers.

Despite the gravity of the criminal activities they encompass, these novels are rollicking escapades. They teem with wacky characters (whose nicknames include Parade Float, Horse Dick, and Booger) engaged in nefarious schemes and wielding a profusion of weaponry. Their shenanigans inflame Pine and Collins who hurl themselves into the fray with exuberant foolhardiness. "It's police business when they want to make it their business. They don't make it their business, then I got to make it *my* business."[279] Statements like that launch the plots onto wild and twisting roller-coaster rides that end in explosions, fires, and free-for-alls.

The dialogue-heavy language is as unfettered and politically incorrect as the plot lines. Hap's take on police corruption is "When I was growing up, a guy with a badge was just assumed to be honest.... These days, Jesus would carry a gun, and the disciples would hold down and corn-hole their enemies."[280] Leonard's view of spousal abuse is "Guy beats a woman on a daily basis, and one day she's had enough, it's okay she sets the guy's head on fire."[281] A business tycoon is one of many who freely express their racism and homophobia. "I know the nigger here is a dick sucker and a pervert too."[282] To which our two heroes respond

> "Ixnay on the iggernay and the ervertpay," I said.
> "Yeah," Leonard said, "I don't like it."[283]

JOSH LANYON: *Adrien English and Jake Riordan* (2000–CURRENT)

Josh Lanyon was born in Great Britain. The Adrien English books are his first published novels. He's a writer and reviewer in Los Angeles.

Detective: Adrien English, bookseller, author of crime stories (gay); LAPD Homicide Detective Jake Riordan (gay)

Settings: Los Angeles and Sonoma, CA. Time period is contemporary with publication dates

Books: *Fatal Shadows* (2000); *A Dangerous Thing* (2002)

Publishers: Millivres Books, Gay Men's Press

LAPD Homicide Detective Jake Riordan and bookseller/mystery writer Adrien English are about as different as two people can be. English is the openly gay scion of a well-to-do California family whose bookstore is reputed to have a superb collection of gay and gothic whodunits. He enjoys reading, listening to opera, and other sedentary pastimes. He has a quick mind and a sharp tongue. Until the start of the series his only experiences with murder came from the books he's read and written.

Riordan is a "man's man" who enjoys fishing, camping, and drinking beer. He thinks that "the only thing worse than opera is someone who hums along with opera"[284] (like English). He deals with violence and death on a daily basis in his job and, after work, engages in leathersex scenes with other men. He fears and detests anything about himself that could suggest he might not be a full-fledged supercop—especially his homosexual desires. He's "a homosexual cop buried so deep in the closet he didn't know where to look for himself."[285]

The differences in their personalities and backgrounds add spice to their personal relationship and detecting partnership. Riordan relies on logic based on physical evidence and interrogation. His belief that detecting should be left to professionals also leads him to shield English from the danger that will surely result from his attempts to emulate fictional sleuths. English is more intuitive, interested in interpersonal relationships, and inclined to use library research as an investigative tool. Both approaches prove their value for solving cases of multiple killings that mix murder with chess, greed with mysticism, and history with legend.

Riordan acts as a buffer between English and the law-enforcement agencies who want to incarcerate him for offenses that range from "constructive possession" of a controlled substance to murder. English is Riordan's pathway to self-acceptance. Even though Riordan is eight years older than English, "I sometimes felt like his mentor or Fag Big Brother...."[286] Indeed, by the end of *A Dangerous Thing* Riordan has not only developed a grudging respect for English, he's taken vital steps towards accepting his love for another man.

LAUREN MADDISON: *Connor Hawthorne and the team* (1999–CURRENT)

Lauren Maddison holds a B.A. in political science and an M.A. in religious studies and is pursuing a doctoral degree. She's Associate Director of the Institute for Spiritual Leadership at the Unity Church in Tustin, California, where she lives. She also has a teaching credential from Emerson Institute.

Detectives: Connor Hawthorne, author and former prosecutor (lesbian); Laura Nez, security specialist and Connor's lover (lesbian); Benjamin Hawthorne, presidential advisor, ex-senator and Connor's father (heterosexual); Capt. Malcolm Jefferson, Washington Metro PD and Connor's friend (heterosexual); Gwendolyn Broadhurst, high priestess of "the Circle" and Connor's grandmother (heterosexual)

Settings: Various U.S and British locations. Time period is contemporary with publication dates

Books: *Deceptions* (1999); *Witchfire* (2001); *Death by Prophecy* (2002); Finalist Lambda Award—Best Lesbian Mystery (2002); *Epitaph for an Angel* (2003)

Publisher: Alyson Publications

The cosmic struggle between good and evil produces the murders and other crimes that occur in these novels. The forces of good are defended by a team led by Connor Hawthorne whose investigative and restorative efforts lie equally in the spiritual and physical spheres.

"The team came to life, one by one, at first to fulfill the needs of my plot.... Later, as the characters took on more depth, they served the story's unfolding at a deeper level than simply having the perfect skill set. I imagined them, and then they began telling the story.... I wanted Connor and the entire cast to emerge as people with various strengths, as well as weaknesses for which others could help compensate. I also gave the reader other people to care about or admire—individuals of different professions, ideologies, ethnic backgrounds, all of them able to work together, especially when the chips are down." Gwendolyn Broadhurst continues her participation in the group even after death—which is consistent with the spiritual bent of the series.

Connor is "still struggling with issues of faith, and also with the idea that there are vast gray areas where logic and rules don't serve as particularly effective guides. She was successful, if not deeply happy, in her former career as a prosecutor because she is, at heart, an achiever. But, like many people in that profession, she burned out and then moved into the relatively solitary life of a novelist.... Her tidy world is turned upside down when she's caught up in myths and legends come to life, and forced to confront the inexplicable.... She's begun to accept her spiritual destiny, however grudgingly. Part of the reason she's been able to do that is because of her relationship with Laura [a Navaho], whose matter-of-fact acceptance of magic and mystery smoothes the way for Connor.... She has yet to assume her rightful place as high priestess of the Circle, or dissolve enough of her human ego to do it with both grace and humility....

"While Connor's lesbianism is not the central issue of any of these mystery novels, it *is* an important quality of *her* character. Her conflicts with her mother and dozens of other people in her life have arisen from that one aspect of who she is. Her calm determination to be exactly who she is colors her interactions with others. Still, I believe we each find our challenges as we go through life. Homosexuality presents a particular set of assets and liabilities for a person living in the world. But so do race, religion, physical disability, gender, height, weight, economic circumstance, education ... etc."

Maddison lists the following as the major themes of the series:

> 1) There is so much more to the existence than what we think is "real" in our limited third-dimensional view. Therein lies the real magic of the universe.
> 2) We can determine how we will deal with conflict, and learn to see it as something we've drawn into our lives for a purpose, rather than becoming professional victims of the deeds of 'others.'
> 3) We have a destiny that we ourselves have chosen at some level.
> 4) We can indeed lead with our hearts and choose not to succumb to impulses toward greed, hatred, prejudice, callousness, and separation.
> 5) We must really avoid taking ourselves too seriously....

"I'd also add laughter. I know, sounds silly. But the ability to see the absurdity in life is critical to preserving one's sanity."

MABEL MANEY: *Nancy Clue, Cherry Aimless, and friends* (1993–1995)

Mabel Maney (1958–) is a visual artist living in San Francisco. She grew up in the midwestern United States and has a Bachelors of Fine Arts from Ohio State University and a Master of Fine Arts degree from San Francisco State University. Her installation art and handmade books earned her fellowships from The San Francisco Foundation and San Francisco State University. The Nancy Clue/Cherry Aimless and Hardly Boys handmade art books were included in the Bad Girls exhibition at New York's New Museum of Contemporary Art and Los Angeles' County Museum. There have been radio broadcasts and stage plays based upon the Nancy Clue series. Maney also writes a series of lesbian parodies of the James Bond spy thrillers.

Detectives: Nancy Clue, "girl detective," and friends

Settings: River Depths, Illinois, and San Francisco. Time period is the 1950s.

Books: *The Case of the Not-so-Nice-Nurse* (1993); *The Case of the Good-for-Nothing-Girlfriend* (1994); *A Ghost in the Closet* (1995)

Publisher: Cleis Press

These novels parody the popular Nancy Drew, Cherry Ames, and Hardy Boys juvenile-detective series. With one exception, the detectives come from the original series—but they've reemerged as lesbians or gay men. Jackie Jones, the exception, is an African American detective in the San Francisco PD. "The originals are so white the pages are practically transparent. I love the idea of giving a black woman in the 1950s official authority." There's an "'all-for-one-and-one-for-all' attitude of the characters, and the creation of a family that won't shun you. Unless, of course, you wear white after Labor Day."

The series had a complex genesis. "In 1991, while spending a few months in bed recovering from a back injury, I decided to reread the Cherry Ames books I so enjoyed as a girl…. They are a homoerotic, fetishistic cheese fest, escapism of the purest form. Who wouldn't want to live in an all-girl dorm, giggle late into the night, and wear a starched uniform and jaunty cap? … I wondered what life would be like with Cherry. The uniform fixation I could work with, and her experience with medication would come in handy, but her slavish devotion to righting wrongs at the expense of her own health … worried me…. I realized our relationship could never work." When Maney began rereading her Nancy Drew books, "I knew I had the Cherry puzzle solved. She would date Nancy, tormenting her with her goodness, medical advice, and cheese puff recipes."

Underneath the humor, the books address quite a few social issues. The most important to Maney are: "The unspoken pain of women and girls. The chance for redemption. Love." The hardest issue to incorporate was incest. "It's hard to bring up in a book with such an air of enforced innocence. The language had to be right on the mark, the characters true to self. If they speak and act as expected, the information can seep in without being so jarring....

"I decided to use the basic framework of the Nancy Drew originals — a crime is committed, outfits are selected, daring stunts follow, and the girls are victorious — as a framework in which to work out what I detected between the lines: Nancy's creepy wifelike devotion to her father, the missing mother, Nancy's suffocatingly small world, of which she is always the center, and her life of privilege far from those lesser souls who wear unflattering, ill-fitting clothes and whose English is peppered with *foreign phrases*. In this case, I consider the subplot not a second or third complication, but the invasion of these characters into a genre in which their presence would be unthinkable. Adding a layer of social and political messages can be a challenge. You don't want to be heavy-handed or step outside the tone of the original. Most important, I think, is to keep your characters true to self. Cherry, the center of the books, stays her simple, innocent self no matter the circumstances. Whether it's Chief Chumly being dipped in bronze ('It's just like the bronze baby shoes mother has on her bureau, only bigger!')[287] or receiving her first kiss from Nancy ('She wished she had worn panties. She had decided against them so as to preserve the line of her dress, but they would be a big help right now!')[288] Cherry is always painfully perky."

PENNY MICKELBURY: *Gianna Maglione and Mimi Patterson* (1994–CURRENT)

Penny Mickelbury (1948–) was the first African American reporter for the *Banner-Herald* (Athens, Georgia). She's covered politics for ABC-TV and the *Washington Post*, and she's written plays, historical fiction, short stories, and two mystery series. Mickelbury writes, lectures, and teaches in Los Angeles and operates a publishing company, Migibooks, with her partner. The Givens Collection of African American Literature (University of Minnesota) is collecting and curating her papers along with those of other selected African American writers.

Detectives: Lt. Giovanna (Gianna) Maglione, Head of Hate Crimes Unit, Washington, D.C., Metropolitan PD and her lover M. Montgomery (Mimi) Patterson, crime reporter

Setting: Washington, D.C. Time period is contemporary with publication dates

Books: *Keeping Secrets* (1994); *Night Songs* (1995); Finalist Lambda Award—Best Lesbian Mystery (1995); *Love Notes* (2002)

Publishers: Kings Crossing Publishers, Migibooks, The Naiad Press

Mimi Patterson is a top-notch crime reporter, and Gianna Maglione heads the Metropolitan PD's Hate Crimes Unit. "I paired the reporter and the cop because they are natural enemies. All the better to explore different angles of the same issues and subjects; but also it provides a natural tension to the interpersonal relationship that exists between the two women. Building and growing a relationship naturally is a difficult process. To do so between 'natural' enemies provides a lovely challenge for a writer: how do these two women maintain the love and respect they have for each other in the face of the professional disdain they *must* have for each other? It provides a constant challenge for me as a writer to keep the relationship between Mimi and Gianna both tense and loving, and it both forces and allows me to explore social, moral and political issues of importance in contemporary society from different viewpoints.

"It is inherently more difficult to write the Mimi/Gianna books because there almost are two separate plots being developed, two streams of character development, two different and separate points of view—but just the one story. And of course, there's only one plot, but viewing it from two points of view often feels like constructing two plots, because they must be realized separately and differently, because the characters must always feel separate and different."

The third-person narrator shifts smoothly between the two women as they pursue their separate investigations, think about each other, and confront the hatred around them. "Mimi's perspective has emerged as the more dominant because.... I wanted to explore various aspects of the culture from different points of view.... I also did not want to write a police procedural, and I wanted to present the cops as more multidimensional and not as either the ... 'my way or the highway' ... or the surly loner who loves the law but hates the rules of law. This emergence of Mimi's perspective as dominant was, however, unintentional, though certainly it exists."

The primary theme of the series is bigotry and the damage it can cause. The wanton murders of African American prostitutes in *Night Songs* gives Mimi "an acute awareness of the way women are treated just because they're women.... Mimi's almost surly response to her bosses at the beginning of *Love Notes* suggests ... she's not taking any more race- or gender-based crap from anybody." Despite the murders of closeted lesbians and gay men in *Keeping Secrets*, Gianna remains in the closet at work. "Gianna knows that all the hatred isn't 'out there.' ... whatever respect and cooperation she's earned from her peers inside the police department is tenuous because she's a woman, and ... she never forgets that those who fought establishment of the Hate Crimes Unit would shut it down if they learned that a lesbian was in charge....

"Both have accepted their relationship as important, necessary, even, to their lives, and know that they must learn to accommodate that reality, though that lesson remains a work in progress.... Regarding the occasional erotic nature of the Mimi/Gianna relationship: they're both passionate beings engaged in intense and passionate work. They're also new lovers. Sex is and probably will be, for a while, an important part of their relationship and, therefore, of the books."

ORLAND OUTLAND: *Doan McCandler and Binky Van de Kamp* (1997–1999)

Orland Outland (1962–) was raised in Nevada and spent a number of years in San Francisco where he began writing. He has seven published books, including his mystery trilogy and novels about gay relationships. He currently lives in Reno, Nevada.

Detective: Doan McCandler, PI and fashion consultant (gay); Binky Van de Kamp, PI and charitable fund manager (heterosexual)

Settings: Large cities in the U.S. Time period is contemporary with publication dates

Books: *Death Wore a Smart Little Outfit* (1997); *Death Wore a Fabulous New Fragrance* (1998); *Death Wore the Emperor's New Clothes* (1999)

Publisher: Berkley Publishing Group

In this series, friendship between a gay transvestite and a heterosexual socialite evolves into an investigative partnership that cracks fashion- and entertainment-related murder cases in three different cities.

"My inspiration for writing the series at all was the Nathan Aldyne books. I loved them. I loved Clarisse Lovelace, obviously. But Dan Valentine was very butch.... My take was the polar opposite. Part of it is that a person like Doan has a lot of leeway.... A person like that is dismissed easily. A drag queen. How nonthreatening is that? The idea that a drag queen could go out there and fix people's wagons was something I hadn't seen."

Doan would take immediate offense at that description of him—with some justification. ("I am *not* a drag queen.... I do *not* wear makeup, I do *not* pretend to be a woman."[289]) "The character was entirely of my own creation, but I had a physical role model for him. It was a performer named Justin Bond who lived in San Francisco when I did.... He's a very feminine-looking man. His early shtick was Julie London. He has long straight hair and wore a dress. He was willowy and feline. He just looked kind of girly but not because of makeup or eyelashes and fingernails. That was my physical model for Doan: someone who was not a drag queen but who did wear a dress."

Binky's character was based on Outland's friend, Nancy. "She was not a disinherited socialite, but we both felt that we were so good at spending money we should have had more of it.... We wrote to entertain ourselves and each other. Like Binky and Doan, we would get together over pastry and champagne and exchange chapters."

Both Binky and Doan mature as the series progresses. "At first Binky is very forthright about being a 'ho.' Men are for using and throwing away. By the third book, she's deeply involved in a relationship. When you meet them in the first book, they are basically in dead-end jobs. Their reasons for getting up in the morning have nothing to do with how they make their living. Whereas by the end of the series, what they are doing certainly has meaning for them and it's fun."

The series uses humor to address serious issues, including outing and homophobia. "The thing that enrages me enough to get me into that fulmination mode always turns out to be some form of hypocrisy. Whether it's a closeted movie star who allows his adopted children to live in psychic misery so he can get a $20 million paycheck or whether it's a media tycoon who takes a political stance and grandstands from there when he really doesn't give a damn about the politics. He just knows that this is where the money is." Included among those targets are the gay activists of the early nineties "who made a very good living being professionally indignant."

Outland does not consider the outrageousness and incongruity of his characters and stories as campy. "I don't know if my books turned out campy, but I sure didn't want them to.... To me, camp is double entendres. A lot of camp is self delusion—a seedy self-delusion. It's sad people deluding themselves that they're living fabulous lives.... Binky and Doan live in a skewed and surreal world, but there were definitely people like them, and I didn't think they were living in a dream world. They don't delude themselves. They live fabulous lives but with the knowledge they are doing it on credit and there will be a price to pay."

ABIGAIL PADGETT: *Blue McCarron and Roxie Bouchie* (1998–CURRENT)

Abigail Padgett, a former court investigator for the county of San Diego, now works as an advocate for the mentally ill, and maintains an avid interest in desert preservation and Native American cultures. Her debut novel, *Child of Silence*, was the first to feature an investigator living with manic depression. Her popular Bo Bradley series features a (heterosexual) child-abuse investigator with bipolar disorder.

Detectives: Dr. Emily Elizabeth (Blue) McCarron, social psychologist and her lover; Dr. Roxanne (Roxie) Bouchie, forensic psychiatrist

Setting: Southern California. Time period is contemporary with publication dates

Book: *Blue* (1998); Finalist Macavity—Best Novel (1998); *The Last Blue Plate Special* (2001)

Publisher: Mysterious Press

These intricate mysteries present bizarre and complex crimes that are solved by a pair of intelligent and talented female detectives. Blue McCarron and Roxie Bouchie are both highly educated, independent-minded feminists. Both are also the products of their families, upbringing, and racial identities.

Blue is white, the daughter of an Episcopal minister and the fraternal twin of an armed robber serving a long jail term. Roxie is black, the illegitimate child of a mentally ill prostitute, whose education was funded by the hard work of her grandmother and the gracious support of her church. When they meet, at the start of *Blue*, McCarron adheres to a monolithic theory delineating the different natures of women and men that grew out of her need to understand her brother's descent into crime. Roxie is driven by the need to follow the logical upward trajectory established for her when she began her escape from the ghetto. By the end of *The Last Blue Plate Special*, they realize that life is more convoluted and mysterious than they had imagined.

Their investigative approaches are constructed from their backgrounds, personalities, and feminist philosophies. Roxie adheres to a logical, deductive style that draws on her medical training and experience peering into the minds of individual criminals. Blue begins with the statistical, data-driven approach of social psychology which allows her to identify patterns and trends. She digests them and lets them percolate. "I had to follow an irrational path paved erratically in glaring coincidences that blazed and vanished like mirages in my field of vision."[290]

Their markedly different styles form a blend that is ideal for the unconventional cases they are hired to probe: determining whether a mild-mannered, elderly woman actually murdered a stranger and stuffed him into a freezer and stopping a serial killer fixated on Biblical strictures and dinner plates who targets prominent women.

The social factor underlying these crimes is sexism, which adopts various guises, including child prostitution, spouse abuse, and rape. The antidote is the feminist-activism of secondary characters.

Nancy Sanra: *Tally McGinnis and Cid Cameron* (1995–2000)

Nancy Sanra (1944–) grew up in Menlo Park, California. She received her undergraduate degree from the University of California and did graduate work in psychology at Columbia University. Before becoming a full-time writer, she worked as a regional sales manager. She lives in Michigan with her life partner.

Detectives: Tally McGinnis, Cidney (Cid) Cameron, co-owners (with Katie O'Neil) of the Phoenix Detective Agency (lesbians)

Setting: San Francisco. Time period is contemporary with publication dates

Books: *No Witnesses* (1995); *No Escape* (1998); *No Corpse* (2000)

Publisher: Rising Tide Press

This series pits private investigators Tally McGinnis, Cid Cameron, and their assistant Katie O'Neil against wily and elusive criminals.

When the series begins, McGinnis is the sole proprietor of the Phoenix Detective Agency where O'Neil is her office manager. Cameron is then a lieutenant in the San Francisco police department. "Tally's youthful, nonthreatening appearance belied her toughness."[291] She's a former police officer who has been working as a private investigator for over seven years. She applies her understanding of human psychology to her investigations, and she has the interpersonal skills needed to interact well with clients. Cameron is a crusty, tough-talking and hard-drinking cop who pulls no punches ("We've got a fresh kill here. Give me details before the trail's as cold as the corpse."[292]). By the end of *No Witnesses,* the first book in the series, Cameron has retired from the SFPD, McGinnis and O'Neil have become lovers, and the three have equal shares of the Agency.

The other major figure in the series is Marsha Cox. Cox is an almost superhuman sociopath who is reminiscent of Professor James Moriarty, Sherlock Holmes' brilliant and evil adversary. The murders she commits are grisly and bizarre, and she uses them to flaunt her criminal prowess. ("True challenges excite me. Conquering what is seemingly unconquerable."[293] For example, she drains the blood of some of her victims using techniques she learned as a mortician, and she leaves one victim on public display, suspended among trees in a public park. Her flare for the dramatic extends to leaving a red rose at the scene of her crimes and sending dead roses to prospective victims.

Most of the major characters in these stories are lesbians. Two investigations involve lesbians accused of killing their lovers, and the third takes place during an Olivia (lesbian) cruise. Forensic evidence is presented and discussed extensively in the stories and forms the basis for the cases for and against the accused.

> ... there were only three wounds: one precise slash to the windpipe and two stab wounds to the heart. No bruising. No other cuts.... He or she knew how to kill quickly."[294]

Despite the context, most of the themes in these stories (e.g., monogamy, drug abuse, stalking, corruption) are not specific to the lesbigay community, which clearly illustrates why stories about gay and lesbian characters should appeal to heterosexual audiences.

SAMUEL M. STEWARD: *Gertrude Stein and Alice B. Toklas* (1985–1989)

Samuel M. Steward (1909–1993) was a professor, writer, tattoo artist, and pornographer. He published extensively under his given name, but he's best known for short stories and novels written under the pseudonym Phil Andros. In the course of his life, he became acquainted with a number of writers and artists, including Gertrude Stein and Alice Toklas. Before his death, he donated a collection of Stein/Toklas memorabilia to the University of California at Berkeley.

Detectives: Gertrude Stein and her lover, Alice B. Toklas
Settings: Paris and southern France
Books: *Murder Is Murder Is Murder* (1985); *Caravaggio Shawl* (1989)
Publisher: Alyson Publications

The stories in this celebrity-mystery series have three core elements: murder investigations, gay male erotica, and Stein and Toklas. All three are covered by a veneer of camp humor that includes outrageous characters and bizarre situations. The investigations also constitute the slim thread that links the Stein-Toklas and erotic elements.

Stein and Toklas become detectives when murder touches their lives. In *Murder Is Murder Is Murder*, they are asked to intervene following the disappearance of their gardener's father—last seen attacking the neighbor who raped his Adonis-like son. In *Caravaggio Shawl*, the women solve the murder of their maid's husband, a guard at the Louvre. They also expose the theft of a Caravaggio painting depicting Orpheus who, according to legend, introduced homosexual love to Greece.

Despite the gender of the main characters, the narrator's perspective is clearly gay and male. Lesbians are identifiable solely by their mannish attire. In contrast, most of the young men in the books (and apparently in France as a whole) are gay Adonises who fall into bed with each other at the pop of a button. Even Stein and Toklas admire the parade of male beauty. "If I weren't the way I was, or if I were a fairy, I'd get him before sundown, come hell or high water."[295] The women also prevail upon their assistant sleuth, Johnny (called "Johnny Jump-up" because he jumps up to light Alice's cigarettes), to extend their investigations to the boudoirs of potential informants. Johnny jumps to do that as well.

The Stein-Toklas element includes characterization of the two women and their French milieu along with a great deal of language play. Literary and art references sprinkled throughout the books give the reader a flavor of the world in which they lived. The language play includes quotes from Stein's works, Stein-like language, and puns on French words and phrases. For example, every time someone calls Toklas "Madame" (the title for older and married women) as opposed to "Mademoiselle" (the title for a young, unmarried woman), her anger escalates until she shoots a sneering, gun-wielding murderer solely because he persists in calling her "Madame."

The stories are set in Paris and the French countryside when the women are in their fifties and have been together many years. There's a sweetness about their relationship that reveals mutual respect and love— and reflects Steward's friendship with them. For example, in *Caravaggio Shawl*, Stein concludes a ruminating walk around Paris with these Stein-like thoughts

> ... a brass nameplate ought really to shine all the time especially if it says Gertrude Stein and Alice B. Toklas on it and it does it certainly does and thats me and her and shes my dear sweet Pussy and I love her and I'm home.[296]

DAVID STUKAS: *Robert Willsop, Michael Stark, and Monette O'Reilley* (2001–CURRENT)

David Stukas (1958–) grew up in the midwestern United States. He earned degrees from Michigan State University and New York's Fashion Institute of Technology and then worked in advertising until 2000. The Robert Willsop series is his first published writing. When he's not writing, Stukas sells real estate. He lives in California with his lover/partner/ best friend in a house they both designed.

Detectives: Robert Willsop, copywriter for an advertising agency (gay); Michael Stark, wealthy playboy (gay); Monette O'Reilley, clerk at Endangered Herbs Society of America (lesbian)

Settings: Various locations. Time period is contemporary with publication dates

Books: *Someone Killed His Boyfriend* (2001); *Going Down for the Count* (2002); *Wearing Black to the White Party* (2003)

Publisher: Kensington Publishing Corp.

These high-energy farces lampoon gay culture, the wealthy, great detectives, and anything else that falls within their pages. "I like to think of my books as comedy murder mysteries with healthy dollops (okay, avalanches) of social satire.... First, I need to make people laugh. I know that's not a theme or issue, but it's something that comes from poking fun at some very serious issues."

At the center of the whirlwind are three amateur detectives. "Robert is the quintessential outsider and observer. He sits back and watches the world go by, amazed at the things people do and the things they get away with. He believes in common sense, moderation in everything, and for comic relief, falls back on the Old Lithuanian sayings of his wacky grandmother, Martha the Obtuse. Robert is so good, so genuine, so real, so caring that he often suffers for it—comically, of course—because these qualities handicap him in a world that rewards the good-looking, the well-heeled, the well-connected and the more aggressive.... While many of the other characters in my books gyrate out of moral control, Robert remains steadfast.... As the observer in my books, Robert also gets to make running social commentary on what he observes—the world according to Robert Willsop....

"Michael is the exact opposite.... Michael has everything that Robert thinks he wants. Robert knows that Michael's lifestyle has a shallow quality. So does Michael. The difference is that Michael revels in being one-dimensional—he's proud of it....

"Monette is ... like Robert in lesbian drag.... She has a good heart, a stable personality, and bundles of energy, but none of these seem to help. She is stuck doing brochure layouts for the Endangered Herbs Society of America, has no girlfriend, and a shitty apartment in the Park Slope area of Brooklyn filled to the ceiling with detective novels she has read. Like Robert, she is eagerly waiting for something big to happen in her life, yet it never does." Because she's an avid mystery reader, she becomes the "great detective" in the stories.

The party culture "does creep up in most of my books in one form or another since these kinds of people tend to swarm about my character Michael Stark. Michael, in fact, is their reigning king.... I'm a lazy author and couldn't find an easier target. You just sit back and take aim. White parties? Bang! Fire Island? Bang! Pretentious restaurants? Bang! Like shooting ducks in a barrel. It gets me some good laughs, plus it perhaps makes people think about how these cultures have—in some ways—distracted the gay community from growing up and accepting themselves as they are."

The "insanity of the world is a recurring theme because it transcends money, friendship, homophobia, sexism—all of it...." This is most clearly expressed through a host of oddball characters engaged in outrageous schemes, ranging from Michael's murderous mother (gay men mysteriously die when she's around) to a host of Bette Davis impersonators.

"I wanted to fill a niche in writing by gay authors. When I would walk into stores like A Different Light or Lambda Rising, I would see that there were tons of books about coming out, self-help, living with AIDS, and erotic fiction. There didn't seem to be a lot of humor. There was even less in the area of humorous mysteries.... So, being a very practical man, I decided to write where there wasn't a lot of competition. After all, I wanted to get published."

THERESE SZYMANSKI: *Brett Higgins and Allie Sullivan* (1997–CURRENT)

Therese Szymanski (1968–) is a novelist, playwright, columnist, erotic-story writer, editor, reviewer, graphic designer, manager of adult businesses, and Jill-of-all-trades. She's from Michigan and has a bachelor's degree from Michigan State University. Her play *And Divided We Fall* (about gays in the military) took first prize in an MSU playwriting competition, and the university premiered it. She edited *Back to Basics: A Butch/Femme Erotic Journey* and wrote a novella. Szymanski lives and works in the Washington, D.C., area.

Detectives: Brett Higgins, manager of adult businesses, and her lover Allison (Allie) Sullivan, various jobs including police officer

Settings: Detroit and central Michigan. Time period is contemporary with publication dates

Books: *When the Dancing Stops* (1997); *When the Dead Speak* (1998); *When Some Body Disappears* (1999); *When Evil Changes Face* (2000); Finalist Lambda Award—Best Lesbian Mystery (2000) *When Good Girls Go Bad* (2003)

Publishers: Naiad Press, Bella Books

This is one of the few series that provides a butch-femme viewpoint. "With Brett and Allie the butch-femme difference is really big.... It's just a part of who I am. It's part of how I see the world.... As I've gotten older and gotten more self-confident I've become more butch.... There's no way I'd want to become a man, though."

Brett and Allie differ in virtually every way. Brett is decidedly butch while Allie is clearly femme. Allie is a high school senior from an affluent family who is planning to become a police officer. Brett grew up on the mean streets of Detroit and manages a number of adult businesses (including a theater featuring erotic dancing) and sometimes performs functions that stray outside the law. "Brett's got a dark side that she keeps struggling with. She keeps trying to be good but she can't quite make it. If she was in the Old West, she'd be wearing a black hat.... She's also a kind of a dark avenger because she takes care of the bad guys....

"Some people have gotten on my case about having a college-educated white girl managing adult businesses in Detroit. It happened. After college I couldn't find a job in my area and ended up managing an adult bookstore, an adult theater, a lesbigay book and gift store, and an adult distributorship.... Those jobs have given me fodder for stories ever since. One time, someone actually asked for a larger butt plug. That ended up in one book. There's a dark humor in the series—especially the earlier books—that comes from that work, too."

In the course of the series the two bust a high school drug ring by masquerading as students, uncover a money-laundering scheme, use Allie (posing as an erotic dancer) to lure a serial killer, and go on the lam. They "were going to move to Aurora, California. Then, I decided that there's not a lot that is set in Michigan, so I had them come back...."

Although the novels are action-oriented and story-focused, a number of themes come through. Brett "doesn't do any of the really slimy stuff, like child porn or drugs. I'm very antidrug as well. Occasionally I would go charging through the theater because I could smell one of the dancers in the upstairs dressing rooms smoking something....

"There are some things in this world that disgust me. Violence against women is one of them. I was fortunate that my parents did not abuse us, but when I look at the statistics about how many girls are abused, it just blows my mind. It happens everywhere, and it's not getting better.... When you deal with erotic dancers a lot of them come from interesting backgrounds including bad, abusive backgrounds. A lot of the dancers I managed at the Wood Six Theater (the Paradise in the series) were on drugs. It's a pity that so many women become erotic dancers.

Some kids, like my nephew's old girlfriend, think that being an erotic dancer is an easy way to make a lot of money without working. I talked her out of it."

Despite these concerns, the spirit of the series is far more positive. "I like seeing women kicking butt and in control and making their own decisions."

MARK RICHARD ZUBRO: *Tom Mason and Scott Carpenter* (1989–CURRENT)

Mark Richard Zubro has been writing gay mysteries since 1989. In addition to the Tom and Scott mystery series he writes a series about a gay police detective (see the section on Police). Like Tom Mason, Zubro is an openly gay junior high school teacher working in a suburb south of Chicago. He lectures frequently about the craft of mystery writing as well as about the problems inherent in being an openly gay school-teacher.

Detectives: Tom Mason, high school English teacher and his lover Scott Carpenter, professional baseball player

Setting: Chicago metropolitan area. Time period contemporary with publication dates

Books: *A Simple Suburban Murder* (1989); Lambda Award—Best Gay Men's Mystery (1989); *Why Isn't Becky Twitchell Dead?* (1990); *The Only Good Priest* (1991); *The Principal Cause of Death* (1992); *An Echo of Death* (1994); *Rust on the Razor* (1996); *Are You Nuts?* (1998); *One Dead Drag Queen* (2000); *Here Comes the Corpse* (2002)

Publisher: St. Martin's Press

This series is strongly gay positive and has a high level of social awareness. It "is still true today although things have gotten better—that we still see mostly stereotypical gay people in popular culture.... I wanted to portray in my books fully developed, fully rounded characters. There could be a drag queen. There could be people dying of AIDS. There could be depressed people, but that's not all."

Tom Mason (the first-person narrator) and Scott Carpenter are designed to fly in the face of those stereotypes about gay men and gay life. Tom is an ex-marine who fought in Vietnam. "Tom is smarter than I am, better at his job, is a better lover, is richer. I tried to create him as a caring schoolteacher. He has to be reasonably bright." Scott is a pro-fessional baseball pitcher who pitched no-hitters in two World Series games. "People ask me why I picked a baseball player for his lover. In essence, I've always wanted to have a baseball player as a boyfriend. That has never happened, and it is never likely to happen. So, I decided to do it in a fantasy world. Scott is an old fantasy of mine come to life."

By the time the series begins, Tom and Scott have been together for eight years and are still very happy. "I knew that Tom and Scott were going to be a happy couple. There was no question about that.... In fact, the first couple of books it turned into a problem because they were always happy and loving. Of course, that is not realistic." Despite their mutual devotion, Tom and Scott begin the series living apart and in the closet. As the series progresses they both come out and, in *Here Comes the Corpse*, they get married.

Many of the crimes are by-products of homophobia or are issues of concern to teenagers and their parents (e.g., sex, drugs, child prostitution, teachers trading sex for good grades, and parental attitudes towards gay children). "I actually don't set out to have a theme when I'm writing something. I write more how it feels.... If you create characters and situations around real issues in real life, then the commentary and theme follow."

Most of these action-packed stories include at least one rollicking chase sequence or fight sequence. Sometimes, the thrill of the chase overpowers the sense of danger that precipitated the chase in the first place. In *The Principal Cause of Death*, for example, Tom and Scott commandeer a horse and buggy to escape a gang of murderous thugs. After Scott grabs the reins, he's described as driving the buggy like a Roman charioteer.

The writing is light and humorous. Much of the humor comes from satirical characterizations. For example, some of Tom's students talk in "teenage mumble," a school administrator looks remarkably like Ichabod Crane, and a nasty parent is a harridan with bad color sense who tries to look twenty years younger than she is. "Quite often, I am picking on people I don't like. That's fun. You can do all kinds of rotten things to very mean people." The criminal perpetrators also tend to be rotten people, but many rotten characters are merely smelly red herrings.

III

Themes Across the Series

This chapter identifies gay and lesbian–related themes in gay/lesbian detective literature. In their interviews, authors were asked to identify the important themes in their novels. Their responses were the starting point for this chapter. Themes for authors not interviewed come from critical reading of the novels.

For some authors themes are a focal point. Joan Drury describes her Tyler Jones series as being "about *all* the ways in which women have been silenced." Despite the importance of themes to their work, however, Drury and most other theme-oriented authors identify constructing a good story populated by interesting characters as their most important goal.

Other authors, including Nikki Baker, see themes as "just kind of the soup of stuff we swim around in every day." Val McDermid states that "I never start off a novel with the idea of having a particular theme or agenda. With me, the story is always what comes first, and it is paramount throughout." Themes that emerge from their novels arise from examination of the plots and the personalities, lifestyles, and philosophies of their characters.

The "soup" that gay/lesbian detectives swim around in is seasoned with ingredients closely related to being lesbian or gay (e.g., coming out, queens, the lesbigay community) and those that reflect the diversity of the community (e.g., BDSM, marriage, and having children) and its members (e.g., ethnicity, racism, aging). References to homophobia and the closet are so widespread that the listings for them have been restricted to specific facets of those themes.

There is also crossover of themes. There are female authors who categorize their series as feminist but women's issues are not the sole domain of female authors. Male authors, including Lev Raphael, John Morgan Wilson, and Mark Richard Zubro write about abortion, sexism, and violence against women. Similarly, authors of both sexes include AIDS/HIV in their series. Both Jaye Maiman and Barbara Johnson join Michael Nava and other male authors who write about series-level characters afflicted with AIDS.

General themes, such as abuse of power, greed, hypocrisy, and the search for truth, are covered in the analyses and interviews found in chapters 2 through 6 rather than in this chapter. The use of characters as role models is also described in the other chapters of this book.

Both main and secondary characters may be flawed or prejudiced. Their attitudes and behavior helped generate the entries in this chapter. For example, Joe R. Lansdale's Hap Collins admits he's homophobic, and Fred Hunter's Alex Reynolds is ageist. Hunter and other authors have commented on the tendency of readers to transfer these attitudes to the authors.

> [Some readers think that] I, the author, was ageist when it's Alex's viewpoint. There is nothing wrong with one of my characters being ageist, because that's a human frailty. But people always attribute those kinds of things to the author.

This applies to attitudes tied to the lesbigay lifestyle as well. For example, Katherine V. Forrest's main character, Kate Delafield, believes she must remain closeted, but Forrest views the closet as a destructive force. When examining themes of a novel or series it is, therefore, critical to remember that opinions of the characters—including main characters—do not necessarily represent those of the author.

Entry formats

The basic structure of an entry is Author Surname. *Novel Title.*
Examples: *Sims. *Damn Straight*
Zimmerman. *Closet*

Multiple novels are separated by a semicolon.
Example: *Redmann. *Death by the Riverside; Lost Daughters*

A star (*) indicates that the author mentioned the theme in the interview or it was found to have an impact on a central character and/or story.

Themes in the works of authors who write multiple series have separate entries.
Example: Zubro. (Tom Mason & Scott Carpenter) *Are You Nuts?*
Zubro. (Paul Turner) *Sorry Now?*

The series is indicated in parentheses after the author's name.

When a theme appears repeatedly in a series, the format is Author Surname. Character Name.
    Example: Forrest. Kate Delafield

If that recurring theme is more central to one novel in the series, its title may be appended to the entry and placed in parenthesis.
    Example: *Hansen. Dave Brandstetter (*Death Claims*)

Authors with identical surnames are differentiated by adding given names or another distinguishing feature. In the following example, John Morgan Wilson is identified by his full name and Barbara Wilson is identified by adding her legally chosen name.
    Examples: Wilson, John Morgan. Benjamin Justice
               Wilson/Sjoholm. Cassandra Reilly (*Trouble in Transylvania*)

Abortion and Adoption

Abortion

*Albarella. *Agenda for Murder*
Beecham. *Second Guess*
*Hartman. Drew Parker & Jen Grey
*Johnson, Steve. Doug Orlando (*Final Atonement*)
*Marcy. *A Cold Case of Murder; Mommy Deadest*
Mildon. *Fighting for Air*
Miller. *Reporter on the Run*
*Redmann. *Deaths of Jocasta*
*Sims. *Damn Straight*
*Welch. *Smoke and Mirrors*
*Zubro. (Tom Mason & Scott Carpenter) *One Dead Drag Queen*

Adoption and baby selling

*Albarella. *Agenda for Murder*
*Duffy. *Fresh Flesh*
Fennelly. *The Closet Hanging*
*Lordon. *Son of a Gun*
*Maiman. *Under My Skin*

*Marcy. *A Cold Case of Murder*
Redmann. *Death by the Riverside; Lost Daughters*
Roeder. *Someone Is Killing the Gay Boys of Verona*
*Sumner. *Crosswords*
York. *Timber City Masks*
*Zubro. (Paul Turner) *Another Dead Teenager*

Age

Age difference

Refers to lovers whose ages are ten or more years apart.

Aldyne. *Cobalt; Vermillion*
*Craft. *Boy Toy*
Fennelly. Matty Sinclair
*Forrest. Kate Delafield
Gilligan. *Danger! Cross Currents*
Hansen. Dave Brandstetter (*The Man Everybody Was Afraid Of*)

Herren. (Chanse MacLeod) *Murder in the Rue Dauphine*
Lordon. Sydney Sloane
*Maiman. *Someone to Watch*
Manthorne. Harriet Hubbley
Michaels. *Dead on Your Feet; Mask for a Diva*
Nava. Henry Rios
*Padgett. *Blue*
Saum. *Murder is Material*
Scoppettone. *Let's Face the Music and Die*
Stevenson. *Death Trick; Tongue Tied*
Sumner. *End of April*
*Szymanski. Brett Higgins & Allie Sullivan
Taylor. *The Last of Her Lies*
Townsend. *One for the Master, Two for the Fool*
Zaremba. Helen Keremos

Aging and ageism

Aldyne. *Vermillion*
*Baxt. *Topsy and Evil*
*Cutler. Mark Bradley & Rayford Goodman
Douglas. Allison O'Neil & Kerry Owyhee
Douglas. (Caitlin Reece) *The Daughters of Artemis*
Fennelly. *The Glory Hole Murders*
Forrest. Kate Delafield (*Apparition Alley*)
Gilbert. *Spiked*
Hansen. Dave Brandstetter (*A Country of Old Men*)
Hart. *A Small Sacrifice*
Hunter. *National Nancys*
Johnson, Bett Reece. *The Woman Who Rode to the Moon*
Johnson, Steve. *False Confessions*
Lordon. Sydney Sloane (*Mother May I*)

Manthorne. Harriet Hubbley
*Marcy. *Cemetery Murders*
*Mickelbury. *Love Notes; Night Songs*
Nava. *Goldenboy*
*Plante. Cynthia Chenery Scott
Powell. Hollis Carpenter
*Sanra. Tally McGinnis & Cid Cameron
Saum. Brigid Donovan
Schmidt. Laney Samms
Scoppettone. Lauren Laurano
*Tell. Poppy Dillworth
Wilson/Sjoholm. Cassandra Reilly (*Trouble in Transylvania*)
Zaremba. Helen Keremos

Older gay men

Aldyne. *Vermillion*
Fennelly. *The Glory Hole Murders*
Gilbert. *Spiked*
*Hansen. *A Country of Old Men*
Herren. (Chanse MacLeod) *Murder in the Rue Dauphine*

Older lesbians

*Craft. *Body Language*
Douglas. Allison O'Neil & Kerry Owyhee
*Dreher. *Shaman's Moon*
*Drury. *The Other Side of Silence*
*Forrest. *The Beverly Malibu*
*Fritchley. *Chicken Feed; Chicken Out*
Gilligan. *Danger! Cross Currents*
*Hart. *Robber's Wine*
Herren. Scotty Bradley
*Manthorne. *Ghost Motel*
*Marcy. *Cemetery Murders*
McConnell. *Mrs. Porter's Letter*
*Mickelbury. *Love Notes*
Mildon. Cal Meredith
*Miller. Lexy Hyatt
*Morell. Lucia Ramos (*Final Rest*)

*Padgett. *Blue*
*Plante. Cynthia Chenery Scott
*Redmann. *Deaths of Jocasta; Lost Daughters*
*Sanra. Tally McGinnis & Cid Cameron (*No Corpse*)
*Saum. Brigid Donovan
*Schmidt. Laney Samms
*Stevenson. *On the Other Hand, Death*
*Steward. Gertrude Stein & Alice B. Toklas
*Sumner. *End of April*
*Tell. Poppy Dillworth
*Wilson/Sjoholm. Cassandra Reilly
York. *Timber City Masks*

AIDS/HIV

Allen. *Takes One to Know One*
Baker. *Long Goodbyes; The Ultimate Exit Strategy*
*Craft. *Eye Contact; Name Games*
Drury. *Closed in Silence*
Dunford. Mitchell Draper
*Dymmoch. Jack Caleb & John Thinnes
Fennelly. *The Closet Hanging*
Forrest. *The Beverly Malibu; Murder by Tradition*
Foster. *The Monarchs Are Flying*
Gilbert. *Spiked*
*Gilligan. Alix Nicholson (*Danger in High Places*)
Grobeson. *Outside the Badge*
Haddock. *Final Cut*
*Hansen. Dave Brandstetter (*Early Graves*)
*Hart. *A Killing Cure; Hunting the Witch*
James. *Posted to Death*

*Johnson, Barbara. Colleen Fitzgerald
Johnson, Bett Reece. *The Woman Who Knew Too Much*
Johnson, Steve. Doug Orlando
*Lynch. *Sue Slate: Private Eye*
*Maiman. Robin Miller
*Manthorne. *Deadly Reunion*
McConnell. *The Burnton Widows*
McDermid. *Final Edition*
*McNab. *Dead Certain; Cop Out*
Michaels. *Time to Check Out*
Mickelbury. *Keeping Secrets*
*Nava. Henry Rios
Outland. Doan McCandler & Binky Van de Kamp
Plante. *Getting Away with Murder*
Redmann. Micky Knight (*Lost Daughters*)
*Scoppettone. Lauren Laurano (*My Sweet Untraceable You*)
*Stevenson. Don Strachey (*Third Man Out*)
Taylor. Maggie Garrett
Townsend. *Masters' Counterpoint*
*Wilson, John Morgan. Benjamin Justice
Wilson/Sjoholm. (Pam Nilsen) *The Dog Collar Murders*
*Zimmerman. Todd Mills (*Hostage*)
*Zubro. Paul Turner (*Sorry Now?*)
*Zubro. Tom Mason & Scott Carpenter

Safe sex

Allen. *Tell Me What You Like*
Craft. *Eye Contact; Name Games*
Dunford. *Soon to Be a Major Motion Picture*
Fennelly. Matty Sinclair
Herren. (Chanse MacLeod) *Murder in the Rue Dauphine*
Manthorne. *Last Resort; Final Take*

Michaels. *A Body to Dye For; Dead on Your Feet*
Nava. *Goldenboy*
Pincus. *The Solitary Twist*
Schmidt. Laney Samms
Stevenson. *Ice Blues; Shock to the System*
Taylor. *We Know Where You Live*
Townsend. *One for the Master, Two for the Fool*

Alcohol and Alcoholism
see Drugs and Alcohol

Alienation

This topic refers to main characters.

*Baker. Virginia Kelly
*Dickson. Jas Anderson
*Douglas. (Allison O'Neil & Kerry Owyhee) *Death at Lavender Bay*
*Herren. (Chanse MacLeod) *Murder in the Rue Dauphine*
*Maiman. Robin Miller
*Nava. Henry Rios
*Redmann. Micky Knight
*Roberts. Cameron McGill
*Welch. Helen Black
*Wilson, John Morgan. Benjamin Justice
*Wings. *She Came in Drag*

Anonymous Sex
see Casual and Anonymous Sex, Cruising

Bars and Baths
see Lesbigay Community

BDSM (Bondage, Discipline, Sadism, Masochism)
see Leather Sex/SM/BDSM

Bisexuals

Aldyne. *Canary*
Davis. *Devil's Leg Crossing*
*Hart. *A Small Sacrifice*
Manthorne. *Deadly Reunion; Last Resort*
McNab. *Death Club*
Outland. *Death Wore a Fabulous New Fragrance*
*Raphael. *The Edith Wharton Murders*
Redmann. *The Intersection of Law and Desire*
Sumner. Tor Cross
*Wilson, John Morgan. *Revision of Justice*
*Wings. *She Came by the Book*
York. *Timber City Masks*
Zaremba. *White Noise*

Blackmail

Outing

*Baker. *The Lavender House Murder*
*Baxt. *A Queer Kind of Death*
Beecham. Amanda Valentine
*Calloway. *2nd Fiddle; 3rd Degree*
Clare. *Street Rules*
*Craft. *Eye Contact; Name Games*

*Dickson. *FreeForm*
*Douglas. (Caitlin Reece) *The Always Anonymous Beast*
*Dymmoch. *The Man Who Understood Cats*
*Fennelly. *The Glory Hole Murders*
*Forrest. *Amateur City*
*Foster. *The Monarchs Are Flying*
Gilligan. *Danger! Cross Currents*
*Hansen. *Death Claims; Early Graves*
*Hart. *A Small Sacrifice; Hunting the Witch*
*Hartman. *Gumshoe Gorilla*
*Herren. (Chanse MacLeod) *Murder in the Rue Dauphine*
*Hunter. *National Nancys*
*James. *Posted to Death*
Johnson, Steve. *False Confessions*
*Maddison. *Witchfire*
Maiman. *I Left My Heart*
*McKay. *The Kali Connection*
*McNab. *Fatal Reunion; Dead Certain; Lessons in Murder*
*Nava. Henry Rios (*The Little Death*)
*Outland. *Death Wore the Emperor's New Clothes*
*Powell. *Houston Town*
*Rand. *Gay Detective*
*Raphael. *The Edith Wharton Murders*
*Redmann. *Death by the Riverside*
Saum. *Murder is Relative*
Silva. *Storm Front*
*Stevenson. *On the Other Hand, Death; Shock to the System; Third Man Out*
Stukas. Robert Willsop, Monette O'Reilley & Michael Stark
*Wilson, John Morgan. *Simple Justice*
*Wings. Emma Victor
*York. *Crystal Mountain Veils*
*Zaremba. *A Reason to Kill*
*Zimmerman. *Tribe*

*Zubro. (Tom Mason & Scott Carpenter) *Are You Nuts?*
*Zubro. (Paul Turner) *The Truth Can Get You Killed*

Various reasons

*Aldyne. *Cobalt; Vermillion*
*Allen. *Takes One to Know One*
*Fritchley. *Chicken Feed*
*Hart. Jane Lawless
*James. Simon Kirby-Jones
*Maiman. *Crazy for Loving; Under My Skin*
*McDermid. *Final Edition*
*McNab. *Death Club*
*Mildon. Cal Meredith
*Plante. *Dirty Money*
*Raphael. *The Edith Wharton Murders*
*Sanra. *No Corpse*
*Saum. Brigid Donovan
*Sumner. *Crosswords*
*Taylor. Maggie Garrett
*Zaremba. Helen Keremos

Bull Dykes
see **Stereotypic Characters**

Butch and Femme

*Allen. Alison Kaine (*Just a Little Lie*)
*Azolakov. Cass Milam
Beecham. Amanda Valentine
Calloway. Cassidy James
Davidson. Toni Underwood
*Davis. Maris Middleton
Forrest. Kate Delafield (*The Beverly Malibu*)
Herren. (Scotty Bradley) *Bourbon Street Blues*

Johnson, Barbara. Colleen Fitzgerald

Lynch. *Sue Slate: Private Eye*

*Maney. Nancy Clue, Cherry Aimless & friends

Manthorne. Harriet Hubbley

Powell. Hollis Carpenter

Redmann. Micky Knight

Richardson. *Double Take Out*

Sanra. Tally McGinnis & Cid Cameron

Schmidt. *Silverlake Heat*

Silva. Delta Stevens

Sims. *Damn Straight*

Steward. Gertrude Stein & Alice B. Toklas

*Szymanski. Brett Higgins & Allie Sullivan

*Tell. Poppy Dillworth

*Townsend. Bruce MacLeod

Wilson, John Morgan. *Justice at Risk*

Wilson/Sjoholm. (Cassandra Reilly) *Gaudi Afternoon*

Wings. *She Came by the Book; She Came to the Castro*

Cancer and Mastectomy

Includes cancer research and activism.

Clare. *Street Rules*

Dymmoch. *The Man Who Understood Cats*

*Forrest. *Murder at the Nightwood Bar*

*Gilligan. *Danger in High Places*

Hansen. *Fadeout*

Hart. Jane Lawless

Maiman. *I Left My Heart; Every Time We Say Goodbye*

*Manthorne. *Ghost Motel; Last Resort*

McNab. *Accidental Murder*

Morell. *Final Rest*

Padgett. *The Last Blue Plate Special*

Scott. *Stronger Than Death*

Taylor. Maggie Garrett

Wings. *She Came in Drag*

Casual and Anonymous Sex, Cruising

*Aldyne. Dan Valentine & Clarisse Lovelace

Baker. *The Lavender House Murder; The Ultimate Exit Strategy*

Calloway. *4th Down*

Clare. *Street Rules*

Craft. *Boy Toy; Eye Contact*

Douglas. (Caitlin Reece) *Ninth Life*

Dunford. *Making a Killing*

*Fennelly. Matty Sinclair

Foster. Harriet Fordham Croft

Fritchley. *Chicken Run; Chicken Feed*

*Gilbert. *Spiked*

Gilligan. *Danger in High Places*

Griffith. *The Blue Place*

*Haddock. *Final Cut*

Hartman. *Gumshoe Gorilla*

Herren. (Chanse MacLeod) *Murder in the Rue Dauphine*

Herren. (Scotty Bradley) *Bourbon Street Blues*

James. Simon Kirby-Jones

Johnson, Steve. *False Confessions*

*Manthorne. Harriet Hubbley

McConnell. *Double Daughter*

*McDermid. *Conferences Are Murder*

Michaels. *Time to Check Out*

*Miller. *Mayhem at the Marina*

Outland. Doan McCandler & Binky Van de Kamp

Raphael. *Burning Down the House; Let's Get Criminal*

*Redmann. Micky Knight

Roberts. Cameron McGill
Roeder. *Someone Is Killing the Gay Boys of Verona*
*Stevenson. Don Strachey
*Steward. Gertrude Stein & Alice B. Toklas
*Stukas. Robert Willsop, Monette O'Reilley & Michael Stark
Welch. *A Day Too Long; Snake Eyes; Still Waters*
Wilson/Sjoholm. Pam Nilsen
Wilson/Sjoholm. Cassandra Reilly
*Wings. *She Came in a Flash*
Zaremba. Helen Keremos
*Zimmerman. *Closet*

Children
see also Family; Internalized Homophobia

Child abuse, molestation and incest

*Aldyne. *Canary*
*Allen. *Give My Secrets Back; Just a Little Lie*
*Baker. *Long Goodbyes*
*Beal. *Angel Dance*
*Calloway. Cassidy James (*6th Sense*)
*Clare. *Bleeding Out*
*Craft. *Boy Toy*
*Cutler. *Shot on Location*
*Davidson. Toni Underwood (*Deadly Gamble*)
*Davis. Maris Middleton (*Shattered Illusions*)
*Douglas. (Caitlin Reece) *A Rage of Maidens*
*Drury. Tyler Jones (*Closed in Silence*)
Dymmoch. *Feline Friendship*

*Fennelly. *The Glory Hole Murders*
*Forrest. Kate Delafield (*Murder at the Nightwood Bar*)
Foster. *Legal Tender*
*Gilligan. *Danger! Cross Currents*
*Griffith. *Stay*
Grobeson. *Outside the Badge*
*Haddock. *Edited Out*
Hansen. Dave Brandstetter
*Hart. *Stage Fright*
*Hartman. *Gumshoe Gorilla*
James. *Posted to Death*
*Johnson, Bett Reece. *The Woman Who Found Grace*
*Johnson, Steve. *False Confessions*
*laFavor. Renee LaRoche
*Lansdale. *Mucho Mojo*
*Lordon. Sydney Sloane (*Father Forgive Me*)
*Lynch. *Sue Slate: Private Eye*
*Maddison. *Deceptions*
*Maiman. Robin Miller (*Every Time We Say Goodbye; Under My Skin*)
*Maney. Nancy Clue, Cherry Aimless & friends
*McAllester. Tenny Mendoza
*McClellan. *Chimney Rock Blues*
McConnell. *The Burnton Widows*
McDermid. *Final Edition*
*McNab. *Chain Letter; Lessons in Murder*
*Mildon. Cal Meredith (*Stalking the Goddess Ship*)
*Morell. Lucia Ramos
*Nava. Henry Rios (*How Town*)
*Plante. *Dirty Money*
*Powell. *Houston Town*
*Redmann. Micky Knight
*Saum. Brigid Donovan (*Murder is Relative*)
*Schmidt. *Sweet Cherry Wine*
Scoppettone. *Everything You Have Is Mine*
*Sims. *Damn Straight*

*Stevenson. *Chain of Fools; Third Man Out*
Steward. *Caravaggio Shawl*
Sumner. *End of April*
*Szymanski. Brett Higgins & Allie Sullivan (*When the Dead Speak*)
*Taylor. *The Last of Her Lies*
*Townsend. *Masters' Counterpoint*
*Welch. *A Day Too Long; Murder by the Book; A Proper Burial*
*Wilson, John Morgan. Benjamin Justice (*Limits of Justice; Revision of Justice*)
*Wilson/Sjoholm. Pam Nilsen
*Woodcraft. Frankie Richmond (*Babyface*)
York. *Timber City Masks*
*Zaremba. *Work for a Million*
Zimmerman. Todd Mills
*Zubro. (Tom Mason & Scott Carpenter) *A Simple Suburban Murder; Rust on the Razor*

Child pornography and prostitution

*Douglas. (Allison O'Neil & Kerry Owyhee) *Swimming Cat Cove*
*Hansen. *Skinflick*
*laFavor. *Evil Dead Center*
*Mildon. *Stalking the Goddess Ship*
*Padgett. *Blue*
*Redmann. *The Intersection of Law and Desire*
Roeder. *Someone Is Killing the Gay Boys of Verona*
*Scoppettone. *Gonna Take a Homicidal Journey*
*Silva. *Weathering the Storm*
*Taylor. *The Last of Her Lies*
*Wilson/Sjoholm. Pam Nilsen (*Sisters of the Road*)
*Zubro. (Tom Mason & Scott Carpenter) *A Simple Suburban Murder*

Gay children and youth

*Aldyne. *Cobalt; Vermillion*
*Azolakov. (Cass Milam) *Cass and the Stone Butch*
*Azolakov. (T.D. Renfro) *Blood Lavender*
*Craft. *Boy Toy*
*Dickson. *Some Kind of Love*
*Fennelly. Matty Sinclair
*Grobeson. *Outside the Badge*
*Hansen. *Skinflick*
*Hart. *Vital Lies*
*Hartman. Drew Parker & Jen Grey
Herren. (Chanse MacLeod) *Murder in the Rue Dauphine*
*Herren. (Scotty Bradley) *Bourbon Street Blues*
*Johnson, Steve. *False Confessions*
*McConnell. *Double Daughter*
*Nava. Henry Rios (*Goldenboy*)
*Roeder. *Someone Is Killing the Gay Boys of Verona*
*Stevenson. Don Strachey
*Townsend. *One for the Master, Two for the Fool*
*Wilson, John Morgan. Benjamin Justice (*Revision of Justice*)
Wilson/Sjoholm. (Pam Nilsen) *Sisters of the Road*
*Zaremba. *A Reason to Kill*
*Zimmerman. Todd Mills
*Zubro. Tom Mason & Scott Carpenter
*Zubro. (Paul Turner) *Another Dead Teenager; Dead Egotistical Morons*

Lesbian children and youth

*Albarella. Nikki Barnes
*Allen. Alison Kaine (*Give My Secrets Back*)
*Calloway. *1st Impressions; 4th Down*
*Clare. *Street Rules*

Davidson. *Deadly Rendezvous*
*Douglas. (Caitlin Reece) *The Daughters of Artemis; A Tiger's Heart*
*Drury. *Closed in Silence*
Foster. *The Monarchs Are Flying*
*Gilligan. Alix Nicholson
*Grobeson. *Outside the Badge*
*Haddock. Carmen Ramirez
*Hart. *Hallowed Murder*
*Hartman. Drew Parker & Jen Grey
*Johnson, Steve. *False Confessions*
Manthorne. *Ghost Motel; Deadly Reunion*
*Miller. Lexy Hyatt
*Plante. *Dirty Money*
Redmann. Micky Knight
*Stevenson. *Death Trick*
*Sumner. *End of April*
*Szymanski. Brett Higgins & Allie Sullivan
*Taylor. *The Last of Her Lies*
Welch. *Fallen from Grace; Open House; Smoke and Mirrors*
Wilson/Sjoholm. Cassandra Reilly
*Wilson/Sjoholm. (Pam Nilsen) *Sisters of the Road*
Wings. Emma Victor
*Zimmerman. Todd Mills

Gay men with children

*Craft. Mark Manning (*Boy Toy*)
Foster. *The Monarchs Are Flying*
*Maiman. *Baby It's Cold*
McNab. *Cop Out; Past Due*
Nava. *The Burning Plain*
*Outland. *Death Wore a Fabulous New Fragrance*
*Roeder. *Someone Is Killing the Gay Boys of Verona*
Stevenson. *Chain of Fools; Tongue Tied*
*Sumner. *Crosswords*

*Zimmerman. Todd Mills (*Tribe*)
*Zubro. Paul Turner

Lesbians with children

Albarella. *Agenda for Murder*
Allen. Alison Kaine (*Takes One to Know One*)
*Davis. Maris Middleton (*Shattered Illusions*)
Douglas. (Allison O'Neil & Kerry Owyhee) *Swimming Cat Cove*
Drury. Tyler Jones (*Closed in Silence*)
*Duffy. *Fresh Flesh*
*Fritchley. Letty Campbell
*Griffith. *Stay*
*Hart. *A Small Sacrifice; Robber's Wine; Vital Lies*
Johnson, Steve. *Final Atonement*
*King. *With Child*
*laFavor. Renee LaRoche
*Lynch. *Sue Slate: Private Eye*
*Maddison. Connor Hawthorne & team
*Maiman. Robin Miller (*Baby It's Cold; Someone to Watch*)
Manthorne. *Last Resort*
*McAllester. Tenny Mendoza (*The Search*)
McConnell. *The Burnton Widows*
McDermid. *Conferences Are Murder*
*McNab. Carol Ashton (*Past Due*)
Nava. *The Burning Plain*
*Pincus. Nell Fury
*Sanra. *No Corpse*
Saum. Brigid Donovan
*Silva. *Storm Front; Weathering the Storm*
Stevenson. *Chain of Fools; Tongue Tied*
*Sumner. Tor Cross
Tell. Poppy Dillworth
*Welch. *A Day Too Long*
Wilson/Sjoholm. Pam Nilsen

*Wilson/Sjoholm. (Cassandra
Reilly) *Gaudi Afternoon*
*Woodcraft. *Good Bad Woman*
*Zimmerman. Todd Mills (*Tribe*)

Classism in the Lesbigay Community

*Baker. *In the Game; The Lavender
House Murder*
*Fennelly. *The Glory Hole Murders*
*Fritchley. Letty Campbell
Gilbert. *Spiked*
Marcy. Meg Darcy
McDermid. *Common Murder*
McNab. *Death Club*
Miller. Lexy Hyatt
*Redmann. Micky Knight
*Sanra. *No Corpse*
Sims. *Damn Straight*
*Stukas. Robert Willsop, Monette
O'Reilley & Michael Stark
Taylor. *We Know Where You Live*
Welch. *Murder by the Book*
*Wilson, John Morgan. Benjamin
Justice
York. *Timber City Masks*

Closet
see also Internalized Homophobia

Virtually all series include this
topic, and in many novels the closet
plays a role in the main plot or a
subplot. This list only includes closeted main characters.
Baker. Virginia Kelly
Baxt. Pharoah Love
Beecham. Amanda Valentine
Clare. L.A. Franco

Forrest. Kate Delafield
Gilbert. *Spiked*
Grobeson. *Outside the Badge*
Haddock. *Edited Out*
Hart. *Hallowed Murder*
Johnson, Bett Reece. Cordelia Mor-
gan & partners
King. *A Grave Talent*
Lanyon. Adrien English & Jake
Riordan
McClellan. Tru North
McNab. Carol Ashton (until *Dead
Certain*)
Mickelbury. Gianna Maglione &
Mimi Patterson
Morell. Lucia Ramos
Richardson. Stevie Houston
Saum. Brigid Donovan
York. Royce Madison
Zubro. Tom Mason & Scott Car-
penter (until *Rust on the Razor*)
Zubro. Paul Turner

Coming Out
see also Closet

To others

*Azolakov. T.D. Renfro
Calloway. *2nd Fiddle; 5th Wheel*
*Craft. Mark Manning
Cutler. *The Face on the Cutting
Room Floor*
*Davidson. *Deadly Butterfly*
*Davis. Maris Middleton
*Dickson. *FreeForm*
*Dreher. *Gray Magic*
Fennelly. *The Glory Hole Murders*
*Foster. *The Monarchs Are Flying*
Gilligan. *Danger in High Places*
*Haddock. *Edited Out*
*Hart. *Robber's Wine*

Self awareness and sexual experience

Community
see **Lesbigay Community**

Cross Dressing/ Transvestites

Dymmoch. *Feline Friendship*
Griffith. *Stay*
Hansen. Dave Brandstetter (*Night-work; Skinflick*)
Hart. *Faint Praise*
*Hartman. *The Gumshoe, the Witch, and the Virtual Corpse*
Hunter. *The Chicken Asylum*
Johnson, Steve. *False Confessions*
Lordon. *Mother May I*
*Maney. Nancy Clue, Cherry Aimless & friends
McKay. *The Kali Connection*
Mickelbury. *Night Songs*
*Outland. Doan McCandler & Binky Van de Kamp
*Plante. *Dirty Money*
Redmann. *Death by the Riverside*
Richardson. *Double Take Out*
*Sanra. *No Corpse*
*Scoppettone. *My Sweet Untraceable You*
*Stevenson. *Death Trick*
*Stukas. *Going Down for the Count*
*Szymanski. Brett Higgins & Allie Sullivan
Townsend. *One for the Master, Two for the Fool*
Wilson, John Morgan. *Justice at Risk*
*Wilson/Sjoholm. (Cassandra Reilly) *Gaudi Afternoon*

Drag queens and kings

*Aldyne. *Canary; Vermillion*
Beecham. *Second Guess*
Davidson. *Deadly Gamble*
Fennelly. *The Glory Hole Murders*
Hartman. *The Gumshoe, the Witch, and the Virtual Corpse*
Herren. (Scotty Bradley) *Bourbon Street Blues*
Lynch. *Sue Slate: Private Eye*
*Maiman. *Crazy for Loving*

Michaels. *A Body to Dye For; Love You to Death*
Outland. Doan McCandler & Binky Van de Kamp
*Redmann. Micky Knight
Stevenson. *Strachey's Folly*
*Stukas. Robert Willsop, Monette O'Reilley & Michael Stark
Wilson/Sjoholm. (Cassandra Reilly) *Gaudi Afternoon*
*Wings. *She Came in Drag*
*Zimmerman. Todd Mills (*Closet*)
*Zubro. (Tom Mason & Scott Carpenter) *An Echo of Death; One Dead Drag Queen*

Cruising
see **Casual and Anonymous Sex, Cruising**

Disabled

Includes both mental and physical afflictions.

*Albarella. *Close to You*
Allen. *Just a Little Lie*
Craft. Mark Manning
Douglas. (Allison O'Neil & Kerry Owyhee) *Death at Lavender Bay*
Douglas. (Caitlin Reece) *Goblin Market*
*Maiman. *Baby It's Cold; Someone to Watch*
*Schmidt. *Sweet Cherry Wine*
Wilson, John Morgan. *Justice at Risk; Simple Justice*
*Wings. Emma Victor
*Zubro. Paul Turner

Diversity

These authors mention diversity as a theme in their novels.

Albarella. Nikki Barnes
Allen. Alison Kaine
Calloway. Cassidy James
Dickson. Jas Anderson
Drury. Tyler Jones
Dunford. Mitchell Draper
Hansen. Dave Brandstetter
Hart. Jane Lawless
Maddison. Connor Hawthorne & team
McConnell. Nyla Wade
McDermid. Lindsay Gordon
Roeder. Sean
Wings. Emma Victor
Zimmerman. Todd Mills

Domestic Violence
see Violence Against Women

Drag Queens
see Cross Dressing/ Transvestites

Drugs and Alcohol

Alcohol and alcoholism

*Albarella. Nikki Barnes
*Aldyne. Dan Valentine & Clarisse Lovelace
*Allen. Tell Me What You Like
Baker. Virginia Kelly
Calloway. 3rd Degree
Clare. L.A. Franco
Craft. Mark Manning (Flight Dreams)

*Cutler. Mark Bradley & Rayford Goodman
*Davis. Maris Middleton (Shattered Illusions)
Douglas. Caitlin Reece
*Dreher. Shaman's Moon; Stoner McTavish
*Drury. Tyler Jones
Duffy. Saz Martin
Dymmoch. Jack Caleb & John Thinnes
Forrest. Kate Delafield (Apparition Alley)
Gilbert. Spiked
Haddock. Edited Out
*Hansen. Dave Brandstetter (The Man Everybody Was Afraid Of)
Hart. Jane Lawless (A Small Sacrifice; Hunting the Witch)
Herren. (Scotty Bradley) Bourbon Street Blues
*Johnson, Bett Reece. Cordelia Morgan & partners (The Woman Who Knew Too Much)
Johnson, Steve. Doug Orlando
*Knight. Lil Ritchie
laFavor. Renee LaRoche
*Lanyon. A Dangerous Thing
Maddison. Connor Hawthorne & team
*Maiman. Robin Miller (Under My Skin)
Maney. Nancy Clue, Cherry Aimless & friends
*Manthorne. Harriet Hubbley
*Marcy. Dead and Blonde
*McClellan. Chimney Rock Blues
McDermid. Conferences Are Murder
McKay. The Kali Connection
McNab. Cop Out
Michaels. Time to Check Out
Mickelbury. Night Songs
Miller. Lexy Hyatt
*Nava. Henry Rios

*Outland. Doan McCandler &
Binky Van de Kamp
*Plante. Cynthia Chenery Scott
Powell. *Bayou City Secrets*
*Redmann. Micky Knight
Sanra. *No Corpse*
*Saum. Brigid Donovan
*Schmidt. Laney Samms
Scott. *Stronger Than Death*
*Stevenson. *Death Trick; Ice Blues;
Shock to the System*
Stukas. Robert Willsop, Monette
O'Reilley & Michael Stark
*Szymanski. *When the Dead Speak*
Taylor. *The Last of Her Lies*
*Welch. Helen Black (*Still Waters*)
*Wilson, John Morgan. Benjamin
Justice
*Wilson/Sjoholm. (Pam Nilsen)
Murder in the Collective
Wings. *She Came Too Late*
Woodcraft. Frankie Richmond
York. *Timber City Masks*
*Zaremba. *A Reason to Kill*
Zimmerman. Todd Mills

Drugs and drug abuse

*Albarella. *Called to Kill*
*Aldyne. Dan Valentine & Clarisse
Lovelace (*Cobalt*)
*Allen. Alison Kaine
*Beal. *Angel Dance*
*Calloway. Cassidy James
*Clare. *Street Rules*
*Cutler. Mark Bradley & Rayford
Goodman (*Shot on Location*)
*Davidson. *Deadly Rendezvous*
*Dickson. Jas Anderson
Dreher. *Something Shady*
Forrest. Kate Delafield
*Fritchley. *Chicken Feed*
*Griffith. *The Blue Place*
Grobeson. *Outside the Badge*

*Hansen. Dave Brandstetter (*Death
Claims*)
*Hart. Jane Lawless (*A Killing Cure;
A Small Sacrifice; Immaculate Mid-
night*)
*Hartman. Drew Parker & Jen Grey
*Herren. (Scotty Bradley) *Bourbon
Street Blues*
*Johnson, Barbara. Colleen Fitzger-
ald
*Johnson, Bett Reece. Cordelia
Morgan & partners (*The Woman
Who Knew Too Much*)
*Knight. Lil Ritchie
*laFavor. *Evil Dead Center*
*Lansdale. Hap Collins & Leonard
Pine (*Mucho Mojo*)
*Lordon. *Father Forgive Me*
*Lynch. *Sue Slate: Private Eye*
*McKay. Lynn Evans
*Michaels. *A Body to Dye For; Time
to Check Out*
*Mickelbury. *Night Songs*
*Mildon. *Stalking the Goddess Ship*
*Nava. Henry Rios (*The Hidden
Law*)
*Outland. *Death Wore the Emperor's
New Clothes*
*Padgett. *Blue*
*Plante. *Dirty Money*
Powell. Hollis Carpenter
*Rand. *Gay Detective*
*Redmann. Micky Knight
*Roberts. Cameron McGill
*Sanra. *No Escape*
*Scott. *Hen's Teeth; Night Mares*
*Silva. *Taken by Storm; Tropical
Storm*
*Stevenson. Don Strachey
Stukas. Robert Willsop, Monette
O'Reilley & Michael Stark
*Sumner. *End of April*
*Szymanski. Brett Higgins & Allie
Sullivan (*When Evil Changes Face*)

*Taylor. Maggie Garrett (*We Know Where You Live*)
*Townsend. *One for the Master, Two for the Fool*
*Welch. Helen Black (*Murder by the Book*)
*Wilson, John Morgan. *Limits of Justice; Simple Justice*
Wilson/Sjoholm. (Pam Nilsen) *Sisters of the Road*
*Wings. Emma Victor (*She Came Too Late*)
*York. *Timber City Masks*
*Zubro. Tom Mason & Scott Carpenter (*Why Isn't Becky Twitchell Dead?*)

Miller. Lexy Hyatt
Pincus. Nell Fury
Sanra. *No Corpse*
Schmidt. *Silverlake Heat*
Sims. *Damn Straight*
Stevenson. *Death Trick*
Stukas. Robert Willsop, Monette O'Reilley & Michael Stark
Szymanski. Brett Higgins & Allie Sullivan
Tell. Poppy Dillworth
*Townsend. Bruce MacLeod
Welch. Helen Black
Wilson/Sjoholm. (Pam Nilsen) *The Dog Collar Murders*
Wings. Emma Victor
Zaremba. Helen Keremos

Erotic Scenes/ Explicit Sex

Most of the entries in this category have one or two explicit sex scenes per novel.

Albarella. Nikki Barnes
Allen. Alison Kaine
Azolakov. T.D. Renfro
Calloway. Cassidy James
Craft. Mark Manning
Davidson. Toni Underwood
Dickson. Jas Anderson
Douglas. Caitlin Reece
Forrest. Kate Delafield
Griffith. *The Blue Place*
Johnson, Barbara. Colleen Fitzgerald
Lanyon. Adrien English & Jake Riordan
Maiman. Robin Miller
Manthorne. Harriet Hubbley
Marcy. Meg Darcy
McNab. Carol Ashton
Mildon. Cal Meredith

Family

*Beecham. Amanda Valentine
*Craft. Mark Manning
*Davidson. *Deady Gamble*
*Davis. Maris Middleton
*Douglas. (Allison O'Neil & Kerry Owyhee) *Death at Lavender Bay*
*Dreher. Stoner McTavish
*Drury. Tyler Jones
*Foster. *The Monarchs Are Flying*
*Fritchley. Letty Campbell
*Haddock. Carmen Ramirez
*Hart. Jane Lawless
*Hartman. Drew Parker & Jen Grey
*Herren. Scotty Bradley
*laFavor. Renee LaRoche
*Lordon. Sydney Sloane
*Maddison. Connor Hawthorne & team
*Maiman. Robin Miller
*Maney. Nancy Clue, Cherry Aimless & friends
*McConnell. Nyla Wade
*Mickelbury. *Keeping Secrets*

*Miller. Lexy Hyatt
*Nava. Henry Rios (*Rag and Bone*)
*Saum. Brigid Donovan
*Stevenson. Don Strachey
*Wilson, John Morgan. Benjamin
  Justice
*Wilson/Sjoholm. Pam Nilsen
*Wilson/Sjoholm. *Gaudi Afternoon*
*Woodcraft. Frankie Richmond
*York. Royce Madison
*Zubro. Paul Turner

Extended/created families

*Azolakov. Cass Milam
*Forrest. Kate Delafield (*Murder at
  the Nightwood Bar*)
Foster. *The Monarchs Are Flying*
*Fritchley. Letty Campbell
*Haddock. Carmen Ramirez
*Herren. Scotty Bradley
*Johnson, Barbara. Colleen Fitzger-
  ald
Lordon. Sydney Sloane
*Maddison. Connor Hawthorne &
  team
*Maney. Nancy Clue, Cherry Aim-
  less & friends
Manthorne. Harriet Hubbley
*Marcy. Meg Darcy
McClellan. *K.C. Bomber*
*McConnell. Nyla Wade
*Miller. Lexy Hyatt
Pincus. Nell Fury
*Tell. Poppy Dillworth
*Wilson, John Morgan. Benjamin
  Justice
*Wilson/Sjoholm. Cassandra Reilly

Homophobia

*Albarella. Nikki Barnes (*Agenda for
  Murder*)
Aldyne. *Cobalt; Vermillion*

*Allen. Alison Kaine (*Tell Me What
  You Like*)
*Azolakov. Cass Milam
Azolakov. (T.D. Renfro) *Blood
  Lavender*
*Baker. Virginia Kelly
*Calloway. *4th Down*
*Craft. Mark Manning (*Eye Contact*)
Cutler. Mark Bradley & Rayford
  Goodman
*Davis. Maris Middleton (*Until the
  End*)
*Dreher. Stoner McTavish
*Drury. Tyler Jones (*Silent Words*)
Duffy. *Fresh Flesh*
*Dymmoch. Jack Caleb & John
  Thinnes
*Forrest. Kate Delafield (*Murder at
  the Nightwood Bar*)
*Foster. Harriet Fordham Croft
Fritchley. Letty Campbell
Gilbert. *Spiked*
*Gilligan. *Danger in High Places*
*Hansen. Dave Brandstetter (*Death
  Claims*)
*Hart. Jane Lawless (*Hallowed
  Murder*)
*Hartman. Drew Parker & Jen Grey
Herren. (Chanse MacLeod) *Murder
  in the Rue Dauphine*
*James. *Posted to Death*
Johnson, Barbara. Colleen Fitzgerald
*Johnson, Bett Reece. *The Woman
  Who Found Grace*
*Johnson, Steve. *False Confessions*
King. Kate Martinelli
laFavor. Renee LaRoche
*Lansdale. *Mucho Mojo*
*Lordon. Sydney Sloane
*Maddison. Connor Hawthorne &
  team
*Maiman. Robin Miller
*Maney. Nancy Clue, Cherry Aim-
  less & friends

*Manthorne. Harriet Hubbley
(*Ghost Motel*)
*Marcy. Meg Darcy
*McAllester. *The Lessons*
McClellan. *K.C. Bomber*
*McConnell. Nyla Wade (*Mrs. Porter's Letter*)
McDermid. *Conferences Are Murder*
*McNab. Carol Ashton (*Cop Out*)
*Michaels. *Love You to Death; Time to Check Out*
*Mickelbury. *Keeping Secrets*
*Mildon. *Stalking the Goddess Ship*
*Miller. Lexy Hyatt
*Nava. Henry Rios
Pincus. *The Solitary Twist*
*Plante. *Dirty Money*
*Powell. *Bayou City Secrets*
*Raphael. *Let's Get Criminal*
*Redmann. Micky Knight
*Richardson. Stevie Houston
*Roeder. *Someone Is Killing the Gay Boys of Verona*
*Saum. Brigid Donovan
*Schmidt. Laney Samms
*Scoppettone. *Everything You Have Is Mine*
Silva. *Weathering the Storm*
*Stevenson. Don Strachey (*Death Trick; Shock to the System*)
*Stukas. Robert Willsop, Monette O'Reilley & Michael Stark
*Sumner. *End of April*
*Szymanski. *When the Dead Speak*
*Taylor. Maggie Garrett
Tell. *Hallelujah Murders*
*Townsend. *One for the Master, Two for the Fool*
*Welch. Helen Black
Wilson, John Morgan. Benjamin Justice
Wilson/Sjoholm. Pam Nilsen
*Wilson/Sjoholm. Cassandra Reilly

*Woodcraft. Frankie Richmond
(*Good Bad Woman*)
*York. Royce Madison (*Crystal Mountain Veils*)
*Zaremba. *A Reason to Kill*
*Zimmerman. Todd Mills (*Hostage*)
*Zubro. Tom Mason & Scott Carpenter (*Rust on the Razor*)
*Zubro. (Paul Turner) *The Truth Can Get You Killed*

Supportive attitudes, acceptance

*Adlyne. *Vermillion*
*Allen. *Takes One to Know One*
Azolakov. (T.D. Renfro) *The Contactees Die Young*
Beecham. Amanda Valentine
Craft. *Body Language; Boy Toy*
*Davidson. Toni Underwood (*Deadly Gamble*)
Davis. *Devil's Leg Crossing*
*Dreher. Stoner McTavish
*Drury. Tyler Jones
*Dymmoch. *Incendiary Designs*
Fennelly. *The Glory Hole Murders*
*Forrest. *Sleeping Bones*
*Foster. *The Monarchs Are Flying*
*Fritchley. Letty Campbell
Griffith. *The Blue Place*
*Hansen. Dave Brandstetter
*Hart. Jane Lawless
*Hunter. Alex Reynolds, Peter Livesay & Jean Reynolds
Johnson, Steve. Doug Orlando
*laFavor. Renee LaRoche
*Lordon. Sydney Sloane
*Maddison. Connor Hawthorne & team
*Maiman. Robin Miller (*Every Time We Say Goodbye*)
Manthorne. Harriet Hubbley
*Marcy. Meg Darcy

McAllester. Tenny Mendoza
*McConnell. *Double Daughter*
McKay. *The Kali Connection*
*McNab. Carol Ashton
Michaels. *Mask for a Diva*
Mickelbury. *Keeping Secrets*
*Miller. Lexy Hyatt
Morell. Lucia Ramos
*Nava. *Goldenboy*
Padgett. *Blue*
*Pincus. Nell Fury
Plante. *Getting Away with Murder*
Raphael. Nick Hoffman
*Redmann. *Lost Daughters*
*Roberts. *Needlepoint*
*Roeder. *Someone Is Killing the Gay Boys of Verona*
*Sanra. Tally McGinnis & Cid Cameron
*Scoppettone. *Everything You Have Is Mine*
*Szymanski. Brett Higgins & Allie Sullivan
Wilson/Sjoholm. *Sisters of the Road*
Woodcraft. Frankie Richmond
*York. Royce Madison (*Crystal Mountain Veils*)
*Zaremba. *A Reason to Kill*
Zimmerman. *Closet*
*Zubro. Tom Mason & Scott Carpenter (*One Dead Drag Queen*)
*Zubro. Paul Turner

Feminism

see **Women's Activism; Sexism and Misogyny**

Friendship

All gay/lesbian detectives have friends. In these novels friendship is an important element.

Albarella. Nikki Barnes
Aldyne. Dan Valentine & Clarisse Lovelace
Allen. Alison Kaine
Azolakov. Cass Milam
Azolakov. (T.D. Renfro) *Blood Lavender*
Calloway. Cassidy James
Craft. *Hot Spot*
Davidson. Toni Underwood (*Deadly Gamble*)
Douglas. Allison O'Neil & Kerry Owyhee
Dreher. Stoner McTavish
Drury. Tyler Jones (*Closed in Silence*)
Dunford. Mitchell Draper
Dymmoch. Jack Caleb & John Thinnes
Forrest. Kate Delafield (*Liberty Square*)
Fritchley. Letty Campbell
Gilligan. *Danger in High Places*
Haddock. Carmen Ramirez
Hart. Jane Lawless
Hartman. Drew Parker & Jen Grey
Herren. Chanse MacLeod
Hunter. Alex Reynolds, Peter Livesay & Jean Reynolds
Johnson, Barbara. Colleen Fitzgerald
Johnson, Bett Reece. Cordelia Morgan & partners
King. *Night Work*
Lansdale. Hap Collins & Leonard Pine
Lordon. Sydney Sloane
Maddison. Connor Hawthorne & team
Maiman. Robin Miller
Maney. Nancy Clue, Cherry Aimless & friends
Manthorne. *Last Resort; Final Take*
Marcy. Meg Darcy

Gay and Lesbian Bashing

Gay men

*Zubro. Tom Mason & Scott Carpenter

Lesbians

*Allen. *Tell Me What You Like*
*Azolakov. (Cass Milam) *Skiptrace*
Calloway. *1st Impressions*
*Davidson. *Deadly Rendezvous*
*Davis. *Possessions*
*Drury. *Silent Words*
*Johnson, Barbara. *The Beach Affair*
*Maiman. *Old Black Magic*
*McAllester. *The Lessons*
*McConnell. Nyla Wade
Richardson. *Over the Line*
*Saum. *Murder is Germane*
*Scoppettone. *Let's Face the Music and Die*
*Szymanski. *When the Dancing Stops*
*Tell. *Murder at Red Rook Ranch*
*Woodcraft. *Good Bad Woman*

Unspecified or both

*Herren. (Chanse MacLeod) *Murder in the Rue Dauphine*
*Herren. (Scotty Bradley) *Bourbon Street Blues*
*Johnson, Barbara. *The Beach Affair*
*McConnell. Nyla Wade (*Double Daughter*)
*Mickelbury. *Keeping Secrets*
*Raphael. Nick Hoffman
Scoppettone. Lauren Laurano
Stevenson. Don Strachey
*Taylor. *We Know Where You Live*
Zubro. (Paul Turner) *Political Poison; Sorry Now?*

Gay and Lesbian Rights, Activism, Politics, and Pride

Beal. *Angel Dance*
Beecham. *Fair Play*
*Calloway. *4th Down*
*Craft. Mark Manning (*Eye Contact*)
Cutler. Mark Bradley & Rayford Goodman
Dymmoch. *The Man Who Understood Cats*
*Fennelly. Matty Sinclair
*Forrest. *Apparition Alley; Murder by Tradition*
*Foster. *The Monarchs Are Flying*
*Gilbert. *Spiked*
*Gilligan. *Danger in High Places*
*Grobeson. *Outside the Badge*
*Haddock. Carmen Ramirez
*Hansen. *The Man Everybody Was Afraid Of*
*Herren. (Chanse MacLeod) *Murder in the Rue Dauphine*
Johnson, Barbara. Colleen Fitzgerald
*Johnson, Steve. Doug Orlando
*King. *A Grave Talent; Night Work*
Lanyon. *A Dangerous Thing*
Manthorne. *Deadly Reunion*
McAllester. *The Lessons*
*McConnell. Nyla Wade (*The Burnton Widows*)
*McDermid. *Conferences Are Murder*
*Miller. Lexy Hyatt
*Nava. Henry Rios (*Goldenboy*)
*Outland. Doan McCandler & Binky Van de Kamp
Plante. *Dirty Money*
Rand. *Gay Detective*
*Raphael. Nick Hoffman (*The Edith Wharton Murders*)
*Roeder. *Someone Is Killing the Gay Boys of Verona*

*Stevenson. Don Strachey (*Third Man Out; Tongue Tied*)
Stukas. *Someone Killed His Boyfriend*
*Szymanski. *When the Dancing Stops*
*Taylor. *We Know Where You Live*
Wilson, John Morgan. *Benjamin Justice*
*Wings. *Emma Victor*
York. *Crystal Mountain Veils*
Zimmerman. *Closet*
*Zubro. Tom Mason & Scott Carpenter (*Are You Nuts?*)
*Zubro. (Paul Turner) *Sorry Now?*

Gay Community
see Lesbigay Community

Gay on Gay Crime
see also Lesbian on Lesbian Crime

*Aldyne. *Canary; Cobalt*
*Azolakov. (T.D. Renfro) *Blood Lavender*
*Baxt. *A Queer Kind of Death*
*Fennelly. *The Glory Hole Murders*
*Gilbert. *Spiked*
*Gilligan. *Danger in High Places*
Hartman. *Gumshoe Gorilla*
*Herren. (Chanse MacLeod) *Murder in the Rue Dauphine*
*Lansdale. *Bad Chili*
*Lordon. *Father Forgive Me*
*Manthorne. *Final Take*
*Michaels. *A Body to Dye For*
*Nava. Henry Rios (*Goldenboy*)
*Rand. *Gay Detective*
*Stevenson. Don Strachey
*Steward. *Caravaggio Shawl*

*Stukas. Robert Willsop, Monette O'Reilley & Michael Stark
*Taylor. *We Know Where You Live*
*Townsend. *One for the Master, Two for the Fool*
*Wilson, John Morgan. *Benjamin Justice*

Gaydar
see Stereotypic Characters

Heterosexism
see also Heterosexual Marriage

Includes both the assumption that someone is heterosexual and pressure to conform to heterosexual behavior.

Aldyne. *Vermillion*
Baker. *The Ultimate Exit Strategy*
*Craft. *Flight Dreams*
Cutler. Mark Bradley & Rayford Goodman
Davis. *Shattered Illusions*
*Foster. *The Monarchs Are Flying*
*McAllester. *The Lessons*
*McNab. Carol Ashton (*Lessons in Murder*)
Richardson. Stevie Houston
*Schmidt. Laney Samms
Silva. *Weathering the Storm*
*Stevenson. Don Strachey
Welch. Helen Black

Heterosexual Marriage
see also Closet; Internalized Homophobia

Lesbians and gay men married to members of the opposite sex.*

*Albarella. *Agenda for Murder*

*Gay/lesbian marriage is included under Relationships with Lovers and Romance.

*Aldyne. *Vermillion*
*Azolakov. Cass Milam
*Baker. *The Ultimate Exit Strategy*
*Beecham. Amanda Valentine
*Calloway. *3rd Degree; 4th Down*
*Craft. Mark Manning (*Body Lan-guage*)
*Davidson. *Deadly Gamble*
*Davis. Maris Middleton
*Douglas. (Caitlin Reece) *The Always Anonymous Beast*
*Dymmoch. *Incendiary Designs*
*Fennelly. *The Glory Hole Murders*
*Foster. *The Monarchs Are Flying*
*Fritchley. *Chicken Out; Chicken Run*
Gilbert. *Spiked*
Grobeson. *Outside the Badge*
*Hansen. Dave Brandstetter
*Hart. *A Killing Cure; Robber's Wine*
*Hartman. *Gumshoe Gorilla*
*Herren. (Chanse MacLeod) *Murder in the Rue Dauphine*
Lordon. *Sister's Keeper*
Maddison. *Deceptions*
*Maiman. Robin Miller (*Someone to Watch*)
*Manthorne. *Ghost Motel; Last Resort*
*McConnell. *The Burnton Widows*
McDermid. *Final Edition*
*McNab. Carol Ashton
*Michaels. Stan Kraychik
*Mickelbury. *Keeping Secrets*
Miller. *Mayhem at the Marina*
Morell. *Final Session*
*Nava. Henry Rios (*The Death of Friends*)
*Outland. Doan McCandler & Binky Van de Kamp (*Death Wore a Fabulous New Fragrance*)
*Pincus. *The Two-Bit Tango; The Solitary Twist*
*Redmann. Micky Knight
Richardson. *Over the Line*

Sims. *Holy Hell*
*Stevenson. Don Strachey (*Shock to the System*)
Sumner. *End of April*
*Szymanski. Brett Higgins & Allie Sullivan (*When Some Body Disappears*)
Taylor. *We Know Where You Live*
*Tell. Poppy Dillworth
*Wilson, John Morgan. Benjamin Justice
*Wings. *She Came in Drag; She Came Too Late*
*Woodcraft. *Good Bad Woman*
*York. *Timber City Masks*
*Zimmerman. Todd Mills (*Innuendo*)
*Zubro. (Paul Turner) *The Truth Can Get You Killed*

HIV
see AIDS/HIV

Homophobia
see also Family

Virtually all series include homophobia. This listing contains special aspects of homophobia only.

At work or school

*Albarella. Nikki Barnes
*Azolakov. (T.D. Renfro) *Blood Lavender*
*Baker. Virginia Kelly
Beal. *Angel Dance*
*Beecham. Amanda Valentine
*Calloway. *4th Down; 8th Day*
*Craft. *Boy Toy; Eye Contact*
*Cutler. Mark Bradley & Rayford Goodman (*Best Performance by a Patsy*)

*Douglas. (Caitlin Reece) *The Always Anonymous Beast*
Fritchley. *Chicken Out*
*Gilbert. *Spiked*
*Gilligan. Alix Nicholson
*Haddock. Carmen Ramirez
Hansen. *Troublemaker*
*Hart. *Hallowed Murder; Hunting the Witch; A Small Sacrifice*
*James. *Posted to Death*
*Johnson, Barbara. Colleen Fitzgerald
*Maiman. *Old Black Magic; Under My Skin*
Marcy. Meg Darcy
*McClellan. Tru North
McConnell. *Double Daughter*
*McDermid. Lindsay Gordon (*Conferences Are Murder*)
*Michaels. Stan Kraychik
* Outland. Doan McCandler & Binky Van de Kamp
*Pincus. *The Hangdog Hustle*
*Plante. *Getting Away with Murder*
Powell. *Bayou City Secrets*
*Rand. *Gay Detective*
*Raphael. Nick Hoffman
*Redmann. Micky Knight
*Richardson. Stevie Houston (*Last Rites*)
Roeder. *Someone Is Killing the Gay Boys of Verona*
Schmidt. Laney Samms
*Scoppettone. *My Sweet Untraceable You*
Scott. *Hen's Teeth*
*Sims. *Damn Straight*
*Stevenson. Don Strachey
*Sumner. Tor Cross
*Szymanski. *When the Dancing Stops*
*Townsend. Bruce MacLeod
*Welch. *Fallen from Grace*
*Wilson, John Morgan. Benjamin Justice

*Wilson/Sjoholm. (Pam Nilsen) *Murder in the Collective*
*Wings. *She Came Too Late*
Woodcraft. *Good Bad Woman*
*York. *Crystal Mountain Veils*
*Zimmerman. Todd Mills (*Closet*)
*Zubro. Tom Mason & Scott Carpenter (*One Dead Drag Queen; The Principal Cause of Death*)
*Zubro. Paul Turner

In law enforcement

*Aldyne. Dan Valentine & Clarisse Lovelace (*Vermillion*)
Allen. Alison Kaine
*Baxt. *A Queer Kind of Love*
Beecham. Amanda Valentine
*Clare. L.A. Franco
Cutler. Mark Bradley & Rayford Goodman
*Davidson. *Deadly Rendezvous*
*Davis. Maris Middleton
*Dickson. Jas Anderson
*Dymmoch. Jack Caleb & John Thinnes
Fennelly. *The Glory Hole Murders*
*Forrest. Kate Delafield
*Foster. *The Monarchs Are Flying*
*Grobeson. *Outside the Badge*
*Haddock. *Edited Out*
*Hansen. *The Man Everybody Was Afraid Of*
*Hart. *Hallowed Murder; Stage Fright*
*Herren. (Chanse MacLeod) *Murder in the Rue Dauphine*
*Hunter. Alex Reynolds, Peter Livesay & Jean Reynolds
*Johnson, Steve. Doug Orlando
King. Kate Martinelli
*Lansdale. *Bad Chili*
Lanyon. Adrien English & Jake Riordan

*Maddison. *Death by Prophecy*
Manthorne. *Deadly Reunion; Last Resort*
*Marcy. Meg Darcy
*McAllester. Tenny Mendoza
*McClellan. Tru North
*McConnell. Nyla Wade
*McNab. Carol Ashton
*Michaels. Stan Kraychik
*Mickelbury. Gianna Maglione & Mimi Patterson
Morell. Lucia Ramos
*Nava. Henry Rios (*The Burning Plain*)
Outland. *Death Wore a Smart Little Outfit*
Pincus. *The Hangdog Hustle*
Rand. *Gay Detective*
Raphael. *Let's Get Criminal*
Redmann. Micky Knight (*Deaths of Jocasta*)
*Richardson. Stevie Houston (*Over the Line*)
*Sanra. Tally McGinnis & Cid Cameron (*No Witnesses*)
Scoppettone. Lauren Laurano
*Silva. Delta Stevens
Sims. *Holy Hell*
*Stevenson. Don Strachey
Steward. *Caravaggio Shawl*
Taylor. *We Know Where You Live*
Townsend. Bruce MacLeod
*Wilson, John Morgan. *Revision of Justice*
*York. Royce Madison
Zimmerman. Todd Mills (*Outburst*)
Zubro. (Tom Mason & Scott Carpenter) *Rust on the Razor*
Zubro. (Paul Turner)*The Truth Can Get You Killed*

Linked with sexism

Dymmoch. *The Man Who Understood Cats*

Forrest. *The Beverly Malibu; Liberty Square; Murder by Tradition*
Herren. (Chanse MacLeod) *Murder in the Rue Dauphine*
King. *With Child*
Maiman. *Crazy for Loving*
Michaels *A Body to Dye For; Time to Check Out*
Nava. Henry Rios (*The Death of Friends*)
Richardson. *Over the Line*
Silva. *Weathering the Storm*
Stevenson. *Ice Blues; Strachey's Folly; Tongue Tied*
Stukas. Robert Willsop, Monette O'Reilley & Michael Stark
Welch. *Murder by the Book*

Reprogramming/returning to heterosexuality

*Allen. *Tell Me What You Like*
Azolakov. (T.D. Renfro) *Blood Lavender*
Herren. (Scotty Bradley) *Bourbon Street Blues*
Johnson, Barbara. *The Beach Affair*
*Johnson, Bett Reece. *The Woman Who Found Grace*
Lynch. *Sue Slate: Private Eye*
*Maiman. *I Left My Heart*
McNab. *Cop Out*
Nava. *The Burning Plain*
*Stevenson. *Death Trick; Shock to the System; Tongue Tied*

Hustlers
see **Prostitution and Pornography**

Incest
see **Children**

Internalized Homophobia

see also Closet;
Heterosexual Marriage

To minimize duplication with the Closet and other themes, this category covers only extreme behaviors and emotions (e.g., virulent homophobia, repressed sexuality, suicide) and protective behavior (e.g., careful behavior in a dressing room of a gym, bartender in a gay bar refusing to talk about the bar's patrons).

Protective

Aldyne. *Vermillion*
Dymmoch. *Incendiary Designs*
*Forrest. *Murder at the Nightwood Bar*
Hunter. *Government Gay*
*Johnson, Steve. Doug Orlando (*False Confessions*)
Manthorne. *Ghost Motel*
*McConnell. *Mrs. Porter's Letter*
McDermid. *Final Edition*
Michaels. *A Body to Dye For*
Miller. *Killing at the Cat*
*Redmann. Micky Knight (*The Intersection of Law and Desire*)
Sims. *Holy Hell*
*Zubro. (Tom Mason & Scott Carpenter) *A Simple Suburban Murder*

Denial, hatred, repressed sexuality, self-hatred, suicide

*Aldyne. *Vermillion*
Allen. *Tell Me What You Like*
*Azolakov. T.D. Renfro
*Baker. *The Ultimate Exit Strategy*
*Baxt. Pharoah Love (*A Queer Kind of Love*)

*Beecham. Amanda Valentine
*Calloway. *4th Down; 5th Degree*
*Davis. *Possessions*
*Dickson. Jas Anderson
*Douglas. (Caitlin Reece) *The Always Anonymous Beast*
Dymmoch. *The Death of Blue Mountain Cat*
Fennelly. *The Glory Hole Murders*
*Forrest. *Murder by Tradition*
*Foster. *The Monarchs Are Flying*
*Grobeson. *Outside the Badge*
*Haddock. Carmen Ramirez
*Herren. (Scotty Bradley) *Bourbon Street Blues*
*Hunter. *National Nancys*
*Johnson, Bett Reece. *The Woman Who Found Grace*
*Johnson, Steve. *False Confessions*
*Lanyon. Adrien English & Jake Riordan
*Lordon. *Father Forgive Me*
*Maiman. *I Left My Heart; Someone to Watch*
Manthorne. *Sudden Death*
*McNab. Carol Ashton (*Lessons in Murder)*
*Michaels. Stan Kraychik (*Mask for a Diva*)
*Morell. *Final Rest*
*Nava. Henry Rios (*The Burning Plain; The Death of Friends*)
*Outland. *Death Wore the Emperor's New Clothes*
*Redmann. *Death by the Riverside*
*Roeder. *Someone Is Killing the Gay Boys of Verona*
*Scoppettone. Lauren Laurano (*My Sweet Untraceable You*)
*Sims. *Holy Hell*
*Stevenson. Don Strachey
*Taylor. *The Last of Her Lies*
*Townsend. *One for the Master, Two for the Fool*

*Welch. Helen Black
*Wilson, John Morgan. Benjamin
  Justice
*Zaremba. *A Reason to Kill*
*Zimmerman. Todd Mills
  (*Outburst*)
*Zubro. (Tom Mason & Scott Car-
  penter) *Are You Nuts?*
*Zubro. Paul Turner (*The Truth Can
  Get You Killed*)

Leather Sex/ SM/BDSM

Negative viewpoint

*Aldyne. *Canary; Vermillion*
*Allen. *Just a Little Lie*
Beecham. Amanda Valentine
Cutler. Mark Bradley & Rayford
  Goodman
*Davidson. *Deadly Rendezvous*
Drury. *The Other Side of Silence*
Hartman. *Gumshoe Gorilla*
Johnson, Steve. *False Confessions*
McClellan. *Penn Valley Phoenix*
Mickelbury. *Night Songs*
*Mildon. *Stalking the Goddess Ship*
*Nava. *The Burning Plain*
Redmann. *The Intersection of Law
  and Desire*
Steward. *Caravaggio Shawl*
Wilson, John Morgan. *Limits of
  Justice*
*Wilson/Sjoholm. (Pam Nilsen) *The
  Dog Collar Murders*

Positive/neutral viewpoint

*Allen. Alison Kaine
*Dickson. Jas Anderson
King. *Night Work*
*Lanyon. *A Dangerous Thing*

Lordon. *Say Uncle*
Maney. Nancy Clue, Cherry Aim-
  less & friends
Michaels. *A Body to Dye For; Love
  You to Death*
*Stukas. Robert Willsop, Monette
  O'Reilley & Michael Stark
*Szymanski. Brett Higgins & Allie
  Sullivan (*When the Dancing Stops*)
*Townsend. Bruce MacLeod
*Wilson/Sjoholm. (Pam Nilsen) *The
  Dog Collar Murders*

Lesbian Bashing
see Gay and Lesbian Bashing

Lesbian Community
see Lesbigay Community

Lesbian on Lesbian Crime
see also Gay on Gay Crime,
Violence Against Women

*Allen. Alison Kaine
*Baker. Virginia Kelly
*Beecham. *Fair Play*
*Calloway. *4th Down*
*Davidson. *Deadly Rendezvous*
*Duffy. *Calendar Girl*
*Fritchley. *Chicken Feed*
*Maiman. *I Left My Heart*
*Manthorne. *Last Resort; Sudden
  Death*
*McDermid. *Final Edition*
*Pincus. *The Two-Bit Tango*
*Raphael. *The Edith Wharton Murders*
*Sanra. Tally McGinnis & Cid
  Cameron
*Silva. *Storm Front*
*Sims. *Holy Hell*
*Taylor. *We Know Where You Live*

*Welch. *A Day Too Long*
*Wings. Emma Victor

Lesbigay Community and Lesbigay Culture

*Aldyne. Dan Valentine & Clarisse Lovelace
*Allen. Alison Kaine
*Azolakov. Cass Milam
*Baker. *The Lavender House Murder*
*Beecham. Amanda Valentine
*Calloway. *2nd Fiddle; 4th Down*
Douglas. Allison O'Neil & Kerry Owyhee
*Douglas. (Caitlin Reece) *The Always Anonymous Beast; The Daughters of Artemis*
*Fennelly. *The Glory Hole Murders*
*Fritchley. *Chicken Feed; Chicken Run*
*Gilbert. *Spiked*
*Gilligan. *Danger! Cross Currents*
*Haddock. *Final Cut*
Hartman. Drew Parker & Jen Grey
*Herren. (Scotty Bradley) *Bourbon Street Blues*
Hunter. Alex Reynolds, Peter Livesay & Jean Reynolds
Johnson, Barbara. Colleen Fitzgerald
Maiman. *Someone to Watch*
McAllester. *The Lessons*
*McConnell. Nyla Wade
*Michaels. Stan Kraychik
*Miller. Lexy Hyatt
Morell. Lucia Ramos
*Nava. Henry Rios
*Outland. Doan McCandler & Binky Van de Kamp
Pincus. Nell Fury
*Plante. *Dirty Money*

*Rand. *Gay Detective*
Redmann. Micky Knight
Roberts. *Needlepoint*
Sanra. Tally McGinnis & Cid Cameron
*Schmidt. Laney Samms
Scoppettone. Lauren Laurano
*Sims. Lillian Byrd
*Stevenson. Don Strachey (*Death Trick*)
Steward. Gertrude Stein & Alice B. Toklas
*Stukas. Robert Willsop, Monette O'Reilley & Michael Stark
Szymanski. *When the Dancing Stops*
*Taylor. Maggie Garrett (*We Know Where You Live*)
*Tell. Poppy Dillworth
Welch. Helen Black
*Wilson, John Morgan. Benjamin Justice
*Wilson/Sjoholm. Pam Nilsen (*The Dog Collar Murders*)
*Wings. Emma Victor
Woodcraft. Frankie Richmond
*Zaremba. *Beyond Hope; Uneasy Lies*

Bars and baths

*Aldyne. Dan Valentine & Clarisse Lovelace
Azolakov. Cass Milam
*Beecham. *Second Guess*
Davidson. *Deadly Rendezvous*
*Fennelly. *The Glory Hole Murders*
*Forrest. *Murder at the Nightwood Bar*
Foster. *The Monarchs Are Flying*
*Gilbert. *Spiked*
Griffith. *The Blue Place*
*Haddock. Carmen Ramirez
Hansen. *Early Graves; Troublemaker*

*Herren. (Scotty Bradley) *Bourbon
Street Blues*
*Hunter. *Government Gay*
*Johnson, Steve. Doug Orlando
*Knight. *Shattered Rhythms*
*Lynch. *Sue Slate: Private Eye*
*Manthorne. Harriet Hubbley (*Sudden Death*)
McClellan. Tru North
*Michaels. *Time to Check Out*
*Miller. Lexy Hyatt (*Killing at the Cat*)
Nava. Henry Rios (*Goldenboy*)
Padgett. *Blue*
Pincus. Nell Fury
*Rand. *Gay Detective*
*Redmann. Micky Knight (*The
Intersection of Law and Desire*)
*Schmidt. Laney Samms
Silva. *Storm Front; Taken by Storm*
*Sims. *Holy Hell*
*Stevenson. *Death Trick*
*Stukas. Robert Willsop, Monette
O'Reilley & Michael Stark
Wilson, John Morgan. *Justice at
Risk*
Wilson/Sjoholm. (Cassandra Reilly)
Trouble in Transylvania
*Zimmerman. Todd Mills (*Closet*)
*Zubro. Tom Mason & Scott Carpenter (*A Simple Suburban Murder*)
*Zubro. (Paul Turner) *The Truth
Can Get You Killed*

Marriage
see Heterosexual Marriage;
Relationships with
Lovers and Romance

Minorities and Ethnicity
see also Diversity

Includes cultural information and
racial/ethnic bias. ">" indicates the

main character is African American,
Hispanic, or Native American.

*Albarella. *Agenda for Murder*
Allen. *Takes One to Know One*
>Baker. Virginia Kelly
>Baxt. Pharoah Love
>Beal. *Angel Dance*
*Calloway. *8th Day*
*Clare. *Street Rules*
Cutler. Mark Bradley & Rayford
Goodman
*Davis. *Until the End*
>Douglas. Allison O'Neil & Kerry
Owyhee
Douglas. Caitlin Reece
Dreher. Stoner McTavish
*Drury. *Closed in Silence*
*Duffy. Saz Martin
*Dunford. *Soon to Be a Major
Motion Picture*
*Dymmoch. *The Death of Blue
Mountain Cat*
*Fennelly. Matty Sinclair
*Forrest. Kate Delafield (*Amateur
City*)
Foster. *Legal Tender*
*Grobeson. *Outside the Badge*
>Haddock. Carmen Ramirez
*Hansen. Dave Brandstetter (*The
Little Dog Laughed; Obedience*)
*Hartman. Drew Parker & Jen Grey
Herren. (Chanse MacLeod) *Murder
in the Rue Dauphine*
Herren. (Scotty Bradley) *Bourbon
Street Blues*
*Hunter. *The Chicken Asylum*
*Johnson, Bett Reece. Cordelia
Morgan & partners (*The Woman
Who Found Grace*)
*Johnson, Steve. Doug Orlando
(*Final Atonement*)
Knight. *Switching the Odds*
>laFavor. Renee LaRoche

>Lansdale. Hap Collins & Leonard Pine
*Lanyon. *A Dangerous Thing*
>Maddison. Connor Hawthorne & team
Maiman. *Under My Skin*
Maney. Nancy Clue, Cherry Aimless & friends
*Marcy. Meg Darcy
>McAllester. Tenny Mendoza
*McConnell. *The Burnton Widows*
McDermid. *Conferences Are Murder*
*McKay. Lynn Evans
*McNab. Carol Ashton (*Inner Circle; Set Up*)
Michaels. *Love You to Death*
>Mickelbury. Gianna Maglione & Mimi Patterson
*Mildon. Cal Meredith
*Miller. Lexy Hyatt
>Morell. Lucia Ramos
>Nava. Henry Rios (*How Town*)
Outland. Doan McCandler & Binky Van de Kamp
>Padgett. Blue McCarron & Roxie Bouchie
*Pincus. Nell Fury
Powell. Hollis Carpenter
Raphael. Nick Hoffman (*Little Miss Evil*)
*Redmann. Micky Knight
*Richardson. Stevie Houston
*Roberts. *Breaking Point*
Sanra. Tally McGinnis & Cid Cameron
Schmidt. Laney Samms (*Sweet Cherry Wine*)
*Scoppettone. Lauren Laurano
*Silva. Delta Stevens (*Storm Rising; Weathering the Storm*)
*Sims. *Holy Hell*
*Stevenson. Don Strachey (*Tongue Tied*)

Stukas. *Someone Killed His Boyfriend*
*Szymanski. *When Some Body Disappears*
Taylor. Maggie Garrett
Townsend. Bruce MacLeod
*Welch. Helen Black (*Open House*)
*Wilson, John Morgan. Benjamin Justice
*Wilson/Sjoholm. (Pam Nilsen) *Murder in the Collective*
*Wilson/Sjoholm. Cassandra Reilly
*York. Royce Madison
>Zaremba. Helen Keremos
Zimmerman. *Outburst*
*Zubro. (Tom Mason & Scott Carpenter) *Rust on the Razor*
Zubro. (Paul Turner)*The Truth Can Get You Killed*

Misogyny
see **Sexism and Misogyny**

Older Gay Men
see **Age**

Older Lesbians
see **Age**

Omnisexuals
see **Bisexuals**

Outing
see also **Blackmail**

*Azolakov. (Cass Milam) *Cass and the Stone Butch*
*Baker. *The Lavender House Murder*

*Davidson. *Deadly Gamble*
*Davis. *Possessions*
*Dunford. *Making a Killing*
*Forrest. *Murder by Tradition;
Apparition Alley*
*Gilbert. *Spiked*
Haddock. *Final Cut*
*Hansen. *Fadeout*
*Hart. *A Small Sacrifice*
Hartman. *The Gumshoe, the Witch,
and the Virtual Corpse*
James. *Posted to Death*
*Johnson, Steve. *False Confessions*
*Maiman. *Someone to Watch*
*Marcy. *Dead and Blonde*
*McNab. *Dead Certain*
*Mickelbury. *Keeping Secrets*
*Morell. *Final Rest*
*Nava. Henry Rios (*Goldenboy*)
*Outland. *Death Wore a Fabulous
New Fragrance*
*Plante. *Getting Away with Murder*
*Richardson. *Double Take Out*
*Schmidt. *Cabin Fever*
Silva. *Storm Front*
*Stevenson. Don Strachey (*Third
Man Out*)
*Townsend. *One for the Master, Two
for the Fool*
*York. *Timber City Masks*
*Zubro. (Paul Turner) *The Truth
Can Get You Killed; Sorry Now?*

Prostitution and Pornography
see also Children

Female prostitutes

*Allen. Alison Kaine
*Baxt. *A Queer Kind of Love*
Beecham. Amanda Valentine

*Cutler. *Rough Cut*
*Davidson. *Deadly Gamble*
*Dickson. *Banged Up*
*Drury. *Closed in Silence*
*Forrest. *Murder at the Nightwood
Bar*
*Lordon. *Say Uncle*
*McAllester. *The Search*
*McConnell. *Mrs. Porter's Letter*
*Mickelbury. *Night Songs*
*Pincus. *The Two-Bit Tango*
Powell. *Bayou City Secrets*
*Richardson. *Last Rites*
*Roberts. *Breaking Point*
*Sanra. *No Corpse*
*Silva. Delta Stevens
*Szymanski. *When the Dancing Stops*
*Taylor. *The Last of Her Lies*
*Wilson/Sjoholm. (Pam Nilsen) *Sisters of the Road*
Woodcraft. *Good Bad Woman*

Male prostitutes/ hustlers/rent boys

*Aldyne. *Vermillion*
*Baxt. *A Queer Kind of Death*
*Dickson. *FreeForm*
*Dymmoch. *The Man Who Understood Cats*
*Fennelly. *The Glory Hole Murders*
*Gilbert. *Spiked*
*Grobeson. *Outside the Badge*
*Hansen. Dave Brandstetter (*Troublemaker*)
*Hartman. Drew Parker & Jen Grey
*Herren. (Chanse MacLeod) *Murder in the Rue Dauphine*
Herren. (Scotty Bradley) *Bourbon Street Blues*
*Johnson, Steve. *False Confessions*
*laFavor. *Evil Dead Center*
McDermid. *Final Edition*
*Michaels. Stan Kraychik

*Calloway. Cassidy James
*Clare. L.A. Franco
*Craft. Mark Manning
*Davidson. *Deadly Butterfly*
*Davis. Maris Middleton
*Dickson. Jas Anderson
*Douglas. Caitlin Reece
*Dreher. Stoner McTavish
*Duffy. Saz Martin
*Fennelly. Matty Sinclair (*Kiss Yourself Goodbye*)
*Forrest. Kate Delafield
*Foster. Harriet Fordham Croft
*Fritchley. *Chicken Run; Chicken Shack*
Gilbert. *Spiked*
*Gilligan. *Danger! Cross Currents*
*Griffith. *The Blue Place*
*Haddock. Carmen Ramirez
*Hansen. Dave Brandstetter
*Hart. Jane Lawless
*Herren. Chanse MacLeod
*Hunter. Alex Reynolds, Peter Livesay & Jean Reynolds
James. Simon Kirby-Jones
*Johnson, Barbara. Colleen Fitzgerald
*Johnson, Steve. Doug Orlando
*King. Kate Martinelli
*laFavor. Renee LaRoche
*Lanyon. *A Dangerous Thing*
*Lordon. Sydney Sloane (*Brotherly Love*)
*Maddison. Connor Hawthorne & team
*Maiman. Robin Miller
*Maney. Nancy Clue, Cherry Aimless & friends
*Manthorne. Harriet Hubbley
*Marcy. Meg Darcy
*McClellan. Tru North
*McConnell. Nyla Wade
*McDermid. Lindsay Gordon
*McKay. Lynn Evans (*Twist of Lime*)
*McNab. Carol Ashton

*Michaels. Stan Kraychik
*Mickelbury. Gianna Maglione & Mimi Patterson
*Mildon. Cal Meredith
*Miller. *Reporter on the Run*
*Morell. Lucia Ramos
*Nava. Henry Rios
*Plante. Cynthia Chenery Scott
*Raphael. Nick Hoffman
*Redmann. Micky Knight
*Richardson. Stevie Houston
*Roeder. *Someone Is Killing the Gay Boys of Verona*
*Sanra. Tally McGinnis & Cid Cameron
*Schmidt. *Silverlake Heat; Sweet Cherry Wine*
*Scoppettone. Lauren Laurano
*Silva. Delta Stevens
*Sims. Lillian Byrd
*Stevenson. Don Strachey
*Steward. Gertrude Stein & Alice B. Toklas
*Stukas. Robert Willsop, Monette O'Reilley & Michael Stark
*Sumner. Tor Cross
*Szymanski. Brett Higgins & Allie Sullivan
*Taylor. Maggie Garrett
*Tell. Poppy Dillworth
*Welch. Helen Black
*Wilson/Sjoholm. (Pam Nilsen) *Murder in the Collective*
*Wings. Emma Victor
*York. Royce Madison
*Zimmerman. Todd Mills
*Zubro. Tom Mason & Scott Carpenter (*Here Comes the Corpse*)
*Zubro. Paul Turner

Monogamy and fidelity

*Aldyne. Dan Valentine & Clarisse Lovelace

Straight women and men

Herren. (Chanse MacLeod) *Murder in the Rue Dauphine*
*Lordon. Sydney Sloane
*Maiman. *Crazy for Loving*
*Manthorne. *Deadly Reunion; Sudden Death*
*Marcy. *Cemetery Murders*
*McNab. *Fatal Reunion; Lessons in Murder*
*Michaels. Stan Kraychik
*Mildon. *Stalking the Goddess Ship*
*Miller. *Killing at the Cat*
*Padgett. *Blue*
*Powell. *Bayou City Secrets*
*Raphael. Nick Hoffman
Richardson. *Over the Line*
*Schmidt. *Silverlake Heat*
Scott. *Night Mares*
*Steward. *Murder Is Murder Is Murder*
*Tell. Poppy Dillworth
*Welch. Helen Black (*Fallen from Grace*)
*Wilson/Sjoholm. (Cassandra Reilly) *Trouble in Transylvania*
*Wings. Emma Victor (*She Came by the Book*)

Religion/Spirituality

*Albarella. Nikki Barnes
*Baker. *The Ultimate Exit Strategy*
*Craft. *Flight Dreams*
*Dymmoch. *Incendiary Designs*
*Haddock. Carmen Ramirez
*Hansen. Dave Brandstetter (*Skinflick*)
*Hartman. Drew Parker & Jen Grey
*Johnson, Steve. Doug Orlando
*King. Kate Martinelli (*To Play the Fool; Night Work*)
*laFavor. Renee LaRoche

*Lanyon. *A Dangerous Thing*
*Maddison. Connor Hawthorne & team
*Maiman. *Baby It's Cold; Old Black Magic*
*Powell. *Houston Town*
*Raphael. Nick Hoffman
Stevenson. *Tongue Tied*
*Welch. Helen Black
*Wings. *She Came in a Flash*
*Zimmerman. *Tribe*
*Zubro. (Tom Mason & Scott Carpenter) *Are You Nuts?*
*Zubro. (Paul Turner) *Sorry Now?*

Anti-Semitism

Calloway. *2nd Fiddle*
*Cutler. *Shot on Location*
Grobeson. *Outside the Badge*
*Johnson, Steve. *Final Atonement*
McNab. *Inner Circle*
Miller. *Reporter on the Run*
*Raphael. Nick Hoffman
*Schmidt. *Cabin Fever*
Stevenson. *Chain of Fools*

Goddess worship/women's religion & spirituality

*Dreher. Stoner McTavish
*Gilligan. *Danger! Cross Currents*
*Hart. *Vital Lies*
*Hartman. Drew Parker & Jen Grey
Herren. Scotty Bradley
*King. *Night Work*
*McKay. *The Kali Connection*
*Maddison. Connor Hawthorne & team
*Mildon. *Stalking the Goddess Ship*
Stukas. Robert Willsop, Monette O'Reilley & Michael Stark
*Tell. Poppy Dillworth

Wilson/Sjoholm. (Cassandra Reilly)
   Trouble in Transylvania

Homophobia

*Albarella. *Agenda for Murder*
*Allen. *Tell Me What You Like*
Beecham. *Second Guess*
Calloway. *2nd Fiddle; 4th Down*
*Craft. *Eye Contact; Flight Dreams*
*Davidson. *Deadly Gamble*
Davis. *Shattered Illusions*
*Haddock. Carmen Ramirez
*Hansen. Dave Brandstetter (*Grave-
   digger; Skinflick*)
*Hart. *Hallowed Murder; A Small
   Sacrifice*
*Hartman. Drew Parker & Jen Grey
Herren. (Chanse MacLeod) *Murder
   in the Rue Dauphine*
*Herren. (Scotty Bradley) *Bourbon
   Street Blues*
*Johnson, Barbara. *Bad Moon Rising*
*Johnson, Steve. Doug Orlando
King. *Night Work*
Knight. *Shattered Rhythms*
laFavor. *Along the Journey River*
*Lansdale. *Mucho Mojo*
*Lanyon. *A Dangerous Thing*
*Lynch. *Sue Slate: Private Eye*
Maiman. *Baby It's Cold; I Left My
   Heart*
*Manthorne. *Deadly Reunion*
*McNab. *Bodyguard; Death Down
   Under*
*Michaels. *Love You to Death*
*Mickelbury. *Keeping Secrets*
*Mildon. *Fighting for Air*
*Miller. *Reporter on the Run*
*Nava. Henry Rios (*The Burning
   Plain*)
*Padgett. *The Last Blue Plate Special*
*Raphael. Nick Hoffman
Redmann. *Deaths of Jocasta*

*Richardson. *Last Rites*
*Roeder. *Someone Is Killing the Gay
   Boys of Verona*
*Saum. Brigid Donovan
*Stevenson. *Tongue Tied*
*Taylor. Maggie Garrett (*The Last of
   Her Lies*)
*Welch. Helen Black
Wings. *She Came by the Book; She
   Came to the Castro*
*York. *Crystal Mountain Veils*
*Zimmerman. Todd Mills (*Tribe*)
*Zubro. Tom Mason & Scott Car-
   penter (*The Only Good Priest*)
*Zubro. (Paul Turner) *Sorry Now?*

Religious Leaders

*Albarella. Nikki Barnes
*Aldyne. *Canary*
*Craft. *Flight Dreams*
*Hartman. *The Gumshoe, the Witch,
   and the Virtual Corpse*
*James. *Posted to Death*
Johnson, Steve. *Doug Orlando*
*Maddison. *Death by Prophecy*
*Nava. *The Burning Plain*
*Richardson. *Last Rites*
*Saum. Brigid Donovan
*Wilson, John Morgan. *Blind
   Eye*
*Zubro. (Paul Turner) *Sorry Now?*
*Zubro. (Tom Mason & Scott Car-
   penter) *The Only Good Priest;
   Rust on the Razor*

Rent Boys
see Prostitution and
Pornography

Repressed Sexuality
see Internalized Homophobia

Reprogramming/ Returning to Heterosexuality
see Homophobia

Roles/Role Playing
see Butch and Femme

Sex Workers
see Prostitution and Pornography

Sexism and Misogyny
see also Women's Activism; Violence Against Women

*Albarella. Nikki Barnes
Aldyne. *Cobalt*
Allen. Alison Kaine
*Baker. Virginia Kelly
Baxt. Pharoah Love
*Beal. *Angel Dance*
*Beecham. Amanda Valentine
Calloway. Cassidy James
*Clare. L.A. Franco
*Cutler. Mark Bradley & Rayford Goodman
*Davidson. Toni Underwood
*Davis. Maris Middleton
*Douglas. The Caitlin Reece
*Drury. Tyler Jones
*Dymmoch. *Feline Friendship*
Fennelly. *The Glory Hole Murders*
*Forrest. Kate Delafield (*Liberty Square*)
*Foster. Harriet Fordham Croft
Gilbert. *Spiked*
*Gilligan. *Danger in High Places*

Grobeson. *Outside the Badge*
*Haddock. Carmen Ramirez
*Hart. Jane Lawless
Hunter. Alex Reynolds, Peter Livesay & Jean Reynolds
James. Simon Kirby-Jones
Johnson, Barbara. *The Beach Affair*
*Johnson, Bett Reece. Cordelia Morgan & partners
Johnson, Steve. Doug Orlando
*King. Kate Martinelli
Knight. Lil Ritchie
laFavor. Renee LaRoche
*Lansdale. *Rumble Tumble*
Lordon. Sydney Sloane
Maddison. *Death by Prophecy*
Maiman. *Baby It's Cold*
*Maney. Nancy Clue, Cherry Aimless & friends
Manthorne. Harriet Hubbley
*Marcy. Meg Darcy
*McAllester. Tenny Mendoza
*McClellan. Tru North
*McConnell. Nyla Wade
*McDermid. Lindsay Gordon
*McKay. Lynn Evans
*McNab. Carol Ashton
*Mickelbury. Gianna Maglione & Mimi Patterson
*Mildon. Cal Meredith
*Miller. Lexy Hyatt
Morell. *Final Session*
Outland. *Death Wore the Emperor's New Clothes*
*Padgett. Blue McCarron & Roxie Bouchie
*Plante. *Getting Away with Murder*
Powell. *Bayou City Secrets*
*Raphael. Nick Hoffman (*The Edith Wharton Murders*)
*Redmann. Micky Knight
*Richardson. Stevie Houston (*Over the Line*)
*Roberts. Cameron McGill

Sexual harassment

SM/S&M
see Leather Sex/SM/BDSM

Stereotypic Characters
see also Heterosexism; Homophobia

"Mannish" lesbians

Gaydar

Douglas. *Swimming Cat Cove*
(Allison O'Neal and Kerry Owyhee)
*Foster. *The Monarchs Are Flying*
Fritchley. *Chicken Out; Chicken Run*
Gilbert. *Spiked*
Gilligan. *Danger in High Places*
Hansen. *Fadeout*
Hart. *Immaculate Midnight; Robber's
Wine*
Hartman. Drew Parker & Jen Grey
Herren. (Scotty Bradley) *Bourbon
Street Blues*
James. *Posted to Death*
Lansdale. *Captains Outrageous*
Maiman. *Crazy for Loving; Someone
to Watch*
Manthorne. *Deadly Reunion; Ghost
Motel*
Michaels. *Mask for a Diva*
Miller. *Mayhem at the Marina;
Reporter on the Run*
Nava. *The Little Death*
*Outland. *Death Wore a Fabulous
New Fragrance*
*Pincus. *The Hangdog Hustle*
Plante. *Getting Away with Murder*
*Redmann. Micky Knight
Roeder. *Someone Is Killing the Gay
Boys of Verona*
Scoppettone. *My Sweet Untraceable
You*
*Sims. *Damn Straight*
Stevenson. *Ice Blues*
*Welch. Helen Black
Wilson/Sjoholm. (Pam Nilsen) *Sis-
ters of the Road*

Queens

*Aldyne. *Cobalt*
*Craft. *Name Games*
*Davidson. *Deadly Gamble*
Dymmoch. *The Death of Blue
Mountain Cat*

*Fennelly. Matty Sinclair
Gilbert. *Spiked*
Haddock. Carmen Ramirez
Hunter. Alex Reynolds, Peter
Livesay & Jean Reynolds
Johnson, Steve. Doug Orlando
Lansdale. *Bad Chili*
*Maney. *A Ghost in the Closet*
*McConnell. *The Burnton Widows*
*Michaels. Stan Kraychik
*Mickelbury. *Night Songs*
Outland. *Death Wore the Emperor's
New Clothes*
*Powell. Hollis Carpenter
*Rand. *Gay Detective*
Redmann. Micky Knight
Steward. *Caravaggio Shawl*
Stukas. *Someone Killed His
Boyfriend*
*Townsend. *One for the Master, Two
for the Fool*
Wilson, John Morgan. *Justice at
Risk*
*Zimmerman. Todd Mills

Straight Men and Women
see Relationships with Lovers and Romance

Suicide
see Internalized Homophobia

Transsexual Prostitutes
see Transsexuals

Transsexuals

*Allen. *Just a Little Lie; Takes One to
Know One*

Transvestite Prostitutes
see Cross Dressing/
Transvestites

Transvestites
see Cross Dressing/
Transvestites

Violence Against Women
see also Sexism and Misogyny

Rape see also Children

*Silva. *Tropical Storm*
*Stevenson. *Ice Blues; Shock to the
  System*
*Szymanski. *When the Dancing Stops*
*Welch. Helen Black (*A Day Too
  Long*)
*Wilson/Sjoholm. Pam Nilsen (*Sisters of the Road*)
*York. *Timber City Masks*

Spouse/partner abuse

*Calloway. *3rd Degree; 6th Sense*
*Cutler. *Shot on Location*
*Davidson. *Deadly Rendezvous*
*Davis. Maris Middleton (*Shattered
  Illusions*)
*Douglas. Caitlin Reece
Dreher. *Stoner McTavish*
*Drury. Tyler Jones (*The Other Side
  of Silence*)
*Dymmoch. *The Death of Blue
  Mountain Cat; Feline Friendship*
*Fennelly. *The Glory Hole Murders*
*Forrest. *Sleeping Bones*
*Foster. Harriet Fordham Croft
*Gilligan. *Danger! Cross Currents*
*Griffith. *Stay*
*Hart. *A Killing Cure; Stage Fright*
*Johnson, Bett Reece. *The Woman
  Who Knew Too Much*
*Johnson, Steve. Doug Orlando
  (*Final Atonement*)
*King. *Night Work*
*Lansdale. *Bad Chili; Rumble Tumble*
*Lordon. *Father Forgive Me; Sister's
  Keeper*
*Maiman. Robin Miller (*Under My
  Skin*)
*Maney. Nancy Clue, Cherry Aimless & friends
*Marcy. *Dead and Blonde; A Cold
  Case of Murder*

*McAllester. *The Lessons*
*McNab. *Cop Out; Death Down
  Under*
*Mildon. *Stalking the Goddess Ship*
*Miller. *Mayhem at the Marina*
Morell. *Final Session*
*Nava. Henry Rios (*Rag and Bone*)
*Padgett. *The Last Blue Plate Special*
*Powell. *Bayou City Secrets*
*Richardson. *Over the Line*
*Roberts. *Breaking Point*
Sanra. Tally McGinnis & Cid
  Cameron
*Saum. Brigid Donovan
*Scoppettone. *Everything You Have
  Is Mine; My Sweet Untraceable
  You*
Scott. *Night Mares*
Silva. *Weathering the Storm*
Stevenson. *Chain of Fools; Ice Blues*
*Szymanski. *When the Dead Speak*
*Welch. *Smoke and Mirrors*
Wilson, John Morgan. *Simple Justice*
Wilson/Sjoholm. (Pam Nilsen)
  Sisters of the Road
Wilson/Sjoholm. (Cassandra
  Reilly) *Trouble in Transylvania*
*Woodcraft. Frankie Richmond
York. *Timber City Masks*
*Zubro. (Tom Mason & Scott
  Carpenter) *A Simple Suburban
  Murder*

Women's Activism

Activism, lesbian feminism, separatism

*Albarella. Nikki Barnes
*Allen. Alison Kaine (*Takes One to
  Know One*)
*Azolakov. Cass Milam
*Beal. *Angel Dance*

*Craft. Mark Manning (*Body Language*)
*Davidson. Toni Underwood (*Deadly Rendezvous)*
*Douglas. Caitlin Reece (*The Daughters of Artemis*)
*Dreher. Stoner McTavish (*Bad Company)*
*Drury. Tyler Jones
*Forrest. Kate Delafield (*Murder at the Nightwood Bar*)
*Foster. *The Monarchs Are Flying*
Fritchley. *Chicken Feed*
*Gilligan. Alix Nicholson
Haddock. Carmen Ramirez
*Johnson, Bett Reece. Cordelia Morgan & partners (*The Woman Who Knew Too Much*)
Johnson, Barbara. Colleen Fitzgerald
Johnson, Steve. Doug Orlando (*False Confessions*)
*King. Kate Martinelli (*Night Work*)
laFavor. Renee LaRoche
*Maddison. *Deceptions*
Manthorne. *Deadly Reunion*
Marcy. Meg Darcy
McAllester. *The Lessons*
*McConnell. Nyla Wade
*McKay. Lynn Evans
*McNab. Carol Ashton (*Body Guard; Death Club*)
*Mickelbury. Gianna Maglione & Mimi Patterson
*Mildon. *Stalking the Goddess Ship*
Miller. Lexy Hyatt
*Morell. Lucia Ramos
Outland. *Death Wore a Fabulous New Fragrance*
*Padgett. Blue McCarron & Roxie Bouchie
Pincus. Nell Fury
*Plante. Cynthia Chenery Scott
*Raphael. Nick Hoffman

Redmann. Micky Knight
Roberts. Cameron McGill
*Schmidt. Laney Samms
Silva. Delta Stevens
*Sumner. *End of April*
Tell. Poppy Dillworth
*Wilson/Sjoholm. Pam Nilsen
Wilson/Sjoholm. Cassandra Reilly
Wings. Emma Victor
*Woodcraft. Frankie Richmond
*York. Royce Madison
Zaremba. *Beyond Hope; White Noise*
*Zubro. (Tom Mason & Scott Carpenter) *The Only Good Priest*

Feminist or feminist viewpoint (self-defined)

In their interviews or in other publications these authors describe their novels as feminist or having a feminist perspective.

Albarella. Nikki Barnes
Beal. *Angel Dance*
Calloway. Cassidy James
Dreher. Stoner McTavish
Drury. Tyler Jones
Forrest. Kate Delafield
Fritchley. Letty Campbell
Hart. Jane Lawless
Johnson, Barbara. Colleen Fitzgerald
Johnson, Bett Reece. Cordelia Morgan & partners
King. Kate Martinelli
laFavor. Renee LaRoche
Lordon. Sydney Sloane
McClellan. Tru North
McConnell. Nyla Wade
McDermid. Lindsay Gordon
McKay. Lynn Evans
McNab. Carol Ashton
Miller. Lexy Hyatt
Padgett. Blue McCarron & Roxie Bouchie

Plante. Cynthia Chenery Scott
Richardson. Stevie Houston
Roberts. Cameron McGill
Schmidt. Laney Samms
Scoppettone. Lauren Laurano
Silva. Delta Stevens
Szymanski. Brett Higgins & Allie
    Sullivan
Wilson/Sjoholm. Pam Nilsen
Wilson/Sjoholm. Cassandra Reilly

Wings. Emma Victor
Woodcraft. Frankie Richmond
York. Royce Madison
Zaremba. Helen Keremos

Youth, Gay and Lesbian
see Children

Notes

I. THE GAY AND LESBIAN CRIME-FICTION SCENE

1. Stein, Gertrude. "What Are Masterpieces and Why Are There So Few of Them." (1936; reprint, in *Context* online edition, no. 5. Normal, IL: Dalkey Archive Press, 2000)

2. "Barbara Wilson," *Seattle Arts Newsletter* 22, no. 1, 1999.

3. "Joseph Hansen." In *Contemporary Authors Autobiography Series*. Vol. 17. Detroit, MI: Gale Research Co., 1993. P. 68.

4. Hansen, Joseph. 2003. Email message sent to the author. 28 February.

5. Redmann, Jean M. *The Intersection of Law and Desire.* New York, NY: Avon Books, 1995. P. 161.

6. Michaels, Grant. *Dead as a Doornail.* New York, NY: St. Martin's Press, 1998. P. 8.

7. Ibid. P. 9.

8. Outland, Orland. *Death Wore a Smart Little Outfit.* New York, NY: The Berkley Publishing Group, 1997. P. 161.

9. Van Dine, S.S. "Twenty Rules for Writing Detective Stories." In *American Magazine*, (September) 1928.

10. Richardson, Tracey. *Last Rites.* Tallahassee, FL: The Naiad Press, Inc., 1997. P. 178.

11. Baker, Nikki. *In the Game.* Tallahassee, FL: The Naiad Press, Inc., 1994. P. 13.

12. Craft, Michael. *Flight Dreams.* New York, NY: Kensington Books, 1997. P. 74.

13. Lansdale, Joe R. *Bad Chili.* New York, NY: Warner Books, 1997. P. 3.

14. Wilson, Barbara. *Trouble in Transylvania.* Seattle, WA: Seal Press, 1993. P. 22.

15. Woodcraft, Elizabeth. *Good Bad Woman.* New York, NY: Kensington Books, 2000. P. 296.

16. Fritchley, Alma. *Chicken Run.* London: The Women's Press, Ltd., 2000. P. 13.

17. Wings, Mary. *She Came Too Late.* Markham, Ontario, Canada: New American Books, 1987. P. 53.

18. Rand, Lou. *Gay Detective.* Fresno, CA: Saber Books, 1961; reprint, under title *Rough Trade,* New York, NY: Paperback Library, 1965. P. 91.

19. Outland, Orland. *Death Wore a Fabulous New Fragrance.* New York, NY: The Berkley Publishing Group, 1998. P. 19.

20. Dreher, Sarah. *Gray Magic.* Norwich, VT: New Victoria Publishers, 1987. Pp. 38–39.

21. Scoppettone, Sandra. *I'll Be Leaving You Always.* New York, NY: Ballentine Books, 1993. P. 187.

22. Stevenson, Richard. *Death Trick.* Los Angeles, CA: Alyson Books, 1981. P. 78.

23. Rand. *Gay Detective.* P. 9.

24. Bergman, David. "Camp." In *glbtq: an encyclopedia of gay, lesbian, bisex-*

ual, transgender, & queer culture. http://www.glbtq.com/literature/camp.html, 2003. P. 1.

25. Rand. *Gay Detective.* P. 24.

II. The Authors and Their Characters

1. Grobeson, Mitchell. *Outside the Badge.* New York, NY: Vantage Press, 2000. P. 11.

2. Morell, Mary. *Final Rest.* Duluth, MN: Spinsters Ink, 1993. P. 128.

3. Stevenson, Richard. *A Shock to the System.* New York, NY: St. Martin's Press, 1995. P. 61.

4. Michaels, Grant. *Love You to Death.* New York, NY: St. Martin's Press, 1992. P. 23.

5. Silva, Linda Kay. *Taken by Storm.* Huntington Station, NY: Rising Tide Press, 1991. P. 179.

6. Stevenson, Richard. *On the Other Hand, Death.* New York, NY: St. Martin's Press, 1984. Pp. 61–62.

7. Zubro, Mark Richard. *The Truth Can Get You Killed.* New York, NY: St. Martin's Press, 1997. P. 12.

8. Silva, Linda Kay. *Storm Shelter.* St. Paul, MN: Paradigm Publishing Company, 1993. P. 4.

9. Forrest, Katherine V. *Murder by Tradition.* Tallahassee, Fl: The Naiad Press, Inc., 1991. P. 30.

10. Lansdale, Joe R. *Bad Chili.* New York, NY: Warner Books, Inc., 1997. Pp. 97–98.

11. Johnson, Steve. *False Confessions.* New York, NY: Signet/Penguin, 1993. P. 33.

12. Silva, Linda Kay. *Weathering the Storm.* St. Paul, MN: Paradigm Publishing, 1994. P. 131.

13. Hunter, Fred. *Government Gay.* New York, NY: St. Martin's Press, 1997. Pp. 6–7.

14. Davidson, Diane. *Deadly Rendezvous.* Huntington Station, NY: Rising Tide Press, 1994. Pp. 1–2.

15. Forrest. *Murder by Tradition.* P. 91.

16. McClellan, Janet. *Penn Valley Phoenix.* Tallahassee, FL: The Naiad Press, Inc., 1997. P. 18.

17. Mickelbury, Penny. *Night Songs.* Tallahassee, FL: The Naiad Press, Inc., 1995. P. 36.

18. Allen, Kate. *Give My Secrets Back.* Norwich, VT: New Victoria Publishers, 1995. P. 13.

19. Allen, Kate. *Tell Me What You Like.* Norwich, VT: New Victoria Publishers, 1993. P. 160.

20. Beecham, Rose. *Fair Play.* Tallahassee, FL: The Naiad Press, Inc., 1996. P. 166.

21. Ibid. P. 76.

22. Davidson, Diane. *Deadly Butterfly.* Tucson, AZ: Rising Tide Press, 2001. P. 42.

23. Ibid. P. 192.

24. Dickson, Jack. *Banged Up.* Brighton, England: Gay Men's Press, 1999. P. 178.

25. Grobeson. *Outside the Badge.* P. 211.

26. Ibid. P. 301.

27. Johnson, Steve. *Final Atonement.* New York, NY: Penguin Books, 1992. Pp. 49–50.

28. McAllester, Melanie. *The Lessons.* Duluth, MN: Spinsters Ink, 1994. P. 221.

29. McNab, Claire. *Lessons in Murder.* Tallahassee, FL: The Naiad Press, Inc., 1988. P. 181.

30. Morell, Mary. *Final Session.* Duluth, MN: Spinsters Ink. 1991. P. 85.

31. Richardson, Tracey. *Double Take Out.* Tallahassee, FL: The Naiad Press, Inc., 1999. P. 166.

32. Townsend, Larry. *Masters' Counterpoint.* Los Angeles, CA: Alyson Books, 1991. P. 5.

33. Townsend, Larry. *One for the Master, Two for the Fool.* Los Angeles, CA: Alyson Publications, 1992. P. 6.

34. York, Kieran. "We Were All Lesbians in Those Days." *Mystery Readers Journal* 9, no. 4, 1993/1994. P. 44.

35. Ibid. P. 43.

36. Ibid. P. 43.

37. York, Kieran. *Timber City Masks.* Chicago, IL: Third Side Press, 1993. P. 33.

38. York, Kieran. *Crystal Mountain Veils.* Chicago, IL: Third Side Press, 1995. P. 35.

39. Zubro, Mark. *Another Dead Teenager.* New York, NY: St. Martin's Press, 1995. P. 3.

40. Douglas, Lauren Wright. *Swimming Cat Cove.* Tallahassee, FL: The Naiad Press, 1997. P. 124.

41. Hansen, Joseph. 2003. Email message sent to the author. 27 May.

42. Pincus, Elizabeth. "Full of Sound and Fury," *Mystery Readers Journal* 9, no. 4, 1993/1994. P. 35.

43. Hansen, Joseph. "Matters Grave and Gay." In *Colloquium on Crime,* edited by Robin Winks. New York, NY: Charles Scribner, 1986. P. 116.

44. Rand, Lou. *Gay Detective.* Fresno, CA: Saber Books, 1961; reprint, under title *Rough Trade,* New York, NY: Paperback Library, 1965 P. 9.

45. Lordon, Randye. *Father Forgive Me.* New York, NY: St. Martin's Press, 1997. P. 164.

46. Zaremba, Eve. *Work for a Million.* London: Virago, 1986. P. 79.

47. Ibid. P. 79.

48. Maiman, Jaye. *Someone to Watch.* Tallahassee, FL: The Naiad Press, 1995. P. 18.

49. Marcy, Jean. *Mommy Deadest.* Norwich, VT: New Victoria Publishers, 2000. P. 48.

50. Stevenson, Richard. *Death Trick.* Los Angeles, CA: Alyson Publications, 1981. P. 53.

51. Pincus, Elizabeth. *The Hangdog Hustle.* Minneapolis, MN: Spinsters Ink, 1995. P. 33.

52. Hart, Ellen. *Wicked Games.* New York, NY: St. Martin's Press, 1998. P. 112.

53. Manthorne, Jackie. *Ghost Motel.* Charlottetown, P.E.I., Canada: Gynergy Books, 1994. P. 164.

54. Scoppettone, Sandra. *My Sweet Untraceable You.* New York, NY: Ballantine Books, 1994. P. 8.

55. Marcy. *Mommy Deadest.* P. 12.

56. Lordon, Randye. *Mother May I.* New York, NY: Avon Books, 1998. P. 6.

57. Duffy, Stella. *Wavewalker.* London: Serpent's Tail. 1996. P. 23.

58. Ibid. P. 18

59. Redmann, J.M. *The Intersection of Law and Desire.* New York, NY: Avon Books, 1995. P. 47.

60. Hansen, Joseph. *A Country of Old Men.* New York, NY: Penguin Books, 1992. P. 2.

61. Griffith, Nicola. *Stay.* New York, NY: Doubleday, 2002. P. 10.

62. Wings, Mary. *She Came to the Castro.* New York, NY: The Berkley Publishing Group, 1997. P. 15.

63. Knight, Phyllis. *Switching the Odds.* New York, NY: St. Martin's Press, 1992. P. 59.

64. Sumner, Penny. *The End of April.* Tallahassee, FL: The Naiad Press, 1992. P. 50.

65. Pincus. *The Hangdog Hustle.* P. 11.

66. Maiman, Jaye. *Baby It's Cold.* Tallahassee, FL: The Naiad Press, 1996. P. 23.

67. Douglas, Lauren Wright. *A Rage of Maidens.* Tallahassee, FL: The Naiad Press, Inc., 1994. P. 177.

68. Pincus, Elizabeth. *The Two-Bit Tango.* Minneapolis, MN: Spinsters Ink, 1992. P. 5.

69. Stevenson. *Death Trick.* P. 9.

70. Ibid. P. 8.

71. Saum, Karen. *Murder is Germane.* Tallahassee, FL: The Naiad Press, 1991. P. 129.

72. Douglas, Lauren Wright. *A Tiger's Heart.* Tallahassee, FL: The Naiad Press, Inc., 1992. Pp. 54–55.

73. Douglas, Lauren Wright. *The Daughters of Artemis.* Tallahassee, FL: The Naiad Press, Inc., 1991. P. 44.

74. Douglas, Lauren Wright. *The Always Anonymous Beast.* Tallahassee, FL: The Naiad Press, 1987. P. 11.

75. Douglas. *The Daughters of Artemis.* P. 43.

76. Ibid. P. 72.

77. Douglas. *The Always Anonymous Beast.* P. 110.

78. Griffith, Nicola. *The Blue Place.* New York, NY: Avon Books. 1998. P. 3.

79. Ibid. P. 35.

80. Nicola Griffith, "Living a Big Life," interview by Victoria A. Brownworth, *Lambda Book Report*, September, 2002. P. 8.

81. Griffith, Nicola. *Stay*. New York, NY: Doubleday, 2002. P. 3.

82. Ibid. P. 18.

83. Nicola Griffith, "A conversation with Nicola Griffith about her novel 'Stay,'" interview by Nan Talese, http://www.randomhouse.com/NanaTalese/exclusive/griffithinterview.html, 2003.

84. Griffith. *Lambda Book Report*. P. 8.

85. Hansen. *Colloquium on Crime*. P. 117.

86. Knight, Phyllis. *Shattered Rhythms*. New York, NY: St. Martin's Press, 1994. P. 50–51.

87. Knight. *Switching the Odds*. P. 98.

88. Ibid. P. 90.

89. Lordon, Randye. *Sister's Keeper*. New York, NY: St. Martin's Press, 1994. P. 192.

90. Ibid. P. 131.

91. Lynch, Lee. *Sue Slate: Private Eye*. Tallahassee, FL: The Naiad Press, Inc., 1989. P. 16.

92. Ibid. P. 2.

93. Ibid. P. 10.

94. Ibid. P. 3.

95. Ibid. P. 48.

96. Maiman, Jaye. *Under My Skin*. Tallahassee, FL: The Naiad Press, Inc., 1993. P. 4.

97. Maiman, Jaye. *I Left My Heart*. Tallahassee, FL: The Naiad Press, Inc., 1991. P. 299.

98. Mildon, Marsha. *Stalking the Goddess Ship*. Norwich, VT: New Victoria Publishers, 1999. P. 13.

99. Ibid. P. 62.

100. Ibid. P. 50.

101. Mildon, Marsha. *Fighting for Air*. Norwich, VT: New Victoria Publishers, 1995. P. 136.

102. Pincus. *Mystery Readers Journal*. P. 35.

103. Ibid. P. 35.

104. Ibid. P. 36.

105. Ibid. P. 8.

106. Pincus, Elizabeth. *The Solitary Twist*. Minneapolis, MN: Spinsters Ink, 1993. P. 13.

107. Ibid. P. 89.

108. Ibid. P. 122.

109. Pincus. *The Two-Bit Tango*. P. 3.

110. Pincus. *The Solitary Twist*. P. 90.

111. Pincus. *The Two-Bit Tango*. P. 5.

112. Ibid. P. 193.

113. Rand. *Gay Detective*. P. 60.

114. Ibid. P. 5.

115. Ibid. P. 9.

116. Ibid. P. 90.

117. Ibid. P. 95.

118. Ibid. P. 15.

119. Ibid. P. 24.

120. Ibid. P. 31.

121. Redmann. *The Intersection of Law and Desire*. P. 203.

122. Saum. *Murder Is Germane*. P. 129.

123. Saum, Karen. *Murder Is Material*. Tallahassee, FL: The Naiad Press, Inc., 1994. P. 150.

124. Sumner, Penny. *Crosswords*. London: The Women's Press, 1994. P. 144.

125. Ibid. P. 113.

126. Sumner. *The End of April*. P. 1.

127. Sumner, P. 23.

128. Ibid. P. 92.

129. Taylor, Jean. *We Know Where You Live*. Seattle, WA: Seal Press, 1995. P. 6.

130. Ibid. P. 105.

131. Taylor, Jean. *The Last of Her Lies*. Seattle, WA: Seal Press, 1996. P. 5.

132. Ibid. P. 149.

133. Ibid. P. 26.

134. Tell, Dorothy. *The Hallelujah Murders*, Tallahassee, FL: The Naiad Press, Inc., 1991. P. 7.

135. Ibid. P. 62.

136. Ibid. P. 64.

137. Ibid. Pp. 146 -147.

138. Welch, Pat. *Snake Eyes*. Tallahassee, FL: The Naiad Press, 1999. P. 199.

139. Welch, Pat. *Still Waters*. Tallahassee, FL: The Naiad Press, 1991. P. 61.

140. Zaremba, Eve. *A Reason to Kill*. Toronto, Ontario, Canada: Second Story Press, 1989. P. 5.

141. Zaremba. *Work for a Million*. P. 55.

142. Zaremba, Eve. "A Canadian

Speaks," *Mystery Readers Journal* 9, no. 4, 1993/1994. P. 45.

143. Ibid. Pp. 45–46.

144. Ibid. P. 5.

145. Wilson, John Morgan. *Revision of Justice*. New York, NY: Doubleday, 1997. P. 157.

146. Zimmerman, R.D. *Closet*. New York, NY: Dell Publishing Group, 1995. P. 48.

147. Mickelbury, Penny. *Night Songs*. Tallahassee, FL: The Naiad Press, Inc., 1995. P. 210.

148. Ibid. P. 15–16.

149. Gilbert, W. Stephen. *Spiked*. London: GMP Publishers Ltd., 1991. P. 206.

150. Haddock, Lisa. *Edited Out*. Tallahassee, FL: The Naiad Press, Inc., 1994. P. 8.

151. Haddock, Lisa. *Final Cut*. Tallahassee, FL: The Naiad Press, Inc., 1995. P. 152.

152. Miller, Carlene. *Killing at the Cat*. Norwich, VT: New Victoria Publishers, 1998. P. 90.

153. Wilson, John Morgan. *Simple Justice*. New York, NY: Doubleday, 1996. P. 218–219.

154. Craft, Michael. *Boy Toy*. New York, NY: St. Martin's Press, 2001. P. 129.

155. Zimmerman, R.D. *Outburst*. New York, NY: Dell Publishing, 1998. P. 79.

156. Sims, Elizabeth. *Holy Hell*. Los Angeles, CA: Alyson Publications, 2002. P. 74.

157. Woodcraft, Elizabeth. *Good Bad Woman*. New York, NY: Kensington Publishing Corp., 2000. P. 27.

158. Stevenson, Richard. *On the Other Hand, Death*. New York, NY: St. Martin's Press, 1984. P. 39.

159. Johnson, Bett Reece. *The Woman Who Knew Too Much*. San Francisco, CA: Cleis Press Inc., 1998. P. 7.

160. Outland, Orland. *Death Wore a Fabulous New Fragrance*. New York, NY: The Berkley Publishing Group, 1998. P. 96.

161. Haddock. *Final Cut*. P. 60.

162. Gilbert. *Spiked*. P. 131.

163. Zimmerman. *Closet*. P. 192.

164. Mickelbury. *Night Songs*. P. 192.

165. Miller, Carlene. *Killing at the Cat*. P. 17.

166. Wings, Mary. *She Came by the Book*. New York, NY: The Berkley Publishing Group, 1996. P. 150.

167. Mortimer, John. "Rumpole and the Man of God," *The Trials of Rumpole*. New York, NY: The Armchair Detective Library, 1991. P. 37.

168. Nava, Michael. *The Hidden Law*. Los Angeles, CA: Alyson Publications, 1992. P. 1.

169. Foster, Marion. *The Monarchs Are Flying*. Ithaca, NY: Firebrand Books, 1987. P. 208.

170. Nava. *The Hidden Law*. P. 5.

171. Ibid. P. 15.

172. Foster, Marion *Legal Tender*. Ithaca, NY: Firebrand Books, 1992. P. 126.

173. Woodcraft. *Good Bad Woman*. P. 152.

174. Nava, Michael. *Goldenboy*. Los Angeles, CA: Alyson Publications, 1988. P. 48.

175. Nava, Michael. *The Death of Friends*. New York, NY: G.P. Putnam's, 1996. P. 209.

176. Foster. *The Monarchs Are Flying*. P. 29–30.

177. Lordon, Randye. *Say Uncle*. New York, NY: St. Martin's Press, 1999. P. 143.

178. Hart, Ellen. *Immaculate Midnight*. New York, NY: St. Martin's Press, 2002. P. 6.

179. Nava, Michael. *The Little Death*. Los Angeles, CA: Alyson Publications, 1986. P. 61.

180. Herren, Greg. *Bourbon Street Blues*. New York, NY: Kensington Publishing Corp., 2003. P. 126.

181. Wilson, Barbara. *Sisters of the Road*. Seattle, WA: Seal Press, 1987. P. 143.

182. Baker, Nikki. *In the Game*. Tallahassee, FL: the Naiad Press, 1991. P. 27.

183. Foster. *The Monarchs Are Flying*. P. 164–165.

184. Gilbert. *Spiked*. P. 86.

185. Ibid. P. 7.

186. Ibid. P. 87.

187. Ibid. P. 28.

188. Ibid. P. 35.

189. McKay, Claudia. *The Kali Connection*. Norwich, VT: New Victoria Publishers, 1994. P. 168.

190. Nava. *The Little Death*. P. 67.

191. Nava, Michael. *The Burning Plain*. New York, NY: Penguin, 1997. P. 73.

192. Nava. *The Hidden Law*. P. 14.

193. Ibid. P. 21.

194. Powell, Deborah. *Houston Town*. Tallahassee, FL: The Naiad Press, 1992. P. 128.

195. Ibid. P. 177.

196. Wilson, John Morgan. *Simple Justice*. P. 138.

197. Woodcraft. *Good Bad Woman*. P. 115.

198. Ibid. P. 55.

199. Zimmerman, R.D. *Hostage*. New York, NY: Dell Publishing Group, 1997. P. 9–10.

200. Zimmerman. *Closet*. P. 32.

201. Zimmerman, R.D. *Tribe*. New York, NY: Dell Publishing Group, 1996. P. 41.

202. Wilson, Barbara. *Murder in the Collective*. Seattle, WA: The Seal Press, 1984. P. 74.

203. James, Dean. *Faked to Death*. New York, NY: Kensington Books, 2003. P. 93.

204. Michaels, Grant. *A Body to Dye For*. New York, NY: St. Martin's Press, 1991. P. 50.

205. Baker, Nikki. *In the Game*. Tallahassee, FL: The Naiad Press, 1991. P. 48.

206. laFavor, Carole. *Along the Journey River*. Ithaca, NY: Firebrand Books, 1996. P. 12.

207. Michaels. *A Body to Dye For*. P. 77.

208. Wilson. *The Dog Collar Murders*. Seattle, WA: The Seal Press, 1989. P. 55.

209. Hart, Ellen. *Wicked Games*. New York, NY: St. Martin's Press, 1998. P. 81.

210. Wilson, Barbara. *Trouble in Transylvania*. Seattle, WA: Seal Press, 1993. P. 273.

211. Dreher, Sarah. *Stoner McTavish*. Norwich, VT: New Victoria Publishers, 1985. P. 5.

212. laFavor. *Along the Journey River*. P. 11.

213. Albarella. *Agenda for Murder*. Tucson, AZ: Rising Tide Press, 1999. P. 43.

214. Ibid. P. 43.

215. Raphael, Lev. *Let's Get Criminal*. New York, NY: St. Martin's Press, 1996. P. 18.

216. Gilligan, Sharon. *Danger in High Places*. Tucson, AZ: Rising Tide Press, 1993. P. 61.

217. Manthorne, Jackie. *Last Resort*. Charlottetown, P. E.I., Canada: Gynergy Books. 1995. P. 89.

218. Schmidt, Carol. *Silverlake Heat*. Tallahassee, FL: The Naiad Press, 1993. P. 27.

219. Fennelly, Tony. *The Glory Hole Murders*. New York, NY: Carroll & Graf Publishers, 1985. P. 37.

220. Azolakov, Antoinette. *Skiptrace*. Austin, TX: Banned Books, 1988. P. 25.

221. Ibid. P. 114.

222. Azolakov, Antoinette. *Cass and the Stone Butch*. Austin, TX: Banned Books, 1987. P. 62.

223. Ibid. P. 64.

224. Azolakov, Antoinette. *The Contactees Die Young*. Austin, TX: Banned Books, 1989. P. 48.

225. Azolakov, Antoinette. *Blood Lavender*. Austin, TX: Banned Books, 1993. P. 56.

226. Beal, M.F. *Angel Dance*. New York, NY: Daughters Publishing Co., 1977. Pp. 258–59.

227. Dreher, Sarah. *Gray Magic*. Norwich, VT: New Victoria Publishers, 1987. Pp. 38–39.

228. Fennelly, Tony. *The Glory Hole Murders*. New York, NY: Carroll & Graf, 1985. P. 101.

229. Ibid. P. 11.

230. Ibid. P. 11.

231. Gilligan, Sharon. *Danger in High Places*. Huntington Station, NY: Rising Tide Press, 1993. P. 42.

232. Gilligan, Sharon. *Danger! Cross Currents.* Huntington Station, NY: Rising Tide Press, 1994. P. 160.

233. Herren, Greg. *Bourbon Street Blues.* New York, NY: Kensington Publishing Corp., 2003. P. 71.

234. Ibid. P. 251.

235. James, Dean. *Posted to Death.* New York, NY: Kensington Publishing Corp., 2003. P. 9.

236. laFavor, Carole. *Along the Journey River.* Ithaca, NY: Firebrand Books, 1996. P. 11.

237. Manthorne, Jackie. *Last Resort.* Charlottetown, P. E.I., Canada: Gynergy Books, 1995. P. 106.

238. Manthorne, Jackie. *Sudden Death.* Charlottetown, P. E.I., Canada: Gynergy Books, 1997.P. 113.

239. Ibid. P. 114.

240. Michaels, Grant. *Dead as a Doornail.* New York, NY: St. Martin's Press, 1998. P. 9.

241. Michaels, Grant. *A Body to Dye For.* New York, NY: St. Martin's Press, 1991. P. 157.

242. Michaels, Grant. *Love You to Death.* New York, NY: St. Martin's Press, 1992. P. 98.

243. Michaels. *Dead as a Doornail.* Pp. 238–39.

244. Ibid. P. 94.

245. Plante, Pele. "An Act of Revolution." *Mystery Readers Journal* 9, no. 4, 1993/1994. P. 36.

246. Ibid. P. 37.

247. Ibid. P. 37.

248. Plante, Pele. *Getting Away with Murder.* Los Angeles, CA: Clothespin Fever Press, 1991 Pp. 137–38.

249. Roeder, Mark A. 2003. Email message sent to the author. 5 November.

250. Roeder, Mark A. *Someone Is Killing the Gay Boys of Verona.* Lincoln, NE: iUniverse.com, 2000. P. iii.

251. Roeder, Mark A. 2003. Email message sent to the author. 5 November.

252. Ibid.

253. Roeder. *Someone Is Killing the Gay Boys of Verona.* P. 135.

254. Schmidt, Carol. *Cabin Fever.* Tallahassee, FL: The Naiad Press, 1995. P. 239.

255. Scott, Manda. *Stronger Than Death.* London: Headline paperback, 1999. P. 140.

256. Ibid. P. 44.

257. Steward, Samuel. *Caravaggio Shawl.* Los Angeles, CA: Alyson Publications, Inc., 1989. P. 151.

258. Lanyon, Josh. *A Dangerous Thing.* London: GMP Publishers Ltd., 2002. P. 8.

259. Lansdale, Joe R. *The Two-Bear Mambo.* New York, NY: Warner Books, 1995. P. 35–6.

260. Cutler, Stan. *The Face on the Cutting Room Floor.* New York, NY: Dutton, 1991. P. 43.

261. Hartman, Keith. *The Gumshoe, the Witch, and the Virtual Corpse.* Decatur, GA: Meisha Merlin Publishing, Inc., 1998. P. 13.

262. Mickelbury, Penny. *Keeping Secrets.* Tallahassee, FL: The Naiad Press, Inc., 1994. P. 101.

263. Lansdale. *The Two-Bear Mambo.* P. 3.

264. Lansdale, Joe R. *Bad Chili.* New York, NY: Warner Books, 1997. P. 2.

265. Outland, Orland. *Death Wore a Fabulous New Fragrance.* New York, NY: The Berkley Publishing Group, 1998. P. 19.

266. Steward, Samuel. *Murder Is Murder Is Murder.* Los Angeles, CA: Alyson Publications, 1985. P. 52–3.

267. Padgett, Abigail. *The Last Blue Plate Special.* New York, NY: Mysterious Press, 2001. P. 165.

268. Aldyne, Nathan. *Cobalt.* New York, NY: Avon Books, 1982. P. 79.

269. Douglas, Lauren Wright. *Death at Lavender Bay.* Tallahassee, FL: The Naiad Press, 1996. P. 74

270. Ibid. P. 66–67.

271. Dymmoch, Michael Allen. *Feline Friendship.* New York, NY: St. Martin's Press, 2003. P. 237.

272. Hunter, Fred. *Government Gay.* New York, NY: St. Martin's Press, 1997. P. 120.

273. Ibid. P. 12.

274. Hunter, Fred. *Federal Fag.* New York, NY: St. Martin's Press, 1998. P. 90–1.

275. Johnson, Bett Reece. *The Woman Who Knew Too Much.* San Francisco, CA: Cleis Press Inc., 1998. P. 5.

276. Ibid. P. 53.

277. Lansdale, Joe R. *The Two-Bear Mambo.* P. 3.

278. Lansdale. *Rumble Tumble.* New York, NY: Warner Books, 1998. P. 42.

279. Lansdale. *Bad Chili.* P. 98.

280. Lansdale, Joe R. *The Two-Bear Mambo.* P. 6.

281. Lansdale. *Rumble Tumble.* P. 6.

282. Lansdale. *Bad Chili.* P. 190–1.

283. Ibid. P. 190–1.

284. Lanyon, Josh. *A Dangerous Thing.* London: GMP Publishers Ltd., 2002. P. 112.

285. Ibid. P. 6.

286. Ibid. P. 8.

287. Maney, Mabel. *The Case of the Good-for-Nothing Girlfriend.* San Francisco, CA: Cleis Press, Inc., 1994. P. 237.

288. Maney, Mabel. *The Case of the Not-So-Nice Nurse.* San Francisco, CA: Cleis Press, Inc., 1993. P. 109.

289. Outland, Orland. *Death Wore a Smart Little Outfit.* New York, NY: The Berkley Publishing Group, 1997. P. 5.

290. Padgett, Abigail. *The Last Blue Plate Special.* P. 259.

291. Sanra, Nancy. *No Escape.* Huntington, NY: Rising Tide Press, 1998. P. 10.

292. Sanra. *No Witnesses.* Huntington, NY: Rising Tide Press, 1995. P. 5.

293. Ibid. P. 190.

294. Sanra. *No Escapes.* P. 22.

295. Steward, Samuel M. *Murder Is Murder Is Murder.* P. 16.

296. Steward. *Caravaggio Shawl.* P. 151.

Bibliography

Binyon, T.J. *Murder Will Out: The Detective in Fiction*. Oxford: Oxford University Press, 1989.

By a Woman's Hand: A Guide to Mystery Fiction by Women. 2nd ed. Edited by Jean Swanson and Dean James. New York: Berkley Prime Crime, 1996.

Contemporary Lesbian Writers of the United States. Edited by Sandra Pollack and Denise D. Knight. Westport, CT: Greenwood, 1993.

Detecting Men. Edited by Willetta Heising. Dearborn, MI: Purple Moon, 1998.

Detecting Women. 3rd ed. Edited by Willetta Heising. Dearborn, MI: Purple Moon, 1999.

Dove, George N. *The Police Procedural*. Bowling Green, OH: Bowling Green University Popular Press, 1982.

The Fine Art of Murder. Edited by Ed Gorman, Martin Greenberg, Larry Segriff, and Jon Breen. New York: Galahad, 1993.

Gambone, Philip. *Something Inside: Conversations with Gay Fiction Writers*. Madison: University of Wisconsin Press, 1999.

Goldthwaite, Donna L. "Murder in the Stacks: Readers' Advisory for Mystery and Detective Fiction." In *Deadly Pleasures: Reading Mysteries*. Online resources of the Springfield Library WMRLS Readers' Advisory Training Workshop http://www.springfieldlibrary.org/stacks/index.html, 2002.

Griffith, Nicola. "A Conversation with Nicola Griffith about Her Novel 'Stay.'" Interview by Nan Talese, http://www.randomhouse.com/NanaTalese/exclusive/griffithinterview.html, 2003.

Hansen, Joseph. "Joseph Hansen." In *Contemporary Authors Autobiography Series*. Vol. 17. Detroit, MI: Gale, 1993. Pp. 59–74.

_____. "Matters Grave and Gay." In *Colloquium on Crime*. Edited by Robin Winks. New York: Scribner, 1986. Pp. 111–126.

Klein, Kathleen Gregory. *The Woman Detective: Gender and Genre*. 2nd ed. Champaign: University of Illinois Press, 1995.

Marling, William. *Hard-Boiled Fiction*. Cleveland, OH: Case Western Reserve University. http://www.cwru.edu/artsci/engl/marling/hardboiled, 2001.

The Oxford Book of American Detective Stories. Edited by Tony Hillerman and Rosemary Herbert. Oxford: Oxford University Press, 1996.

The Oxford Companion to Crime and Mystery Writing. Edited by Rosemary Herbert. Oxford: Oxford University Press, 1999.

Rowe, Michael. *Writing Below the Belt*. New York: Masquerade, 1995.

Rudolph, Janet A. "The Gay and Lesbian Detective." *Mystery Readers Journal* 9, no. 4, 1993/1994.

Slide, Anthony. *Gay and Lesbian Characters and Themes in Mystery Novels*. Jefferson, NC: McFarland, 1993.

Van Dover, J. Kenneth. *Murder in the Millions*. New York: Frederick Ungar, 1984.

Willis, Chris. "The Woman Detective, 1859–1910." M.A. thesis. Birkbeck College, University of London, 1992.

Windrath, Helen. *They Wrote the Book: Thirteen Women Mystery Writers Tell All*. Duluth, MN: Spinsters Ink, 2000.

Winn, Dilys. *Murder Ink, Revived, Revised, Still Unrepentant*. New York: Workman, 1984.

Young, Ian. *The Male Homosexual in Literature: A Bibliography*. Metuchen, NJ: Scarecrow, 1982.

Zimmerman, Bonnie. *The Safe Sea of Women: Lesbian Fiction 1969–1989*. Boston: Beacon, 1990.

Index

Author names (and pseudonyms) are listed alphabetically by last name. They are in bold type. The name or pseudonym used for their mysteries is followed by a dash and the name of the series' main character in *bold italics* (e.g., **Hart, Ellen**—*Jane Lawless*). Authors with more than one series have a separate listing for each series (e.g., **Zubro, Mark Richard**—*Tom Mason and Scott Carpenter*; **Zubro, Mark Richard**—*Paul Turner*). Character names are in bold italics and listed alphabetically by first name and also by last name. A character listing refers the reader to the author's name, e.g., *Alex Reynolds* (see **Hunter, Fred**).